The C Programming Language

Including ANSI C, Portability, and Software Engineering

Douglas A. Troy
Miami University

James D. Kiper
Miami University

SCOTT, FORESMAN AND COMPANY

Glenview, Illinois   Boston   London

Library of Congress Cataloging-in-Publication Data

Troy, Douglas A.
  The C programming language.

  Includes index.
  1. C (Computer program language)   I. Kiper, James D.
II. Title.
QA76.73.C15T76   1989   005.13'3   88-33670
ISBN 0-673-39803-X

  2 3 4 5 6 7 8 9 10 - MUR - 94 93 92 91 90 89

Printed in the United States of America

IBM is a registered trademark of International Business Machines Corporation.
MICROSOFT is a registered trademark of Microsoft Corporation.
UNIX is a trademark of AT&T Bell Labs.
PDP, VAX, and DEC are trademarks of Digital Equipment Corporation.

Preface

The C programming language has grown out of the confines of the UNIX environment to become a widely accepted general-purpose programming language. In fact, C had become so popular that, in 1983, the American National Standards Institute (ANSI) formed a committee to produce a standard definition for the language. At the time of the writing of this text, this standard is in the final stages of public comment and is on the verge of acceptance. Many C compiler vendors have already incorporated the major changes proposed by the standard into their C compilers.

The proposed ANSI standard not only establishes a concise definition of the C language, but also has made some significant changes to the language. Their purpose is to promote portability, reliability, maintainability, and efficient execution of C language programs on a variety of computing systems.

This text presents the language as specified in the proposed ANSI standard and discusses the differences between the standard and older versions. Each chapter of the text also addresses portability and software engineering issues concerned with producing reliable and maintainable C programs.

The book concentrates on the presentation of the C language and the production of readable C programs. It is written for use by students who have had programming experience, preferably in another high-level language such as Pascal. The text also presents programming concepts, such as abstraction and recursion, that are helpful in the effective use of C. It is not a book about algorithms or data structures, but it does contain examples of the implementation of such structures as arrays, linked lists, and trees using C. The text could thus be used in a second high-level programming course or in a course in which C is the implementation language, such as systems programming or scientific programming.

The text covers many C language topics that are not presented in beginning C language texts, including the standard libraries, dynamic properties of C such as memory management, and signal processing. Each chapter contains an extensive list of discussion questions, exercises, and a variety of programming problems.

Chapters 1 through 3 present an overview of the C language sufficient for writing many programs. Functions, separate compilation, operators, expressions, simple input/output (I/O), single-dimension arrays, and the preprocessor are all introduced in the first three chapters.

Chapter 4 presents a more thorough discussion of the operators, types, and expressions that were introduced in the first three chapters. Chapter 5 is a complete discussion of the preprocessor. Chapter 6 describes the related topics of arrays, pointers, and strings. Chapter 7 covers structures and unions.

Chapter 8 is a presentation of the C I/O library. Portions of this chapter may have been covered earlier, but as some of the examples utilize structures, it is helpful to have read Chapter 7 before reading Chapter 8.

Chapter 9 covers bit fields, bit manipulation operators, enumerated types, and the type qualifiers const and volatile.

Chapter 10 is a discussion of the most commonly used standard library functions. It may be desirable to utilize portions of this chapter along with earlier chapters, depending upon the goals of the course.

Chapter 11 covers dynamic memory management and the standard way of writing functions that may receive a variable number of parameters.

Chapter 12 presents advanced control flow, including local and nonlocal gotos, the use of pointers to functions and dispatch tables, and signal processing.

The appendices provide references to the standard library functions, keywords, operator precedence and associativity, and the collected syntax diagrams for the language.

Acknowledgments

Many resources were used to compile this text. The *Draft American National Standard Programming Lauguage C* provided the primary source of information about the C language. The original definition of the C Language is described in *The C Programming Language,* first edition, by Kernighan and Ritchie. This text provides the prestandard specification of the language. The C language syntax diagrams used in the text are based on diagrams by David Smith and used with the permission of David Smith and AGS Computers, Inc. Many reviewers furnished valuable suggestions and comments. In particular, Prof. Gary Fostel, North Carolina State University (Raleigh), provided exhaustive reviews and suggestions for improvements for which we are grateful.

Contents

              Structures and I/O   247
     7.3   Unions   249
              Definition and Motivation   249
              Declaration of Unions   250
              Referencing Members of a Union   251
              Usage Examples   252
     7.4   Portability and Software Engineering Issues   255
     7.5   Summary   260
              Keywords   261
              References   261
              Discussion Questions   262
              Exercises   263
              Programming Problems   265

8   Standard I/O Library   271

     8.1   Standard Libraries   271
     8.2   Header Files   271
     8.3   Linking the Standard I/O Library   272
     8.4   Files and File Access   272
              Streams   272
              File Access   273
              File Organization   273
              Text and Binary Files   274
     8.5   File-Access Functions   274
     8.6   Character and Line I/O   276
              Single Character I/O   277
              Line I/O   279
     8.7   Formatted I/O   280
              Formatted Output   281
              Formatted Input   285
              Internal Memory Conversion   291
     8.8   Direct I/O   293
     8.9   File Positioning   296
     8.10 Operations on Files   301
     8.11 Error Handling   302
              Error Indicators   302
              Buffering of I/O   303
     8.12 Portability and Software Engineering Issues   304
     8.13 Summary   307
              Keywords   309

11   Dynamic Aspects of C Programming   393

12   Advanced Control Flow   443

**The C Programming
Language**

1 Introduction

This chapter introduces the C language, its history, evolution, and use for writing portable software. The chapter begins with an overview of the history of C and the evolution of standard C. The general characteristics of C are presented in comparison with other programming languages. Although C programs are usually written in the context of some overall host system, they sometimes are used on bare machines. These two environments are discussed. The chapter includes an introduction to C and a discussion of how C source programs are translated into executable programs. The chapter concludes with a discussion of issues relating to the development of portable, quality software.

1.1 THE ROOTS OF C

The C programming language was designed as a general-purpose language with features to support system programming. In its first applications, C was used as the implementation language for system software, such as operating systems, compilers, and editors. Subsequently, implementation of other applications, including database software, spread sheet programs, engineering applications, and word processing software, has demonstrated its utility. C is the primary language of the popular *UNIX™ system,* but runs in many other environments, from personal computers to mainframe computers.

The roots of C can be found in a language called *BCPL* (Basic Combined Programming Language) developed by Martin Richards of Cambridge, England. In 1970, computer scientists at Bell Laboratories developed a variant of BCPL for use in writing an early UNIX operating system, which was being developed on a Digital Equipment Corporation (DEC) PDP-11™. These Bell scientists called this language *B*.

B was a typeless language in which there was only one kind of data object: the machine word. Each word in main memory could be accessed using "pointer" variables. This simple view of the hardware proved to be inadequate, primarily because the memory of the PDP-11 was byte addressable and supported both arithmetic and floating-point operations. B lacked the ability to address bytes. It also lacked the ability to distinguish between integer and floating-point values, and thus could not support floating-point and integer arithmetic conveniently.

1

These deficiencies led to the refinement of B and the resulting new language was named *C*.

C was developed at the American Telephone and Telegraph Company's (AT&T) Bell Laboratories in 1972 by Dennis Ritchie. The major change in the evolution of B into C was the addition of data typing to the language. Each data definition or declaration in C specifies a data type that determines the set of values that an object can represent and the operations that can be applied to the object.

1.2   STANDARD C

The C language was originally described in *The C Programming Language* by Brian W. Kernighan and Dennis M. Ritchie. Since that time, C has experienced a slow but steady evolution resulting from its use within Bell Labs and extending to the wider community as the UNIX operating system came into widespread acceptance and use.

During the decade of the 1980s, C became popular in its own right as a language for the development of microcomputer and personal computer software applications. A primary reason for this popularity is that C was one of the few viable replacements for assembly language for microcomputer software development. (See Section 1.3 for a discussion of the character of C and assembly language.) Another reason is that compilers for C are easier to develop than for many languages because of the nature of C and the availability of existing C compilers on which to build.

The popularity of C encouraged the development of many C compilers by various software vendors. Most of these compilers used the Kernighan and Ritchie work as a baseline language standard. Though it is an excellent work, the Kernighan and Ritchie book does not completely specify all aspects of the language. Additionally, as the usage of C grew, requests for extensions to the language were suggested by users. These factors lead to the production of similar but incompatible implementations of C.

In 1983, the American National Standards Institute *(ANSI)* formed a committee charged with developing a single, clearly defined standard for the C language, known as the X3J11 Technical Committee. In 1987, the committee produced the draft proposed standard for public comment. The work of the X3J11 committee has not changed the character of C, but has attempted clearly to define the syntax and semantics, to eliminate obsolete features of the language, and to add new features that will allow more reliable program development (i.e., software engineering improvements).

In 1987, the International Standards Organization *(ISO)* initiated a working group on C to produce an ISO standard for the language. It is expected that the ISO and ANSI standards will be identical.

This text will present the language as proposed in the ANSI standard. In cases where the ANSI standard differs significantly from the Kernighan and Ritchie definition, both versions will be presented. Thus, the book can be used with either version of the language. Most C compiler vendors have updated their products to comply with the standard, or are in the process of doing so. (The interested reader may want to explore another variant of C called C++ that is marketed by AT&T. C++ is not an implementation of the standard. See the chapter references for more information.)

1.3 THE CHARACTERISTICS OF C

Each computer processor implements a particular instruction set. Instructions include operations that move values in memory, perform arithmetic, compare values in memory, and control the flow of execution. There is no standard instruction set in the industry. Thus, an IBM mainframe, a DEC minicomputer, and an Intel microprocessor all implement different instruction sets.

The programming language that most closely corresponds to a machine's instruction set is called an *assembly language*. Assembly languages are thus closely tied to each particular computer manufacturer's hardware. Assembly languages are called low-level languages because of their close correspondence to a machine's instruction set. Assembly languages have traditionally been used by system programmers to implement system software such as operating systems and compilers because this software often requires an intimate knowledge and use of a machine's instruction set. One drawback of assembly language is that major reprogramming is required in order to modify an assembly language program to run on machines with different instruction sets.

Application programmers have long enjoyed the benefits of high-level languages such as FORTRAN, COBOL, Pascal, and Ada. These languages are not tied to a particular computer's instruction set. Instead, their syntax allows a more natural expression of program operations and control, and rely on a compiler program to convert the high-level language program, called source code, into assembly or machine-level instructions.

The development of high-level languages, such as FORTRAN and COBOL, allowed programs to be moved, or ported, across different machines by taking the source code to a new machine and recompiling the code. However, early high-level languages like FORTRAN and COBOL were designed to solve application programming problems, and did not support the facilities needed for system programming, requiring systems programmers to rely on assembly language as their medium of expression. Thus, application software was usually more portable than system software.

To aid the development of system software, the C language provides many features typically found in assembly languages. One such feature is access to most of the machine-level operators, including bit manipulation and indirect addressing. (Indirect addressing involves the use of pointers to values in memory.) Other important assembly-like features that are found in C are macro processing and conditional compilation. The language itself is rather compact, eschewing many high-level operations, such as built-in input/output (I/O) statements. These features of C have led some programmers to characterize the language as a low-level language, similar in nature to assembly language.

To facilitate the natural expression of algorithms and data structures, the language also supports the common control and data structures found in modern high-level programming languages such as Pascal and Ada. For example, C contains the traditional if-then-else, while, and case control statements and it directly supports arrays and structures. (A structure is a collection of one or more different kinds of data items.) These facilities of the language characterize C as a high-level language.

Thus, C allows the programmer to work "close to the machine" when necessary, but to do so in a natural and structured way. C could be characterized as a compromise language because it strikes a balance between the unrestricted access to the machine found in assembly language and the problem-oriented constructs found in high-level languages.

The definition of the language does not include all of the higher level operations found in many high-level programming languages. C contains very few built-in operators that directly manipulate data structures; for example, there are no built-in string or array manipulation operators in C. Additionally, the language definition does not specify any built-in I/O facilities. These features, which would require a larger language and could be machine or application dependent, were omitted from the language proper and are instead defined and implemented as subroutines. (In C, subroutines are referred to as *functions*.) A collection of related functions is called a *library*. The typical C compiler is supplied with one or more libraries containing I/O functions, math functions, and other useful routines. The ANSI standard specifies a large group of library functions that are to be included with a standard C compiler. Chapters 6, 8, and 10 through 12 of this text contain a discussion of these functions.

To summarize, C began as a small language designed for writing system software. Its usage has now grown beyond the original vision into many areas of programming, especially in microcomputer application development. It is an established language, as evidenced by its successful use for over 15 years, but still evolving. The culmination of this evolution is the specification of the ANSI standard definition.

1.4 THE IMPORTANCE OF PORTABILITY AND MAINTAINABILITY

The C language helps to solve the portability problem for systems programs in several ways. First, as C is a "compiled language" and not tied to any particular assembly language, one can port a C program between dissimilar machines by recompiling the source code using a C compiler that generates the proper machine code. Second, the small size and relative simplicity of the language allow the C compiler itself to be easily ported between machines. This is particularly important with respect to microcomputers, where new machine designs are constantly appearing on the market. Third, such features of the language as conditional compilation and separate compilation of program units allow the programmer to identify and isolate machine dependencies to aid the porting process. Finally, the specification of the ANSI standard has helped to guarantee that language features and function libraries will be portable across various individual compilers.

Maintainability has been recognized as a critical issue in the software industry. Barry Boehm, one well-respected software engineer, has indicated that the cost of software maintenance accounts for the largest portion of a computer system's lifetime cost. By using a standard C compiler, or at least being cognizant of implementation-dependent issues of the language, a programmer can develop more maintainable and cost-effective C programs. Portability and software engineering issues relating to maintainability are addressed throughout this text.

1.5 THE C PROGRAM TRANSLATION ENVIRONMENT

We distinguish between two separate environments: that on which the program is being written and processed, called the *translation environment,* and that on which the program will ultimately execute, called the *execution environment.* We will now discuss the translation environment.

In the translation environment, we require a program called a translator that transforms the C program text into some executable format. Most implementations of C translators are *compilers,* although C language *interpreters* are available.

When using a compiler, one begins writing a C program by entering C language code into one or more text files called *source files*. These files can be created by an editor, such as *vi* or *emacs,* or by using a word processor. Word processors provide more powerful text-formatting capability than do editors. Often, a word processor will store formatting information within the text. This information cannot be included in programming language source text, and can usually be avoided by selecting the proper word processor option (such as the ASCII text option in WordStar).

Source programs are then translated into a format called *object files* by using a compiler. The object files are not directly executable because they typically contain *unresolved references* to external objects such as library functions. Recall that the C language does not itself define I/O operators, many math operators, and other desirable operations. When a C programmer calls a function to do these things, the compiler generates a reference to a function; the compiler does not generate the code for the function. Object files are further processed by a *linkage editor* or *loader*. The linkage editor combines object modules (either directly or by extracting them from libraries), in order to resolve all external function and data references, and produces an *executable program*. Figure 1.1 illustrates this process. (Sometimes these two steps, translation and loading or linking, are invoked by a single command so that the user is not aware of the distinction. An example of this is the UNIX system cc command.)

Interpreters can speed the development and debugging process because they eliminate the need to generate machine-level executable code. Instead, an interpreter translates source code into an intermediate format and then directly "executes," or interprets, this code. Also, incomplete or syntactically incorrect programs can be executed to the point of the error, facilitating partial testing and debugging. The penalty involved is that interpreter execution is usually an order of magnitude or more slower than execution of a compiled and link edited program. For this reason, final production systems are rarely executed by interpreters.

During the translation phase, the compiler might produce object code either for the machine on which development is taking place or for a different target machine. In the latter case, the compiler is referred to as a *cross-compiler*. Because the machine on which development is taking place may differ from that

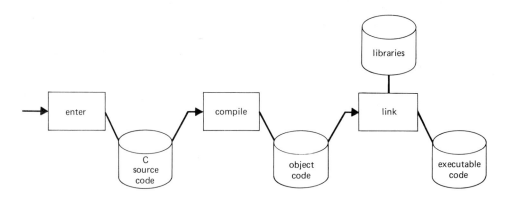

Figure 1.1. Program translation process

on which the program will execute, we distinguish between the translation environment and the execution environment.

1.6 THE EXECUTION ENVIRONMENT

An execution environment under the control of an operating system is called a *hosted environment* and one without an operating system is called a *freestanding environment*. Execution of a program on a personal computer under the control of MS-DOS or on a minicomputer running the UNIX operating system is an example of a hosted environment. Loading and executing an executable C program on a bare machine represent a freestanding execution environment.

The freestanding environment is encountered in special-purpose industrial and military applications. For example, a single program running in a hand-held microprocessor-based calculator without the benefit of any other software is a freestanding execution environment. Such software is sometimes called *embedded software*. Since this environment is typically used in specific and specially defined cases, the definition of the behavior of program start-up and termination is left to each implementation of the particular C compiler—the language standard does not define this behavior.

The hosted environment is the most common program execution environment. The language standard specifically addresses the behavior of C programs during start-up and termination in this environment. For example, the standard specifies an interface between the host operating system and a C program that allows start-up information to be passed from the operating system into a C program during run time. Consider the following UNIX operating system command, which is usually implemented by a C program:

```
cp file1 file2
```

Given this command, the operating system will execute the cp (i.e., copy) program and pass to it the strings "file1" and "file2." The way in which these strings are passed to the cp program is indicated by the language specification. The standard also defines the method for returning a value to the operating system upon program termination. This interface will be addressed in detail later in the text, in particular, see the discussion of argc and argv in Chapter 6 and the getenv() function in Chapter 10.

1.7 GETTING STARTED

There is no better way to get a feel for C than to code, enter, and test a program. Program 1.1 illustrates a simple C program.

```
#include <stdio.h>
/* Traditional first C program */

main()
{
        printf("This program is working!\n");
        exit();
}
```

Program 1.1

The structure of C programs and the meaning of the code in programs like Program 1.1 will be addressed in detail in Chapter 2. For the present, a brief explanation is presented here.

The first line specifies that the file stdio.h is to be processed as a part of this program. This file is sometimes necessary in order to do any I/O. An alternative notation for this line on some PCs is #include "stdio.h". The file stdio.h is not coded by the programmer but is typically supplied with the compiler.

The second line is a comment, not an executable statement. Comments are delimited by the /* */ characters.

The actual entry point for the program is indicated by the line main(). This is a function definition. A function is indicated by the parentheses and a definition by the braces that follow the name. The executable statements in the main() function are enclosed in the braces { and } and constitute the body of the function.

There are only two executable statements in main(), and both are *function calls:* one call to the printf function and the other to the exit function. Statements are delimited with a semicolon. The printf() function is used to output data to the user's terminal or screen. exit() terminates the program and returns control to the host operating system. A pair of parentheses appended to an identifier in an executable statement indicates a function call. In C, there is no keyword such as call to indicate a function call.

The printf call passes one *parameter* to the function. In this example, the parameter is a string to be displayed. Strings are enclosed in double quotes. In this case, the string is terminated by a new-line (line-feed) character (this is indicated by the \n symbol).

The call to exit passes no parameters, but the parentheses are still required to indicate a function call (exit() can be given a parameter that will be returned to the host environment). Both printf() and exit() are found in a *standard library* of C functions supplied with the compiler. A linkage editor will be used to load printf() and exit().

Notice that the () have two possible meanings in this example. In a definition, as in main(), the parentheses indicate that a function is being defined. In an executable statement, the parentheses indicate that a function is to be called. The meaning is derived from the context.

In order to translate and execute this program, you will have to learn a bit about your translation and execution environments. A straightforward environment is one in which the translation and execution environments are the same. Let us assume this environment and consider a specific example that will allow us to test Program 1.1.

We will assume a UNIX-like environment. To enter, translate, and execute the program on a UNIX-based system using a compiler, one would begin by entering the above program into a text file whose name is suffixed with the characters ".c". The file name "program1.c" is a reasonable file name. Next, translate and link edit the source code by using the UNIX command "cc" (this command actually runs the UNIX C compiler and the UNIX linkage editor):

```
cc program1.c
```

The result of this command is an executable file named "a.out" (a.out is the default executable file name on UNIX systems). Execute this program by typing its name

```
a.out
```

and you should see the program output displayed on your terminal.

If you are working with a personal computer-based system, you may need to run the compiler and linkage editor yourself (in contrast with the UNIX "cc" command that runs both of these programs). For example, to invoke the Lattice C compiler on the IBM PC (running the PC-DOS operating system), one enters the command "lcs":

```
lcs program1
```

This command produces an object file named "program1.obj" that must be linkage edited by using the IBM-PC linkage editor:

```
link c.obj program1.obj, program1.exe, ,lcs.lib
```

Referring to this command, "c.obj" is an object file supplied with the compiler that provides the hosted environment interface (commonly called the root module), "program1.exe" is the output of the linkage editor, and "lcs.lib" is the name of the standard C library. The program could be tested under PC-DOS by entering its name

```
program1
```

and the expected output should be displayed on the PC monitor.

The reader should investigate the steps needed to translate and run a program in his or her own environment and then experiment with Program 1.1 (see Exercise 8 and Programming Problem 1).

1.8 ISSUES IN WRITING PORTABLE SOFTWARE

We have seen that C was developed as a tool for writing system software that can be easily ported between dissimilar machines. The C language provides the tools for this process, but it does not in itself guarantee that any program written in C will be portable. The development of portable software requires that the programmer exercise care in the design and coding of the program so that areas that present potential portability problems either can be avoided or can be identified and isolated in the source code.

Categories of portability issues as identified in the C standard are summarized below.

1. A program can be nonportable if it utilizes a C language construct that is unspecified. *Unspecified behavior* is the action of a correct program construct for which the language standard imposes no requirements. For example, the language does not specify the order in which function parameters are to be evaluated. A program that depends upon a particular order of evaluation for correct results would be nonportable.
2. A program can be nonportable if it utilizes an *implementation-defined* program construct. Implementation-defined behavior is specified by each particular execution environment. For example, C allows the programmer to retrieve and set individual bits within a byte, but it is up to each compiler to specify the order in which bits are numbered within a byte for such reference.
3. A program can be nonportable if it utilizes a program construct that is either not specified by the standard or exceeds the minimum requirements set forth by the standard. For example, the standard requires that the first 31 characters of an identifier be treated as significant. Use of more than 31 characters with a compiler that exceeds this minimum requirement could lead to portability problems.

A primary objective of this text is to identify portability issues and to suggest ways of addressing such issues. Each chapter will present an analysis of portability considerations relating to the topics of that chapter.

1.9 THE IMPORTANCE OF SOFTWARE ENGINEERING ISSUES

Given the current state of the art of software development, more time is spent on program maintenance than on the original program development. The term "maintenance" refers to any changes made to the program after it has been placed in operation. This includes enhancements to add new functionality and corrections to errors in the program.

As maintenance, by definition, occurs after design and implementation, the modifier of the code is frequently someone who was not involved in the original development. It is vital to the maintenance task that the existing software be understandable. If the original is designed by means of good software engineering concepts, the modifications or enhancements can be more smoothly and efficiently incorporated.

The C programming language does not enforce many accepted software engineering concepts. In particular, the flexibility that makes C useful in system programming actually is contrary to accepted software engineering philosophy. This does not imply that well-engineered, easily modified programs cannot be written in C. However, to do so requires discipline by the programmer.

At the end of each chapter, methods, techniques, and disciplines useful for constructing well-engineered software in C that are pertinent to that chapter will be discussed. Some of these are contrary to the common practice in C, but are vital in writing modifiable software.

1.10   SUMMARY

C was developed as a general-purpose programming language to address the needs of the developers of system software and evolved from early systems programming languages into its present ANSI standard form.

The language is characterized as a high-level language that supports many features, such as bit manipulation, indirect addressing, and conditional compilation, traditionally associated with assembly languages.

C is important because it is a tool that can be used to write portable system software. Portability is important because it allows programs to be easily moved between dissimilar computer systems.

We distinguished between the program translation and execution environments because they may differ. The translation environment includes the language translator (either interpreter or compiler) and other software, such as linkage editors and text editors, that are needed to produce an executable program.

The usual steps required to compile and link a C program were illustrated.

Two execution environments were identified: freestanding and hosted. In the freestanding environment, a program executes without the support of an operating system. Freestanding environments are implementation specific and not addressed by the language standard. The hosted environment involves an interface with an operating system, and is specified by the C language standard.

A first C language program was presented and two specific examples of the steps required to compile and execute the program were described.

The chapter concluded with a presentation of general categories of issues that must be considered in order to produce C programs that are portable, and with a discussion of the motivation for applying software engineering concepts to C program development.

Keywords

ANSI	interpreter
assembly language	ISO
B	library
BCPL	linkage editor
C	loader
compiler	object file
cross-compiler	parameter, of a function
embedded software	portable software
executable program	separate compilation
execution environment	source file
freestanding environment	standard C library
function	translation environment
function call	translator
function parameter	UNIX system
hosted environment	unresolved references
implementation defined	unspecified behavior

References

Boehm, B. W. 1981. *Software Engineering Economics*. Englewood Cliffs, N.J.; Prentice-Hall. This book discusses, among other topics, the costs associated with software development and maintenance.

Draft American National Standard X3.159-198x, Programming Language C. Copies may be obtained from Global Engineering Documents, Inc., 2805 McGaw Irvine, CA 92714 (1-800-854-7179).

Murray, R. B. 1986. An introduction to C++: Object-oriented programming. *The C Journal* (InfoPro Systems) 2(2):14–18.

Kernighan, B. W., and D. M. Ritchie. 1978. *The C Programming Language,* Englewood Cliffs, N.J.; Prentice-Hall.

Plauger, P. J. 1987. Writing freestanding C programs. *The C Journal* (InfoPro Systems) 2(4):10–19.

Ritchie, D. M., S. C. Johnson, M. E. Lesk, and B. W. Kernighan. 1978. The C Programming Language. *Bell Sys Tech J* 57(6). A similar paper can be found in: *Western Elec Eng* 25(1):14–27, 1981.

Stroutsrup, B. 1986. *The C++ Programming Language*. Reading, Mass.: Addison-Wesley Publishing Company.

Discussion Questions

1. Discuss the characteristics of assembly languages that make them much less portable than higher level languages.

2. Why is system software such as operating systems, compilers, and linkage editors often written in assembly language?

3. Discuss the tasks performed by each of the following programs: text editor, compiler, linkage editor, and operating system.

4. Why are object files not executable?

5. From the standpoint of an organization such as a corporation or government agency, why are standards (such as ANSI standard C) important? Consider standards from the point of view of a hardware manufacturer and/or a software manufacturer. Are standards an advantage to a manufacturer? Could standards be considered a disadvantage to a manufacturer?

6. Review the concept of functions and parameters. Note that the parentheses pair is needed to indicate a function call even if no parameters are passed to the function. How do other languages with which you are familiar indicate a function call?

7. Distinguish among the following three kinds of errors:
   Compile-time errors
   Link (loading) errors
   Run-time errors
   For example, the program

```
#include <stdio.h>
/* Traditional first C program */

main()
{
        prntf("This program is working!\n");
        exit(0);
}
```

will compile cleanly, but will result in a linkage-editor error (since printf is misspelled). An example of a run-time error is a division by zero. Why is the C compiler unable to find the above printf misspelling or a division by zero that involves two variables?

Exercises

1. List the characteristics of the C language that allow the development of portable system software.

2. In considering the hosted environment, state an example of why one might want to return a value from a program to the operating system.

3. In general, would you expect a program written for a freestanding execution environment to be more portable or less portable than a program written for a hosted environment? Why?

4. Is your language translator a compiler or an interpreter? What characteristics determine this?

5. Describe the commands on your computer system that will allow you to perform the following operations:
   a. Execute your compiler or interpreter
   b. Execute your linkage editor (if you are using a compiler).
   c. Assign a name to the executable file (if you are using a compiler).

6. Describe the usual naming conventions for the following on your computer system:
   a. The name of C source files.
   b. The name of object files (for compiler environments).
   c. The name of executable files. What is the operating system command to run an executable file?

7. Study your translation and execution environments and ascertain their characteristics as follows:
   a. Determine the character code in use (ASCII or EBCDIC).
   b. Determine the word size of your execution machine.
   c. Find out how to get a hard copy listing of your program. List the command that will generate a hard copy listing.
   d. Does your printer produce listings in both upper- and lowercase? Does your printer have the { and } characters?
   e. Some translation environments allow the programmer to generate a cross-reference listing. What is the command, if any, that will generate a cross-reference listing in your environment? What information can you obtain from a cross-reference?

f. Find out if you can get an assembly language expansion of the source code that is generated from your compiler. What is the compiler option that will generate an assembly language expansion? How could this help in debugging?

8. Try to spot some common syntax errors in the code shown below.

Example 1:

```
#include <stdio.h>
/* Traditional first C program /

main()
{
      printf("This program is working!\n");
      exit(0);
}
```

Example 2:

```
#include <stdio.h>
/* Traditional first C program */

main()
{
      printf("This program is working!\n");
      exit(0);
)
```

Example 3:

```
#include <stdio.h>
/* Traditional first C program */

main()
{
      printf("This program is working!\n")
      exit(0);
}
```

Programming Problems

1. Enter and run Program 1.1 on your computer system.

2. Modify Program 1.1 as shown below and run it. Compare its output with that from the original program. What is the difference?

```
#include <stdio.h>
/* Traditional first C program */

main()
{
      printf("This program is working!");
}
```

3. You may want to enter and compile the programs listed in Exercise 8 and observe the diagnostic messages that are presented by your compiler. Are the messages descriptive of the errors? Enter the erroneous program shown in Discussion Question 7. What is the message that is generated from the linkage editor that indicates the unresolved reference?

2 Language Overview

Chapter 2 presents the basic building blocks of a C program. They include the lexical elements of the language, such as identifiers and constants. The structure of a C program is revisited in some detail and an overview of many of the common operators and statements are presented. Simple I/O and an introduction to preprocessor directives are included.

2.1 SYNTAX

The rules that the programmer must follow in order to construct a meaningful program are called the *syntax* rules of the language. This chapter will present the foundation for the C language syntax, followed by an overview of a sufficient amount of the language to allow further experimentation and program development.

Syntax Diagrams

In this text, the syntax of C will be specified by using a combination of a graphic notation known as *syntax diagrams* and a textual description of the constraints that may apply to a particular syntactic element. For example, the diagram in Figure 2.1 defines the syntax rule for a *comment*.

Each individual diagram defines either a category of syntactic elements or the actual syntax of a specific construct, such as an identifier, operator, expression, or statement. Each diagram is labeled for reference by other diagrams.

COMMENT

Figure 2.1. Syntax diagram for a comment

To use a syntax diagram, the reader should begin at the upper left and follow the diagram either from left to right or in the direction of the arrowheads. Each time the flow passes through an oval or circle, the symbols specified within are used to generate a syntactic element. Characters in the syntactic element that must appear exactly as shown are enclosed in a circle and are called *terminal symbols*. Thus, Figure 2.1 indicates that a comment must begin with the two characters /*.

Continuing with Figure 2.1 after the /*, we can either continue straight to the terminal symbol */, or, just before reaching this terminal, we can branch down and proceed toward the symbol called non-comment terminator; thus, we have an option specified by the diagram. Suppose that we follow this branch and encounter a non-comment terminator symbol. This symbol represents a syntactic category, sometimes called a *nonterminal symbol,* and is so indicated by the oval. Nonterminals represent a category of syntactical elements that are defined by another syntax diagram with the corresponding label. In this example, non-comment terminator would represent any of the valid symbols in the host environment's character set except for the comment terminator */ (since comments cannot be nested in C). The implications of the restriction on comment nesting are further discussed in Sections 2.6 and 5.7.

Notice that the line that goes through the nonterminal symbol leads back up to and just after the /* symbol. We can thus continue looping through that nonterminal, each time selecting another character to produce a comment, but at some point, the path leading to the */ terminal must be followed to complete the comment.

Figure 2.2 illustrates valid and invalid comments as defined by the diagram.

We will use syntax diagrams together with examples to clarify the syntax of the language. Appendix D presents the complete language syntax.

```
Valid Comments                          Invalid Comments

/**/                                     /*   This is
                                              a /* nested
/* /* */                                         comment */
                                         */
/* A comment */

/*

     A multi line comment.

*/
```

Figure 2.2. Examples from the comment syntax diagram

2.2 LEXICAL ELEMENTS

Character Set

The lowest level symbols of the language are the characters from the host environment's character set. These must include the uppercase and lowercase characters of the English alphabet, the decimal digits, and the following punctuation characters:

    ! " # % & ' ( ) * + , - . / : ; < = > ? [\ ] ^ _ { | } ~

Also included are the space character, horizontal and vertical tabs, form feed, and an end-of-line indicator. The end-of-line may be a single character or multiple characters (such as carriage return, line feed), but is usually treated as a single character called the *new-line* character.

 The characters above must be combined according to the syntax rules to produce valid constructs called lexical elements. The smallest lexical element is called a *token* and there are six categories of tokens in the language: identifiers, keywords, punctuators, constants, string literals, and operators. These tokens will be introduced in the sections that follow.

Identifiers

Identifiers are used to name program variables, functions, and other program constructs. Figure 2.3 presents the syntax for an identifier.

IDENTIFIER

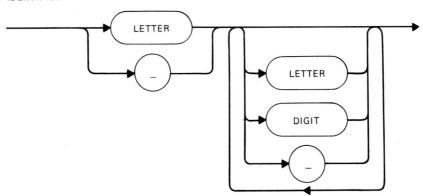

Figure 2.3. Identifier syntax

Notice that the first character of an identifier cannot be a digit. Also, C is case sensitive. This means that the identifier temp1 is considered to be different from TEMP1, or even Temp1. Finally, certain identifiers, called *keywords,* are reserved for use by the compiler. The keywords are presented below.

The maximum number of significant characters that can be used in an identifier depends upon the uses of the identifier. In particular, C programs are often composed of multiple source (or object) files. Identifiers that are used only in a single file are called internal. Identifiers shared across files are called external. The ANSI specification requires that the translator treat at least the first 31 characters of an internal identifier as significant. Older C translators may recognize fewer than 31 characters. External identifiers may be restricted to as little as six significant characters. Significance refers to the number of characters actually recognized by the translator. Identifiers may exceed the significant length, but any additional characters are for source code readability purposes only. There is no specific limit on the maximum number of characters in an identifier. The use of internal and external identifiers will be discussed in detail in Chapter 3.

Keywords

Keywords are a special class of identifiers that have predefined meanings to the translator. Keywords may not be used as names for programmer-defined identifiers. Table 2.1 presents the list of C keywords. Notice that they are specified entirely in lowercase.

Punctuators

A *punctuator* is one of the following symbols:

        [ ] ( ) { } * , : = ; ... #

Punctuators are used to delimit various syntatic units and to indicate certain

Table 2.1. Keywords

auto	default	float	register	switch
break	do	for	return	typedef
case	double	goto	short	union
char	else	if	signed	unsigned
const	enum	int	sizeof	void
continue	extern	long	static	volatile
		noalias	struct	while

operators. The role of each punctuator in the syntax will be addressed as we study the associated declarations and expressions throughout the text.

Another group of lexical elements, constants, will be discussed after we introduce the concept of type.

2.3 TYPES

All data objects and the variables that reference data objects are assigned a *type*. The type defines: (1) the number of bits needed to represent an object; (2) how the object is stored in the computer's memory; (3) the set of values to attribute to the pattern of bits; and (4) the set of operations that can be performed on those values. For example, in the C statement

```
x = 12;
```

the variable x and the constant value 12 are both assigned a type. The way that x and 12 are stored in memory and the operations that can be performed on these two objects are determined by their type.

There are many different types in C. The most common are the *simple types,* which include *character, integer,* and *floating point.* Other types include aggregate types and derived types. In this chapter, we will consider variables and constants with the above three simple types. Types are further discussed in other sections of the text, especially in Chapters 3 and 4.

Data representing whole numeric values can be stored in a program using the integer type. Numeric values that require a fractional part are represented using floating-point types. Character types are used for entities that represent a value from the computer's character set. The following sections illustrate some of the uses of types.

2.4 CONSTANTS

Constants are used in programs to represent values that do not change during program execution. In C, we distinguish between constants of the following types: integer, floating, character, and enumeration. We now present the syntax for each type of constant, except enumeration constants, which are discussed in Chapter 9.

Integer Constants

Integer constants can be coded in three number systems, as shown in Figure 2.4. *Decimal constants* must begin with a nonzero digit. A leading zero followed by

INT CONSTANT

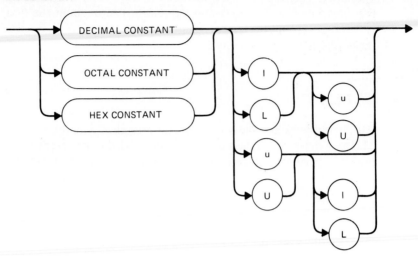

DECIMAL CONSTANT

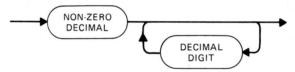

HEX CONSTANT

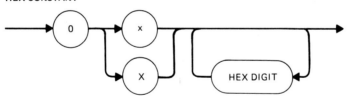

OCTAL CONSTANT

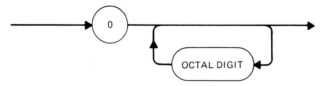

Figure 2.4. Integer constants

a sequence of one or more digits represents an *octal constant* and a leading 0x or 0X represents a *hexadecimal constant*. Octal constants consist of the digits 0 through 7 and hexadecimal constants consist of the digits 0–9, a–f, or A–F. Table 2.2 presents some examples.

The suffixes l (ell) and L indicate a double precision or long constant and the suffixes u and U indicate unsigned constants. The meaning of long and unsigned attributes will be discussed in Section 3.6, where data types will be addressed in greater detail.

Notice that the syntax makes no provision for a negative constant. Negative values are attained by using a negation operator (discussed in Section 2.7).

Floating Constants

Floating constants are used to represent values that contain fractions. Floating constants must be expressed in base-10 using the syntax shown in Figure 2.5.

Floating constants are distinguished from integer constants by either the presence of the decimal point, the exponent part (e or E) of the number, or the floating suffix (F or f).

Floating constants can be specified in three different floating-point types: float, double, and long double. Of the three floating-point types, float types can represent values with the lowest precision and range, and long doubles the values with the greatest precision and magnitude. Thus, the set of values that can be represented by a constant of type float is a subset of type double. Double constants can, in turn, represent a subset of values of the type long double.

The exponent part specifies scientific notation, that is, a power of ten by which the preceding value is scaled. Table 2.3 presents some examples.

The default type for a floating constants is double. The f or F suffix indicates that the constant is type float (lower than the default precision) while the l (ell) or L suffix indicates a double precision floating constant whose type is called long double (greater than the default precision).

Table 2.2. Examples of Integer Constants

Decimal	Octal	Hexadecimal
127	0173	0X7b
512	01000	0X200
65535U	0177777U	0XFFFFU
107155L	0321223L	0X1A293L

FLOAT CONSTANT

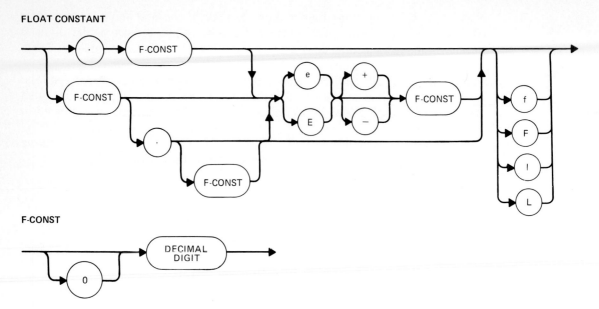

F-CONST

Figure 2.5. Floating constant

Table 2.3. Example of Floating Constants

Double	Float	Long Double
3.14	3.14F	3.14L
0.34	0.34F	0.34L
32E16	32E8F	32E24L
1.2E–10	1.2E–4F	1.2E–20L

Character Constants

Character constants are used to represent a sequence of one or more character codes using the character set of the target machine (e.g., ASCII, EBCDIC). Character constants are enclosed in single quotes, as shown in Figure 2.6.

Assuming the ASCII character set (see Appendix B), Table 2.4 presents some example character codes along with their internal representation.

Characters that are preceded by a back slash indicate *escape sequences*. Certain escape sequences (see Table 2.5) are used to represent unprintable characters such as format effectors and control characters. The digit sequence \ddd (ddd represents from one to three octal digits) can be used to specify the code for any single character in octal notation and the digit sequence \xdd (typically one to two hexadecimal digits) represents a hexadecimal character code. Note that a char-

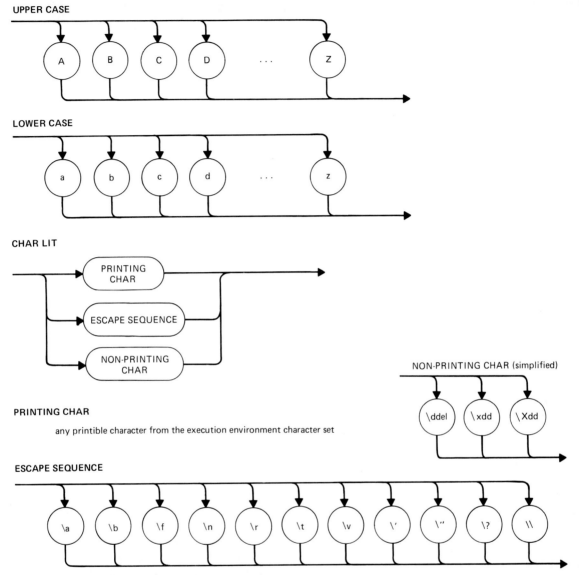

Figure 2.6. Character constants

acter constant cannot span a line of the source file, so that to code a new-line
character in a character constant, one must use an escape sequence.

Character constants are stored as the integer values used to represent the
corresponding character codes on the particular machine (e.g., ASCII or
EBCDIC). A character constant has type integer because its value represents the
integer encoding of the characters in the machine's character set.

Table 2.4. Representation of Character Constants

'a'	97
'A'	65
'0'	48
' '	32
'.'	46
'abc'	97,98,99 (3-byte sequence)

Note: See the discussion in the portability section about character constants that consist of more than a single character.

Table 2.5. Escape Codes

\'	Single quote		\a	Alarm (bell)
\"	Double quote		\b	Backspace
\?	Question mark		\f	Form feed
\\	Backslash		\n	New line (Line feed)
\ddd	Octal code		\r	Carriage return
\xdd	Hexadecimal code		\t	Horizontal tab
\0	Null byte		\v	Vertical tab

2.5 STRING LITERALS

A *string literal* represents a sequence of one or more characters such that the characters are stored contiguously in primary storage and terminate with the null byte ('\0'). The null byte is added by the translator and is not written in the source text. The null byte is one distinction between a string literal and a character constant. The other is that the individual characters of a string literal are stored as characters each of which has the type character, whereas character constants have the type integer. A string literal is really a vector of characters.

String literals are specified by enclosing a sequence of zero or more characters, including the escape codes discussed above if desired, within double quotes. (The double quotes distinguish the string literal from the character constant.) Table 2.6 presents some examples of strings literals along with the corresponding internal representation (again assuming ASCII).

Notice that the number of bytes represented by a string literal is usually one greater than the number of characters between the double quotes because of the terminating null that is added automatically by the language translator. The qualifier usually was used because escape sequences obviously require multiple characters in the source code to represent a single character in the literal.

Table 2.6. Example of String Literals

```
"ABC"
|65|66|67|0|

"\a\aError: %d\n"
|7|7|69|114|114|111|114|58|32|37|100|10|10|0|

"\001header\002text\003"
|1|104|101|97|100|101|114|2|116|101|120|116|3|0|
```

2.6 COMMENTS AND WHITE SPACE

Comments have been illustrated in Program 1.1 and in Section 2.1. To recap, comments are initiated with the characters /* and terminate with the */. Comments may not be used within character constants or string literals as the comment characters would be interpreted as part of the constant. Comments may span lines but they may not be nested.

White space is composed of space characters, tabs, form feeds, new lines, and comments. White space is ignored by the language translator except when required to separate adjacent lexical elements such as identifiers and keywords, or when used within character constants and string literals.

2.7 INTRODUCTION TO OPERATORS AND EXPRESSIONS

Operators and Expressions

An *operator* is a symbol that specifies an operation to be performed that yields a value. Operators act upon *operands*. An *expression* is a sequence of operators and operands that specifies how to compute a value. An operand can be a variable, a constant, or another expression.

The C language is rich in operators (there are 42 of them) and it would be premature to present them all at this point in the text. For the present, we will consider the operators presented in Table 2.7.

The following sections will introduce the above operators and their usage in expressions.

The Value and Classification of Expressions

In C, all expressions have a *value*. An expression can be as simple as the name of a variable. For example, the expression, x has as its value the value referenced

Table 2.7. Some C Operators

Arithmetic		Relational	
++	Increment	>	Greater than
--	Decrement	<	Less than
-	Unary minus	>=	Greater or equal to
*	Multiplication	<=	Less than or equal to
/	Division	==	Equality
+	Addition	!=	Not equal to
-	Subtraction		
	Assignment		Function Call
=	Simple assignment	()	Function call

by x. The value of the expression a + b is the sum of the contents of a and b. It is important to know the value of expressions, as such values are often used as operands within larger expressions. We will often return to this concept when discussing operators.

Operators can be classified according to the number of operands upon which they act. Operators that require exactly one operand are called *unary;* operators that require two operands are called *binary*. Of the operators in Table 2.7, ++, --, unary minus (–), and function call () are unary, and the remainder are binary.

The following sections present a brief introduction to the above operators.

Relational Operators

The *relational operators* in Table 2.7 are binary operators used to compare the values of their operands. The value of a relational expression such as

```
operand1 relational-operator operand2
```

is an integer equal to either 1 or 0. In C, zero represents false and nonzero represents true.

Assignment Operator

The *assignment operator* is a binary operator that assigns the value of an expression to an object in memory. The syntax is

```
lvalue = expression
```

The expression on the left-hand side of the assignment operator must reference an object in memory. An expression that represents an object in memory is called an *lvalue*. The value of an assignment expression is the value that is assigned.

Unary Increment and Decrement

The binary arithmetic operators and the unary minus operator from Table 2.7 have the usual algebraic meaning.

The unary increment and decrement are unusual. The increment operator, ++, is often used with identifiers as shown in the following expressions:

Postfix Version		*Prefix Version*
`identifier++`	or	`++identifier`

The value of the postfix version expression is the initial value of the identifier. However, as a side effect, the value of the identifier is updated with the identifier's initial value plus one, as in the assignment statement: identifier = identifier + 1;. The value of the prefix version is the new (incremented) value, plus the fact that the variable is updated as a side effect. Consider the following statements:

```
count = 0;
sum = count++;
total = ++count;
```

This sequence of statements would set sum equal to zero, and both count and total to two.

The decrement operator, −−, is analogous to the unary increment. Given the expression

| `identifier--` | or | `--identifier` |

the value of the left expression is the initial value of the identifier. The value of the right-hand expression is the new decremented value. Both expressions have the side effect of updating the value of the variable. Other uses of these operators are considered later in the text.

Function Call Operator

The postfix () after an identifer indicates a *function call* (also called a subroutine call). Expressions separated by commas may be listed within the parentheses to indicate values to be passed to the function. The value of a function call expression is the value (if any) returned by the function.

Table 2.8. Partial List of Operator Precedence

Function call operator ( )
Postfix increment and decrement ++ −−
Prefix increment and decrement ++ −−
Unary minus −
* /
+ −
< > <= >=
== !=
= (assignment operator)

Operator Precedence

When coding expressions involving more than a single operator, it is important to determine the order in which operators are applied. *Operator precedence* rules provide such an ordering. Operators with a higher precedence class are applied before those in a lower class. For now, it is adequate to note that C obeys the usual algebraic precedence sequence, summarized by Table 2.8, where operators at the top of the table have precedence above those lower in the table. Binary operators of equal precedence are evaluated left to right.

Expressions may be enclosed in parentheses in order to defeat the default precedence. The subexpression (b + c) in the expression

        (b + c) * a

will be evaluated before the application of the * operator. This order is opposed to the nonparenthesized expression, where * would be applied before + using the default precedence.

A more complete discussion of operators and their order of evaluation in expressions (including precedence and associativity) is presented in Chapter 4.

2.8   C PROGRAM STRUCTURE

Modules

C programs are coded into one or more source files known as *modules*. These modules need not be translated at the same time in order to produce the final executable program. In fact, most C programming applications are made up of many modules, usually translated (compiled) at different times, with many of the commonly used compiled modules (object modules) being stored in collections called libraries.

When coding a module, many kinds of entities are created and named. Examples of entities include variables and functions, each of which must be named so that they can be later referenced elsewhere in the code. The programmer introduces names and their meaning through the use of *declarations*. In fact, at the highest level, a C program can be described as one or more declarations. See Figure 2.7.

A declaration can be used to define an entity or to reference an entity that is defined elsewhere. For example, you can declare a function, including its body of executable statements. This is a *defining declaration*. You could also declare a function in a module and simply call it. Such a declaration is called a *referencing declaration*. The definition is contained in some other module. Data, such as variables, can also be introduced in the form of either defining or referencing declarations. Stated another way, a defining declaration introduces a name, its attributes, and the entity itself to which the name refers. A referencing declaration simply introduces a name and its attributes and leaves the definition to some other module.

Notice in Figure 2.7 that there are two data definitions: e-data definitions and i-data definitions. E-data definitions are written outside of any functions. I-data definitions are coded inside of a block (or function body). This location, or context, is important, and is explored in detail in Section 3.3.

The syntax for a function definition is also illustrated in Figure 2.7. Notice that the body of a function is composed of declarations and executable statements. For a function, the declarations can be referencing declarations for functions or data, but defining declarations for data only. A function may not be defined (nested) within a function as in Pascal.

The next section presents an example of a C module and its constituent declarations.

C Program Walkthrough

To illustrate these ideas, let us examine a C module. It is useful to have the computer tell a little about itself. Program 2.1 prints a partial table of character codes from the execution environment. (This code will be revisited in the next section, where alternative program constructs are presented.)

This program prints a header line, then it goes through a loop as the value of ch goes from 32 to 126 inclusive, printing the value of ch as a character code, and as a decimal, hexadecimal, and octal number. The first few lines of the output appear below.

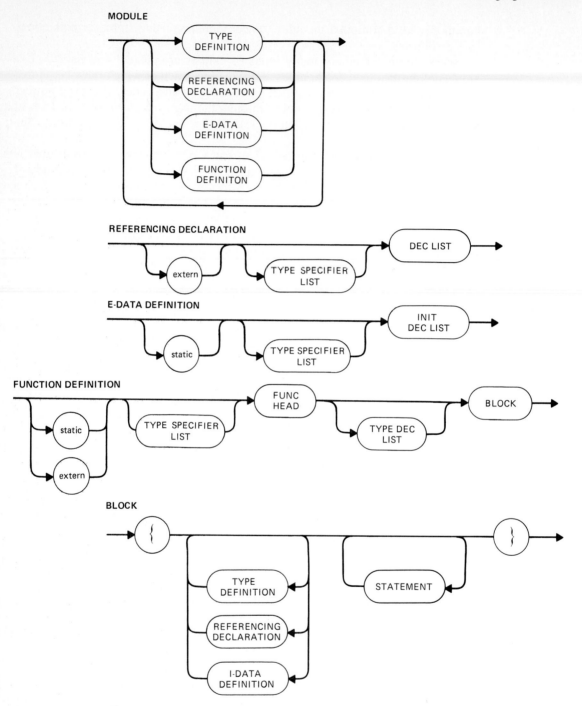

Figure 2.7. High-level module syntax

```
/*
 *      Print a table of characters and their associated codes.
 *      The ASCII character set is assumed in this program.
 */

#include <stdio.h>

main()
{
        char ch;          /* a character code */

        printf("character\t decimal code\t hex code\t octal code\n");

        ch = 32;

        while (ch < 127)
        {
                printf("     %c\t\t %d\t\t %x\t\t %o\n", ch, ch, ch, ch);
                ch++;
        }
        printf("\ndone.\n");
        exit();
}
```

Program 2.1. Character code table

character	decimal code	hex code	octal code
	32	20	40
!	33	21	41
"	34	22	42
#	35	23	43
$	36	24	44
	.	.	
	.		
	.		

We will now walk through this program and analyze its structure.
To begin, comments are presented to document the function of the program.
Next comes the line:

```
#include <stdio.h>
```

This line is called a *preprocessor directive*. Preprocessor directives are written with lines whose first non-white-space character is a # symbol. In general, preprocessor directives can be used to include one source file within another,

specify conditional compilation, and implement macro replacement. The processing of these directives occurs before the program is actually translated, hence the
name "preprocessor."

In Program 2.1, the #include directive specifies that the contents of the source
file stdio.h are to be processed at this point as if it were a part of the program. The
file stdio.h is supplied with the C compiler, and you may want to investigate its
contents. Its primary purpose is to define symbols (using more preprocessor
directives) that will be used in conjunction with the C standard library.

The file stdio.h may be found either in a directory of system header files or in
your working directory. In a multiuser environment, system-supplied header files
such as stdio.h are often stored together in a commonly accessible directory. The
directive #include <stdio.h> indicates that the header file is located in this
common directory. On a PC, system header files could be stored in your working
directory. The directive #include "stdio.h" indicates this. Depending on the
location of the system-supplied header files, use either the <stdio.h> or "stdio.h"
syntax.

The next part of our example presents a functioning declaration. A declaration
specifies the attributes that are to be associated with an identifier and the way that
they will be interpreted by the language. In the declaration

```
main()
{
        . . .
}
```

the identifier main is defined. The fact that main is a function is indicated by the
( ) pair following the function name. Every C program in the hosted execution
environment must have one and only one function named main that serves as the
program entry point when execution is initiated by the operating system.

The braces indicate a *block* (also called a compound statement) and are used to
delimit the body of the function. A block is made up of optional declarations
followed by a sequence of executable lines of code known as *statements*. The fact
that the declaration of main() is a defining declaration and not a referencing
declaration is due to the presence of the braces that constitute the code that will
make up the function.

The first line within the block of Program 2.1 is a *defining declaration* for the
variable ch:

```
char ch;
```

This definition is read as follows:

```
                     ┌─── Define a variable named ch
      char ch;       │    that has data type
                     └─── of char (character).
```

Table 2.9. Simple Type Specifiers

int	Single integer value
char	Single character value
float	Single floating-point value

The keyword *char* is one of several keywords that are used to specify the type of a program entity. This and other simple *type specifiers* are listed in Table 2.9.

Note the use of the semicolon to terminate the declaration. Semicolons are used in C to terminate most declarations and statements. However, semicolons are not used to terminate preprocessor directives (note the #include directive).

Most of the names that are used in a C program must be declared. Keywords are an obvious exception. Other declarations are supplied in the system header files such as stdio.h. This is the case for library functions such as printf().

The first executable statement in Program 2.1 is a *function call* to a function named printf:

```
printf("character\t decimal code\t hexadecimal code\t octal code\n");
```

The function call is indicated in a statement by the function call operator: ( ). Data values that are passed to the function, called *actual parameters,* are listed within the parentheses. In this case, a single string literal is passed to the printf() function as an actual parameter.

The printf() function will be linked with our module by the linkage editor. The object module for printf() is found in the standard library that is supplied with the compiler.

The purpose of printf() is to "print" formatted output (hence the "f" suffix). The function can be used simply to output text and also to perform conversion and data formatting, as will be illustrated shortly.

During execution, printf() sends its output to the standard output device, usually the programmer's terminal or monitor. The concepts of a standard input and output device should be addressed by your particular operating system and C compiler execution-environment documentation.

Notice the multiplicity of usage for the parentheses illustrated by this expression and the declaration of the main() function. Parentheses are used in declarations to indicate that a name refers to a function and also in expressions to indicate a function call. This is an example of the same symbols representing a punctuator (declaration) in one context and an operator (function call) in another.

The next statement in the example is called a *while statement*. The general syntax of the while statement is shown in Figure 2.8.

The statement (the loop body) in Figure 2.8 will be executed as long as the expression (the loop-control expression) evaluates to a nonzero value. (In C, 0 is used to represent false and any nonzero value to represent true.) The loop-control

WHILE

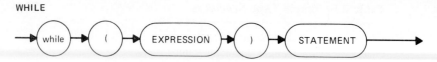

Figure 2.8. While statement

expression is evaluated once at the start of the statement execution and again after each execution of the loop body.

The while statement from Program 2.1 is outlined below:

```
while (ch < 127)
{
    . . .
}
```

In comparing this code with the syntax from Figure 2.8, the reader will note that the statement to be iteratively executed in this code is a block, as indicated by the braces. As it was necessary to execute more than one statement during each loop iteration, the use of a block was required in order to group this set of statements into a single syntactic unit. If the body consisted of only one statement, the braces would not have been necessary. The loop body must modify the loop-control expression or an infinite loop will result.

In examining the loop-control expression, we note that the relational operator $<$ was used to compare the value in ch with the integer constant 127. Iteration will continue as long as the value of ch is less than 127.

Within the loop body, note the printf( ) statement call:

```
printf("    %c\t\t %d\t\t %x\t\t %o\n", ch, ch, ch, ch);
```

This is an example of a formatted print. The first parameter is a string literal called the control string. The symbols in the control string that begin with the % symbol are known as *conversion specifications* and are used to indicate the intended location, formatting, and conversion that should be applied to the output data values in the printf( ) call. The conversion specifications correspond in left to right order with the arguments that follow the string literal. The first specification (%c) corresponds to the first occurrence of ch, the second specification (%d) to the second occurrence of ch, and so on. During execution, the conversion specifications are used to produce the formatted values of the corresponding arguments. For example, if ch contains the value 65, then %c indicates a conversion to character representation (A in ASCII), %d indicates decimal conversion (65), %x hexadecimal (41), and %o octal (101). See Figure 2.9 for further illustration.

Some common conversion specifications and their meanings are summarized in Table 2.10.

```
character              decimal code    hex code    octal code
                       32              20          40
      !                33              21          41
      "                34              22          42
      #                35              23          43

                                .
                                .
                                .
      0                48              30          60
      1                49              31          61
      2                50              32          62

                                .
                                .
                                .
      A                65              41          101
      B                66              42          102
      C                67              43          103

                                .
                                .
                                .
      a                97              61          141
      b                98              62          142
      c                99              63          143

                                .
                                .
                                .
      {                123             7B          173
      |                124             7C          174
      }                125             7D          175
      ~                126             7E          176

done.
```

Figure 2.9. Output of Program 2.1

Table 2.10. Some printf Conversion Specifications

%c	Single character conversion
%d	Decimal integer conversion
%u	Unsigned integer conversion
%x	Hexadecimal integer conversion
%o	Octal integer conversion
%f	Floating-point conversion

Characters in the printf control string other than conversion specifications are output as they appear—notice the use of the escape sequences to specify horizontal tabs (\t) and a new-line character (\n).

To increment the value in ch in the loop, we use the unary increment operator

```
ch++;
```

which could be written more conventionally as

```
ch = ch + 1;
```

The ++ operator is a short-hand notation that is often used by C programmers.

Pascal programmers might notice that the above statement involves values with two different types, char for ch and integer for the constant 1. C permits mixed-mode arithmetic, performing automatic conversion of types when required. Type conversion is further addressed in Chapter 4.

The last printf( ) in the program gives a visual completion message to the user.

Execution of the program terminates following the call to exit( ) and control then returns to the host environment operating system. If the exit( ) call is omitted, the program will terminate at the last executable statement of the function.

The abbreviated output of this program resulting from execution on a computer using ASCII is illustrated in Figure 2.9.

2.9   ADDITIONAL STATEMENTS AND DIRECTIVES

We have seen compound statements (blocks), expression statements, and the while statement so far in our program examples. Figure 2.10 illustrates the syntax of some additional C statements.

The *while* and *for* statements are known as *iteration statements*. The *if* statement is known as a *selection statement*.

For Statement

The *for statement* gathers the loop initialization, control, and modification expressions into a single statement. For this reason, many C programmers prefer it to the while statement. For example, Program 2.1 rewritten using the for statement would yield Program 2.2.

Notice that the for statement includes the loop initialization as the first expression, the loop-control expression as the second expression, and an expression that is executed after the body of the loop as the third expression (typically, the loop-control modification).

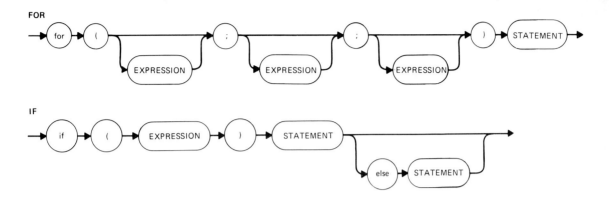

Figure 2.10. Additional statements

If Statement

The *if statement* embodies the if-then-else construct: the expression in parentheses (the controlling expression) is evaluated; if it is nonzero, then the first statement is executed; if the expression is zero (false), then one of two possibilities present themselves. If no else clause is present, execution simply proceeds to the next statement in the program. If the else clause is present, it specifies a statement that is to be executed when the controlling expression evaluates to zero (false).

```
/*
 *  Print a table of characters and their associated codes.
 */
#include "stdio.h"

main()
{
    char ch;           /* A character code. */

    printf("character\t decimal code\t hex code\t octal code\n");
    for (ch = 32; ch < 127; ch++)
    {
        printf("   %c\t\t %d\t\t %x\t\t %o\n", ch, ch, ch, ch);
    }
    printf("\ndone.\n");
    exit();
}
```

Program 2.2. Using the for statement

```
/*
 *  Input a string and display its associated character codes.
 */

#include <stdio.h>
#define BLANK ' '              /* lowest printable code */

main()
{
    int ch;

    printf("Enter a string : ");
    ch = getchar();
    while (ch != EOF)
    {
      printf("character\t decimal code\t hex code\t octal code\n");
      while (ch != '\n')
      {
        if (ch < BLANK)
        {
            printf("\n\n");
        }
        else
        {
            printf("\n%c\t\t %d\t\t %x\t\t %o\n", ch, ch, ch, ch);
        }
        ch = getchar();
      }
      printf("\nEnter a string : ");
      ch = getchar();
    }
    exit();
}
```

Program 2.3. Interactive character code conversion

Let us now rewrite Program 2.1 so that it is interactive. Instead of displaying a table of character codes, it will allow the user to enter a string of characters and then display the corresponding character codes. This version is shown in Program 2.3.

Program 2.3 begins by displaying a header line. It then accepts a string of characters from the user and displays each character along with the corresponding code in decimal, hexadecimal, and octal.

The program will execute, accepting strings and displaying codes, until the user enters an end-of-file indication. On UNIX systems, the end-of-file is entered from the keyboard by typing a control-D character; on MS-DOS systems, the end-of-file is a control-Z. (Check your system documentation if you use another operating system.) In the code, the end-of-file is indicated by the symbol EOF that is defined in the "stdio.h" include file.

Macros

The second line in Program 2.3

```
#define BLANK ' '
```

is a preprocessor directive called a *macro* that equates the symbolic name BLANK to the character constant ' '. After this directive, BLANK can be used anywhere in the code in place of ' '. EOF is also implemented as a macro that is #defined in the file stdio.h. Before actual compilation, the preprocessor replaces occurrences of BLANK and EOF (outside of string literals and comments) with their #defined values.

Functions That Return Values

Program 2.3 introduced one of the C language functions commonly used to input data: getchar(). Here we see an example of a function call that results in a value. This value is assigned to a variable in the assignment expression:

```
ch = getchar();
```

The type of ch was declared to be int because getchar () returns a value of this type. Integers are returned by getchar() because: (1) character codes are represented by integers and (2) to indicate exceptions, getchar() returns negative integer values. Negative values are used for exceptions because these cannot be used for character codes. For example, getchar() returns EOF, defined in stdio.h to (−1), to indicate end-of-file. The type char may or may not be permitted to hold a negative value (this is implementation dependent). Thus, the value return from getchar() should be assigned to a variable of type integer.

Within the innermost while loop of Program 2.3, the if statement is used to avoid attempting to print unprintable ASCII values. If the value of ch is less than a BLANK, we instead output a blank line. Remember, BLANK is a macro that is simply replaced with its #defined string by the preprocessor as a part of the compilation process. Thus, the code

```
if (ch < BLANK)
```

is expanded to

```
if (ch < ' ')
```

Recall also that ' ' is a character constant. Its type is integer, and its value is the

ASCII encoding for a blank: 32. The if statement compares the ASCII code in ch with 32. If ch is less than 32, the "then" part of the if statement is executed.

Program 2.3 introduced the concept of character input. Let us now consider the processing of character input that represents numeric values, and the conversion required to render such values amenable for use with arithmetic operators.

2.10 CHARACTER-TO-BINARY-CONVERSION EXAMPLE

Character Codes

It is often necessary to input a string of characters that represents a numeric value and to perform computations on the number so represented. In this case, the ASCII or EBCDIC character codes that represent the digits must be converted from their character code to the binary (integer) representation of the corresponding digits.

Character-to-Binary Conversion

You will notice (see Appendix B) that in both the ASCII and EBCDIC character sets, the character codes for the digits 0–9 are assigned sequential values. For example, the ASCII codes are 48–57 and the EBCDIC codes are 240–249. To convert the character code for a digit from its character code to binary, simply subtract the code for a zero. For ASCII

```
ch = getchar();
value = ch - 48;
```

For EBCDIC

```
ch = getchar();
value = ch - 240;
```

Both ch and value have type int in the code above.

A problem with the above two examples is that they are not portable between environments with different character sets. A better choice for the code thus is

```
ch = getchar();
value = ch - '0';
```

These statements will input one character (presumably a digit) and convert it to its binary value.

To input a sequence of digits that represent an integer and convert that number to binary format for use with arithmetic operators, we could use the code fragment in Figure 2.11.

```
/* Input a sequence of digits an
 * convert the number to an integer.
 */

value = 0;
ch = getchar();
while (ch != '\n')
{
    value = (value * 10) + (ch - '0');
    ch = getchar();
}
```

Figure 2.11. Character-to-binary conversion

This code will input a string of digits until a new line is entered, convert them to binary, and accumulate the integer value of the string in the variable value. The multiplication by ten takes into account the place value of each succeeding digit in the string. Library functions to perform this conversion are available, but require array data structures that we are not yet prepared to introduce. For the present, we will have to use our version as illustrated in Figure 2.11.

Before we apply the code from Figure 2.11, we shall consider an alternative coding style for this algorithm that is preferred by most C programmers.

2.11 USING EMBEDDED ASSIGNMENT EXPRESSIONS

Recall that in Section 2.7 we said that the value of the assignment expression

```
lvalue = expression
```

is the value that is assigned to the object on the left-hand side of the operator. In C, assignment expressions can be *embedded* into other expressions both to assign a value and to use that value with yet another operator.

Consider the code in Figure 2.12, which is the same algorithm as illustrated in Figure 2.11, but using the embedded assignment statement.

In this code, the value of the assignment expression (ch = getchar()) is used as an operand with the not-equal-to operator. The expression (ch = getchar()) requires enclosure in parentheses because the assignment operator has lower precedence than the not-equal-to operator. Thus, the expression (ch = getchar()) is processed first, resulting in a call to the getchar() function and assignment of the returned value to the variable ch. The value of the assignment expression is the value that is being assigned—that is, the value returned from getchar(). This is the value that is compared with '\n' (new line). Thus, the while loop executes as

```
/*  Alternative style, using embedded assignment */

value = 0;
while ((ch = getchar()) != '\n')
{
     value = (value * 10) + (ch - '0');
}
```

Figure 2.12. Using embedded assignment

long as the value returned from getchar( ) is not a new-line character. A common
C programming error is to write the above while statement as

```
while (ch = getchar()  != '\n')
```

This will result in the value returned from getchar( ) to be compared with '\n', and
the resulting value (1 or 0) assigned to ch as != has higher precedence than =.

The code in Figure 2.12 is often used rather than that in Figure 2.11 because the
former eliminates the necessity for a duplicate call to getchar( ). Figure 2.12 is a
more compact notation.

We shall apply the code from Figure 2.12 to write a program that accepts two
numbers on separate lines from the standard input and displays their product and
quotient to the standard output. See Program 2.4.

Note that we performed the above operations using integer arithmetic. The use
of floating-point arithmetic is left as an exercise for the reader. Conversion of
character data to floating point is much more difficult because of the variety of
forms that the floating-point data can take. It may be best initially to restrict the
number of forms you accept.

An obvious improvement to Program 2.4 would be to isolate the character-to-
binary-conversion code into a function. We should also add some data validity
checks to ensure that digits are indeed entered. This will be done in Chapter 3 in
the context of another example.

2.12 PORTABILITY AND SOFTWARE ENGINEERING ISSUES

Style

Any programming language provides a notation for the description of an algorithm. This notation, no matter how well conceived or defined, can be abused to
produce unreadable code. The following guidelines apply to any programming
language.

```
/*
 *   Accept two numbers and display their product
 *   and integral quotient.
 */

#include <stdio.h>

main()
{
    int a, b;                  /* values to multiply, divide */
    int product, quotient;
    int ch;

    a = 0;
    b = 0;

    printf("Enter first number (A) : ");
    while ((ch = getchar()) != '\n')
    {
        a = (a * 10) + (ch - '0');
    }

    printf("Enter second number (B) : ");
    while ((ch = getchar()) != '\n')
    {
        b = (b * 10) + (ch - '0');
    }

    product = a * b;

    if (b != 0)
    {
        quotient = a / b;
        printf("\nA * B = %d\t A / B = %d\n",product, quotient);
    }
    else  /* avoid attempt to divide by zero */
    {
        printf("\nA * B = %d\tdivison by zero is undefined\n", produc
    }
    exit();
}
```

Program 2.4. Product and quotient example

Identifier names—variable, function, construct names—should be descriptive. The length of a name is not always an indicator of its descriptive ability. The context of the program often determines the meaningfulness of a name. In scientific programming, the variables x and y are quite acceptable for describing the x and y coordinates of a point. In fact, these names are actually preferable to the longer x-coordinate and y-coordinate. In a business application, the converse may be true.

In C, the underscore character is a convenient symbol to use for a name that one might like to construct from two or more words. A variable that holds a running total could be named running_total and the current cursor position could be named cursor_pos. When the number of characters that can be used for a variable name is limited (such as to six for certain kinds of identifiers in some C implementations), the programmer can often construct informative but abbreviated names by removing the vowels. For example, quantity could be coded as qnty.

Variable names should be chosen that have a "psychological distance" from one another. It is better to have names that differ in only the first character than names that differ in only the last character.

Whenever special constants are used in a program, for example, the value of pi or a tolerance value, these should be given a name via the #define directive. By defining the value of a constant in one place, changes to that value can be achieved easily. Also, the name of the constant can be chosen to be more meaningful than the value itself.

It is common practice among C programmers to write variable names using lowercase and macro symbols using uppercase. With this convention, it is easy to determine whether an identifier is a true variable or simply a symbolic representation of a constant value.

The statements that make up the body of a loop or conditional statement should be indented to highlight the extent of control. Compare the two styles illustrated below.

With Indentation and Braces

```
if (divisor == 0)
{
    printf("Division by zero is undefined\n");
}
else
{
    printf("Quotient = %f\n", dividend / divisor );
}
printf("Execution complete\n");
```

Without Indentation and Braces

```
if (divisor == 0)
printf("Division by zero is undefined\n");
else printf("Quotient = %f\n", dividend / divisor );
printf("Execution complete\n");
```

Indentation makes it easy to locate the code that is executed when the condition (divisor == 0) is either true or false.

Notice that the braces are not required in the first example. They are required when the body contains more than a single statement. However, consistent use of braces to delimit the body of ifs and loops is good practice because it lays a foundational groundwork that will accommodate the addition of statements to the body at a later time.

Another stylistic convention that adds to the readability of a program is to use a blank line to highlight logical blocks of code. The code fragment shown in Figure 2.13, from Program 2.4, illustrates the use of blank lines to group statements that perform related functions and to delimit groups from one another.

C Language Variations

The characters that are allowed in identifiers and the maximum allowable number of significant characters in an identifier that is supported by an implementation of the language may exceed those listed in this text. Obviously, the use of such extensions can lead to nonportable code, and their usage is thus discouraged.

Character constants are limited to a single character in some older, nonstandard C compilers. Additionally, we noted that the value of a character constant that

```
int a, b;                    /* values to multiply, divide */
int product, quotient;
int ch;

a = 0;
b = 0;

printf("Enter first number (A) : ");
while ((ch = getchar()) != '\n')
{
    a = (a * 10) + (ch - '0');
}

printf("Enter second number (B) : ");
while ((ch = getchar()) != '\n')
{
    b = (b * 10) + (ch - '0');
}

product = a * b;
```

Figure 2.13. Using blank lines

consists of more than a single character is implementation dependent. For these reasons, the use of multiple characters within character constants is strongly discouraged.

The ANSI standard specifies that adjacent string literals will be concatenated to form a single literal. Thus, the example shown below is equivalent to "\t\tVersion 1.1\n\n" and the corresponding ASCII representation is also illustrated.

```
"\t\tVersion "
"1.1\n\n"
|11|11|86|101|114|115|105|111|110|32|49|46|49|10|10|0|
```

This is an addition to the C language made by the standard, and is not supported by many prestandard compilers. For maximum portability and maintainability, we recommend that this feature be avoided.

Some C compilers support nested comments. Although this is a convenience when "commenting out" code during testing, a better way to accomplish this is to use conditional compilation (to be discussed in Chapter 5). For example, consider the following code segment, with comments added, from Program 2.4:

```
/* Get the first operand from the user */
printf("Enter first number (A) : ");
while ((ch = getchar()) != '\n')
{
   a = (a * 10) + (ch - '0');
}

/* Get the second operand from the user */
printf("Enter second number (B) : ");
while ((ch = getchar ()) != '\n')
{
   b = (b * 10) + (ch - '0');
}

product = a * b;
```

Suppose that we wanted temporarily to disable the code that inputs values and simply test the remainder of the code with zero-valued operands. One might be tempted to "comment out" this code as follows:

```
/*                                    ←Attempt to comment out
   /* Get the first operand from the user */
   printf("Enter first number (A) : ");
   while ((ch = getchar()) != '\n')
   {
      a = (a * 10) + (ch - '0');
   }
```

```
                    /* Get the second operand from the user */
                    printf("Enter second number (B) : ");
                    while ((ch = getchar ()) != '\n')
                    {
                        b = (b * 10) + (ch - '0');
                    }
        */                                    ←—End of comment out
                    product = a * b;
```

Notice that the comment characters are now mismatched:

```
/*
    /* Get the first operand from the user */←—Terminates comment
    └──────This is ignored
```

The result is that the following code (printf( ), while) is outside of the comment. As with other extensions, nested comments should be avoided.

Particular implementations of the C compiler often contain a few additional keywords. Nonstandard keywords can be a problem both in porting software to the nonstandard environment (because the code may have used that word as an identifier) and when porting software out of such an environment (as the keyword no longer will be recognized). Nonstandard keywords should be avoided or isolated by using conditional compilation (discussed in Chapter 5).

Some systems may support nonstandard escape codes for character representation. These can be avoided by using the octal or hexadecimal escape code equivalent, but this can introduce a portability problem when moving the code between machines with different code sets.

Recall that preprocessor directives are introduced with the #. Examples are #include <stdio.h> and #define EOF (–1). Many C compilers require that the # be coded in the first column of a line, not the first non-white-space character as specified by the ANSI standard. While in the transition phase to the new standard, greater portability can be obtained by following this old convention.

The entry point for a program running in a hosted environment is the main( ) function. For programs that run in the freestanding environment, the entry point is not specified and is thus left as an implementation specific issue. Software written for such a freestanding environment must address the question of the specific entry point for each different environment.

The topic of data type was introduced in this chapter. The magnitude of value that variables of the various types may span is implementation dependent and is related to the specific hardware in the execution environment. To determine the limiting magnitudes for the integer and floating point types, refer to the standard include files limits.h and float.h. The following are some macros from limits.h for an 16-bit PC C compiler:

```
#define INT_MAX    32767      /* maximum (signed) int value */
#define INT_MIN   -32767      /* minimum (signed) int value */
#define LONG_MAX  2147483647  /* maximum (signed) long value */
#define LONG_MIN -2147483647  /* minimum (signed) long value */
```

When deciding between a type, such as int or long, the programmer can refer to limits.h and float.h to ascertain the range of values that can be represented by the type. The minimum numerical limits as specified by the standard are listed in Appendix A.

2.13 SUMMARY

In this chapter, we considered the foundations for the syntax of the C language. Syntax diagrams were introduced as a formal way of defining the syntax.

The tokens that are used to compose C programs were defined: identifiers, keywords, punctuators, constants, string literals, and operators. Next, several examples were presented that illustrated the structure of a C module. We noted that a module consists of data and function declarations.

Data definitions were then examined and the simple type specifiers (keywords) int, char, and float were introduced. Next, C operators and statements were introduced. The increment, decrement, relational, multiplication, division, and modulus operators were presented and a subset of statements (expression statements, the while statement, the for statement, and the if statement) were illustrated in the examples.

The C printf() and getchar() functions were introduced that perform, respectively, formatted output to the standard output device and character input from the standard input device. Examples of interactive programs were also presented. The #include preprocessor directive was again examined and the #define preprocessor was introduced.

Finally, some portability issues related to the material presented in the chapter were considered. As a general rule, the reader was warned to avoid nonstandard language extensions, especially those relating to the syntax of the language tokens. We noted also that the numerical magnitudes of the various data types that were discussed in the chapter are implementation dependent, but the limits are specified in the include files limits.h and float.h.

Keywords

actual parameter	character constant
assignment operator	character type
binary operator	comment
block	constant

conversion specification
declarations
defining declaration
decimal constant
embedded assignment
escape sequence
expression
floating constant
for statement
floating-point type
function call
function call operator
function declaration
getchar( )
hexadecimal constant
identifier
if statement
include directive
integer constant
integer type
iteration statement
lvalue
macro
main function
module

new-line character
nonterminal symbol
octal constant
operand
operator
operator precedence
preprocessor directive
printf( )
punctuator
referencing declaration
relational operator
selection statement
simple types
statement
string literal
syntax
syntax diagram
terminal symbol
token
type
type specifier
unary operator
value of an expression
while statement
white space

References

Draft American National Standard X3.159–198x, Programming Language C. Copies may be obtained from Global Engineering Documents, Inc., 2805 Irvine, CA 92714 (1-800-854-7179).

Plauger, P. J. 1988. Types play central role in new Standard C. *C Users J* 6 (3): 17–23. R&D Publications, Inc., McPherson, Kans.

Discussion Questions

1. Discuss the concept of a type. Why is it important to distinguish between types such as integers and floating point? Discuss how internal storage representation and arithmetic operators differ for integers and floating-point values.

2. Discuss the representation of integers in binary, octal, decimal, and hexadecimal base systems. Review place value and conversion between bases. Is the internal representation of the number 10 different from 012?

3. Motivate the need to convert between the character (ASCII or EBCDIC) representation of the digits and the internal (binary) representation of such numbers. For example, if the digit 2 is typed on a keyboard, what is the value that is returned from a call to getchar()? How does this value differ from the value stored in the variable x following the assignment $x = 2$?

4. Discuss the concept of the value of an expression. Is the value of an expression always obvious? Consider, for example, the value of the expressions a + b, a++, a > b, and a = b.

5. Compare events that happen at compile time with those that happen during execution. For example, compare the processing performed for preprocessor directives, data definitions, and operators within expressions. Are there any expressions that might be evaluated at compile time?

6. C allows arithmetic operations on character constants and character types. This may seem strange to a person familiar with Pascal or BASIC. Why does C permit arithmetic on character objects but still uses the operator in a consistent manner?

7. Discuss issues of good coding style. Why indent code within braces? When are comments appropriate? How can white space be used to improve the readability of a program? Why is it important to write a program so that it can be read easily?

Exercises

1. Express the following constant values using the appropriate C language syntax:
   a. The value 196000 in scientific notation. Put your decimal point after the 1.
   b. An integer constant that represents the binary value 01010011 as a hexadecimal integer constant.
   c. A character constant that represents the Acknowledgment control code (in ASCII, this code has the integer value 6).
   d. A character constant that represents the single new-line character.
   e. A string literal that could be used as a prompt so that the cursor remains on the current line after the message.

   f. A string literal that could be used with printf( ) that would cause a page eject using a form-feed character.

   g. A string literal, to be used with printf(), that would output the string: Please enter "DONE" when finished. [*Hint:* To display double quotes, you may need to use an escape sequence.] The string should end with a new-line.

2. What is the difference in internal representation between the character constant 'a' and the string literal "a"?

3. In what order will the operators in the following expressions be evaluated?
   a. a + b * c
   b. c = a + b
   c. c == a + b
   d. c = getchar( ) != '\n'
   e. a++ == 10
   f. c = a++ * 2

4. All C expressions have a value. That value can be used within other expressions, such as in assignment statements, as a function call parameter, and so on. Consider the following variables:

```
int a, b, x, y, z;
```

Suppose that these variables are initialized as follows:

```
a = 0; b = 1; x = 2; y = 0; z = 3;
```

State the value of each of the following expressions. Treat each expression as independent of the others.

Expression	Value
a + b	
x = a	
a++	
++a	
a == y	
- -x	
z * a + b	

5. How many iterations will the following loop perform?

```
count = 0;
while (count++ < 10) print("counting...\n");
```

6. Rewrite the two statements in Exercise 5 as a for statement.

7. In Section 2.10, we discussed the conversion of characters to binary values. In particular, the expression:

```
(ch - '0')
```

was presented as a portable expression that would convert character representations for digits to the corresponding binary values (assuming contiguous, ascending assignment of character codes). Explain why this statement is portable whereas the alternatives discussed in the text are not.

8. Experimentally determine the number of significant characters for identifiers in your environment by writing a program.

Programming Problems

1. Write a C program that counts from 2 to 100, displaying each integer as it counts. The program should use the for statement to do the initialization, loop, and counting.

2. Write a C program that counts from 200 to 0. Again, use a single executable statement to do the initialization, loop, and counting.

3. Write a program that it outputs a conversion chart for degrees Celsius to Fahrenheit, beginning with 0 degrees Fahrenheit through 100 degrees Fahrenheit. The formula for this conversion is

```
C = 5(F- 32)/9
```

Declare the variables C and F to be of type float.

4. Most C libraries have a function called putchar() that is used to output a character. Putchar() is used as follows:

```
putchar(c)
```

where c is the identifier (or constant) that represents the character to be output.

Write a C program using getchar() and putchar() that will read characters from the standard input and echo them back to the standard output. Echo all characters as typed, except convert all lowercase alphabetic characters to uppercase. It is easy to do this without making assumptions about the coding scheme. The ASCII and EBCDIC character sets are listed in Appendix B. Use the ~ character as a sentinel to terminate your program.

5. Write a program that will read a C program [use getchar()] and extract only the comments. The comments should be displayed on the standard output. You may use either printf() or the function putchar() that was described in Problem 4. Remember, a C comment begins with /* and ends with */, may span several lines of source text, or may even be embedded in a statement. Also, /* and */ should be ignored if they appear within string literals or character constants. Do not allow embedded comments. If available, use command line redirection to cause the input to come from any of your current C programs. (A program such as this that transforms its standard input in some way and then sends the results on to its standard output is called a *filter*.)

6. Use the code from Program 2.4 and some code of your own to build an interactive desk calculator. Use infix notation, but restrict expressions to simple expressions that have only two operands (constants), one operator, and no parentheses. Allow addition, subtraction, multiplication, or division.

7. Rewrite Program 2.4 so that it operates using floating-point values. You will have to declare the appropriate variables as type float. You will also have to rewrite the integer-to-binary-conversion code so that it will accept a decimal point and so that floating-point values can be entered as input to the program.

8. Write a program that will accept a line of text from the standard input; count the number of words, lines, and characters in the file; and then output these numbers to the standard output by using printf(). For simplicity, assume that words are delimited by either a single blank, or a new-line or end-of-file character. Lines are delimited by a new-line character. Find out how to enter end-of-file from the standard input and use this to terminate your input. The function getchar() will return a value represented by the symbol EOF (defined in stdio.h) when an end-of-file is entered from the standard input. If you are using a UNIX system, you may want to check your output using the wc utility.

9. Recall that by the Pythagorean theorem, given a right triangle with legs a and b and hypotenuse c,

$$c^2 = a^2 + b^2$$

Develop a program that will determine whether a triangle is a right triangle, given the three sides. Make the program interactive so that it accepts integral values for the three sides from the standard output, and outputs either Yes or No as to whether the sides represent a right triangle.

10. The factorial of a nonnegative integer, n, called n!, is defined as follows:

```
0! = 1
1! = 1
2! = 2 * 1
     .
     .
     .
n! = n * (n-1) * (n-2) * ... * 2 * 1
          or
n! = n * (n-1)!
```

Write a program, using a loop, to compute a table of factorials for 1! through 10!.

3 Declarations Functions and Data

Declarations are used to introduce the name of a data object or function to the compiler. We will use the word "entity" to refer to data objects or functions in a program. Just as people use introductions to give a person's name and information about that person, C uses declarations to introduce an entity's name and information about it. The information that a declaration can provide includes type, scope, linkage, duration, and initialization. We will examine declarations and the information that they convey in this chapter. Large C programs are often broken down into functions that are coded in separate source files and independently compiled. This chapter will illustrate the use of separate compilation of functions. To assist us in writing more meaningful programs, we will reexamine the simple arithmetic data types and their variants, and we will introduce the array type, the switch (case), and do-while statements. Design techniques called abstraction and information hiding will be illustrated that take advantage of some of the power of the C language facilities discussed in this chapter. After studying the material here, the reader will be in a position to write fairly sophisticated C programs.

3.1 MULTIMODULE C PROGRAMS

Section 2.8 introduced the organization of a C program. In this text, we call a file of C source code a module. A C program can be composed of one or more individual modules that are coded and compiled separately and later linked together to form the complete executable program.

A module is composed of declarations and (optionally) preprocessor directives. The relationship between a C program and its modules, data, and function declarations is shown in Figure 3.1.

Notice that a C program is composed of one or more modules. Modules, in turn, are composed of data and function declarations. Some declarations actually define an entity such as a data object or a function. Other declarations reference an entity that is defined elsewhere in the module or another module. This is the reason for the distinction between declarations that are definitions and those that are declarations. The next section illustrates this structure through example.

57

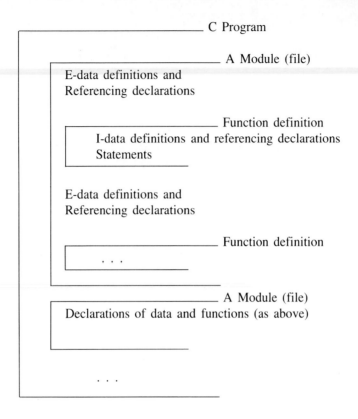

Figure 3.1. Organization of a C program

3.2 WRITING FUNCTIONS

Declaring Functions

As an example of the organization illustrated in Figure 3.1, consider a simple function that accepts a single lowercase character and converts it to uppercase. To test the converter, we will need a *driver* function, leading us to the two-function skeleton module illustrated in Program 3.1.

Let us examine the code illustrated in Program 3.1.

The first line is a preprocessor directive that instructs the preprocessor to include the contents of file stdio.h in this module. The file stdio.h contains directives and declarations that are used with the I/O functions. For the present

```
contents of convert.c:

#include <stdio.h>

main()
{
   int ch;                  /* character to be converted */
   int convert( int );      /* upper case converter function */

   /* driver code goes here */
}

/* function to convert lower to upper case */

int convert( int c );
{
     /* code to convert case goes here */

     return( c );
}
```

Program 3.1. A two-function module

time, just assume that the information in this file enables us to use the I/O
functions properly.

   The remaining code consists of C language declarations. The first such declaration is the defining declaration of the function named main.

   Consider the declarations within main( ). The first, int ch, is a defining declaration for the variable ch that specifies that ch will refer to an integer. The second,
int convert(int), is a referencing declaration for a function named convert. The
meaning of this declaration is illustrated below.

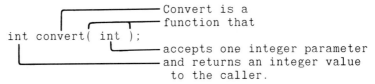

The declaration can be divided into two parts:

1. The *type specifier:* int. For a function, the type specifier gives the data type
   for the value returned from the function. For a data object, the type specifier
   indicates the type of value to be stored in the object.
2. The *declarator:* convert(int). This specifies the name and other characteristics of an entity. In this example, the parentheses indicate that convert is a

function. The keyword int inside the parentheses indicates that convert( ) requires a single parameter of type int when it is called.

The declaration of convert( ) is a referencing declaration because the declaration has no body associated with it. In fact, no body is permitted because function definitions cannot be nested. Henceforth, whenever convert is used in main( ), it is understood that this is a reference to a function requiring a single integer valued parameter and that convert returns an integer value.

In ANSI C, a referencing declaration for a function is called a *function prototype*. The task of actually defining the code for convert( ) is left to the subsequent *defining declaration:*

```
int convert( int c )
{
        /* code to convert case goes here! */
        return c;
}
```

The defining declaration gives the function name, its return type, the list of parameter names and types, and the function body. The number and type of parameters and the type of the function return value must agree with any function prototype declarations. The parameter names that are declared in the declarator (within parentheses) will be used to hold a copy of the parameter values passed by any calls to the function. The name of the parameters need not match the names used in any calling functions.

Returning Values from Functions

The *return statement* in convert( ) is used to exit the function and to send a value back to the caller. The general syntax is

```
return expression
```

When executed, the expression is evaluated and the resulting value is returned as the value of the call in the calling function. Notice that the return statement is an executable statement, and does not necessarily have to be (but usually is) the last statement in a function.

Let us now code the bodies for main( ) and convert( ). Refer to Appendix B, the ASCII character code table, and note that the lowercase characters a–z are assigned the character codes 97–121, and the uppercase characters A–Z are given the values 65–89. Thus, to convert between the cases, either add or subtract the difference between the same characters in both cases. For example, given a lowercase ASCII character code in the variable c, the code

$$c = c - (\text{‘a’}-\text{‘A’}) \quad \text{or} \quad c = c - \text{‘a’} + \text{‘A’}$$

would convert the code in c from lowercase to uppercase. Program 3.2(a) reflects this observation.

The driver will accept a single line of lowercase characters and then call convert( ) once for each character entered. The corresponding uppercase character that is returned by each call to convert( ) is output using printf( ).

Using Multiple-Source Files

Considering Program 3.2(a), convert( ) is the useful function; main( ) is really a "throwaway" driver. It would be easier to reuse convert( ) if it were not coded within the same source file as main( ). Thus, a better way to code the above two functions would be to use two separate source files, as illustrated in Program 3.2(b).

Notice that we are now using two source files: driver.c to hold main( ) and toupper.c to hold convert( ). Thus, we can edit and compile these two modules independently. For example, the UNIX command

```
cc -c driver.c
```

will compile driver.c to produce the object file driver.o. The -c flag on the above command means "compile only." Without the -c flag, the cc command would

```
#include <stdio.h>

main()
{
    int ch;
    int convert( int );

    while ((ch = getchar()) != '\n')
    {
        printf("char = %c\n",convert(ch));
    }
    exit();
}

/* Convert lower case to upper case */
int convert( int c )
{
    c = c - 'a' + 'A';
    return( c );
}
```

Program 3.2(a). Case converter function and driver

```
contents of driver.c:

#include <stdio.h>

main()
{
   int ch;
   int convert( int );

   while ((ch = getchar()) != '\n')
   {
      printf("char = %c\n",convert(ch));
   }
   exit();
}

contents of toupper.c:

/* routine to convert lower case ASCII to upper case *,

int convert( int c )
{
    c = c - 'a' + 'A';
    return( c );
}
```

Program 3.2(b). Using multiple-source files

attempt to compile and link the driver module. Similarly, the command cc -c toupper.c would produce an object file named toupper.o.

The file driver.o is not executable. One reason that it is not is that it is missing the code for both convert() and printf(). The linkage editor (or linker) program will be used to combine the needed modules to produce an executable file. To combine our object files and produce an executable file named upcase, we could use the UNIX command:

```
cc -o upcase driver.o toupper.o
```

This will instruct the linker to combine driver.o, toupper.o, and the C library containing printf.o to produce the executable file upcase.

Linkage

Program 3.2(b) contains several declarations, as follows:

```
main()                          Defining declaration for the
{                               function named main
  . . .
}

int ch;                         Defining declaration for the variable ch

int convert( int );  Prototype (referencing) declaration for
                     the function convert.

int convert( ... )   Defining declaration for convert function
{
  . . .
}

int c                           Defining declaration for the function
                                parameter c
```

Notice that some declarations, such as "int ch" and "int c," stand alone. Other declarations introduce the same name, for example, "int convert(int)" and "int convert(int c) { . . . }."

Multiple declarations for the same function or data object can be coded provided that each declaration has *linkage*. Declarations that stand alone are said to have *no linkage*. These names are declared once. An example of a variable with no linkage is the variable ch, shown above. An entity can have *internal linkage*. A declaration with internal linkage refers to the same function or data object as other declarations of the same name in the same module. An object or function with *external linkage* can refer to the same function or object as other declarations of the same name in any module. The function convert() in the example above has external linkage. The feature of external linkage allows us to code convert() in one module and reference it in another. Names that are introduced in a referencing declaration must have either internal or external linkage, as a referencing declaration implies the existence of a defining declaration elsewhere.

The C language has several rules that determine the linkage for a function or object. We will examine these rules in Section 3.3, after looking at another application of the use of multiple modules.

3.3 INFORMATION CONVEYED BY DECLARATIONS

Data Abstraction and Information Hiding

Many advantages are to be gained by breaking a large program into multiple functions and modules. The ease of editing and potential for reusability of a module are advantages over a large monolithic program. Another advantage is that we can implement the design techniques of *information hiding* and *abstract data types*.

Information hiding is a design technique that suggests that effective modularity can be achieved by defining a set of independent modules that communicate with one another only the information that is necessary to achieve the desired software function.

Data abstraction allows a designer to represent a data object in terms of those operations (functions) that can be applied to it. With data abstraction, we implement a data structure in a module and provide C functions that furnish operations on that data type at a level such that the user of the data structure does not have to be concerned with the physical (in terms of code) representation of the data structure. Essentially, the functions "hide" the physical data structure from other modules in the program. Abstract data types provide a method for implementing information hiding.

As an example, consider a module that provides a LIFO (last in, first out) stack data structure. A stack is a linear list with a top and depth. Data can be added, or pushed, into the top of the stack and, in turn, removed, or popped, from the top. Thus, the last item pushed into the stack will be the first popped out. The depth of the stack is the maximum number of items that can be pushed in without intervening pops.

Using the concepts of information hiding and abstract data types, we could provide a single C module that affords push( ) and pop( ) functions. The module will contain the necessary data structures to represent the stack and a variable to keep track of its depth, but the details of these data objects can be hidden in the module. The skeleton for such a module is illustrated in Program 3.3.

In the eyes of a user of this module, push( ) and pop( ) implement a data type that is an abstraction of a LIFO stack. The user of push( ) and pop( ) need not be concerned with the way that data is actually stored or retrieved from the stack.

The following sections examine this code and further elaborate upon the information conveyed by the declarations illustrated in Program 3.3.

Context of Declarations

In Figures 2.7 and 3.1, we described the high-level syntax for C programs and modules. Modules are composed of three kinds of declarations:

1. Referencing declarations. These can be *inside* or *outside* of functions (or blocks).
2. E-data definitions. These are coded *outside* of functions.

contents of stack.c:

```
    static int top = 0;       /* pointer to top of stack */
    static int stack[10];     /* the stack itself */
    int serrno;               /* an error code indicator */

    int push( int element )
    {
        /* code for push goes here */
    }

    int pop( void )
    {
        int result = 0;

        /* code for pop goes here */
    }
```

Program 3.3. Skeleton version of stack module

3. Function definitions. These are *outside* of any functions—they cannot be nested within a function. Function definitions can contain referencing declarations and/or I-data definitions.

Notice that there are two contexts for declarations: inside or outside of functions (or blocks). A third context not shown on our diagrams is a definition of a *function parameter* within the parentheses of a function declaration. Table 3.1 summarizes these three contexts.

Declarations within each context take on different default attributes. These attributes include scope, linkage, and duration. The next two sections examine scope and linkage.

Table 3.1. Contexts for Declarations

File level declaration. A declaration outside of any function declaration. Examples from Program 3.3 are the declaration of top, stack, serrno, push( ), and pop( ).

Function parameter level declaration. Declarations contained in the parentheses of a function declaration. In Program 3.3, the variable name "element" has parameter level context.

Block level declaration. Declarations written within the braces of a function (or any other block in a function). The example from Program 3.3 is the declaration of result in pop( ).

Scope

The context of a declaration determines the scope of the name that is being declared. *Scope* is the portion of a program in which a name is visible; that is, it can be used. The scope rules that apply to the three contexts are shown in Table 3.2.

As indicated in Table 3.2, top, stack, serrno, push() and pop() are visible from their declarations to the end of the file. Thus, push() and pop() may use the variables top, stack, and serrno. The variable "element" can only be used within push() because it has parameter scope. The variable "result" can be used only within pop() because it has block scope.

Because of the scope rules, one declaration can mask another, permitting the same name to be used to represent more than one object. Consider Program 3.4.

Table 3.2. Scope Rules

1. Names declared in file level declarations are visible from the end of the declaration to the end of the module. This is called *file scope*.

2. Names declared as function parameters are visible only in the body of the associated function definition. This is called *parameter scope*.

3. Names declared with block scope are visible from the declaration to the end of the block. This is *block scope*.

```
#include <stdio.h>

main()
{
   int i;

   i = 0;
   printf("i = %d\n",i);
   for (i = 0; i < 2; i++)
   {
      int i;

      i = -2;
      printf("i = %d\n",i);
   }
   printf("i = %d",i);
   exit();
}
```

Program 3.4. Variables with different scopes

This example defines two different variables named i. Inside of the for loop, the innermost i is visible. Outside of the loop, the outer i is visible. Thus, the for loop should perform two iterations. The output of Program 3.4 is as follows:

```
i = 0
i = -2
i = -2
i = 2
```

Default Linkage and Explicit Linkage

The context of a declaration also determines the default linkage given to an object. The rules for default linkage are listed in Table 3.3.

Notice that internal linkage does not appear in Table 3.3. Internal linkage is assigned explicitly to an entity by using the storage class keyword "static" in the declaration. Internal linkage is used to enforce information hiding, because it guarantees that a data object or function cannot be referenced outside of the module. Functions can also be declared as static. Such a function can only be referenced from within the module in which it is coded.

The linkage for each name in Program 3.3 is summarized as follows:

External:	serror, push( ), and pop( )	(by default)
Internal:	top and stack	(by explicit use of static)
No linkage:	element, result	(by default)

The storage class keyword "extern" can be used on referencing declarations to indicate explicitly that a given declaration is not a defining declaration. Figure 3.2 shows the syntax diagrams for referencing declarations and E-data definitions.

The number of characters that are recognized as significant for names with external linkage can be limited to as few as six, in contrast with the 31 that can be used in other names. The restriction is due to the constraints imposed by some linkage editors.

Notice in Figure 3.2 the nonterminals dec list and init-dec-list. These include

Table 3.3. Default Linkage Rules

1. No linkage. Function parameters and data objects within a block.

2. External linkage. Data objects declared outside of any function and functions that have not been previously declared as static.

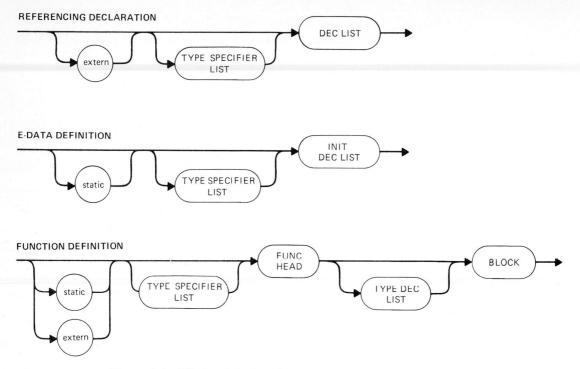

REFERENCING DECLARATION

extern

TYPE SPECIFIER LIST

DEC LIST

E-DATA DEFINITION

static

TYPE SPECIFIER LIST

INIT DEC LIST

FUNCTION DEFINITION

static

extern

TYPE SPECIFIER LIST

FUNC HEAD

TYPE DEC LIST

BLOCK

Figure 3.2. File level declarations

the declarator that gives the name of the entity and other information about that entity. The syntax for a declarator is illustrated in Figure 3.3.

The next section examines the meaning of some of the options in Figure 3.3.

Declarators: Initialization and Arrays

Now consider further the declaration of the variable top shown in Figure 3.4. This declaration defines the variable top to have type integer, with file scope (due to the context) and internal linkage (due to the keyword "static"). The declarator in this example also contains the *initializer:* = 0. The variable top is thus not only defined (i.e., created) but given an initial value of zero before the start of program execution. We will use top to keep track of the number of elements in the stack.

The declaration of stack defines an *array* of integers. It reads as shown in Figure 3.5.

It is assumed here that the reader has used arrays previously in another language. An array in C comprises a contiguously allocated set of objects of one type. In C, objects that consist of more than a single object (like arrays) are called *aggregates.* Again, because of the context of the declaration and the use of the

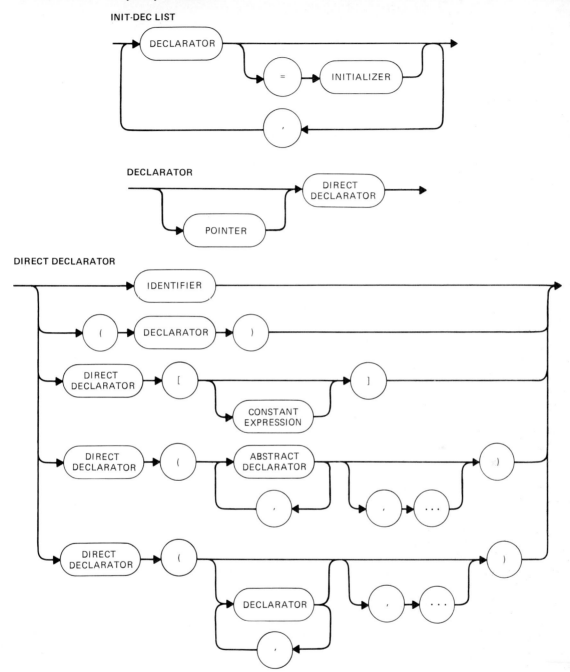

Figure 3.3. Declarator and init-dec-list

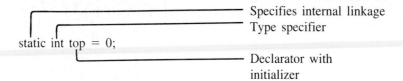

Figure 3.4. A declarator with initialization.

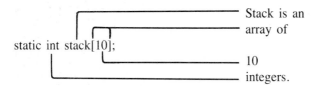

Figure 3.5. Array declaration

keyword "static," the variable stack has file scope and internal linkage. We will discuss access to the individual array elements when we examine the body of push( ) and pop( ).

The third declaration, int serror, defines a variable that will be used to hold a status code to indicate the success or failure of the push( ) and pop( ) functions. This variable has file scope, but in contrast with top and stack, it is given the (default) linkage of external. This means that serrno can be used in another module, given an appropriate referencing declaration in that module.

The declaration of push( ) in Program 3.3 is as follows:

```
int push(int element)
{
}
```

This function definition states that push( ) has external linkage (the default), that it will return an integer value, and that push( ) accepts a single integer valued parameter from the caller. The value of the parameter will be stored in the variable named element. The scope of a function parameter is the block that makes up the function body, and it has no linkage (it cannot be referenced in another declaration).

The declaration of pop( ) is as follows:

```
int pop( void )
{
        int result;
}
```

This declaration is similar to push ( ), except that the type specifier "void" is used in the parameter list. Void indicates that this function requires no parameters. The use of void to indicate no parameters is optional (it can be skipped, and some older compilers do not support it), but we recommend its use as a form of self-documentation. Another use of void is to declare that a function returns no value. For example, the declaration

```
void exit( int );
```

indicates that exit( ) returns no value.

Using Macros and Header Files

Let us make the following additional design decisions about our stack module:

1. push( ) will return -1 if the stack is full, otherwise it will return 1. It will also store these values into serrno.
2. pop( ) will return either the top value on the stack or 0 if the stack is empty. It will set serrno equal to -2 if the stack is empty, or 1 otherwise.

We thus have several symbolic values: the size of the array (10), an overflow indicator (-1), an empty condition (-2), and a success indication (1). These values can be given symbolic names using the preprocessor directive #define as illustrated in Figure 3.6.

In the example in Figure 3.6, the symbol DEPTH has been associated with the digit 10, EMPTY with (-2), and so on. The #define directive does not create a program variable, but simply attaches a name to a string of characters. These names cannot, typically, be used as the target for assignment statements. The use

```
contents of stack.h:

/* Macros and declarations for the stack module */

#define DEPTH 10          /* stack size */

/* The following values are stored in serrno */
#define SUCCESS    1
#define EMPTY     (-2)
#define OVERFLOW  (-1)

/* The following are the stack function prototypes */
int push( int );
int pop( void );

/* The following is the external error number indicator */
extern int serrno;
```

Figure 3.6. Using #define and #include files

of uppercase characters for preprocessor-declared identifiers is simply a convention employed by most C programmers in order easily to distinguish a preprocessor symbol from a program variable.

Why name these constants? Constants such as storage limits and return values should be symbolically referenced so that they can be changed at a later time, if necessary, in one location and not at each reference. For example, if we use EMPTY in place of -2 throughout the code, and if it is later required to change the empty indication to -32000, one can make the change to the #define directive and simply recompile the module.

Notice in Figure 3.6 that the #define directives are coded into a file named stack.h. This is done so that these symbols can be #included in both the stack module (stack.c) and in any modules that will use the stack functions. Coding the #defines into an #include file eliminates the need to recode these directives in the modules that use push( ) and pop( ).

Notice also in the header file listed in Figure 3.6 the referencing declarations:

```
int push( int );
int pop( void );
extern int serrno;
```

These were coded in stack.h so that modules that call push( ) and pop( ) and include this header file will receive the appropriate prototype declarations of the functions, and also to specify that push( ), pop( ) and serrno have external linkage (by the default linkage rule). We employ the convention of using the extern keyword on all referencing declarations for data objects as a form of documentation.

Complete Stack Module

Consider the completed code for the stack module in Program 3.5. Notice that push( ) and pop( ) can use the variables top, stack, and serrno because of their file scope.

```
contents of stack.c:

#include "stack.h"

static int top = 0;
static int stack[DEPTH];
int serrno;            /* status code indicator */

/*
 *    This function will accept an integer and
 *    attempt to push it onto the stack.  It sets
 *    serrno to either SUCCESS or OVERFLOW (if the
 *    stack is full) and returns the value of serrno.
 */
```

Program 3.5. LIFO stack module (continues)

```
int push( int element )
{
   if (top == DEPTH)
   {
     serrno = OVERFLOW;
   }
   else
   {
     stack[top++] = element;
     serrno = SUCCESS;
   }
   return(serrno);
}

/*
 *   This function will attempt to pop an element off
 *   the stack.  It sets serrno to SUCCESS or EMPTY,
 *   and if it is successful, it returns the popped value.
 *   If unsuccessful, the return value is set to zero.
 */
int pop( void )
{
   int result = 0;

   if (top > 0)
   {
     result = stack[--top];
     serrno = SUCCESS;
   }
   else
   {
     serrno = EMPTY;
   }
   return result;
}
```

Program 3.5. (continued)

Storage Duration

Another facet of declarations in C is *storage duration,* sometimes called *lifetime*. The storage duration of a variable determines the time during program execution over which that variable retains its value. Storage duration can be specified in a declaration either by default (according to context) or explicitly by using a storage class keyword.

Variables declared outside of any program block are given *static* storage duration, which means that these variables will retain their values throughout program execution. Such entities are created before program execution in "static storage" and thus retain their values across function calls. The variables top, stack, and serrno in Program 3.5 have static duration.

Variables that are declared as function parameters or inside of a block and are not explicitly given a storage class are given *dynamic* storage duration. Variables of this type are allocated upon entry into the block (typically on a run-time stack or in registers) and are deallocated upon exit from the block (thus, the term "dynamic," as they are created during run time). The value stored in dynamic variables cannot be relied upon across invocations of a block (or function in our example). That is, the value is not guaranteed to remain the same from the end of one function invocation to a subsequent invocation of the same function. The variables "element" and "result" in push( ) and pop( ) from Program 3.5 have dynamic duration.

Initialization of static objects is treated differently than is initialization of dynamics. Static objects are always initialized—either implicitly to zero in the absence of an explicit initialization or explicitly to the value indicated in an initializer one time prior to program execution. The declaration int top = 0; in Program 3.5 illustrates explicit initialization of a static.

Dynamic objects do not receive an implicit initialization. If none is given in the declarator, then the initial value of such objects is undefined. If initialized, dynamic variables are set to their initial value each time that the block in which they are declared is entered during run time. In the case of function parameters, the value is reinitialized for each call to the function using the value from the caller. The declaration int result = 0; in pop( ) illustrates initialization of a dynamic variable.

The storage class keywords can be used to make explicit or to override the default duration for variables declared within a block. Figure 3.7 presents the syntax for I-data definitions. The keywords such as static and auto are storage class keywords.

For example, a declaration such as

```
int pop( void )
{
  static result = 0;
}
```

would cause result to be given static duration instead of dynamic duration. This means that result would maintain its value across invocations of the pop function and would only be initialized once. Statics can be used in functions when a function must remember something of its state between calls. The keyword "auto" represents the default. It makes dynamic duration explicit. Thus, auto is rarely used in practice. The register storage class is discussed in Chapter 9.

I-DATA DEFINITION

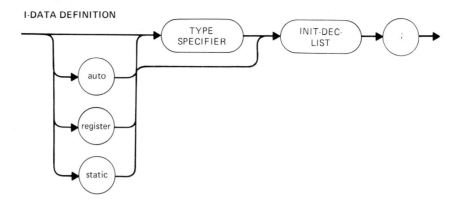

Figure 3.7. I-data definition

Default Type

One last point should be made about declarations. If the type specifier keyword is omitted from a function definition, the default type of int is assumed. Thus, the following two declarations are equivalent.

```
int push( int element )        push( int element )
{                              {
}                              }
```

The reader is encouraged always to declare the type of an entity as a matter of good coding practice.

It is apparent that declarations in C convey a lot of information, sometimes much of it by default. It is very important to study declarations and become familiar with their syntax and semantic rules.

Program 3.5 illustrates the use of the array reference operator. Let us now examine this operator.

3.4   ARRAY REFERENCE OPERATOR

Consider the following statements from Program 3.5:

```
stack[top++] = element;     and     result = stack[--top];
```

Both expressions represent a reference to an individual member in the stack array. In C, array members are referenced by using the array reference operator: []. The array reference operator takes an integer valued expression known as a *subscript* and uses this subscript to fetch a member of the array.

The value of the subscript should be in the range of 0 through size-1, where size is the number of members in the array definition. We say "should" because C does not enforce subscript bounds checking, even though it is a coding error if the value of the subscript exceeds the bounds of the array. The error may be detected immediately by a run-time error (such as memory reference error) or it may go undetected for quite a while, depending upon the nature of the program. The elements of the stack array can be accessed as stack[0] through stack[DEPTH-1]. Notice also that the [] pair can be used either as an array reference operator in an expression or as a part of an array declaration in a declarator.

The subscript expression top++ illustrates the *postfix-increment* operator. The value of this expression is the value contained in top *before* the increment operation. Top is incremented and updated with a value one greater than its previous value, but *after* the value of the expression is fetched, hence the name "postfix-increment."

The subscript expression --top illustrates the use of the *prefix-decrement* operator. Its value is the result after the decrement operation, and the operand top is updated with the new value.

These two statements are equivalent to the more conventional statements:

```
stack[top] = element;          top = top - 1;
top = top + 1;                 result = stack[top];
```

Increment can also be used as a prefix operator (e.g., ++top) and decrement can be used as a postfix operator (e.g., top--).

Experienced C programmers make heavy use of the increment and decrement operators.

3.5   A MULTIMODULE EXAMPLE

One common use of the stack data structure demonstrated in Program 3.5 is in the evaluation of arithmetic expressions. Early compiler writers realized that an expression such as A / B + C * D − E could be interpreted in several ways (based on precedence rules). Even if they required programmers fully to parenthesize such expressions, they were still faced with the difficult problem of translating such expressions into machine language.

One solution, still commonly used, involves the use of postfix notation, also known as reverse-Polish notation (RPN) in honor of its inventor, the Polish

Infix	*Postfix (RPN)*
A + B	A B +
(A + B) / C	A B + C /
(A * B) * (C + D)	A B * C D + *

Figure 3.8. Reverse-Polish notation.

mathematician Lukasiewicz. In this notation, arithmetic operators immediately precede their operands, and questions of parentheses and precedence become moot. For example, Figure 3.8 illustrates some examples of RPN expressions and their corresponding infix counterparts.

To evaluate an expression written in RPN notation, operands are pushed onto a stack as they are encountered in an expression. When a binary operator is encountered, it is applied to the top two operands on the stack (these values are popped off) and the result is pushed onto the stack. The result of the expression is found on top of the stack after completion of the expression evaluation.

contents of stack.h:

```
/* Macros and declarations for the stack module */

#define DEPTH 10          /* stack size */

/* The following values are stored in serrno */
#define SUCCESS    1
#define EMPTY     (-2)
#define OVERFLOW  (-1)

/* The following are the stack function prototypes */
int push( int );
int pop( void );

/* The following is the external error number indicator */
extern int serrno;
```

contents of rpn.c:

```
#include <stdio.h>
#include "stack.h"
```

Program 3.6. RPN expression interpreter (continues)

```
main()
{
    void rpn_expr( void );

    printf("Enter an expression : ");

    rpn_expr();

    exit();
}

/**
 *  Accept an expression in RPN notation and evaluate it.
 **/
void rpn_expr(void)
{
    int ch;
    int first_operand, second_operand;
    int result;

    ch = getchar();
    while (ch != '\n')
    {
        if (ch == '+')
        {
            first_operand = pop();
            second_operand = pop();
            result = second_operand + first_operand;
            push(result);
        }
        else if (ch == '-')
        {
            first_operand = pop();
            second_operand = pop();
            result = second_operand - first_operand;
            push(result);
        }
        else if (ch == '*')
        {
            first_operand = pop();
            second_operand = pop();
            result = second_operand * first_operand;
            push(result);
        }
        else if (ch == '/')
        {
            first_operand = pop();
            second_operand = pop();
```

Program 3.6 (continued)

```
          result = second_operand/first_operand;
          push(result);
          }
          else /* ch is an operand */
          {
              push(ch - '0');
          }
          ch = getchar();
      }
      result = pop();                  /* result is on top of stack */
      printf("\n\nYour result is %d\n", result);
      return;
  }
```

contents of stack.c:

```
#include "stack.h"

static int top = 0;
static int stack[DEPTH];
int serrno;            /* status code indicator */

/*
 *  This function will accept an integer and
 *  attempt to push it onto the stack.  It sets
 *  serrno to either SUCCESS or OVERFLOW (if the
 *  stack is full) and returns the value of serrno.
 */
int push( int element )
{
   if (top == DEPTH)
   {
     serrno = OVERFLOW;
   }
   else
   {
     stack[top++] = element;
     serrno = SUCCESS;
   }
   return(serrno);
}

/*
 *  This function will attempt to pop an element off
 *  the stack.  It sets serrno to SUCCESS or EMPTY,
 *  and if it is successful, it returns the popped value.
 *  If unsuccessful, the return value is set to zero.
 */
```

Program 3.6 (continued)

```
int pop( void )
{
    int result = 0;

    if (top > 0)
    {
      result = stack[--top];
      serrno = SUCCESS;
    }
    else
    {
      serrno = EMPTY;
    }
    return result;
}
```

Program 3.6. (continued)

Program 3.6 illustrates a simple implementation of an RPN interpreter. The program consists of two modules: the RPN interpreter (contained in the source file rpn.c) and the stack functions (contained in the source file stack.c). In addition, the header stack.h is used in both rpn.c and stack. c to assure the use of consistent macro and referencing declarations.

The reader will note that the program processes only single-digit integer values and yields only integer results. Extensions to the program to process multidigit values and floating-point values, and to error check, are left as exercises.

Notice that the abstract types of push( ) and pop( ) are used in the RPN code without regard for the underlying data structure used for the stack. If, in the future, the data structure for the stack must be modified, such as to change its size or change it from an array to a linked list or a file, these changes could be made to the stack module, and, as long as the interfaces to push( ) and pop( ) remain unchanged, the RPN code would be unaffected. This is the power of data abstraction and information hiding.

3.6 VARIATIONS ON ARITHMETIC TYPES

There are two arithmetic types: integers and floating types. C supports various sizes of these two types. Figure 3.9 shows the syntax for type specifiers.

Table 3.4, which is adapted from Plauger's paper "Types Play a Central

TYPE SPECIFIER LIST

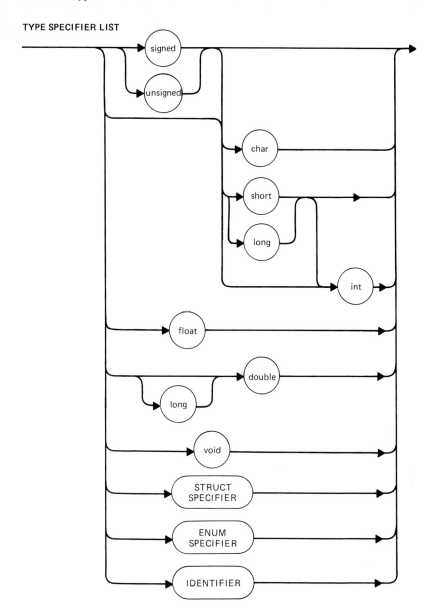

Figure 3.9. Type specifiers

Role in Standard C," gives some meaning to the types to be discussed in this section.

Notice the groupings of the type specifiers in Table 3.4. Each grouping represents different ways of specifying the same type. This means that short, short int, signed short, and signed short int are all the same type!

Table 3.4. Simple Type Variations

Signed Integers		Unsigned Integers	Floating Point
signed char	char	unsigned char	float
short		unsigned short	double
short int		unsigned short int	
signed short			
signed short int			
int		unsigned int	long double
signed int			
long		unsigned long	
long int		unsigned long int	
signed long			

Integer Types

The variations of the integer types come in two broad categories: signed and unsigned. For a signed integer, the most significant bit is used for the sign indicator. For the unsigned varieties, no sign bit is used, so these unsigned integers can represent positive values with a magnitude of one power of two greater than the signed variety. Of course, an unsigned integer cannot represent a negative value.

An object declared as a char is large enough to store any single character on the computer. Whether objects of type char are treated as signed or not is implementation dependent. This is the reason why the char type in Table 3.4 is placed between the signed and unsigned char types. When an object of type char is used in an expression, its value is treated as an int. This is where the signed versus unsigned implementation of chars is important. If chars are implemented as a signed type, then the value '\377' (octal notation) will be treated as a negative value in an expression. The same value will be treated as 255 if chars are implemented as unsigned types. The behavior can be explicitly controlled by using either the signed char or unsigned char type specifier. Both signed and unsigned char objects are allocated the same amount of space with the provision that signed chars may represent negative values.

Objects of type int represent the natural, or most popular, size integer on the execution machine. The number of bits used for shorts, ints, and longs is implementation dependent. The minimum guarantees specified by the standard are

```
char     8  bits
short   16  bits
int     16  bits
long    32  bits
```

The relationships in the set of values that objects of the integer types may represent are expressed in Figure 3.10. The $<=$ symbol here indicates a subset and the $|\ |$ symbols indicate absolute value.

For the signed types, the distinction as to whether the relationship is a proper subset is implementation dependent. The file limits.h specifies the ranges for the integer types for each implementation.

```
char <= short int <= int <= long int
|char| <= unsigned char
|int|  <= unsigned int
|long| <= unsigned long
```

Figure 3.10. Maximum magnitudes of integer types

Floating-Point Types

Floating-point values can be expressed in three magnitudes, as illustrated in Table 3.4. The relationship between their precision and magnitudes is shown in Figure 3.11. As with integers, the relationship may be a subset or a proper subset. This is implementation dependent.

The file float.h specifies the ranges for the floating types for each implementation.

```
float          6 decimal digits
double        10 decimal digits
long double   10 decimal digits
```

```
float precision  <= double precision
float magnitude  <= double magnitude
double precision <= long double precision
double magnitude <= long double magnitude
```

Figure 3.11. Maximum magnitudes of floating-point types

SIZE OF EXPRESSION

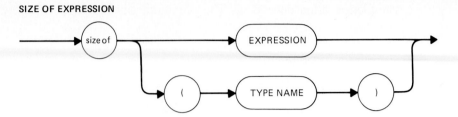

Figure 3.12. sizeof operator

Sizeof Operator

To illustrate the relationships shown in Figures 3.10 and 3.11, we can use a simple C program and the *sizeof* operator (introduced here for the first time) to determine the number of bytes allocated to objects of the simple type for a particular execution environment. sizeof is a compile-time operator. Its syntax is shown in Figure 3.12. Its value is the size in bytes of its operand. The operand may be either an expression or a type specifier keyword, but if the operand is an expression, sizeof just looks at its type and determines the number of bytes that that type would require.

The type of the value generated by sizeof is a special type: size_t. size_t is declared (or #defined) in many of the standard header files, such as stdio.h and stdlib.h, to be an integer type—often an unsigned int or an unsigned long (depending on the implementation). Unsigned types are used because the size of certain objects (such as large char arrays) can exceed the magnitude of a simple integer. We will assume here that the type of size_t is an unsigned integer. See Program 3.7.

```
main()
{
        printf("Keyword\t\tSize in Bytes\n\n");

        printf("char\t\t\t%u\n",sizeof(char));
        printf("int\t\t\t%u\n",sizeof(int));
        printf("short\t\t\t%u\n",sizeof(short));
        printf("long\t\t\t%u\n",sizeof(long));
        printf("float\t\t\t%u\n",sizeof(float));
        printf("double\t\t\t%u\n",sizeof(double));
        exit();
}
```

Program 3.7. The size allocated by simple types

The output of the program written on a machine based on the 16-bit Intel 8086 is shown in the following.

```
Keyword          Size in Bytes

char             1
int              2
short            2
long             4
float            4
double           8
```

The magnitudes that can be represented within variables of each of these types on some other popular machines and C implementations is presented in Table 3.5.

3.7   SWITCH, BREAK, AND DO-WHILE STATEMENTS

C has additional control statements that are not necessary in order to write a program, but that are very convenient. We will introduce these statements here.

Switch Statement

The *switch* statement provides the control structure generically known as the "case" construct. The syntax is illustrated in Figure 3.13.

Table 3.5. Simple Arithmetic-Type Magnitudes

	8088/8086	DEC VAX
char*	0 to 255	0 to 255
short	−32,767 to 32,767	−32,767 to 32,767
int	(same as short)	−2,147,483,647 to 2,147,483,647
long	−2,147,483,647 to 2,147,483,647	(same as int)
float magnitude		
max. positive	10E38	10E38
min. positive	10E-38	10E-38
double magnitude		
max. positive	10E308	10E38
min. positive	10E-308	10E-38

*Note: Assuming unsigned char

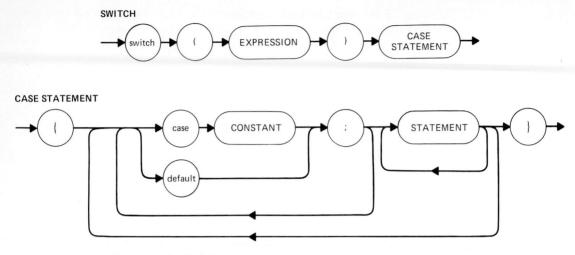

Figure 3.13. Switch statement

The switch statement can be used to select a group of statements to be executed based upon the value of an integer expression. Consider the skeleton statement shown in Figure 3.14.

Execution of the switch statement begins by evaluating the expression in the

```
switch (integer_expression)
{
  case constant-expression-1:
     statement;
            .
            .
            .
  case constant-expression-2:
     statement;
            .
            .
            .
  case constant-expression-n:
            .
            .
            .
  default:
     statement;
            .
            .
            .
}
```

Figure 3.14. Switch statement format

parentheses, which must yield an integer value. The case prefixes are then examined in top-to-bottom order, comparing the constant expression following the case keyword with the value of the switch expression. If a match is found, control is transferred to the first statement within that case. If no match is found and the default case is present (it is optional), then control is transferred to the first statement following the default. If no match is found and no default is specified, none of the statements in the block will be executed.

Once execution of a case begins, it continues until the end of the switch statement or until control is modified using either a break or goto statement. This means that control will flow from one case into the next unless control is modified.

Note that the expression following the case keyword must be a constant expression that evaluates to an integer value. This means that no program variables are permitted in the case expression. Also, the case expressions need not be in any specific order (i.e., ascending or descending order).

Figure 3.15 illustrates the use of the switch statement on the code from the RPN module in Program 3.6.

Switch can be used to simplify the coding of a multiway if statement when the value being tested is an integer value. Notice that the various groups of statements that constitute each case do not require enclosure in braces. The case keywords serve to delineate the groups of statements.

Break Statement

Observe the *break* statement at the end of case in Figure 3.15. Once execution of a case begins in the switch, statements are executed one after the other. If it is desired to execute only those statements in a given case grouping (which is the usual case), the flow of control must be interrupted at the end of the case. The best way to do this is to use the break statement. The break statement can be used in switch, while, for, and do-while statements to cause control to "break out" of the statement and to be sent to the next statement in the program. The effect of the break statement on the flow of control of the switch statement is shown in Figure 3.16.

Without the break statement, control will simply flow from one case to the next. This is sometimes desirable. Additionally, it is often desirable to execute the same code for more than one case value. In Figure 3.17, a switch statement is illustrated that could be used to process the response from a user to a menu prompt.

In Figure 3.17, if ch contains either an uppercase or a lowercase A, the add command code is executed, and control leaves the switch statement. If an uppercase or lowercase S is entered, the save command is processed, but then control falls into the quit command case. Any of the letters Q, q, E, or e can be used to execute the quit command code.

Without Switch	With Switch

```
Without Switch                        With Switch

ch = getchar();                       ch = getchar();
while (ch != '\n')                    while (ch != '\n')
{                                     {
                                          switch (ch)
  if (ch == '+')                          {
  {                                         case '+':
    first_operand = pop();                    first_operand = pop();
    second_operand = pop();                   second_operand= pop();
    result = second_operand +                 result = second_operand +
            first_operand;                            first_operand;
    push(result);                             push(result);
  }                                           break;
  else if (ch == '-')
  {                                           case '-':
    first_operand = pop();                    first_operand = pop();
    second_operand = pop();                   second_operand= push();
    result = second_operand -                 result = second_operand -
            first_operand;                            first_operand;
    push(result);                             push(result);
  }                                           break;
  else if (ch == '*')                       case '*':
  {                                             .
     ...                                        .
  }                                           break;
  else if (ch == '/')                       case '/':
  {                                             .
     ...                                        .
  }                                           break;
  else /* ch is an operand */               default:
  {                                           push(ch - '0');
          push(ch - '0');                     break;
  }                                       } /* end of switch */
  ch = getchar();                         ch = getchar();
}                                     } /* end of while */
```

Figure 3.15. Using the switch statement

Do-While Statement

The *do-while statement* is the C version of the generic "repeat-until" statement. The syntax is illustrated in Figure 3.18.

The code fragment in Figure 3.19 illustrates the use of the do-while to read in a line of characters that are terminated by a new-line.

```
          switch(expression)
          {
            case expr-1:
                statements;
/<------    break;
|           case expr-2:
|               statements;
|               break;
|                 .
|                 .
|                 .
|       }
\-->
```

Figure 3.16. Action of the break statement

```
switch (ch)
{
  case 'A':
  case 'a':
     /* Process the add command */
     break;
  case 'S':
  case 's':
     /* Process the save and exit command */
     /* Code goes here for save */
     /* Then flows into the exit case */
  case 'Q':
  case 'q':
  case 'E':
  case 'e':
     /* Process the exit (quit) command */
     break;
}
```

Figure 3.17. Flow of control within switch

DO-WHILE

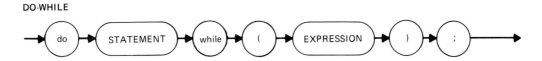

Figure 3.18. Do-while statement syntax

```
int a_char;

do
{
    a_char = getchar();
    process( a_char );
} while ( a_char != '\n' );
```

Figure 3.19. Using do-while

Although a while or for statement can always meet the need for an iterative statement, the do-while is sometimes a natural fit for certain algorithms.

3.8 PORTABILITY AND SOFTWARE ENGINEERING ISSUES

In this chapter, we have been using the ANSI syntax for both defining and prototype function declarations. Before the introduction of the ANSI standard, a different syntax was followed. Figure 3.20 illustrates these two versions of the syntax.

Besides a difference in the syntax, there is also a difference in functionality between standard and prestandard C.

Prestandard C permits a referencing declaration to specify the return type but no information about the parameters. This permitted function calls with the incorrect number and/or type of parameters to be made (which usually causes run-time errors). Additionally, there was no consistency checking between calls to the

Referencing Declarations

ANSI Prototype Format   Old Format

```
    int push( int );                          int push();
```

Defining Declarations

ANSI Format   Old Format

```
int push (int element)                   int push(element)
{                                        int element;
    /* body */                           {
}                                                /* body */
                                         }
```

Figure 3.20. Old and new function declaration syntax

same function, so the same function could be called with different parameter types in different places. Finally, in old C, certain parameter types could not be passed at all because C performed the following automatic "widening" for parameter types:

Type at Call	*Type Passed*
char, short	int
unsigned char	unsigned int
unsigned short	unsigned int
float	double

Thus, parameters of type char, short and float could not be passed at all.

In standard C, the prototype declaration mechanism allows the compiler to verify the number and type of function parameters so that the proper types are passed. It also permits types to be passed as declared in the prototype, so that parameters of type char, short and float can be passed. In fact, even if a prototype is not declared for a function, a standard C compiler will assume one for it at the first call. This has been dubed the *"Miranda"* prototype rule: If you remain silent about your parameters, a function prototype will be appointed for you. The Miranda prototype utilizes the automatic "widening" rules for types that were described above for old C. Thus, the function call

```
a_func('c', 4, 5.4)
```

would be given the Miranda prototype

```
int a_func(int, int, double)
```

since the character and floating point parameters would be widened to type int and double. This prototype would then be used for subsequent calls to that function in the same module.

It is important to note that from the standpoint of portability, code written to use function prototypes will not be downward compatible with old versions of C.

We noted in this chapter that variables can be initialized in their defining declarations. Static storage objects are initialized prior to the start of the program. From a software engineering standpoint, the programmer should not rely on the use of default initialization (as with statics) because this initialization is not visible to the reader of the code. Explicit initialization, even to zero for statics, is recommended. Well-engineered software should make important properties of the program as apparent as possible.

The process of linkage allows the easy sharing of data structures across source files. Sharing data can help to optimize program performance, but it can also have negative consequences from the standpoint of program maintainability and reusability. If performance constraints are not an issue, the design concepts of information hiding and abstract data types can be used to create modules that are easier to maintain and reuse. In a C module, we can declare data structures with internal linkage using the static keyword, and allow access to the data structure only through the associated functions. This will limit the code that modifies the data structure and thus isolate the code that would have to be modified in the event that the data structure were redefined.

Information hiding can also be applied to program variables and parameters. Whenever possible, identifiers should be defined to have block scope. The advantage of a variable with block scope is that it cannot be unintentionally modified by other parts of the program as no other parts have access to that data. Information should have the most restrictive scope possible to accomplish the task. If block scope is too restrictive, then file scope with internal linkage is the next preferred choice. Sharing of data should occur through function call parameters whenever possible, since function parameters provide explicit identification of the values being shared.

C makes many assumptions about the scope, duration, and linkage of objects according to the context of the declaration. For example, functions and data declared outside of a function are by default given external linkage. Following the suggestion that data used within a single module be given internal linkage, the programmer must make explicit use of the storage class keyword "static" to assign internal linkage and override the default linkage.

Although it has been previously discussed, it is appropriate to highlight the importance of header files in the context of software engineering. This practice can result in the development of more maintainable code by isolating the changes to common preprocessor directives and declarations. When names are declared in a single header file and that file is included everywhere it is needed, a modification to the declarations is required in only one place. C permits redundant declarations that do not conflict. This alllows, for example, the coding of prototype declarations of functions in a header file and inclusion of that file in the source file that has consistent defining declarations of those functions.

A typical error in C programming is to include a semicolon in the #define declaration, as in

```
#define EMPTY  (-2);  /* Stack empty symbol */
```

Unlike C language statements and declarations, preprocessor directives *do not* require a terminating semicolon, unless they are to be a part of the macro. Using the above #define in the statement in

```
if (serrno == EMPTY) printf("Stack Error\n");
```

would result in the expanded statement

```
if (serrno == (-2);) printf("Stack Error\n");
```

which is a syntax error.

We saw in Table 3.4 that there are many permutations for the variations of the simple arithmetic-type specifiers. In fact, the order of the keywords can be permuted in a declaration, resulting in many different ways to specify the same type. Also, storage class specifiers such as extern and static can be added to a declaration. We suggest that if storage class is used, it should be specified first in a declaration. The type qualifiers (short, long, unsigned, etc.) should come next, followed by the type specifer.

When designing programs for portability, remember that the implementation of the various simple arithmetic types is machine dependent. There are guaranteed minimum magnitudes, as discussed in this chapter. Also, as noted in Chapter 2, the include files limits.h and float.h contain the specification of the numerical limits of the various data types introduced in this chapter. It is, of course, always advisable to verify the magnitude that various program variables may accept when porting an application across machines by comparing the values in limits.h and float.h of the two machines. For example, suppose that a program written for a VAX utilized integer values in the range + or – 500,000. Suppose further that all integer variables were declared as type int. This program could not be directly ported to an IBM PC because ints on the PC range from –32,767 to 32,767. A better choice for the type declaration would have been long. The files limits.h and float.h are required in standard C compilers and may not be present in prestandard versions of C.

The sizeof operator is specified to have a special type named size_t. This type was invented by ANSI C to help to increase portability of code that uses the sizeof operator, so that the programmer will always know the type of its value. In older compilers, sizeof might produce an int type, long type, or some signed or unsigned variation. With size_t, this is still true, but in most cases, variables or functions that have the value of type size_t can simply be recompiled in a new environment and the types will still be consistent. Sizeof can, however, cause some portability problems when used in the printf( ) statement, because printf( ) requires that we know the underlying type of size_t so that we can use the correct conversion specification. For example, to output the value of sizeof, we might need to use the specification %u (unsigned), %lu (unsigned long), or, possibly, a signed integer type specification. The programmer will have to examine stdio.h or the compiler documentation to determine the correct conversion specification.

3.9   SUMMARY

At the highest level, a C program consists of one or more modules. Modules consist of a sequence of data and function declarations.

Declarations are used to introduce the name of a data object or function and to associate a list of attributes the entity. These attributes include:

1. The data type of the object.
2. The duration of the object: static or dynamic.
3. The linkage associated with the object: none, internal, or external.
4. The scope of the object: file, parameter, or block scope.
5. The kind of program entity: a variable, a function, or an array.

The data type of an object is specified by using a type keyword such as int, char, or float, and the variations of these simple types. The numeric magnitude that is supported by objects of these types is implementation dependent, but their limits are specified in the vendor-supplied files limits.h and float.h.

Duration is the time during program execution that a variable will maintain its value. Variables with static duration maintain their values throughout program execution. Variables with dynamic duration are created when a function or block is entered and destroyed when the block ends. The duration of a variable is determined either by the placement of the declaration in the file or by the use of the keywords "auto" or "static." Variables declared outside of any block are given static duration. Variables declared inside of a block are given dynamic duration unless explicitly declared as static.

Internal and external linkages can be used to introduce a function or variable in more than one place. External linkage allows the definition of a function or data structure in one module (file) and then its reference in another module. Internal linkage allows an entity to be referenced in more than one place but only within a single module (file). Linkage is determined by the context of the declaration in the file and the optional use of storage class specifier keywords. Entities declared outside of a function are given external linkage by default unless the declaration includes the keyword "static." Static assigns internal linkage. Function parameters have no linkage—they cannot be referenced in another declaration. Variables defined within a block are given no linkage.

The scope of a variable is the portion of a file in which that object is visible. Objects declared outside of a block have a scope that begins with the declaration and extends to the end of the file. Objects declared within a block are given block scope. The scope of a function parameter is the block that constitutes the function body.

We noted that a part of the declaration called the declarator specifies the name and interpretation of the object. The three examples of declarators that were considered are simple program variables, functions, and arrays.

The declarator for a program variable consists of the name of the variable and an optional initialization list. The declarator for a function was made up of the function name, a parentheses pair, with an optional list of parameter declarations contained therein. The declarator for a single-dimensional array was made up of the array name and the square bracket pair containing a constant integer expression that indicates the number of elements in the array.

Static objects are initialized once prior to program execution, whereas automatic objects are initialized each time the block in which they are declared is entered during program execution. Static objects are given implicit initialization to zero in the absence of an explicit declaration. Automatic objects are not implicitly initialized.

In further consideration of the use of preprocessor directives, it was noted that the #define directive can be used to associate a symbolic name with a token. In addition, the #include directive is very helpful when a program is broken up into several files. Common #define directives can be placed in a header file and that file may be #included in every necessary file, thus isolating these definitions in a single physical location.

Two new operators and statements were introduced. These operators are

```
Array member reference: []
sizeof
```

The precedence of these operators in relation to the other operators introduced to this point is summarized in Table 3.6, with highest precedence at the top of the table. Gaps in the table indicate groupings of operators of equal precedence.

The sizeof operator yields a value that is the number of bytes that an object or type specifier requires. The type of the value produced by sizeof is the special type size_t. This type is declared in header files like stdio.h and stdlib.h to be either unsigned int or unsigned long (the choice is implementation defined).

The switch statement is a convenient way to express a multiway branch when the value being tested is an integer. The break statement is needed in cases of the

Table 3.6. Operator Precedence

Function call and array reference	( ), []
Postfix increment and decrement	++, --
Prefix increment and decrement sizeof, unary minus	++, -- sizeof, -
Multiplication and division	*, /
Addition and subtraction	+, -
Less than and greater than Equality and not equal	<, >, <=, >= ==, !=
Assignment	=

switch to terminate each case. The do-while statement is the C implementation of the repeat-until.

Keywords

abstract data types
aggregate
array
array reference operator
auto
automatic duration
block level declaration
block scope
break statement
data abstraction
declarator
defining declaration
double
do-while statement
driver
dynamic duration
external linkage
file level declaration
file scope
function definition
function parameter level declaration
function parameter scope
function prototype
information hiding

initialization
internal linkage
linkage
long
Miranda prototype
module
no linkage
postfix-increment
prefix-decrement
referencing declaration
return statement
scope
short
signed integer
sizeof operator
storage class
storage duration (lifetime)
subscript
static duration
storage duration
switch statement
type specifier
unsigned

References

Harbison, S. P. and Steele, G. L. 1984. *A C Reference Manual* Englewood Cliffs, N.J.: Prentice-Hall. (Discussion of old C widening rules.)

Jaeschke, R. February 1988. Exploring the subtle side of the "sizeof" operator. *C Users J.* 21–25. R&D Publications, McPherson, Kans.

Plauger, P. J. December/January 1988. Declaring Functions in Standard C, *C Users J.* 15–19 R&D Publications, McPherson, Kans. (Discussion of Miranda prototypes.)

Plauger, P. J. March/April 1988. Types play central role in new Standard C. *C Users J.* 17–23. R&D Publications, McPherson, Kans.

Plauger, P. J. February 1988. What's in a Name? *C Users J.* 21–25. R&D Publications, McPherson, Kans.

Pressman, R. S. 1987. *Software engineering: A practitioner's approach* (2nd ed.). New York: McGraw-Hill, pp. 225–35. Discusses the use of data abstraction and information hiding for effective module design.

Discussion Topics

1. Discuss the advantages of breaking a large software project into modules and coding the modules into separate source files.

2. Separate files can be used to implement abstract data types. Thus, data structures can only be accessed through the use of the functions provided by the module. Discuss the advantages of this approach as an alternative to letting user modules directly access the data structure. In C, how can we enforce hiding of the data structure within a module?

3. Many beginning C programmers attempt to connect separate modules together using the #include directive, thus confusing the use of header files and the linkage of object modules. For example, they use such statements as "include stack.c" in order to use the functions declared in that source file. Discuss the proper use of header files and contrast this with the way in which object files are combined using the linkage editor.

4. Discuss the way that C references the individual elements of an array. In particular, discuss the range of the subscript (i.e., 0 to size-1) and notice that the subscript can be thought of as an offset from the starting element of the array. Discuss the fact that many C compilers do no bounds checking on array subscripts.

5. The stack module illustrated in this chapter supports only a single stack. It is possible to extend this module to support multiple stacks. Discuss additional data structures, parameters, or functions that might be needed to extend the stack module in this manner.

6. Use of the function prototype declaration allows the compiler to check the number and types of function parameters in a function call at compiler time. Old-style C does not provide this information in a referencing declaration for a function. Discuss the advantages of the prototype format from the standpoint of software quality and maintenance.

7. Extern does not necessarily indicate external linkage. Consider the following program:

```
static int i = 10;
main()
{
    extern int i;

    printf("%d\n",i);
}
```

The output of this program is 10. The extern storage class specifier inherits the linkage of any previous declarations for a given entity. If the static declaration of i were not present, then the extern declaration would have inherited external linkage. Discuss the use of extern as a form of code documentation for referencing declarations.

8. The type size_t is the type of the value that is produced by sizeof. The type of sizeof should be able to represent a value that is at least as large as the maximum array subscript, since sizeof(arrayname) produces the size in bytes of the named array. Discuss the various uses of sizeof. For example,

```
sizeof( variable_name ),

sizeof( type specifier),

sizeof( array_name ), and

sizeof( array_name[l] )
```

Exercises

1. Determine whether your language processor supports function prototype declarations.

2. Explain why the function prototype format for function referencing declarations provides superior error detection over the old-style C function declaration.

3. Define the following terms:
   Scope
   Duration
   Linkage

4. List the three possible scopes for an entity.

5. List the two possible storage durations.

6. List the variations on linkage.

7. Declarations have many defaults, depending on the context in which they are written. List the three contexts.

8. What is the default linkage that is given to a file level definition of a function?

9. What is the default storage duration that is given to a file level data object definition.

10. What is the default linkage given to a function parameter?

11. What is the default storage duration for a data object that is defined within a block (such as a function body)?

12. Consider the following code that is similar to Program 3.6.

```c
#include <stdio.h>

int push( int );
int pop( void );
extern int serron;

main()
{
    int rpn_expr( void );

    printf("Enter an expression : ");

    rpn_expr();

    exit();
}
/**
 *   Accept an expression in RPN notation and evaluate it.
 **/
int rpn_expr( void )
{
    int ch;
    int first_operand, second_operand;
    int result;
        .
        .
        .

}
```

Answer the following questions about this code.
a. What is the scope of main()?
b. What is the scope of pop()?
c. What is the scope of ch?
d. What is the storage duration of result?
e. What is the linkage of push()?
f. What is the linkage of rpn_expr()?
g. What is the storage duration of serrno?

13. The keyword "static" has two uses. It can be used to specify both storage class and linkage. Answer the following questions about static.
a. When static is used on a file level declaration, does it describe duration or linkage?
b. When static is used on a block level declaration of a data object, does it describe duration or linkage?

14. Why is it a good practice to code common preprocessor directives, such as those in stdio.h or stack.h, in an independent file, rather than simply coding the directives directly into each source file that needs them?

15. Distinguish between a defining declaration and a referencing declaration. Consider both data and function declarations.

16. The symbols [] and () can be used in C as either part of a declarator or as an operator. Explain what [] and () mean in both of these cases.

17. What is the purpose of a linkage editor (or linker)? Why is such a program usually necessary?

18. In the examples in this chapter, we declared the array stack using a #define to indicate the size of the array. Why not just code the declaration as int stack[10] instead of int stack[MAX_STACK]?

19. The most extensive scope available in C is file scope. Given that this is the case, how can we arrange for code within one source file to access objects or functions that are defined in another source file?

20. Determine the number of significant characters that are supported in your environment for identifiers with external linkage.

21. What are the outputs of the following two code fragments?
    Fragment 1:

```
a = 3;
case (a)
{
   case 4: printf("*");
   case 3: printf("*");
   case 2: printf("*");
   case 1: printf("*");
}
```

Fragment 2:

```
a = 3;
case (a)
{
   case 4: printf("*");
           break;
   case 3: printf("*");
           break;
   case 2: printf("*");
           break;
   case 1: printf("*");
}
```

Programming Problems

1. Code and execute Program 3.7 on your system. Compare the sizes of the various data types.

2. Write a function that will read a sequence of digits representing an integer from the standard input, convert it to int type, and output the integer value using printf(). Test the code by writing a simple driver function that calls your function and uses prinf() to output the value returned from your converter function. You may assume that valid data will be entered by the user. (Although this is not a reasonable assumption, we are deferring a discussion of error checking to the next chapter.)

3. Write a function that will read a sequence of digits along with a decimal point that represents a floating-point value and convert the value to type float. Do not attempt to process scientific notation, but allow a leading decimal point to begin the number. Test the code by writing a simple driver function that calls your function and uses printf() to output the value returned from your function. Be sure to update the conversion specifications in the printf() function call and the declarations of the data structures, functions, and directives.

4. Incorporate the function that you wrote in Problem 3 into Program 2.4. Modify the necessary declarations in this new version of Program 2.4 so that it uses floating-point values. Be sure to update the conversion specifications in the printf() function calls.

5. Modify Program 3.6 so that the main function calls rpn_expr() in a loop so that the user can repeatedly enter expressions. Make a provision for exit from the loop.

6. Modify Program 3.6 to use the function written in either Problem 2 or 3. You will have to allow the function to have a single-character "look-ahead" so that the numbers can be delimited by the operators. The library function ungetc() (unget character) can be used to put a character just read by getchar() back into the input stream. Call ungetc() as follows: ungetc(ch, stdin) where ch is the character to put back into the input stream and stdin is a symbol representing the standard input, defined in stdio.h.

7. Program 3.6 does not process error conditions. Modify the program so that it will check the RPN input for proper syntax. Supply appropriate diagnostics to inform the user of the location and type of syntax error. Supply code to detect stack overflow, underflow, and zero divide. For example, you should check the value of serrno after each call to pop() and test the return value after each call to push(). For calls to push(), you might use an if statement such as that illustrated below.

```
if (push(result) == OVERFLOW) ...
```

Do not allow the evaluation of the RPN expression to continue if push() or pop() encounters an error.

8. Extend Program 3.6 to support additional operators such as integer exponentiation (you may use either the ^ symbol or the ** token for this operator) and unary negation (use a symbol other than the – symbol).

9. Modify Program 3.6 to allow the user to enter an arithmetic expression in ordinary infix notation. Your program should convert this string to RPN and then use a variation of the code from Program 3.6 to evaluate it. Input may consist of the operators +, –, *, and /, along with either single- or multidigit constant values. Follow ordinary algebraic operator precedence in the infix expression and allow entry of parentheses to modify the precedence.

   [*Hint 1:* To convert the expression to RPN, use an additional stack. This stack will contain only operators and parentheses.]

   [*Hint 2:* Generalize the functions push() and pop() so that they accept as a parameter (or parameters) the desired stack on which to operate—this way you will not have to duplicate these functions.]

10. Develop a set of C functions that implement a FIFO queue discipline. Write a main function to test your code. Be sure to hide all data structures associated with the queue inside the FIFO module by using statics. Design the queue so that it accepts a single type of data. You might use ints or floats (but not both at the same time).

11. A commenting style provided by some software houses is to precede C functions with a brief description as shown below:

```
/**
 *   sqrt() approximates the square root of its
 *   parameter using Newton's method.
 **/
float sqrt( float value )
{
      . . .
}
```

Notice that the function comment begins with the characters /** and ends with **/. This provides a way for automated extraction of function comments from code and the production of a reference manual. Write a C filter that will accept a C program on the standard input and output only the function header comments along with the function declaration. For example, the output from the above code would be

```
/**
 *   sqrt() approximates the square root of its
 *   parameter using Newton's method.
 **/
float sqrt( float value )
```

Output several new lines between each function header.

12. A perfect number is an integer that is equal to the sum of its factors other than itself. Write a program that will list the perfect numbers between 1 and 100. To do so, first write a function that accepts two integers, a numerator and a denominator, and returns true (nonzero) if the denominator is a factor of the numerator, and returns zero otherwise. Next, write a driver function that utilizes your factor-testing function.

4

Types, Operators, and Expressions

This chapter begins with a review of the concept of types in a programming language. The C typedef declaration class is introduced as a method of giving a name to a type. With this background, a more extensive analysis of C operators is presented. This includes a review of those operators that already have been introduced, and the introduction of a large number of additional operators that are useful in arithmetic, logical, and comparison expressions. The precedence and associativity rules of these operators are presented and illustrated. The relationship between types and expressions is discussed with an explanation of C's type conversion mechanism, that is, casting. The chapter ends with a section that presents some useful programming development techniques, including recursion, and a section summarizing various software engineering and portability considerations with these operators.

4.1 TYPES AND TYPEDEF

Types

A *type* in a programming language is a description of a set of values and a set of legitimate operations upon those values. Thus, the type int is the set of integer values from INT_MIN to INT_MAX, and the set of legal operations upon integers. These operations include addition (+), subtraction (–), multiplication (*), division (/), modulo (%), and the comparison operators (<, >, <=, >=, !=, ==). These operators are one of the primary topics of this chapter. (The constants INT_MIN and INT_MAX are defined in the header file limits.h. If a compiler uses 16 bits to represent integers, INT_MAX typically has the value 32767 and INT_MIN has the value –32767.)

An alternative, but complementary, definition of a type is that it is a template or pattern to be used by the compiler in allocating storage for the identifier. This definition is an intuitive one that emphasizes the compiler's use of types, but

104

slights the fact that the type of an identifier follows it throughout program execution.

The types that have been used to this point in this text are int and its varieties (long int, short int, signed, and unsigned), char (signed and unsigned), float and its varieties (double, long double), and arrays. The reader should have some idea about the kind and size of values that can be represented by each of these types. In this chapter, we will discuss the operations that are valid for each data type. In subsequent chapters, additional types will be introduced.

Each identifier in a C program has to have a type associated with it before it is used. This is one purpose of a declaration. Although programmers may be accustomed to the flexibility of some older languages such as FORTRAN, which do not require such declarations, the collective experience of software developers has demonstrated the value of requiring type declarations. (Notice that in languages like FORTRAN, identifiers still have types, but the type is often implicitly assigned to an identifier through a default.) A language such as C that requires the explicit declaration of identifiers can provide much more static analysis by the compiler and tools like lint. Static analysis is the process of checking for errors or potential problems in the source code for a program, rather than in the executing code. The diagnostics produced can be much more precise about the source of the error than can an error message during execution. Thus, types are an integral part of C and are one of the reasons that C has been successful as a programming language. (The standard has introduced more type checking potential into C than was provided by older C compilers. A prime example is the function prototype, which allows a C compiler to do additional type checking to ensure that parameters and return values of function calls agree with that of the function definition.)

The typedef Storage Class Specifier

The chief syntactic construct of C that helps in the managing of types is the *typedef* class specifier. Typedef declarations are a method of giving a new name to a type; that is, a synonym for a type. It does not create a new type. The use of a typedef can aid the understandability of a program by giving meaningful names to types. It is also useful in assigning the same type to multiple objects at different locations in a program. This is most appropriate for a type that requires a complex specification as the typedef can provide a shorthand notation in which typographic errors are less likely. (Type specification will become more complex with the introduction of arrays and pointers in Chapter 6 and structures in Chapter 7.)

A type is given a new name by preceding a declaration with the reserved word "typedef." The identifier at the end of the definition is this new name for the type, rather than being the name of a variable.

```
typedef float score, average(float[100]);
score grades[100];
extern average find_ave;
```

Figure 4.1. Use of a typedef declaration

    In this example, the first line creates two type synonyms: score is a synonym for float and average is a synonym for a function which returns a float. The next two lines use these type names in creating an array of 100 integers called grades and an external function find_ave() which returns a float.

    A type name created with a typedef can be used as any other type specifier. In particular, such an identifier can be used as an operand to the sizeof operator. The scope of a type name created with a typedef is the same as that of any other variable identifier.

Type Void

We complete this discussion of types by reviewing the type *void*. This special void type is permitted in C primarily as a documentation feature. The void type specifies an empty set of values. No object may have type void. This type is useful in indicating that a function returns no values, or that a function has no parameters. Thus, the declarations int f1(void); and void f2(int x); are more informative than the declarations int f1(); and f2(int x);. These latter declarations either say that f1 has no parameters or that the parameters to f1 are not specified here, and that f2 returns no value or that the type of value returned by f2 is not specified here. The use of "void" removes this ambiguity. Notice that in the absence of a type declarator for the return value, C assumes that the function returns an int.

    The type void can also be used in a cast to indicate that the value of an expression is to be ignored. At first consideration, the reason for ignoring the value of an expression may not be apparent. However, an expression is sometimes used only for the side effects that are produced in evaluating the expression. From a software engineering point of view, this is rarely a good idea.

4.2   INTRODUCTION TO OPERATORS AND EXPRESSIONS

C provides a large assortment of flexible operators that can be used to build very complex and powerful expressions. In this chapter, we will discuss the applicable rules for construction and interpretation of these expressions. We will begin by reviewing definitions of the necessary terminology.

Recall the definition of the terms *operator, expression,* and *operand* from Section 2.7. An operator is a symbol that represents some processing to be performed. An expression is a combination of one or more variables, constants, or function calls separated by operators. An operand is one of the expressions upon which the operation is to be performed.

Section 2.7 also introduced some of the C unary and binary operators. A third class of operators, those requiring three operands, are called *ternary operators.* The *result* of an expression is the value that is produced by the application of the operator to the operands. When learning new operators, it is important to understand not only the function performed by the operator, but also the types that are appropriate for operands and the type of the result produced.

C precedence rules were also introduced in Section 2.10. We will extend our definition of that term to include the concept of *precedence class.* The precedence rules of the language divide the operators into a set of ordered classes. Operators in a given class all have the same precedence, and operators in a higher precedence class are applied before those in a lower class. Within a class, *associativity rules* are used to determine which operator is applied first. The precedence and associativity rules for C tend to be those that you would expect from a study of algebra.

Operators often modify the contents of an object in memory. An example of such an operator is the *assignment operator.* Since the assignment operator is a binary operator, it is important to distinguish between the operand on the left-hand side of the assignment operator and that on the right-hand side. As the operand on the left has to represent an object in memory, it ultimately must represent a memory address. In C, such an operand is referred to as an *lvalue.* Because an lvalue must represent a memory location, the following are invalid assignment statements.

```
x + y = 3.0; /*invalid assignment*/

5 = x; /*invalid assignment*/
```

These assignment statements will produce a compilation error.

The operand of the right-hand side of an assignment is used to determine a value. It may be an lvalue, a constant, a literal, a variable, a function call, or some expression that is a combination of these.

We will now consider the C operators. For completeness, we will mention the majority of the operators of C in this section. Some of these have been discussed in previous chapters and the discussion of others will be further amplified in subsequent chapters. This chapter will discuss the meaning of operators and precedence and associativity rules, and the interactions among types and operators.

4.3   UNARY OPERATORS

Unary operators can be classified as arithmetic, logical, type manipulation, bit manipulation, pointer operators, function call, and array reference.

Unary Arithmetic Operators

The *arithmetic unary operators* are the unary minus (i.e., arithmetic negation) and the increment and decrement operators. The meaning of the unary minus is the typical arithmetic meaning as in -7 and $-n$, where n is a variable of an arithmetic type (character, integer, and floating types). It causes a positive value represented by its operand to be changed to a negative, or a negative to a positive.

The increment and decrement operators provide a convenient means of performing a very common operation. The increment operator $++$ adds one to the value of its operand; the decrement operator $--$ i.e., two minus signs in a row) subtracts one from the value of its operand. (One exception to this involves the size of the increment when applied to a pointer variable. This exception is discussed in Chapter 6.) The operand for an increment or decrement must be an lvalue since the value of a memory location is being modified.

Recall that the increment and decrement operators can be applied in two formats: postfix and prefix. In the prefix format, the operator appears before the lvalue and is applied before the lvalue is used. In the postfix format, the lvalue appears before the operator and the operator is applied after the lvalue is used. Figure 4.2 illustrates this difference.

In both cases shown in Figure 4.2, the value of the variable y is incremented to 8. But in the left column, the variable x has the value 8, whereas in the right column, the variable z has the value 7. In calculating the value to be assigned to x, the prefix use of the increment operator means that the increment is performed to y before the value is used. In determining the value for z, the postfix increment means that the value of operand y is used before the increment operator is applied. The decrement operator has an analogous pair of formats and interpretations.

Unary Logical Operator

The solitary *logical unary operator* is logical negation that is represented by the exclamation point symbol (!). Its semantics are that it changes a true value to a

```
y = 7;                  y = 7;
x = ++y;                z = y++;
```

Figure 4.2. Examples of increment operators

false and a false to a true. Since C represents false by a zero value and true by a nonzero value, this actually means that the logical negation operator changes a zero value to a nonzero value (generally one), and that it changes a nonzero value to zero.

Program 4.1 uses the logical negation operator. Notice that the typedef operator has been used to create a synonym for int with the name boolean. Then the variable in_order in the improved_bubble_sort() function is declared with this type. Furthermore, the #define preprocessor directive is used to create two constant identifiers called TRUE and FALSE. In keeping with the C conventions, TRUE is given the value 1 and FALSE is given the value 0. The statement "in_order = TRUE;" gives the boolean (int) variable in_order the value 1. The logical negation operator is used to change a true value to a false, or vice versa.

```c
#include <stdio.h>
#include <string.h>

#define FALSE 0
#define TRUE 1
#define MAX_NUMBER 100

typedef int boolean;

int getint(void);
void get_score( int n);
void improved_bubble_sort( int n, int scores[]);
void print_scores( int n, int scores[]);
void input_scores( int n, int scores[]);

int scores[MAX_NUMBER];

main()
{
    int n;

    printf( "Enter the number of students: ");
    n = getint();
    while (n > MAX_NUMBER)
    {
        printf("ERROR! Number of students cannot be greater than");
        printf(" %d.\n", MAX_NUMBER );
        printf("Please re-enter!\n");
        n = getint();
```

Program 4.1. Improved bubble sort (continues)

```
    } /* end while */

    input_scores( n, scores );
    improved_bubble_sort( n, scores );
    print_scores( n, scores );

} /* end main */


void improved_bubble_sort( int n, int score[] )
{
    int i,j;
    boolean in_order;
    int temp;

    i=1;
    in_order = FALSE;
    while (!in_order)

        {
            in_order = TRUE;

            for( j=0; j<n; j++)
            {
                if (score[j] < score[j+1])
                {
                    temp = score[j];
                    score[j] = score[j+1];
                    score[j+1] = temp;
                    in_order = FALSE;
                } /* end if */

            } /* end for */
        } /* end while */
} /* end improved_bubble_sort */

void input_scores( int n, int scores[])
{
    int i;

    for( i=0; i<n; i++)
    {
        scores[i] = getint();
    }
}/* end get_score */
```

Program 4.1. (continued)

```
void print_scores( int n, int score[])
{
    int i;

    printf("The scores in order are : \n");
    for (i=0; i<n; i++)
    {
        printf( "%d\n", score[i] );
    } /* end for */
}

int getint()
{
    int value, ch;

    value = 0;
    while ( (ch = getchar() ) != '\n')
    {
        value = value*10 + (ch - '0');
    }

    return( value );
}
```

Program 4.1. (continued)

Unary Type Manipulation Operators

There are two unary operators that fall into the category of type manipulation.
The sizeof operator that was introduced in Chapter 3 determines the number of bytes of storage allocated to the operand. This size depends upon the type of that operand. This operand is often used with more complicated data structures, but can also be used with a type specifier like "int" or "float" to determine the number of bytes of memory allocated to a variable of that type. This was illustrated in Program 3.7. This operator can also be used with an object's name as an operand to determine the amount of memory used by that object. It is good practice to use the sizeof operator as it increases the portability and maintainability of a program. In Figure 4.3, if the length of the array named vector is modified, the for loop will still iterate once for each array member.

The second unary type manipulator is the *cast* operator. This operator provides an explicit means of *type conversion*. Type conversion is the operation of changing the type of an object. When a type specifier surrounded by parentheses precedes an expression, the value of the resulting expression is the value of the operand with the type modified. This may result in a change in value or a loss of

```
for (i = 0; i < sizeof(vector)/sizeof(vector[0]);i++)
{
            . . .
}
```

Figure 4.3. Using the sizeof operator

precision. For example, if the float variable r has the value 5.732, the expression "i=(int)r;" will give i the value 5. This operation is called casting and is illustrated by the syntax

```
(type_specifier) expression
```

The value of the above expression will be the value of expression converted to the type given by type_specifier. (Note that the type of expression remains unchanged, but the new expression formed from the type conversion operator applied to expression has the type of type_specifier.) This type_specifier can be any type keyword such as char, int, short, long, float, double, or a structure name, union name, or pointer type. (Pointers are discussed in Chapter 6; structures and unions in Chapter 7.) It can also be a type name created with a typedef class specifier.

Consider the example shown in Figure 4.4. In this example, the values of the variables count and total are converted in temporary memory from integers to floats before the division. Without this type conversion, the answer would have been truncated before assignment to average with a loss of significant digits. (The type of count and total remains int.)

Casting is often used to adapt the type of actual parameters to that required by the corresponding formal parameters for function calls. This conversion is necessary in pre-ANSI standard compilers that do not support the function prototype declaration. In the presence of a function prototype, type conversions are made implicity, although it is better practice to use an explicit type conversion. For example, the library function sin(), which gives the sine of a number in radians, requires a parameter with type double. To find the sine of an integer variable x, use the call in Figure 4.5.

The value of integer variable x is retrieved and is then converted in temporary storage to a double. This double value is then passed to the sin() function. The type and value of the variable x are left unchanged.

```
int count, total;
float average;

average = (float) count / (float) total;
```

Figure 4.4. Use of a cast

```
int x;
double answer;

answer = sin((double)x);
```

Figure 4.5. Use of a cast in a function call

Type conversion often results in a change in precision. A change from a smaller to a larger type (that is, from a type that uses less storage to one requiring more storage) can result in a value of potentially greater precision. The converse situation results in a potential loss of precision or a more dramatic loss of information.

Double-precision values are converted to single precision by rounding of the double-precision mantissa—that is, the fractional part, not the exponent—to fit the size of the single precision. Conversions from floating-point types to integer type is accomplished by truncation of the fractional part. These two categories of conversions result in a loss of precision. A more critical loss occurs when large integers are converted to small because the excess high-order bits are removed.

In the examples in Figure 4.6, the value in the double variable d is converted to an int value. In the first conversion, the fractional portion of the number is lost. There is some loss of information, but the magnitude of the converted number has not been greatly altered. If we assume a MAX_INT of 32676, which is typical on 16-bit machines, then the second answer will result in a complete loss of the magnitude of the number. The most significant digits and the fractional digits are truncated.

One further execption to the conversion scenarios given above deserves clarification. When the conversion is from an unsigned to a signed type or from a smaller signed type to a larger signed type, some compilers perform sign extension. If the most significant bit of an unsigned type variable (or a smaller signed variable) is a one, when converted to a larger signed integer, this sign may be extended across the additional high-order bits that are added. This gives the converted value the correct value as a negative number. Consider the example in Figure 4.7.

```
double d;
int i1, i2;

d = 2756.874;
i1 = (int) d;      /* loss of precision since the value is truncated.*/

d = 47927.5678;
i2 = (int) d;      /* complete loss of the magnitude of the number. */
```

Figure 4.6. Loss of precision in type conversion

```
char c;
int x;

c = '\xFF';    /* Gives c the hexadecimal value FF,    */
               /* or binary 11111111                   */

x = (int) c;
```

Figure 4.7. Conversion with sign extension

If sign extension is performed, the memory location for variable x will contain a string of 16 ones, giving x a negative value. Conversely, if sign extension is not performed, the memory location for x will contain eight zeros followed by eight ones, giving x the value 255. This is a potential source of abstruse errors of which the C programmer should be aware.

The following situation illustrates the potential problems with sign extension. The function getchar( ) returns a value of type int, because it can return the value EOF, which is a negative integer (such as -1). It is a mistake to declare getchar( ) as returning a char type, even though this may seem natural. With the declaration "char ch" and the statement "ch=getchar( )," the test "if (ch == EOF) . . ." may never be true. When the value -1 is returned, the value of ch is converted to all ones to represent the negative one value. When this value is compared with the int value EOF, it is converted to an integer. If the sign is not extended, the value will be eight zeros followed by eight ones (assuming a 16-bit integer). This value is not -1, so that the test is never satisfied.

Type conversion and the various rules regarding operand types and expression results for the various operators are further addressed in Sections 4.8 and 4.9.

Unary Function Call and Array Reference Operator

The *function call operator* ( ) and the subscripted *array reference operator* [ ] have been discussed previously. An expression followed by the ( ), including an optional list of actual parameters, indicates a call to a function. An expression followed by the array reference operator [subscript_expression] indicates a reference to the $(i + 1)^{st}$ member of an array, where i is the integer value of the subscript expression. (Array indexes in C begin with zero.) The subscript expression must evaluate to an integer value. Further usage of the array reference operator and the relationship between arrays and pointers will be discussed in Chapter 6.

Unary Bit Manipulation Operator and Pointer Operators

The final unary operators are the bitwise negation operator ~ and the address and the indirection operators & and *. The meaning and usage of these operators will be discussed in subsequent chapters. (Bitwise operators are presented in Chapter 9; pointers in Chapter 6.)

Unary Operator Precedence and Associativity

The precedence of the unary operators is shown in Figure 4.8. Notice that the unary operators have higher precedence than all other categories of operators.

The operators [ ] and ( ) associate left to right. The remaining unary operators associate right to left. Left-to-right association means that, when several of these operators having the same precedence level appear in an expression, they are evaluated as they are encountered in a left-to-right order.

This concludes the discussion of the unary operators until the pointer operators are considered in Chapter 6. Binary operators will now be considered.

4.4 BINARY OPERATORS

The general form of *binary operators* is

```
expression1 binary-operator expression2
```

Binary operators in C fall into the categories of arithmetic, relational, bit manipulation, logical, and assignment. We will consider the arithmetic, relational, and logical operators in this section. Section 4.5 is devoted to the assignment operators and Chapter 9 will address the bit manipulation operators.

```
[] ()                        Array reference and function call
++ --                        Postfix increment and decrement
++ -- sizeof ! - ~ & *       Prefix increment and decrement and
                             other unary operators

<all other operators>
```

Figure 4.8. Unary operator precedence

Binary Arithmetic Operators

The arithmetic binary operators are listed in Figure 4.9.

Of these, only the modulus operator needs a further explanation of meaning. The expression

    i % j

gives the integer remainder of the value of the integer variable i divided by the value of the integer variable j. The modulus operator accepts only integer operands and results in a value of type int. (For positive integers, this is the same as the mod operator of mathematics, but for negatives, they differ. In mathematics "x mod m" is always defined to be a positive number, whereas in C, the answer is negative if the dividend is negative.) Figure 4.10 gives examples of the use of the mod operator.

Examine the values produced by the mod operator in the preceding examples. In particular, note the sign of the result from the last three cases. These results can be verified by examining the long division performed in Figure 4.11.

The type of the operands of the other binary arithmetic operators in Figure. 4.9 can be char, short, int, float, long, double or long double in signed and unsigned varieties.

C does permit mixed-mode expressions, that is, the use of operands of different types for one operator. For a complete discussion, see Section 4.9.

The precedence of the binary arithmetic operators follows that of the unary operators. Within the set of binary operators, the multiplicative operators (*, /, %)

+	addition
−	subtraction
*	multiplication
/	division
%	modulus

Figure 4.9. Arithmetic binary operators

x	y	x mod y
12	4	0
7	5	2
5	12	5
34	11	1
33	17	16
−33	17	−16
−33	−17	−16
33	−17	16

Figure 4.10. The mod operator

$$
\begin{array}{r}
1 \\
-17\overline{\smash{)}-33} \\
-17 \\
\hline
-16
\end{array}
\qquad
\begin{array}{r}
-1 \\
17\overline{\smash{)}-33} \\
-17 \\
\hline
-16
\end{array}
\qquad
\begin{array}{r}
-1 \\
-17\overline{\smash{)}\ 33} \\
17 \\
\hline
16
\end{array}
$$

Figure 4.11. Derivation of the results of some mod operations

have a higher precedence than the additive operators (+ −). The arithmetic operators within a precedence class associate left to right.

As in algebra, multiplication and addition are commutative. One must beware that, although these operations are commutative, the order of evaluation of the expressions composing their operands is not specified by C. This is particularly problematic in the presence of side effects, especially with the increment and decrement operators. In the case of the statement

$$z = x + (x = \sin(y))$$

the order of evaluation has a dramatic effect upon the value that results. If the expression to the right of the + operator is evaluated first, a side effect is to change the value of the variable x before it is evaluated for use in this expression. The above statement should split into two statements so that the side effects could be more easily controlled.

The associativity of operators can also cause severe problems. Consider the following two expressions:

```
x * y / z      /*the default order*/
x * (y / z)    /*order specified by parenthesis*/
```

If these variables have int type, these two expressions may have different values. This is caused by the effect of the truncation that occurs when two integers are divided. Thus, one cannot make assumptions about the order of evaluation of expressions even though the operator is commutative or associative.

Binary Relational Operators

The binary, *relational operators* are those that are used to compare the values of their operands. These operators are the listed in Figure 4.12.

The result of each of these is always 0 for false or 1 for true. In order to determine the result of a comparison, the normal arithmetic order holds for all the arithmetic types; a lexicographic (alphabetic) ordering based on the underlying representation (e.g., ASCII or EBCDIC) is used for character data.

Operands of any simple type can be compared using the binary relational operators, but not the aggregate types (structures, unions, entire arrays). Figure

```
>           greater than
<           less than
>=          greater than or equal
<=          less than or equal
==          equal
!=          not equal
```

Figure 4.12. Binary relational operators

4.13 demonstrates a simple comparison using character data. (Notice that c1 and c2 are typed as int because getchar() returns a negative value if there is an exception in reading, e.g., end of file.)

The precedence of the relational operators is shown in Figure 4.14. The relational operators associate left to right within a precedence class.

The relational operators allow much more flexibility in expressions than the corresponding operators in many other languages (e.g., Pascal). The C programmer should be aware that, although the syntax of C is much more forgiving in this regard, this flexibility allows for the introduction of errors that are difficult to find, and for which the compiler often gives no diagnostics. For example, Figure 4.15 presents a syntactically correct C statement, provided that the necessary data declarations are present.

```
int c1, c2;
c1 = getchar();
c2 = getchar();
if (c1 < c2)
{
     /* if statement body */
}
```

Figure 4.13. Comparison of character data

```
unary operators
arithmetic binary operators
bitwise shift operators (see Chap. 9)

<   >   <=   >=
==   !=

other operators
```

Figure 4.14. Precedence of relational operators

```
int x;

x = -1;
if( x + ( 5 < 10 ))
{
     /* condition #1 body
}

x = -1;
if ( x + 5 < 10 )
{
     /* condition #2 body
}
```

Figure 4.15. Precedence differences in if statements

   In the first if statement in Figure 4.15, the less-than operator gives a true value (1), which is then added to the value of the variable x. Since the resulting value of x is 0 (false), the body of the if statement is not executed. In the second if statement, the addition operator is executed first because it has a higher precedence than the less-than operator. The value of the expression "x + 5" is 4. This is then compared with 10. The result is nonzero (true), so that the condition body is executed.

Binary Logical Operators

The binary, logical operators are the logical AND operator, which is represented by the symbol &&, and the logical OR operator represented by ||. The operands for these operators are interpreted as boolean in the normal manner (i.e., zero for false, nonzero for true). The semantics of && and || are the standard interpretations as illustrated in Figure 4.16. (Note that || represents logical or, not the logical exclusive or.) In this table, any nonzero value could be substituted for 1 in the first two columns with the same results.

x	y	x&&y	x||y
0	0	0	0
0	1	0	1
1	0	0	1
1	1	1	1

Figure 4.16. Semantics of the logical AND and OR operators

The C standard specifies that the operands for the logical AND (&&) and the logical OR (||) operators be evaluated in left-to-right order and that there is a "sequence point" after the evaluation of the left operand. A sequence point is a particular place in an expression at which all previous side effects are guaranteed to be completed before further processing proceeds. This means that, in this situation, the left-hand operand is evaluated completely before evaluation of the right-hand operand begins. In the case of the logical AND operator, if the left operand evaluates to false (zero), then the right operand is not evaluated and the result of the expression is false (zero). Analogously, for the logical OR operator, if the left operand evaluates to true (nonzero), then the right operand is not evaluated and the expression result is true. This is important if the right operand has some side effect!

This "short-circuit" evaluation of the && and || expressions is useful in avoiding run-time errors, as in the statement in Figure 4.17.

This loop fills an array a with elements obtained from one line of input by the getchar() function. A run-time error is avoided in the case that the new-line is not found because of the short-circuit evaluation of the logical AND. If there are more characters on the input line than can be stored in the space allocated for array a, the loop terminates. If both operands were always evaluated and the value of c was never equal to '\n', then a run-time error would result when the value of x equaled or exceeded MAX_SIZE.

The experienced programmer will recognize that this short-circuit version of the logical AND and logical OR operators is not typical of other programming languages. This short-circuit version is generally beneficial. It solves the kind of problem mentioned above, and adds some efficiency of operation (since the second operand expression of the AND does not have to be evaluated if the first operand is false; nor does the second operand of the OR if the first is true). The

```
#include <stdio.h>
#define MAX_SIZE 30

int x;
char c;

char a[MAX_SIZE+1];

for (x = 0;  (x < MAX_SIZE) && ( (c = getchar() ) != '\n' ); x++)
{
    a[x] = c;

}
a[x] = '\0';
```

Figure 4.17. A use of the "short-circuit" logical AND operator

only disadvantage is that, since the second operand is not always evaluated, any side effects of that second expression cannot be depended upon. On the other hand, a style of programming that depends upon the side effects is generally to be avoided from a software engineering perspective.

The precedence of the logical operators is illustrated in Figure 4.18. The logical operators, as well as all of the binary operators discussed up to this point, associate left to right. Consider the code fragment in Figure 4.19, which illustrates the rules of precedence and associativity.

In this example, the order of operations is $+$, $<$, $!=$, $==$, $\&\&$, $||$. Even though the precedence rules in Figure 4.19 are used correctly, this cryptic form is unacceptable with respect to understandability. The preferred method is to use parentheses to make it more understandable. Figure 4.20 gives the same statement with parentheses.

```
unary operators
arithmetic binary operators
bitwise shift operators        (Chapter 9)
relational operators
bitwise boolean operators      (Chapter 9)

&&
||

other operators
```

Figure 4.18. Precedence of logical operators

```
int x,y;

x=7;
y=0;

if ( x + 5 < 10 || y != 7 && x == 7 )
{
        printf("%d%d\n", x, y );
}
```

Figure 4.19. Use of the precedence of && and ||

```
if((x+5<10)||((y!=7)&&(x==7)))
{
        printf("%d%d",x,y);
}
```

Figure 4.20. Parenthesized use of && and ||

Bitwise Binary Operators

The bitwise shift operators $<<$ and $>>$ and the boolean operators & and | are discussed in Chapter 9.

4.5 ASSIGNMENT OPERATORS

C provides an unusual assortment of *assignment operators,* all of which have the general format:

```
lvalue assignment_op expression
```

In each case, an assignment operator gives a new value to the lvalue on the left-hand side by determining the value of the expression on the right-hand side.

In the simple assignment, the value of the expression is given to the object to which the lvalue refers. Since the assignment expression itself has a value, assignment statements can be embedded inside of more complex expressions, as illustrated in many previous examples, including Figure 4.17. Another result of this property is that multiple assignment expressions can occur in one statement, as in Figure 4.21.

This expression results in the value of the expression "average * n" being assigned to the objects sum, total, and answer. This results because the assignment operators associates right to left. All of the operands except the right-most must be lvalues.

Additional assignment operators are formed by combining the simple assignment operator = with each of the arithmetic binary operators. The symbols to represent these assignment operators are

```
+= -= *= /= %=
```

The meaning of these operators is explained by the semantic equivalence of the two statement forms:

```
lvalue = lvalue operator expression

lvalue operator = expression
```

```
int sum, total, answer, average, n;

n = 10;
average = 75;
sum = total = answer = average * n;

printf( "sum %d total %d answer %d average %d n %d\n", sum, total,
        answer, average, n);
```

Figure 4.21. Multiple assignment statements

Notice that the operator and the "=" symbol are juxtaposed with no intervening spaces in the second form.

This second form has the syntactic advantages of its conciseness and the efficiency advantage that the lvalue is evaluated only once. In Figure 4.22, the statement in the left column is semantically equivalent to the corresponding statement in the right column.

There is an additional group of assignment operators formed from the binary bitwise operators. These will be discussed in Chapter 9.

Program 4.2 demonstrates the use of an assignment operator in the loop that accumulates the total test scores for a student. The statement "total += score[i]"

```
int total, score, count;
float average, factor;

total = total + score;              total += score;
average = average / count;          average /= count;
factor = factor * 10;               factor *= 10;
```

Figure 4.22. Use of the assignment operators

```c
#include <stdio.h>

#define MAX_STUDENTS 100

main()
{
    int getint( void );
    int no_students, i;
    int score[MAX_STUDENTS];
    int total;
    float average;

    printf("Please enter the number of students: ");
    no_students = getint();

    while (no_students > MAX_STUDENTS )
    {
        printf("ERROR! Number too large.\n");
        printf(" The maximum number of students is %d. \n",
            MAX_STUDENTS);
        printf("Please re-enter : ");
        no_students = getint();
```

Program 4.2. Finding a test average (continues)

```
        } /* end while */

        i = 0;
        total = 0;
        while( i < no_students )
        {
               score[i] = getint();

               total += score[i];
               i++;

        } /* end while */

        average = (float) total / (float) no_students;
        printf( "The class average is %f%.", average );

} /* end main */

int getint()
{
    int value, ch;

value = 0;
while ( (ch = getchar() ) != '\n')
    {
            value = value*10 + (ch - '0');
    }

    return( return );

}
```

Program 4.2. (continued)

causes the test score in the array element score[i] to be added to the current value of the variable total. The result of this addition is stored in the variable total.

This strcpy() function discussed previously accomplishes an array assignment by copying each character individually from one char array to the other. It assumes that the array to be copied is terminated by a null byte, and that the target string has been allocated sufficient space.

The precedence of these assignment operators is the lowest of all of the operators mentioned to this point. (The comma operator to be discussed in Section 4.7 is the only operator with a lower precedence.) These assignment operators associate right to left.

4.6 TERNARY OPERATOR

The one *ternary operator,* that is, the one operator that requires three operands, is the *conditional operator.* This operator is used to construct conditional expressions. The use of this operator is called a conditional expression because its value conditionally depends upon the value of the first operand. It can be considered an "if" statement for expressions. Its syntax is illustrated by the following template:

```
expression1 ? expression2 : expression3
```

This operator is mentioned here for completeness. It is important to realize that many software engineers consider this operator difficult to understand, and, therefore, to be avoided by the use of more conventional conditional operators.

The semantics of this operation are that expression1 is evaluated. If the resulting value is nonzero, representing "true," then expression2 is evaluated, and this value becomes the value of the entire expression. If the value of expression1 is evaluated to be zero, representing false, expression3 is evaluated, and this value becomes the value of the entire expression.

The precedence of the conditional operator is lower than the relational and logical operators but higher than the assignment operators. Because of this low precedence, the parentheses in the examples in Figure 4.23 are not necessary, although they add to the readability of the expression.

The first example in Figure 4.23 uses this operator to assign the maximum of the values of the two variables x and y to the variable max.

Notice that only one of the two last expressions in a ternary expression is evaluated. This property is useful if there are conditions in which the evaluation of a particular expression may have severe side effects, or cause an error. For example, in the second example in Figure 4.23, division by zero is avoided. If j is equal to zero, the value of the expression is zero; otherwise the division is performed.

```
int max, x, y, i, j, k, m, n;

max = (x > y) ? x : y;      /* max is set to the larger of  */
                            /* x and y                      */

i = (j == 0) ? 0 : k/j;     /* i is set to k/j if j is not 0; */
                            /* otherwise it is set to 0.      */
n = (n < 0) ? m++ : m--;    /* if n is negative then m is     */
                            /* incremented; otherwise m is    */
                            /* decremented.                   */
```

Figure 4.23. The conditional (ternary) operator

```
x == 0 ? y == 0 ? x : y : x/y;
x == 0 ? ( ( y == 0) ? x : y ) : x/y;
```

Figure 4.24. Nested conditional operators

unary operators
arithmetic binary operators
bitwise shift operators
relational operators
bitwise boolean operators
logical operators

?:

assignment operators
other operators

Figure 4.25. Precedence of conditional (ternary) operator

In the third example, the value of m is either incremented or decremented depending on the value of "n < 0."

The ternary operator associates right to left. Consider the example in Figure 4.24.

The two expressions in Figure 4.24 are equivalent; the second just provides parentheses to clarify the order. The inner conditional expression is evaluated first to produce the value x if y==0 is true and the value y if y==0 is false. Then x==0 is evaluated. If true, then the value of the conditional expression y==0 ? x : y becomes the value of the expression. If x == 0 evaluates to "false," then x/y is evaluated as the value of the expression. These examples illustrate the cryptic nature of this operator.

The relative precedence level of the conditional (ternary) operator is summarized in Figure 4.25.

4.7 COMMA OPERATOR

The last operator to be considered in this chapter is the operator with the lowest precedence, the *comma operator*. This operator is used to separate multiple

```
int sum, i;

for ( i = 1, sum = 0; i < 10; sum += i, i++ );

for ( i = 1, sum = 0; i < 10; i++)
{
    sum += i;
}
```

Figure 4.26. Use of the comma operator in a for loop

expressions within one statement, particularly in the "for" statement. Considering its name, it is not surprising that the symbol for this operator is a comma.

Given the expression form

```
expression1 , expression2
```

the value and type of this comma expression are the value and type of the right expression, that is, of expression2. Both expressions are evaluated. If either involves an embedded assignment operator or a call to a function, the side effects of that assignment or function take effect.

This operator is frequently used in for loops to move the body of a loop into the loop header. The first example in Figure 4.26 illustrates this technique by using the comma operator twice.

The second loop is equivalent to the first with only one use of the comma operator. The first expression reflects the conciseness that is typical of the current practice in C programming. Notice the use of the semicolon at the end of the first loop. This specifies a null statement as the loop body. Without this semicolon, the next statement would become the body of this for loop.

The second for loop is better from a style perspective since the important task of the loop appears in the body whereas the loop header uses the comma operator only in an initialization. The ramifications of this style are further discussed in the software engineering section of this chapter.

As mentioned previously, the comma operator has the lowest precedence of all C operators. Its associativity is left to right. In an expression in which several comma operators are used in sequence, the value of the expression is the right-most expression, although all expressions are evaluated.

4.8 OPERAND AND RESULT TYPES

In understanding operators, it is important for the C programmer to be aware of the type of the operands required and the results produced by each operator. Table 4.1 can serve as a useful reference in learning these correspondences. The entries

Table 4.1. Operand Type and Result

Operator	Type of Operand	Type of Result
–(unary minus)	Any arithmetic type	Same as operand
!	Any simple type	int (1 for true, 0 for false)
++−−	An lvalue	Same as the lvalue
* /	Any arithmetic type	Promoted to larger of the operand types
%	int, short int, long int	Promoted to larger of the operand types
+−	Any arithmetic type or pointer	Promoted to larger of the operand types
Relational	Any simple type or pointer	int (1 for true, 0 for false)
Logical	int, short int, long int	int (1 for true, 0 for false)
Conditional	First operand has to be short int, or char; others can have any type	Type of whichever of the second or third operands is selected
Assignment	lvalue on left side, any compatible type on the right	Type of the right operand
Comma	Any type	Type of the right operand

for +, − and relational operators in this table have references to "pointers." These are included for completeness. (Pointers will be discussed in Chapter 6.) The terminology used in Table 4.1 is discussed next.

4.9   IMPLICIT TYPE CONVERSION RULES

The C programming language provides some *automatic* (or *implicit*) *type conversion* facilities. The C language defines several rules that govern automatic type conversions, which will be discussed subsequently. However, the general principle is that the "smaller" type is promoted or widened to the "larger" type.

```
int x;
long int y;

printf( "%ld", x + y );
```

Figure 4.27. Automatic type conversion of integers

The term "smaller" means the type that requires less memory and that consequently can represent fewer values. In particular, the type int is smaller than the type long int. (For a given implementation, int and long int may be the same size, but logically int type is considered smaller.) Thus, in the example shown in Figure 4.27, the type of the result of the addition operator will be long int.

The rules that govern type conversions are applicable in four situations:

1. Any time that expressions of different types are used as operands of an arithmetic operator.
2. When an arithmetic operator is applied to an operand of type "char" or "short int" (signed or unsigned).
3. When a function is called with char and/or float arguments in a context in which no corresponding function prototype is present, or when the types given in the prototype do not agree with those in the function call.
4. When the types of the expression on the right side of an assignment are not identical to, but are compatible with, those of the lvalue on the left side.

Operands of Differing Types

The first rule, pertaining to the first situation above, is called the "usual arithmetic conversion." Table 4.2 describes this implicit type conversion in arithmetic expressions.

Table 4.2. Implicit Type Conversions

If One Operand Has Type:	Then the Other Operand and the Result Are Converted to:
long double	long double
double	double
float	float
unsigned long int	unsigned long int
long int	long int
unsigned int	unsigned int
char, short int, int	int

To use this table, begin at the top to find the first row that is satisfied. This same information is conveyed in a more precise manner in the following pseudo-code algorithm.

If either operand has type "long double,"
then
> the other is converted to "long double" and the result is "long double."

Else if either operand is of type "double,"
then
> the other operand is converted to "double" and the result is "double."

Else if either operand is of type "float,'
then
> the other operand is converted to "float" and the result is "float."

Else if either operand is of type "unsigned long int,"
then
> the other operand is converted to "unsigned long int" and the result is "unsigned long int."

Else if either operand is of type "long int,"
then
> the other operand is converted to "long int" and the result is "long int."

Else if any operand is of type "char," "short int," or their signed or unsigned varieties
then
> Perform the integral promotions.
> if either operand has type "unsigned int" after this integral promotion
> then
>> the other operand is converted to "unsigned int."

Else the operands and the result are of type "int."

Arithmetic Expressions with char or short int

The second rule, pertaining to the second item, is that of *integral promotion,* which states:

> A "char," "short int," or an "int" bit field, or their signed or unsigned variations are converted to "int."

(Bit fields will be discussed in Chapter 9.) The only exception to this is that if the type "int" cannot represent all the possible values of the original type, then the

```
char ch;
float f;

funcl(ch,f);
```

Figure 4.28. Implicit type conversion in a function call

conversion is made to "unsigned int" rather than to "int." (For example, an unsigned short int would be converted to an "int" if "int" is represented by 32 bits and "short int" by 16. Conversely, an "unsigned int" would have to be converted to an "unsigned int" since an "int" could not represent all the possible values.) These integral conversions preserve the sign. Whether the type "char" is signed or unsigned is implementation defined and thus may vary from compiler to compiler.

Function Parameter Promotions

The third type conversion promotion rule pertains to actual parameters (arguments) used in a call to a function. These conventions are called *"default argument promotions."* (Actual parameters are those used in the call of the function; formal parameters are those specified in the declarations.)

> In the absence of any function prototype declarator in the scope, integral promotions are performed on the actual parameters to a function. In addition, any actual parameters of type "float" are widened to "double."

In Figure 4.28, the variable ch is promoted to "int" and the variable f is promoted to "double." (These variables, ch and f, are the actual parameters.) If a function prototype of the form "void functl(char ch_par, float float_par);" precedes this function call, then the promotions are not performed.

Assignment Statement Between Differing Types

When the types of the left side and of the right side of an assignment operator are not identical, an attempt is made implicitly to convert the type of the right to that of the left. Such a conversion is not always possible. The situations in which implicit conversion is possible are represented by Table 4.3.

The first line of this table is interpreted to mean that any expression with any of the arithmetic types, (short, int, long, float, double, long double) can be used on

Table 4.3. Implicit Type Conversion Permitted in Assignment Statements

Type of Left Side	Type of Right Side
Any arithmetic type	Any arithmetic type
Any pointer type	The integer constant 0
Pointer to A	Array A
Pointer to function	Function

the left side of an assignment operator if the right operand is also an arithmetic type. These two arithmetic types do not have to be the same. The type of the left will be implicitly coerced to that of the right. The remaining lines of the table give other combinations that are possible that will be addressed in Chapter 6, where pointers are discussed in more detail.

As in the discussion of casting (i.e., explicit type conversion) in Section 4.3, the problems of loss of precision and errors in converting from a "larger" to a "smaller" type can also occur in implicit type conversion. Section 4.13 discusses the software engineering considerations of using implicit as compared with explicit type conversions.

4.10   FUNCTION PARAMETER EXPRESSIONS

The order of evaluation of expressions constituting actual parameters in a function call is implementation dependent. In Figure 4.29, the function call in the left column may result in different parameter values, depending on the particular C compiler, because of the side effect created by the second parameter. In particular, the left function call may be equivalent to either of the other two sets of statements, depending on the compiler. If a particular order of evaluation is required, intermediate statements should be used, as in the two right-hand columns of Figure 4.29.

```
funct(x,x++);        funct(x+1,x);        funct(x,x);
                     x++;                 x++;
```

Figure 4.29. Order of parameter evaluation

Table 4.4. Summary of Precedence and Associativity Rules

	Operator	Associativity
Reference	() []	Left to right
Postfix unary	++--	Right to left
Other unary	++---!	Right to left
	(type)	
	sizeof	
Multiplicative	* / %	Left to right
Additive	+ -	Left to right
Relational	< <= > >=	Left to right
Equality	++ !=	Left to right
Logical AND	&&	Left to right
Logical OR	||	Left to right
Conditional (ternary)	? :	Right to left
Assignment	= + = --=*= / =	Right to left
	%=	
Comma	,	Left to right

4.11 SUMMARY OF PRECEDENCE AND ASSOCIATIVITY OF OPERATORS

Table 4.4 summarizes the details of the *precedence rules* and *associativity* of the operators that have been discussed thus far and provides a convenient point of reference. The operators are listed in order of highest to lowest precedence. This list of operators includes some that have not been discussed yet. These will be covered in Chapter 7. Operators in each category have equal precedence.

4.12 USEFUL PROGRAM DEVELOPMENT TECHNIQUES

In this chapter, we have introduced many new operators and reviewed others. In this section, we present some techniques that can be useful in developing C programs. The next section will describe potential problems with the use of these operators that should be avoided for software engineering and portability reasons. (This section will suggest constructive method of program development, and the next will present preventative methods.)

Incremental Software Development

A software design technique that is often used is top-down design. In this technique, the problem is attacked in a "divide and conquer" mode in which the problem is iteratively broken into successively smaller pieces until the pieces are small enough to be coded. Notice that this is a design technique. The result of design is generally some form of pseudocode. The implementation phase of development begins with this pseudocode and produces a working program. An implementation technique that is complementary to top-down design is *incremental development*.

In incremental development, the main program is code first with "stubs" for all the functions called by the main program. A stub is a syntactically valid function with a null body, or only a print statement to be printed when this function is called. Its name and list of parameters are complete. When the main program and its stubs are completed, and have been compiled, they are tested. This has the advantage of incremental testing. Errors can be discovered earlier when they are less expensive to fix.

Next, one of the stubs is chosen for development. It is coded in the same way. The body of the function is written with stubs for any functions it calls. Then the entire program is tested again. This development technique proceeds until all functions have been coded.

Incremental development is well supported by C. The main program can be coded first in the file, with functions to follow. (In Pascal, all function- and procedure-defining declarations must precede their call.) In C, the only concession to the rule that identifiers must be declared before use is that a function prototype for each function should precede its use if the function definition does not. Actually, a function that returns no value, or that returns an int, does not have to have a function prototype. C assumes that all functions return an int unless otherwise stated. However, this default mechanism should not be used because of the loss of understandability and modifiability that it causes.

Recursion as a Software Development Method

A powerful coding technique that can often result in quite eloquent algorithms is *recursion*. Recursion is the process of a function calling itself (direct recursion), or a function calling another function, which eventually results in another call to the original function (indirect recursion). Recursion can provide an alternative to iteration. Program 4.3 uses recursion to reverse a string of characters that are input from the terminal. Thus, if the original input is "abc," then the output is "cba."

This same task can be accomplished by reading the characters into an array, and then printing the array in reverse order. The recursive solution has the advantage of having no upper bound to the length of the input string. The array solution is bound by the size of the array.

```
#include <stdio.h>

main()
{
    void reverse( void );

    reverse();

    exit(0);

}/* end main program */


void reverse( void )
{
    int ch;

    ch = getchar();
    if (ch != '\n')
    {
        reverse();
        putchar( ch);
    } /* end if */

    return;

} /* end reverse() */
```

Program 4.3. Recursive reverse

The key to avoiding an infinite recursion is to provide a terminating case that does not involve recursion, and to guarantee that this case is eventually reached. The terminating situation in the reverse program is when a new-line character is read.

In this recursive function, there is a local variable ch. This has, by default, automatic duration. Therefore, each time that the function reverse() is called, a new copy of this variable is created. The previous versions of ch remain allocated in dynamic storage to be recovered when control is returned to the accompanying invocation of reverse(). This produces the LIFO behavior necessary to reverse the string.

Another common example of recursion is the calculation of the factorial of an integer. This is illustrated in Program 4.4. This program inputs an integer from the user, then calls the recursive function factorial (). The terminating condition for factorial is when n $==$ 0 or n $==$ 1.

```c
#include <stdio.h>

main()
{
    long int i;
    int n;
    long int factorial( /*int*/ );

    printf( "Enter an integer --> ");
    n = getint();

    while ( n <0 )
    {
        printf("ERROR! Cannot take the factorial of a");
        printf(" negative integer.\n");
        printf("Please re-enter. \n");
        n = getint();

    }

    i = factorial( n );
    printf( "n factorial = %ld \n", i );

    exit(0);

} /* end main program */

long int factorial( int n )
{
    long int fact;

    if ( ( n == 1 ) || ( n == 0 ) )
    {
        fact = 1;
    } /* end if */
    else
    {
        fact = n * factorial( n-1 );
    } /* end else */

    return( fact );

} /* end factorial */
```

Program 4.4. Recursive factorial function

4.13 PORTABILITY AND SOFTWARE ENGINEERING ISSUES

The fact that the C programming language is not strongly typed provides much flexibility in the mixture of variables and expressions of various types. This flexibility is at a cost of less compiler type checking, and can potentially be the source of many errors.

The existing state of practice among many C programmers is to utilize the implicit typing facilities, such as type conversion, to a great extent. Although this produces short, powerful statements, it does not conform well to established methods of software engineering. In view of the modification and maintenance problems that are inherent in the software development industry, good engineering practice demands the use of explicit rather than implicit constructs wherever possible. In this situation, explicit type conversion—casting—is preferable to implicit type conversion. In this way, the maintenance programmer is easily made aware of the fact that type conversions are occurring. A frequent source of errors is the mismatch in types of actual parameters and formal parameters in function calls in the absence of prototypes. If the actual parameters are cast to the correct type rather than implicitly converted, this type of error may be avoided, or, at the minimum, discovered more easily.

Standard C compilers allow the use of function prototype declarations as discussed in Section 3.2. Function prototypes give in explicit form the type of the formal parameters to a function. If function prototypes are included in the source file, the C compiler can implicitly convert the type of the actual parameters to agree with that of the formal parameter. These newer C compilers usually provide header files that give function prototypes for all of the standard functions. The appropriate header file should be included whenever a standard function is used. These function prototypes do not replace the need in software engineering for explicit conversion of the type of actual parameters, but merely provide one more safeguard that the types will be converted correctly. (Function prototype declarations that are in include files will not appear in the source listing with the function calls. The maintenance programmer will have to search the header files to examine the declarations.)

In the discussion of the ternary conditional operator, we mentioned that this operator has problems in terms of understandability. The examples in Figures 4.23 and 4.24 illustrate the cryptic nature of this operator. The examples of Figure 4.23 are repeated in Figure 4.30 on page 138 with functionally equivalent alternatives using the more traditional conditional statement.

Another current practice of C programmers that militates against maintainable, understandable programs is the use of the comma operator to move the body of a loop into the loop header. This is a cryptic technique that serves only to disguise the loop body, and, as a result, makes the program more difficult to understand. Compare the simple, functionally identical loops shown in Figure 4.31, which were previously given in Figure 4.26.

```
int max, x, y, i,          int max, x, y, i,
j, k, m, n;                j, k, m, n;


max = (x > y) ? x : y;     if (x>y)
                           {
                                   max = x;
                           }
                           else
                           {
                                   max = y;
                           }

i = (j == 0) ? 0 : k/j;    if (j==0)
                           {
                                   i = 0;
                           }
                           else
                           {
                                   i = k/j;
                           }

(n < 0) ? m++ : m--;       if (n < 0)
                           {
                                   m++;
                           }
                           else
                           {
                                   m--;
                           }
```

Figure 4.30. Conditional statements and expressions

Although the first may appear slightly more concise, the loop body is not nearly as apparent. It is clear, in the second example, that adding together the values of i is the primary function of this loop. This temptation to push the body, or a portion of it, into the loop header is sometimes exacerbated by the convenience of the use of embedded increment, decrement, and assignment operators.

The header file limits.h contains a set of constants to specify such values as the largest integer, smallest integer, largest long, longest short, and so on. For example, the identifier INT_MAX contains the largest integer value (which is typically 32767 if int's are represented in 16 bits) and INT_MIN for the smallest int (which is typically −32767). These constants should be used when possible to achieve greater portability. Pascal programmers will recognize the similarity between INT_MAX in C and maxint in Pascal. Program 4.5 illustrates the use of this INT_MAX value. The header file float.h gives limits for floating types.

```
int sum, i;

for ( i = 1, sum = 1; i < 10; sum += i, i++ );


for ( i = 1, sum =1; i < 10; i++)
{
      sum += i;
}
```

Figure 4.31. Use of the comma operator in a for loop

One important characteristic of quality software is ease of use. For example, if invalid data is entered, the software should present understandable diagnostics. Program 4.5 illustrates a function that can be used to accept integer data from the standard input device.

The function robust_int_input() solves the problems that can occur with the input of an int variable. For example, in Program 3.1, if an error occurs in typing (e.g., a character other than one of the valid digits is entered), that program fails. The function robust_int_input() gives a polite error message in this case, and allows the user to try again. Another error that this function avoids is an attempt to input a value into an int variable that is too large; that is, larger than INT_MAX. Notice that this function has to determine that this error is about to happen before adding the next digit to the accumulator total. If the digit were added to total first, the error would have occurred before it could be reported or avoided.

A similar function could be developed around the use of the standard function atoi() or the more generic function strtol(). These functions can convert a character string of digits stored in an array to an integer. They are discussed in Chapter 8.

A common error that often occurs with integer division is based on the fact that division of two integers results in the truncation of the result to an integer. Thus, 7/2 results in the int value 3. This is true even if the result is to be assigned to a real variable; for example, a float or double. If d is a double and i1 and i2 are int variables, then the expression "d = i1 /i2" will cause the result of the division to be truncated before assignment to the double variable d. This truncation can be avoided by casting i1 and i2 to double before the division. The statement "d = (double) i1 / (double) i2;" will avoid the truncation. Notice that casting only one of the int variables would have the same effect because of the implicit type conversion rules. However, casting both operands is preferred as it makes explicit all the necessary conversion. Conversely, the statement "d= (double) (i1 / i2);" would not have the desired effect as the truncation occurs before the cast.

For floating-point values (i.e., float, double, and long double), Table 4.5 describes the minimum acceptable range of values in standard C.

Notice that these constraints are identical for all three floating-point data types.

```c
#include <stdio.h>
#include <limits.h>

#define TRUE 1
#define FALSE 0

typedef int boolean;

main()
/* main program to test the function robust_int_input() */
{
     int i;
     int robust_int_input(void);

     do
     {
         printf("Please enter an integer.\n");
         printf("Enter zero to quit.\n");
         i = robust_int_input();
         printf( "i= %d\n", i );

     } while (i != 0);

     exit(0);

} /* end main */


int robust_int_input(void)
{
     char ch;
     int total;
     boolean error;

     error = TRUE;

     while ( error )
     {
         error = FALSE;   /* assume that there are no errors to start *
         total = 0;
         ch = getchar();

     while (ch != '\n')
     {
         if ((total > (INT_MAX / 10) ) ||
             (total == (INT_MAX / 10) ) &&
             ( ( ch - '0' ) > (INT_MAX % 10 ) ) )
```

Program 4.5. Robust integer input (continues)

```
/* the digit just entered will make total bigger than INT_MAX, so
not add it on, but give an error message */
            {
                    printf( "ERROR! Integer entered is too large. \n");
                    printf( " Please re-enter the entire integer. \n");
                    error = TRUE; /* found an error */
                    while (getchar() != '\n');
                    break;
            } /* end if */

            if ( ( ch >= '0' ) && ( ch <= '9' ) )
            {
                    total = total * 10 + ( ch - '0' );
                    ch = getchar();
            }
            else
            {
                    printf( "ERROR! Invalid character entered. \n");
                    printf( " Please re-enter the entire integer. \n");
                    error = TRUE; /* found an error */
                    while (getchar() != '\n');
                    break;
            } /* end else */
        } /* end while */

    } /* end while */

    return (total);

} /* end robust_int_input() */
```

Program 4.5. (continued)

Table 4.5. Minimum Magnitudes of Floating Types

Property	Float	Double	Long double
Minimum number of decimal digits of precision	6	6	6
Minimum exponent range	−37 to 37	−37 to 37	−37 to 37
Minimum range	1E-37 to 1E37	1E-37 to 1E37	1E-37 to 1E37
Minimum number such that $1.0 + x \ != x$	1E-5	1E-5	1E-5

The range and precision of "float" are guaranteed to be less than or equal to those of "double" and the range and precision of "double" are guaranteed to be less than or equal to those of "long double." The standard does *not* guarantee that the range and precision of "float" are strictly less than those of "double," and those of "double" are strictly less then those of "long double."

Another, related, implementation dependency is in the number of bits in a word of memory, and the number and order of bytes in a computer word. Many existing computers have 16-bit word lengths and another large group of computers have 32 bit words. These are not the only possibilities. There are computers with 8-bit, 36-bit, and many other sizes. Compilers on all of these machines can support the ANSI standard. In most computers, the bits are ordered with the least significant bit on the right and the most significant bit on the left. There are a few computer architectures in which this order is reversed. In a similar way, most computers store the most significant byte of a computer word at the left end of that word. However, there are some (e.g., the PDP-11™) that store the most significant byte on the right. All of these choices are acceptable to the C ANSI standard. However, programmers who write programs that make assumptions about these underlying orders have to be careful to produce portable code. In general, programs should not be written that depend on the underlying execution environment. There are situations in which this guideline cannot be followed, as for the system programmer. But these exceptions are rare for the applications programmer.

The fact that the order of evaluation of the operands for the commutative arithmetic binary operators (+, −) is not specified was discussed in Section 4.3. This fact is particularly important as a portability issue. Similar situations occur in the evaluation of function parameters, assignment operators, and subexpressions within an expression. In each of these situations, the order of evaluation is not specified. Since the order is not specified in the C standard, two compilers may implement different orders. Thus, a program that works correctly when translated by one compiler may fail when translated by another compiler if a particular order was assumed. Assumptions about the order of evaluation should not be relied upon. If the order is important because of side effects of the evaluation, then the operation should be decomposed into two statements.

There are some points in the execution of a program that can be depended upon to have all side effects completed before execution proceeds. Such a point in a program is called a *sequence point*. In addition to the end of each statement, sequence points in C are

a. A function call.
b. The comma operator.
c. The conditional operator ?

d. The logical and operator &&.
e. The logical or operator ||.

These are the sequence points defined in the C standard. A compiler that adheres to that standard will implement these sequence points. The C programmer can be assured that all side effects from previous expressions are complete, and that no subsequent evaluations have yet begun. With nonstandard C, these are points for potential portability problems.

4.14 SUMMARY

Types were the first topic of this chapter. This term was defined and illustrated. The typedef class specifier was then presented. This class will become more useful in subsequent chapters, but its syntax and simple examples of its use were presented here.

This chapter has described many of the operators in the C programming language, including the unary, binary, ternary, assignment, and comma operators. (The bitwise operators and pointer operators were mentioned. These will be discussed more completely in subsequent chapters.) In addition to describing the syntax and semantics of these operators, the precedence and associativity rules of these operators were presented. Figure 4.32 presents a summary of expression and operator syntax.

The complicated automatic type conversion rules were presented and discussed. The general philosophy is that the types of expressions are widened to the larger type when necessary. It is also possible for the programmer explicitly to control the conversion of types by means of the casting operator. The programmer needs to be aware that this can result in the loss of precision if the conversion is from a larger to a smaller type. The advantages of explicit type conversion over implicit conversion were discussed in the software engineering section.

In addition to the advantages of explicit casting, the software engineering section discussed the use of the comma operator and of embedded increment and decrement operators. The current state of practice of programming in C has made acceptable some uses of the flexibility of implicit type conversions that result in short programs. This small gain has been at the expense of understandability and maintainability.

The portability section presented the standards for ranges and precision of various types of expression. The C standard sets some minimal standards to which standard C compilers must adhere. In some other areas, the standard is silent. This leaves the implementation to the discretion of the programmer. These areas are those to which a programmer must pay attention if portable programs are a goal.

144

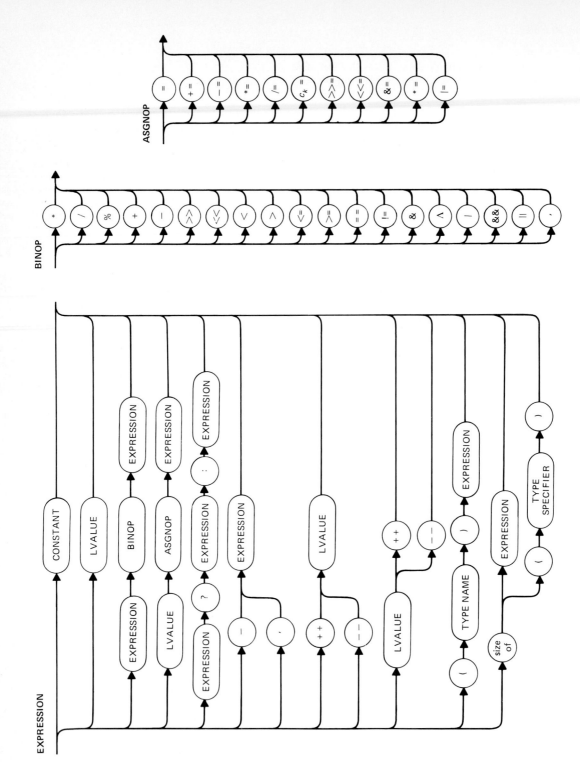

Figure 4.32. Expressions and operators

Keywords

argument promotion
arithmetic operator
array reference operator
assignment operator
associativity rule
binary operator
casting
comma operator
conditional operator
expression
function call operator
implicit (automatic) type conversion
incremental development
integral promotion
logical operator

lvalue
operand
operator
precedence class
precedence rules
recursion
relational operator
result
sequence point
ternary operator
type
type conversion
typedef
unary operator
void type

References

Draft American National Standard x3.159–198x, Programming Language C. This is the ultimate authority on questions of syntax and semantic of C language. Copies may be obtained from Global Engineering Documents, Inc., 2805 McGaw, Irvine, CA 92714.

Jaeschke, R. 1988. For certain uses typedef is far superior to define. *C Users J.* 34–36. InfoPro Systems.

Plauger, P. J. 1988. Types play central role in new standard C. *C Users J.* 17–21. InfoPro Systems.

Pratt, T. W. 1984. *Programming Languages, Design and Implementation* (2nd ed.). Englewood Cliffs, N.J.: Prentice-Hall. This textbook contains a detailed discussion of types.

Tennent, R. D. 1981. *Principles of Programming Languages,* London: Prentice-Hall International. This textbook contains a detailed discussion of types.

Discussion Questions

1. Explain why it is useful to know the number and type of the formal parameters of a function in order to make a successful call to that function. How do prototypes help assure that functions are called properly.

2. What is meant by the term "explicit type conversion"?

3. What are the advantages of explicit type conversion over implicit (or automatic) type conversion? Are these advantages for the computer compiler writer or for the programmer?

4. Can you give any reason for the decision by the designers of C to promote a char argument to an integer or to promote a float argument to a double in an expression?

5. What is the major problem when converting a value from a larger to a smaller type? Give an example.

6. There is a signed char data type. For what purpose would such a type be useful?

7. Give an example to demonstrate that the associativity of operators makes a difference. That is, give an expression that gives different values depending upon the associativity of its operators.

8. Explain exactly what happens in the computer's memory when the statement r=i is executed if r is declared as a float and i as an int.

9. Explain why the "short-circuit" evaluations of logical AND and OR are useful. Can you think of an instance in which it would be useful to have a logical operator that did not have a short-circuit evaluation?

10. Define the term "lvalue." What do you suspect is the motivation behind the name "lvalue"?

11. How can typedef be used for portability?

12. What are the advantages and disadvantages of the use of the comma operator?

13. Why is type conversion, either explicit or implicit, necessary when data of multiple types is used in a single arithmetic expression.

14. Determine the largest and smallest values of int, long int, short int, and char in both their signed and unsigned varieties. (This will require examination of the header file limits.h.) What are the names of the constants that represent these values? (In many compilers, these are actually implemented with the #define preprocessor directive, and should be called macros. The difference between macros and constants will be discussed in the next chapter.)

Exercises

1. Define the following terms:
   a. Operator
   b. Operand
   c. Precedence
   d. Associativity

2. Classify the following C operators as either unary, binary, or ternary. If the symbol can represent more than a single operator, distinguish and classify each case.
   a. +
   b. ++
   c. ==
   d. ?:
   e. +=
   f. &&
   g. −
   h. sizeof
   i. ()
   j. %
   k. >=
   l. !

3. Given the code fragments shown below, state the value of each variable following execution of each fragment. Some expressions may require you to make assumptions about the underlying execution environment. If this is the case, state the appropriate assumptions so that you can compute the value of each expression. (Try these first without use of the computer. Then use the computer to check your work.)

   a.
   ```
   int x = 1;
   int y = 2;
   int i, j, k;
   float a, b, c;

   i = x / y;
   a = x / y;
   b = (float)x / y;
   c = (float)(x / y);

   j = x == y;
   k = x < y;
   ```

   b.
   ```
   int i, j, k;

   i = sizeof(int) >= sizeof(long)
   j = sizeof(float) < sizeof(double)
   k = sizeof(double) >= sizeof(long double) ? 4 : 8
   ```

```
c.   char c1 = 'A';
     char c2 = 'B';
     char d1 = '0';
     char d2 = '5';

     x = c1 > c2;
     y = d2 - d1;
d.   int x = 1;
     int y = 2;
     int z = 3;
     int i;

     i = x++;
     y +=x;
     z += --y;
e.   int x = 1;
     int y = 2;
     int z = 3;

     i = !x;
     j = y > z && ++y == 3;
```

4. Some languages provide an integer division function for integers that gives the integer quotient after division and another division operator for integers that converts the result to a real number. (In Pascal, these are the div and / operators, respectively.) C does not provide two division operators. How can these two types of integer division be accomplished in C?

5. a. In the absence of function prototype declarations, C may automatically make certain type conversions upon actual parameters in function calls. Given the following code fragment, explain what conversions, if any, will be performed on each of the actual parameters.

```
char c;
int i;
long l;
float f;
double d;
long double ld;

funct(c, i, l, f, d, ld);
```

   b. Suppose that we want to pass each of the above parameters to the function using their declared types. Write the appropriate function prototype declaration for funct() that will assure that each type is passed properly.

6. Write a logical expression using either the && or || operator that will have value 1 (true) if the identifier ch (a character) has the following values:
   a. A digit (i.e., between 0 and 9).
   b. An uppercase alphabetic (A through Z).
   c. A printable ASCII character (characters less than a blank and greater than a tilde (~) are not printable).

7. Without knowledge of the type of an array or its size, write an expression that will yield the number of members in the array.

8. Given the expression

   ```
   expression1 && expression2
   ```

   explain the conditions under which (a) expression1 will be evaluated but not expression2; and (b) both expression1 and expression2 will be evaluated.

9. Given the expression

   ```
   expression1 || expression2
   ```

   explain the conditions under which (a) expression1 will be evaluated but not expression2; and (b) both expression1 and expression2 will be evaluated.

10. The assignment operators and binary arithmetic operators can be combined as

    ```
    lvalue op= expression
    ```

    where op is an arithmetic binary operator. From the standpoint of execution time (assuming a nonoptimizing compiler), explain why this assignment expression would be superior to the conventional form of

    ```
    lvalue = lvalue op expression
    ```

11. Modify the program in Program 4.5 so that it can handle negative values as well.

12. The Fibonacci sequence is the sequence of integers whose first two elements are each the number 1. Subsequent elements of the sequence are calculated by adding together the previous two elements. That is, $f_n = f_{n-1} + f_{n-2}$. The first seven elements of the Fibonacci sequence are 1, 1, 2, 3, 5, 8, 13. Write a recursive C program to calculate the nth element of this series where n is a value input from the terminal.

Programming Problems

1. If an amount of money P is invested at an interest rate of i, compounded periodically, the amount accumulated after n periods is given by

   $$a = P(1 + i)n$$

   Write a program that will allow the user interactively to enter the principal, interest rate, and the number of periods from the standard input. Decide whether you will accept the values as integer values or floating-point values and then write the program accordingly. [*Hint:* If you wish, you may investigate the library functions on your system to find one that will help you do the exponentiation; alternatively, you may use repeated multiplication within a loop.]

2. An approximation for the square root of a is given by Newton's method:

   $$x_0 = a/2$$
   $$x_{i+1} = 0.5(x_i + a/x_i) \qquad i = 1,2,3, \dots$$

   Write a function that will accept a single floating-point value and return its square root as the value of the function and write a main program that can be used to test the function. You will have to determine when to terminate the algorithm. For example, you may want to compare successive estimates and terminate the algorithm when the difference between successive estimates is within some predefined delta value. However, be sure that the function does not iterate forever and that your function does not attempt to take the square root of a negative number.

3. The resistance of several resistors in parallel is given by

   $$R = \frac{1}{1/R1 + 1/R2 + 1/R3 + \dots}$$

   Write an interactive program that will accept values for $R1$, $R2$, and so on, and output the value of R indicated by the above relation. Allow the user to enter the resistance in terms of kil-ohms (e.g., 10K, 1K), megohms (e.g., 1M, 10M), or simply ohms.

4. An algorithm for determining the day of the week for a date in this century is as follows: Divide the last two digits of the year by 4, discarding the remainder. Add the last two digits of the year. Add the day of the month. Add 1 for January (0 if leap year), 4 for February (3 if leap year), 4 for March, 0 for April, 2 for May, 5 for June, 0 for July, 3 for August, 6 for September, 1 for October, 4 for November, 6 for December. Divide by 7. The remainder is the day of the week (0 for Saturday, 1 for Sunday, etc.).

Write a program to determine and ouput the day of the week for any date in the form MM/DD/YY. Be sure your program checks for improper input.

5. The length of time to pay off a loan (i.e., to amortize the loan) can be determined from knowledge of the initial principal, the annual interest rate, the payment, and the payment frequency (i.e., number of payments per year). One method is iteratively to determine the present balance after each payment until that payment is zero. Write such a program that will print out the time to amortize in years and months, given the initial principal, the annual interest rate, the payment, and the payment frequency as input.

6. Write a program that allows the user to input any int value, and converts that number to the corresponding roman numeral. (In case you have forgotten, M = 1,000, D = 500, C = 100, L = 50, X = 10, V = 5, and I = 1.)

7. Suppose that two cars are approaching each other on a straight road. Each is driving 30 mph. When these two cars are ten miles apart, a fly leaves the front grill of one, flying 60 mph. When the fly reaches the front grill of the other car, it rests for one minute, then turns around to return to the first car at 60 mph. This process continues until the two cars crash and the fly is exterminated. How far has the fly traveled? (In a classic version of this problem, the fly does not rest before returning. In that situation, the easy solution is to calculate the length of time until the cars crash and use that, along with the fact that the fly travels at 60 mph, to calculate the distance. The fact that the fly rests for one minute at each car complicates the situation.)

8. The Taylor series for sin(x) is

$$\sin(x) = x - x^3/3! + x^5/5! - x^7/7! + \ldots$$

Use a finite number of terms of this series to give values of sin(x) where x is a value input by the user.

9. The Euclidean algorithm for finding the greatest common divisor of two integers x and y is based upon the fact that there are two other integers a and r such that

$$x = y*a + r$$

and with $r < y$. These facts can be used iteratively to determine the greatest common denominator (gcd) of x and y. For example, to find the gcd of 66 and 24:

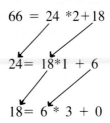

$$66 = 24 *2 + 18$$

$$24 = 18*1 + 6$$

$$18 = 6 * 3 + 0$$

The answer is the last nonzero remainder. In the above example, the gcd(66, 24) is 6.

10. The "Caesar cipher" is a method of encoding a message that was supposed to have been used by Julius Caesar to disguise messages sent to his subordinates across the Roman Empire. This method consists of replacing each letter by the letter obtained by shifting a fixed number of positions in the alphabet. If the shift key was 2, the letter A would be replaced by the letter C, J would be replaced by L, and Z by the letter B. (Notice the wraparound from the end to the beginning of the alphabet.)

Write a program that will allow a user to encode or decode a Caesar cipher. The user should be permitted to type in a shift key followed by a string of characters (a message) that will then be printed out in encoded format. This same program can be used to decode a message by multiplying the shift key by −1.

11. An approximation to the definite integral of a function from a to b is given by the trapezoid method in the formula

$$I = (h/2)[f(x_0) + 2f(x_1) + 2f(x_2) + \dots + f(x_n)]$$

where

$h = (b - a)/n$
n = number of trapezoids used
$x_0 = a$
$x_1 = a + h$
$x_2 = a + 2h$
$\vdots$
$x_n = b$

Write a program that estimates the definite integral of $1/(1 + x^2)$.

12. A planimeter problem. Given a line segment drawn from 5 to 7 along a reference line marked in units from an arbitrary origin, it is obvious that the line segment is two units long. In fact, however, we obtain this answer by taking the imaginary two-unit long line and subtracting an imaginary five-unit long line: 7 − 5 is 2.

A *planimeter* is a mechanical device that employs the two-dimensional equivalent of this geometric trick to determine the area enclosed by merely tracing the perimeter.

For example, consider the following walk:

Move	Command	
Right 3	r	3
Up 1	u	1
Left 1	l	1
Up 2	u	2
Left 3	l	3
Down 2	d	2
Right 1	r	1
Down 1 (closed)	d	1
Down 1	d	1
Left 1	l	1.
Up 1	u	1
Right 1 (closed)	r	1

The enclosed areas are, as one would expect, nine units and one unit.

You are to write a program that accepts a list of motion commands tracing a series of perimeters, computes and prints the areas enclosed by each, and prints the total area enclosed by all perimeters.

Each motion command is to be entered on a line by itself in the form given in the table: a single character in the first column indicating the direction (u, d, l, r), followed by an integer that indicates a distance to move in that direction.

There is no command separating the moves tracing one perimeter from those tracing the next, but each perimeter is a closed walk—each starting and ending at the same point—and this fact should be used to distinguish one perimeter from the next. (This problem appeared as a contest problem at the 1986 East Central Region Scholastic Programming Contest of the Association for Computing Machinery.)

13. For this program, you are to write a program to implement an extended-precision calculator—one that performs addition, subtraction, and multiplication on numbers of somewhat arbitrary length.

The input is a sequence of expressions, one per line. Each expression is composed of one or more numbers (decimal integers) separated by one of the binary operators '+', '−', or '*' (corresponding, respectively, to the operations above). All three operators have equal precedence and associate to the left. Blanks may appear anywhere except within a number.

Your program should read each input line, perform the indicated operation(s), and print the result.

To make this problem slightly easier, you may assume that neither the answer, nor any input value, nor any intermediate result will be negative. The input lines will be no longer than 80 characters and neither numbers nor intermediate results will be longer that 40 digits. (This problem appeared as a contest problem at the 1986 East Central Region Scholastic Programming Contest of the Association for Computing Machinery.)

5 The C Preprocessor

This chapter presents an in-depth look at the preprocessor. There are three categories that emcompass most of the directives in the preprocessor: token replacement (macros), file inclusion, and conditional compilation. These categories will be used for the purpose of exposition and each of the preprocessor directives will be illustrated. Some of the capabilities that do not conveniently fit into these three categories are grouped into a miscellaneous category. This includes some built-in macros and special uses of the preprocessor. Suggestions concerning interesting usages of the preprocessor and pitfalls to avoid are also examined. At the end of this chapter, the reader will be ready to apply the preprocessor's facilities to his or her C programming applications.

5.1 THE PURPOSE OF THE C PREPROCESSOR

The preprocessor is a step or phase of C program compilation that conceptually processes the source code before actual translation begins. In some implementations of C, the preprocessor is actually a separate program that reads the source file and passes on a new (preprocessed) source file to the compiler. In other implementations, the preprocessor and the compiler are packaged as a single program. In Chapter 1, when the usual steps that are required to use a compiler (edit/compile/link) were described, the preprocessing phase was not explicitly noted because it is typically transparent, although on some systems an intermediate file may be produced by the preprocessor.

We have been using the preprocessor since the introduction of the first program in Chapter 1. Recall that the first line of your source files often began with the directive: #include "<stdio.h>." As mentioned in Chapter 2, this is an example of a *preprocessor directive*. A preprocessor directive is a command to the preprocessor. The preprocessor reads C source code, processes and then removes preprocessor directives from the code, and passes the resulting C code, devoid of preprocessor commands, on to the actual compiler or translator.

At this point, the reader may have surmised that the preprocessor statements are not, strictly speaking, a part of the C programming language. Preprocessor directives, in fact, have their own syntax that is independent of the C language.

Why have a preprocessor? The preprocessor enhances the language by providing four general classes of capabilities:

1. *Macro replacement* (also called token replacement).
2. *Source file inclusion* capability.
3. *Conditional compilation.*
4. Miscellaneous directives.

Directives within these categories allow the programmer to save program development time and to create programs that are more portable, more readable, and easier to maintain and debug.

The remainder of this chapter will describe the purpose for and use of preprocessor directives, along with some guidelines for using the preprocessor. The chapter concludes with a discussion of portability and maintainability issues.

5.2 PREPROCESSOR DIRECTIVE SYNTAX

The programmer communicates with the preprocessor by the use of preprocessor directives. The syntax of preprocessor directives represents the only part of the C source code where the concept of a line is important, because preprocessor directives must begin with a # as the first non-white-space character on a line. Additionally, a preprocessor directive typically requires only one line of source text. We hedged the previous sentence because continuation of directives is permitted by some compiler versions (including the ANSI standard). Continuation will be presented later in the preprocessor hints section of this chapter.

Aside from the fact that the first non-white-space character of a preprocessor directive must be the # symbol, preprocessor directives may not be coded within character constants, string literals, or comments. Otherwise, directives may appear on any line of the source file.

One of the most common uses of the preprocessor is the macro capability.

5.3 MACRO REPLACEMENT

Macro replacement is a service provided by a preprocessor that allows the association of a symbolic name with a string of language tokens. This association is performed at compile time, and a reference to the symbolic macro name results in its replacement with the corresponding source text during program translation. Notice that macro processing provides a way of manipulating the source text. Most assembly languages provide a macro capability, but few high-level languages contain one.

The C preprocessor provides two directives to define and undefine macros:

#define and #undef. See Figure 5.1 for a presentation of the syntax of these directives.

It is convenient for the purposes of explanation to distinguish between the #define directive that includes an argument list and one that does not. We call a macro that includes the argument list a *functionlike macro* because it allows for specification of *arguments* that are similar in appearance to a function's parameters. Macros without an argument list are called *objectlike macros*.

Figure 5.2 includes some directives from a stdio.h header file. The first three examples are objectlike macros and the last is a functionlike macro.

These directives associate the symbolic name following the keyword "define" with a string of tokens called the *body* of the macro. The use of uppercase identifiers for the symbolic name is not required (as indicated by the last example); it is a stylistic convention so that macros can be distinguished from other identifiers and functions within a program. A generous amount of white space is recommended between the macro name and the body to enhance readability.

Notice that preprocessor directives do not require the terminating semicolon. A semicolon, if included in the macro, will be treated as part of the macro's body as

TOKEN REPLACEMENT

Figure 5.1. #define and #undef syntax

```
#define BUFSIZ        512
#define EOF           (-1)
#define FILE          struct_iobuff
#define rewind(fp)    fseek(fp, 0L, 0)
```

Figure 5.2. Macro examples

the macro definition terminates with the last non-white-space character that precedes the new-line. For example, consider the macro definition

```
#define MAX_LINES      10;
```

along with the invocation

```
if (counter > MAX_LINES) printf("overflow detected\n");
```

The preprocessor will expand this statement as

```
if (counter > 10;) printf("overflow detected\n");
```

which is a syntax error.

After its definition, whenever the symbolic name of the macro appears elsewhere in the C program in the same format as the definition (except within character constants, string constants, or comments), the preprocessor will replace the name with the associated macro body. This is called an *invocation* of the macro. "In the same format" means that objectlike macros must be invoked without any arguments or parentheses and functionlike macros must be invoked with parentheses and the same number of arguments as appeared in the definition.

When a functionlike macro is invoked, the text that makes up the arguments at the invocation replaces the arguments in the definition. For example, given the macro

```
#define showit( value )  printf("%d\n", (value) )
```

then the invocation

```
showit( sum / average )
```

will be expanded into

```
printf("%d\n", (sum / average) )
```

Notice that this is not the way that function parameters are processed for a function call. For a function call, the expression sum / average would have been evaluated and the resulting value passed to the function.

Consider the directives in Figure 5.2 in conjunction with the statements shown in Figure 5.3.

Notice that what appears to be a call to a function named rewind() in Figure 5.3 is actually a call to fseek(). When the macro rewind was expanded, the argument was substituted for the argument specified in the definition of the macro. Notice that it is the actual token that replaces arguments in a macro, not the value of the argument. Notice also that EOF is not recognized by the preprocessor when it appears within a string literal.

Using macros can make a program easier to read and maintain. For example, if you used the symbol BUFSIZ illustrated in Figure 5.3 in a program where the buffer size is referenced (such as in declarations, function calls, and loop itera-

MACRO REPLACEMENT USING #define

Before Preprocessing	After Preprocessing

```
char buf[BUFSIZE];                      char buf[512];
FILE *fp;                               struct _iobuff *fp;

if (fread(buf,BUFSIZ,1,fp) == EOF)      if (fread(buf,512,1,fp) == (-1))
{                                       {
    printf("EOF on file\n");                printf("EOF on file\n");
    rewind(fp);                             fseek(fp, 0L, 0);
}                                       }
```

Figure 5.3. Macro expansion

tions), it would be simple to change the size of the buffer and any associated code from 512 to 1024. Simply change the body of the #define directive and recompile. Without the symbol, you would have to locate every place in the program where 512 appeared and change it to 1024. Note that using macros does not save recompilation.

Although the most common use of macros is to give symbolic names to constants, the rewind directive illustrated in Figure 5.2 represents a functionlike macro that uses an argument. Consider the following functionlike macro definition that could be used to define the computation of the area of a circle.

```
#define AREA(r)  (3.14 * (r) * (r))
```

The formal argument (r in this example) will be replaced at the invocation of AREA by whatever *token string* is used as an actual argument. For example, we could code

```
base = AREA( start - end );
```

This would expand into

```
base = (3.14 * (start - end) * (start - end));
```

The preprocessor does not compute the value of (start − end) and substitute this as the value for the argument as a function call would for its parameters. Instead, the token string (start− end) is simply substituted for each occurrence of the argument r in the macro definition.

The programmer must be aware of this method of argument substitution to avoid improper expressions in the resultant expansion. For example, suppose the above macro body were coded without the parentheses.

```
#define AREA(r)  3.14 * r * r
```

When this version is expanded using the above invocation, the result is

```
base = 3.14 * start - end * start - end;
```

which may not yield the intended result. When defining a macro involving an arithmetic expression, it is a good rule always to enclose any argument references in parentheses to avoid precedence errors.

A note on the syntax of functionlike macros is in order. The left parenthesis and the name of the macro in the #define directive must not be separated by any white space. White space will put the parenthesis in the body of the macro. For example, the macro definition

```
#define AREA (r)  3.14 * (r) * (r)
```

when invoked in a statement such as a = AREA(base); would expand to

```
a = (r)  3.14 * (r) * (r);
```

which is not the intended result.

When functionlike macro names are referenced in the program text, they must be coded along with the parentheses and associated argument list in order to be recognized. For example, the appearance of AREA in the source text as shown below would not represent an invocation of the macro.

```
base = AREA;
```

Any number of arguments may be coded in the definition of a functionlike macro. Consider the following macros used to find the distance between two points on a plane.

```
#define SQ(x) (x) * (x)
#define DISTANCE(x1,y1,x2,y2) sqrt(SQ((x2)-(x1))+SQ((y2)-(y1)))
```

DISTANCE employs four arguments. It expands into a function call to a presumed sqrt (square root) function. Using the invocation

```
DISTANCE(0,1,2,3)
```

the first pass of the invocation would be expanded as

```
sqrt(SQ((2)-(0))+SQ((3)-(1)))
```

After expansion, macros are rescanned by the preprocessor for the presence of additional macros. In the example above, the expansion of DISTANCE contains the invocation of the macro SQ. Thus, the final expansion would yield

```
sqrt(((2)-(0))*((2)-(0))+((3)-(1))*((3)-(1)))
```

Notice again that the argument references for both SQ and DISTANCE were coded within parentheses. If SQ had been defined as

```
#define SQ(x) x * x
```

and invoked using the code

```
SQ(x2 - x1)
```

the expansion would yield

```
x2 - x1 * x2 - x1
```

which does not yield the intended result because of operator precedence rules.

Although a macro definition may contain invocations of other macros, macros are not allowed to be recursive. In fact, many C compilers do not recognize this fact and degenerate into an infinite loop, repeatedly attempting to expand a recursive invocation.

The process of rescanning macro expansions does not permit an expansion into something that is intended to be another preprocessor directive. The macro

```
#define DEFAREA #define AREA(r)   (3.14 * (r) * (r))
```

may be invoked, but upon expansion, DEFAREA would not result in the definition of the AREA macro because the expanded #define statement would not be processed as a directive.

ANSI C preprocessors support the following two predefined macros that can be referenced by the programmer without coding a #define statement. These two macro names are

```
__LINE__    /* decimal constant:  current source line number */
__FILE__    /* string constant: current source file */
```

Some older C compilers use a single underscore instead of the double underscore for these macros, as follows:

```
_LINE_    /* decimal constant:  current source line number */
_FILE_    /* string constant:  current source file */
```

Macro definitions typically remain in effect until the end of the source file (including all #included header files). They can be removed from definition by use of the #undef directive. It may be desirable to remove a macro definition so that the name can be used as a C language identifier, or so that it later can be redefined. The #undef directive is illustrated in the following code:

```
#define  PI  3.1
#define  AREA(r)  (PI * (r) * (r))
base = AREA(start - end);
#undef PI
#define  PI  3.14
base = AREA(start - end);
```

This expands into

```
base = (3.1 * (start - end) * (start - end));
base = (3.14 * (start - end) * (start - end));
```

The primary use of #undef is in conjunction with conditional compilation, which is discussed in Section 5.5.

Some old C compilers allow redefinition of macros without an intervening #undef statement. Standard compliant processors, allow this only if the subsequent definitions are identical to the original (thus allowing duplicate definitions that are often unintentional). To change the definition of a macro using a standard compiler, the macro must first be undefined using #undef. It is recommended that redefinition be avoided if possible.

Other, more esoteric issues relating to the definition of macros have been introduced by the ANSI specification. These features are discussed in Section 5.6.

In programs that are made up of many modules, the same macros are often used in many separate source files. Consequently, we need a way of sharing these macro definitions without recoding them in every single source file. The file inclusion capability, discussed next, provides just such a capability.

5.4   SOURCE FILE INCLUSION

The file inclusion capability allows the programmer to create a single source file of common C source code and preprocessor directives so that such code may be shared by many source files. These files are called "include files" or "header files."

Inclusion of one file in another is accomplished by use of the #include directive. The syntax is shown in Figure 5.4.

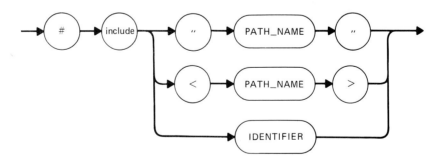

Figure 5.4. #include syntax

Note that this syntax provides for three basic versions of the directive:

```
#include "file-path-name"    /* quoted-string version */
#include <file-path-name>    /* angle-bracket version */
#include identifier          /* macro name version */
```

Here, file-path-name is an implementation-defined string that represents the name of a file to be inserted into the source file in place of the #include directive.

The angle-bracket form of the directive informs the preprocessor to search for the file in a specified set of "system directories," whereas the string literal version of the directive searches the working directory from which the source file was fetched. (We are assuming that the translation environment of the compiler has some sort of file system that supports file names.)

On UNIX machines, the file-path-name can include a sequence of directories separated by slashes, for example, /usr/include/ctype.h. On MS-DOS machines, the path name could include a drive specifier and a back-slash separated list of directories, such as, b:\headers\ctype.h.

The macro name version of the directive is assumed whenever the quoted string or angle-bracket version is not used. In this case, the identifier following the include directive must be a previously #defined macro that eventually expands into either the quoted string or angle-bracket version of the directive. This particular form of the #include directive may not be supported by all compilers, but is specified by the ANSI standard. This will be illustrated in the next section, as it is often used in conjunction with conditional compilation.

The programmer should avoid declaring identifiers that result in allocation of storage (i.e., defining declarations) and executable code in an include file. Since include files are usually #included in many source files, executable code and declarations that allocate storage would be duplicated in each file. Codes commonly found in an include file are #defines, function prototype declarations, extern data declarations, typedefs, structure, and union tag declarations (the last two constructs are introduced in subsequent chapters of this text).

An include file may itself contain #include directives. The allowable depth of such nested #includes may vary between preprocessor implementations, but a depth of five or six is not uncommon.

5.5   CONDITIONAL COMPILATION

It is often desirable selectively to enable or disable compilation of certain portions of program source code at compile time. For example, it might be desirable to code a program so that it can be compiled for either UNIX-based or MS-DOS-based target environments. Obviously, two versions of the source code could be maintained in separate files, but if most of the code is common to the two implementations, this would be an expensive way to manage the situation. Another alternative is conditional execution, where during execution only portions of the code are executed. However, this would result in slower execution of the program and a larger executable file than would be necessary if only the desired code were included for the particular implementation. It would also require compilers that are very well standardized.

Another common example is the use of "debug" or "trace" code. When doing the initial development on a system, it is often helpful to code these trace statements into the code for testing purposes. Later, when the program is translated for production, it is necessary to remove this "temporary" code. The source code could be edited, but an easier approach is to use conditional compilation (especially given the high probability that the trace code will be needed again as soon as it is edited out of the source).

Conditional compilation provides the capability either to pass particular source code through to the compiler or to eliminate source code based on some compile-time condition. This conditional inclusion capability allows programmers to write code for different environments or to include trace code and then selectively to enable or disable such code.

The syntax of the conditional compilation preprocessor directives is illustrated in Figure 5.5.

Table 5.1 describes the function of each of these directives.

Consider the #if, #endif pair. We could use these directives to implement *trace code* as illustrated in the following.

Source Code	*Preprocessed Code*
``	
#define TRACE	
main()	main()
{	{
#ifdef TRACE	
printf("Main entered\n");	printf("Main entered\n");
#endif	
process();	process();
}	}
process()	process()
{	{
#ifdef TRACE	
printf("Process entered\n");	printf("Process entered\n");
#endif	
return;	return;
}	}
``	

The #ifdef is used in this example to determine whether the associated identifier (TRACE in this example) has been defined. If so, the source code between the #ifdef and the #endif is passed through to the compiler. If TRACE was not

CONDITIONAL COMPILATION

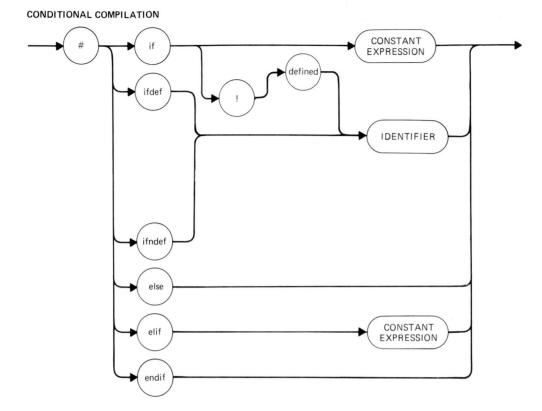

Figure 5.5. Conditional compilation directives

defined, or its definition removed using #undef, the conditional code would have been eliminated before translation.

This example illustrates the most common use of the macro definition that contains no body. Many compilers provide an option for defining such macros on the compiler command line using the -D flag:

```
cc -DTRACE source.c
```

-DTRACE is equivalent to #define TRACE, but allows the programmer the luxury of defining or not defining the symbol without editing the source file. This allows the trace code easily to be enabled or disabled.

#ifndef is similar to #ifdef, but will include code if the associated identifier is not currently defined.

#else and #elif can be used when code for two different target environments may be required. Consider the following situations. The include files for the UNIX version of a utility program are found in the directory /usr/include, and the

Table 5.1. Conditional Compilation Directives

Directive	Purpose
#if constant-expression	Compile code if the expression is nonzero (true).
#ifdef identifier	Compile code if the identifier is currently #defined.
#if defined identifier	Same as above.
#ifndef	Compile code if the identifier is not currently #defined.
#if !defined identifier	Same as above.
#elif constant-expression	Used with #if, #ifdef, and #ifndef to form an "else if" (#elif is not supported by older C versions).
#else	Used with #if, #ifdef, #ifndef, and #elif for negative condition.
#endif	Terminates the scope of #if, #elif, #ifdef, #ifndef, and #else.

code for the MS-DOS version is to be found in c:\headers. Assume that the default version is for UNIX. The code could be written using either of the following two techniques.

```
          Technique 1

#ifdef MSDOS
#include "c:\headers\ctype.h"
#include "c:\headers\math.h"
#else
#include "/usr/include/ctype.h"
#include "/usr/include/math.h"
#endif

          Technique 2

#ifdef MSDOS
     #define CTYPE "c:\headers\ctype.h"
     #define MATH  "c:\headers\math.h"
#else
     #define CTYPE "/usr/include/ctype.h"
     #define MATH  "/usr/include/math.h"
#endif

#include CTYPE
#include MATH
```

If MSDOS is #defined, then the DOS style #includes will be processed; otherwise, the UNIX-style version will be processed. Of course, any program text can be used within the conditional compilation code, not just preprocessor directives as shown in the above example. We could have used a string of #elseif directives (or #ifs in older implementations), if we had wanted to support more than two target environments.

```
        New style                           Old style

#ifdef MSDOS                        #ifdef MSDOS
   DOS-target code                     DOS-target code
#elif VMS                           #endif
   VMS-target code                  #ifdef VMS
#elif CMS                              VMS-target code
   CMS-target code                  #endif
#else                               #ifdef CMS
   Default environment                 CMS-target code
#endif                              #endif
                                    #ifdef UNIX
                                       UNIX-target code
                                    #endif
```

The #elif (else-if) directive is supported on many newer C compilers and ANSI-compliant compilers. Older compilers that do not support #elif require repeated usage of #ifdef/#endif as illustrated in the left-hand code above.

The #if directive is used to test the value of a constant expression. The constant expression may contain other macro invocations but must evaluate at compile time to an integer value, and cannot involve the sizeof operator. Suppose, for example, that we want to use a different sort algorithm depending upon the amount of internal memory available in the target machine. For example, we could use an internal sort if the amount of memory is greater than 256K, but use a disk-based sort if the available memory is less than this amount. We could code

```
#if MEM_SIZE > 256000
```

Internal memory sort code

```
#else
```

Disk-based sort code

```
#endif
```

The expression associated with the #if is evaluated at compile time (it must involve only constants). All integer constants in the expression are treated as long constants. If the value of the expression is zero, the condition is considered false; otherwise, it is considered true.

A preprocessor unary operator, "defined," is provided that evaluates to one if the associated name is defined, and to zero if it is not. For example, the directive

```
#if defined MSDOS
```

is equivalent to the directive

```
#ifdef MSDOS
```

and #if !defined MSDOS is equivalent to #ifndef MSDOS.

5.6   MISCELLANEOUS DIRECTIVES

Many compilers provide some additional directives that we have classified as miscellaneous. The most common is #line, which allows the programmer to instruct the preprocessor to change its thinking about the current source line and file name. The syntax is shown in Figure 5.6.

The directive #line 12 "main.c" informs the preprocessor that the next source line was found on line 12 of the source file main.c. The file-name part of the directive is optional. This information may then be used by the translator in subsequent diagnostic messages. A synonym for the #line directive in some old versions of C is the # symbol, that is, # integer filename is equivalent to #line integer filename. The #line directive is used primarily in software tools that generate C source code.

Less common directives, found in ANSI standard implementations of the language, are #error and #pragma. #error causes the preprocessor to output a message that includes the remainder of the line. It is used to generate a diagnostic message from the preprocessor stage. #pragma is used in an implementation-defined manner to allow vendor-dependent compiler options in the source code. The syntax of these directives is illustrated in Figure 5.7.

The ANSI specification has introduced three new predefined macros

```
__DATE__     /* string constant:  date of translation */
__TIME__     /* string constant:  time of translation */
__STDC__     /* decimal constant:  1 indicating ANSI conformance */
```

in addition to __LINE__ and __FILE__ described previously.

LINE DIRECTIVE

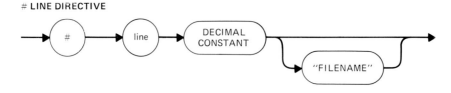

Figure 5.6. #line directive

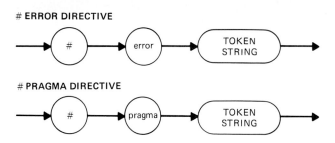

Figure 5.7. #error and #pragma directives

Two macro definition operators have been introduced by the standard: # and ##. In functionlike macros, when a macro argument name is preceded by a #, the actual parameter is replaced by a string constant containing the spelling of the actual. For example,

```
#define STRING_LIT(s) #s
printf(STRING_LIT(Hello));
```

would be expanded into

```
printf("Hello")
```

because the formal parameter, s, is replaced by the actual parameter, Hello, and then enclosed in double quotes. This is a useful operator because it is otherwise impossible to code a macro argument into a string literal (arguments inside of string literals and character constants are not recognized by the preprocessor).

Consider another example. The following sequence of characters is the standard (another ANSI standard, not the C standard) control sequence to position the cursor of a monitor to <row>,<column>.

```
<escape>[<row>;<column>H
```

For example, the string <escape>[1;25H, when output to the monitor, would position the cursor to row 1, column 25. The <escape> character can be represented using the hexadecimal escape sequence '\x1b', so to position the cursor to row 1, column 25, the following printf() call could be used:

```
printf("\x1b[1;25H");
```

Presumably, it will be desirable to position the cursor to other places on the screen, so we could define a macro to represent the cursor position string thus,

```
/* for compilers that support the # operator */
#define POS(r,c) "\x1b[" #r ";" #c "H"
```

where the argument r represents the row and c represents the column. An invocation such as printf(POS(15,40)) would expand into

```
printf("\xlb[" "15" ";" "40" "H")
```

which, due to concatenation of adjacent strings by ANSI compliant compilers would become:

```
printf("\xlb15;40H")
```

The macro body could not have been coded as "\1b[r;cH" because the macro arguments r and c would not be recognized inside of the string literal, except with a few pre-ANSI compilers.

The ## operator can be used to inform the preprocessor that two tokens are distinct, but upon expansion they are to be concatenated. For example, assume that a program had variables named row1 through row24. The following macro could be used to display the value of any one of these variables given the row number, n

```
#define ROW(n) printf("row%d = %d\n",n,row##n)
```

The invocation ROW(15) would expand to

```
printf("row%d = %d\n",15,row15);
```

which would output the value of the variable named row15. The macro body could not have been coded as printf("row%d = %d\n",n,rown) because the "n" in "rown" would not be recognized as a macro argument.

In some older C programs, the reader may find tokens in macros, such as row and n above, separated by a degenerate comment /**/. This method does not work in all cases because some compilers replace comments by white space before translation.

5.7   PREPROCESSOR HINTS

It is important to remember that when a header file is updated, all source files that #include that header file may have to be recompiled. This is necessary because changing a header file is equivalent to changing the associated source files, since the contents of the header file are simply processed as source program. Neglecting to recompile could result in an out-of-date object module being linked into a program. (Utility programs such as the UNIX system "make" program will automatically compare file modification dates between source and header files and recompile source files that are older than their header files.)

The C preprocessor has been used to change the appearance of the C language itself. For example, some programmers who are used to Pascal may prefer the keywords "begin" and "end" as opposed to the C language { and } symbols. This could be accomplished by using the macros

```
#define begin  {
#define end   }
```

and then coding

```
main()
begin
     printf("Main entered\n");
end
```

This practice is not wise, however, because other C programmers may not like your alternative style, and your program will be more difficult to read and maintain.

When defining portions of expressions, it is not a good idea to include the terminating semicolon in the macro body, which can result in errors, as illustrated in Section 5.3.

Considering runtime execution performance, macros provide an advantage over using functions for frequently used, but short, code sequences. Macros result in in-line code without the overhead of code needed for function calls.

Many compiler versions support continuation of long macros so that their definition can span several lines of code. This is accomplished by ending the line to be continued with a back slash (\). Consider:

```
#define  trace(row,col,count)  printf(" row = %d, \
          col = %d, count = %d\n",row,col,count)
```

Macros can be continued in this way, with the final line terminated with a new line.

An alternative for using "trace" code is conditionally to define the trace statement itself. For example,

```
#ifdef TRACE
#define trace(mesg)  printf(mesg)
#else
#define trace(mesg)
#endif
```

If we compile the above code using the compilation flag -DTRACE or by including the directive #define TRACE prior to the code, then the directive

```
#define trace(mesg) printf(mesg)
```

is processed. If the code is compiled with TRACE undefined, then the directive

```
#define trace(mesg)
```

is processed, which creates a macro called trace that has no body. Using this technique, we can code the trace statements in the program without using conditional compilation directives:

```
main()
{
     trace("Entered main\n");
     process();
}
```

If TRACE is defined, the printf() will be compiled in the program. If TRACE is not defined, then a null statement will be compiled (which has no effect in this context).

One technique often encountered in debugging is the practice of "commenting out" a block of code. This is often used to isolate a bug or temporarily to skip a time-consuming unit of code during development. This practice can be dangerous because most compilers do not support nested comments. (The ANSI standard prohibits nesting of comments.) If the code to be "commented out" happens to contain a comment, an error will result because of mismatched /* */ pairs. A better way to skip code temporarily is to use conditional compilation. Simply enclose the code in question with an #ifdef, #endif pair and use some symbol that is not defined, or an #if 0, #endif pair. This will avoid any problems with nested comments.

Many preprocessors allow multiple arguments at the site of macro invocation to be enclosed in parentheses to force them to be treated as a single argument. Consider the following code fragment:

```
#define LENGTH(start,finish)  abs((start) - (finish))

LENGTH(x,y);

LENGTH((x,y));
```

The first invocation would be expanded as expected. The second invocation would be expanded by inserting the string (x,y) in place of the argument start, leaving no argument to insert for finish. This feature is useful if it is necessary to invoke a macro that includes an argument that contains expressions separated by the comma operator.

5.8 PORTABILITY AND SOFTWARE ENGINEERING ISSUES

Macro definitions that are used in more than one source file are usually coded in #include files. Macros used within a single source file but in more than one function in that file are usually written at the top of a source file so that they can be easily located by the reader of a program.

A problem in program documentation and maintenance is to locate all places in the code where a particular diagnostic message is generated, or even to try to find all possible diagnostic messages. If diagnostic messages are all defined in a single header file using macros (or if, at least, an array index or diagnostic message number is defined for each message) and the macros are used in the code, the job of isolating all possible messages is simplified. It is also recommended that a single function be used for the production of diagnostics. A call to this function would be written in any code where it is necessary to output such a message. Such a function could take the appropriate diagnostic macro symbol as parameter. This technique isolates the generation of diagnostics in a single place in the program so that such messages can be later located for documentation, change, or redirection of output (e.g., into a log file).

The original specification of the preprocessor in [Kernighan and Ritchie, 1978] devoted only two pages to a description of the preprocessor. This has been rectified by the production of the ANSI C language standard, but prestandard versions of C often vary in the way that they handle details of the preprocessor. These differences can create portability problems when moving software between compiler implementations. The following is a discussion of some of these differences.

Some preprocessor implementations require that the initial # symbol that initiates directives be coded in column 1 of the source code. The language standard allows the # to be preceded by any amount of white space. Some C implementations disallow white space between the # and the directive name. To maximize portability, we suggest that the # be coded in column 1 and that white space between the # and the directive name be avoided.

Certain implementations do not allow for continuation of macros using the \ character. The ANSI standard does support continuation.

Pre-ANSI standard versions of the compiler sometimes support recognition and substitution of actual arguments in functionlike macros within character and string literals. This is not supported in the standard, and instead the # operator is required for enclosing macro arguments within a string. If a compiler is available that recognizes arguments within strings, the use of this feature should be avoided.

Another common "feature" in many compilers is to allow macro names to be redefined by simply reusing the name in another #define directive without first undefining the name with the #undef macro. The standard does not allow this, and requires that a name must first be explicitly undefined before it is redefined. The best rule for portability considerations is to follow the standard and first undefine names that are to be later redefined.

The conditional compilation directives #elif, #pragma, #error, and #line may not be supported by pre-ANSI standard translators. Additionally, the predefined macros __DATE__, __TIME__, and __STDC__ may not be supported, or the predefined macros may be coded with single underscores (e.g., _DATE_).

A common practice by programmers and some C compiler vendors is to use macros to create user-defined types. For example, as an aid to portability, programmers sometimes create symbolic names for the common type specifiers. Suppose that one needed to be sure that integers were allocated 32 bits. One could create the macro

```
#define INT32    int
```

for a machine that did indeed allocate 32 bits to an integer and declare all integer entities using INT32 instead of int. Then, if the code were ported to a machine on which ints were 16 bits and longs 32, the macro could be changed to

```
#define INT32    long
```

and the code recompiled. This would achieve the desired portability.

Another example of this practice can be found in certain compiler vendor header files. For example, in the Microsoft™ file stdio.h, the following macro is specified:

```
#define FILE struct _iobuf
```

In DEC's C implementation, size_t is created using a #define as follows:

```
#define size_t int
```

This use of macros is discouraged, and typedef should be used instead. The above types should be created as follows:

```
typedef int INT32;
typedef int size_t;
typedef struct _iobuf FILE;
```

Although there are instances in which macros and types created with typedef seemingly can be interchanged, there are cases where the macro method fails. This is particularly true in cases where names are created for derived types involving pointers and structures. Detailed examples will be provided in Chapters 6 and 7, where these types are explored. For the present, we will state the rule that when defining new names for types for the sake of portability, typedef should be used in place of macros.

5.9 SUMMARY

The input and output of the preprocessor is C source code. The input source code may contain preprocessor directives in addition to C language source code. The output contains no directives, as these are read, processed, and replaced by the preprocessor.

Directives can be grouped into four categories: macro replacement, source file inclusion, conditional compilation, and miscellaneous directives. Macro replacement is implemented using the #define and #undef directives. File inclusion requires the #include directive. Conditional compilation utilizes the directives #if, #ifdef, #ifndef, #else, #elif, and #endif. Miscellaneous directives include #line, #error, #pragma, various built-in macros, and the preprocessor operators # and ##.

File inclusion and macros are the most heavily used of the preprocessor facilities. File inclusion is especially helpful when using function libraries, because the function prototype declarations and associated macros can be written into an include file and used whenever the library is required. Conditional compilation is useful for writing code that can be easily ported to various target execution environments.

Keywords

arguments
conditional compilation (inclusion)
functionlike macro
invocation
macro
macro body
macro invocation
macro replacement

objectlike macro
preprocessor
preprocessor directive
token replacement
token string
trace code
source file inclusion

References

Draft American National Standard X3.159–198x, Programming Language C, Copies may be obtained from Global Engineering Documents, Inc., 2805 McGaw, Irvine, CA, 92714 (1-800-854-7179).

Harbison, S. P., and G. L. Steele, 1984. *A C Reference Manual*. Englewood Cliffs, N.J.: Prentice-Hall.

Jaeschke, R. 1988. For certain uses typedef is far superior to #define. *C Users J*. 6(3): 34–6. R&D Publications, McPherson, Kans.

Kernighan, B. W., and D. M. Ritchie. 1978. *The C Programming Language*. Englewood Cliffs, N.J.: Prentice-Hall.

Maurer, H. A., and M. R. Williams, 1972. *A Collection of Programming Problems and Techniques*. Englewood Cliffs, N.J.: Prentice-Hall.

Rogers, J. 1985. The C pre-processor, *C Users J*. 1(3),: 43–8, InfoPro Systems, Denville, N.J.

Discussion Topics

1. How does the preprocessor aid in the development of portable software? Discuss the way that conditional compilation can be used to code programs that can be compiled for different target environments.

2. On many systems, the preprocessor is a separate program (a filter) from the compiler. Could you use the C preprocessor for applications other than writing C code?

3. Functions are useful for consolidating into a single callable unit segments of code that are repeated in many places. In this way, the repeated segments are only coded once, and a function call is used in place of the code. Function calls have overhead because the parameters must be passed, control transferred, and other housekeeping performed. If the repeated segment of code is small, such as a single expression, the overhead of the function call may add significantly to the execution time of the program. Thus, for small segments of repeated code, it is often better to use a macro instead of a function, since macros will save the effort of entering the repeated code, but will not incur the overhead of a function call. Discuss the trade-offs between using functions and macros as a way of consolidating repeated segments of code.

Exercises

1. Consider the following macro definition:

```
#define   AREA(length,width)     (length * width)
```

   Write the expansions of this macro using the actual parameters shown below.

```
AREA( 20, 10 )
AREA( base - height, left - right)
```

   What is a better way to code the macro?

2. The syntax of the #if directive is

```
#if <constant-expression>
```

   The constant expression cannot contain the sizeof operator. Why, do you suppose, is sizeof not allowed?

3. Find out the cursor control commands for your terminal or monitor. For example, if you are using an IBM PC, the following sequences are supported:

```
<escape>[r;cH        /* position cursor to row r, column c */
<escape>[nA          /* move the cursor up n lines */
<escape}[nB          /* move the cursor down n lines */
<escape>[nC          /* move the cursor forward n columns */
<escape>[nD          /* move the cursor back n columns */
<escape>[2J          /* erase all of the screen */
<escape>[k           /* erase to end of line */
```

    a. Code macros to represent the cursor control sequences for your machine or for the IBM PC as described above. (To use these on the PC, include the line device=ANSI.SYS in the CONFIG.SYS file!)

    b. Suppose that you were charged with writing an editor that could be compiled to run on a CRT that supports cursor control or compiled to run on a dumb CRT that does not have such support. Using conditional compilation and appropriate #define directives, code two alternatives for "clear screen": one that uses the cursor control sequence and another that simply outputs 23 blank lines in order to clear the screen by scrolling.

4. Why do changes to #include files often necessitate recompilation of other source files?

5. Code a macro called PRINT that will output its argument as a string (assume support for the # and ## operators, if necessary).

6. Explain why it is better to use conditional compilation to eliminate some section of code in a source file rather than using the technique of "commenting out" that is frequently used by programmers in other languages.

7. Locate some of the header files that were supplied with your compiler and examine the preprocessor directives coded therein. Such files might include stdio.h, ctype.h, math.h, signal.h, string.h, and limits.h. Are #define directives or typedef statements used to create new type names?

8. Given the macro definitions

```
#define MAXUSERS          8
#define MAXPROCESS        10 + 5 * MAXUSERS
#define KBYTES( r )       r / 1024
#define NULLBYTE          '\0';
```

    and the statements

    a.   MAXUSERS = 16;

    b.
```
     If (ucnt > MAXPROCESS)
     {
        printf("Too many processes, max = %d\n",MAXPROCESS);
     }
```

c.   k_available = KBYTES(last - first);
d.   If (ch == NULLBYTE) printf("End of line\n");
Answer the following questions about this code.

    (1) Write the letters that correspond to the syntactically correct C statements.

    (2)   Given: int first = 0, last = 20480;
         Will statement c compute the number of K bytes of memory?

    (3) KBYTES could be recoded as

```
int kbytes(int kb)
{
        return(kb / 1024);
}
```

         Will the statement k_available = kbytes(last - first) compute the number of K bytes of memory?

    (4) Considering only execution time efficiency, identify which of the following implementations is more efficient.

        (a)   k_avail = kbytes(last);
        (b)   k_avail = KBYTES(last);

Programming Problems

1. Suppose that we are given a list of ratios (weight on planet/weight on earth) showing the relationship between the weight of an object on the earth to that on the other planets and the moon. The following table gives the ratios.

Planet	Ratio
Mercury	0.3
Venus	0.8
Earth	1.00
Moon	0.2
Mars	0.4
Jupiter	2.6
Saturn	1.2
Uranus	0.9
Neptune	1.1

Code an #include file called gravity.h and #define symbols that represent the gravity ratios in the table. Write a program that consists of three separate source files: main.c, ratios.c, and weights.c. Ratios.c should contain a function that will allow the user to request the output of the ratio for a given planet.

Weights.c should allow the user to enter a weight and planet and then display the expected weight on the specified planet. Both ratios.c and weights.c must include the file gravity.h and use the #define symbols for the ratios. Main.c is a driver program that gives the user the opportunity to display either a ratio or a weight. If you decide to use an array to hold the ratios, initialize the array using the symbols as follows:

```
float rations[] = {MERCURY, VENUS, etc... };
```

2. Write a program that will add two binary numbers digit by digit. Allow the user to input the two binary numbers. Read the digits into two arrays, perform the addition putting the result into a third array, and then output the result to the screen. Use a #define symbols to declare the size of all arrays, loop iterations, and other maximum sizes so that the program can be expanded to handle various size binary numbers by changing the #define values and recompiling. Compile and demonstrate a ten-digit and a 20-digit version of your program. Another option for this problem is to include conditionally compiled printf() calls that will display the intermediate results of the addition as each digit is processed. Compile versions of the program that both include and exclude these printf()s.

3. Write a program that will read simple chemical formulas from the standard input and compute and output using printf() the atomic weights for the formulas. Use the following elements and weights:

   C   12.01
   H   1.008
   I   126.9
   N   14.01
   O   16.00
   S   32.06

The formula of water is H2O. The atomic weight is 18.016. Another weight, for example, is CH3COOH. Create a header file that includes the symbols for the weights, include the header file into any source files that require the weights. Include conditionally compiled printf() calls that show the intermediate result of the atomic weight as each character of the formula is processed. Compile and demonstrate both a debug and a production version of your program.

4. Read Exercise 3. Code the cursor control sequences for your terminal or PC into a header file. Write a test program that tests each of the possible cursor-movement and screen-control functions.

6 Arrays, Pointers, and Strings

This chapter presents some of the key concepts of the C programming language: arrays and pointers. These form the building blocks for the diverse data structures that are one of the strengths of C. Single-dimensional arrays have been introduced and used in earlier chapters. In this chapter, the discussion of arrays, including multidimensional arrays, will be completed. Pointers are an integral construct in C. A pointer is a variable that contains an address of a memory location. The syntax of pointer declaration and use will be discussed and illustrated. There is a very close relationship between pointers and arrays, which will be explained in this chapter. The chapter will conclude with software engineering and portability considerations of arrays and pointers.

6.1 AGGREGATE TYPES

Simple types are those types that are atomic in the sense that they cannot be decomposed into components of a more basic type. (The simple types are char, int, short int, long int, float, double, and long double in both the signed and unsigned versions, enumerated types, and pointers.) The *aggregate types* are those that can be decomposed into components that have their own type. The aggregate types fall into several classes.

1. Arrays of homogeneous objects.
2. Structures of heterogeneous objects (Chapter 7).
3. Unions of dynamically altering objects (Chapter 7).

Derived types are those that can be constructed from the aggregate and simple types by combining them in various ways with appropriate syntactic rules. These combinations can produce a variety of data structures that are useful for problem solving. (That is, it is possible to define arrays of pointers, pointers to functions, structures of arrays, arrays of structures, pointers to an array of structures, and so on.) The types discussed in this chapter are arrays and pointers.

180

6.2 ARRAYS

Array Definition, Declaration, and Use

The *array* data structure has become an accepted convenience of programming that is built into almost all high-level programming languages. As in most other languages of this genre, an array in C is logically conceived to be an ordered, homogeneous collection of data elements, or *members,* which can be collectively retrieved by a single name or individually referenced by an index. The adjective "homogeneous" in this context refers to the fact that all the constituent data elements have the same type. This common type of the data elements is called the *base type* of the array.

Physically, an array in C is a group of consecutive memory locations. The subscripting array reference operator [] is used with a subscript to retrieve individual array members. Array subscripts in C must be integer expressions that begin at 0.

Single-dimensional arrays were introduced in Chapter 3. Such an array, or *vector,* in C (i.e., an array with one index) is declared by giving the base type, the name of the array, and the number of constituent elements enclosed in square brackets. Figure 6.1 illustrates vector declarations.

The declarations in Figure 6.1 produce an array, A, of ten elements, each of which is an integer; an array, B, of 100 doubles; and an array, C, of seven characters. If a particular machine represents an integer in 4 bytes of memory, a double in 8 bytes, and a character in 1 byte, then array A occupies 40 bytes, B occupies 800 bytes, and C occupies 7 bytes.

To refer to a particular element of an array, the array name is followed by the integer index (subscript) enclosed in square brackets. Figure 6.2 shows syntactically valid references to elements of the above arrays.

If the statements shown were used in the scope of the array definitions of Figure

```
int A[10];
double B[100];
char C[7];
```

Figure 6.1. Single-dimensional array declarations

```
A[7] = 5;
printf(" %f \n", B[0]);
C[6] = '\t';
```

Figure 6.2. Array member reference

6 the first statement would assin the value 5 to the eighth element of array A. (Remember that index values in the C language always begin with 0.) The second would print on the standard output the double that is the first value of array B. This assumes that this element has been given a value previously. The last statement assigns the value of the tab character to the last (i.e., the seventh) member of the array C.

The use of index values outside the declared ranges—that is, outside the range 0 to 9 for A, 0 to 99 for B, and 0 to 6 for C—will not result in a syntax error. The C compiler will generate a reference to a portion of memory that was not allocated to that array. This most likely will result in a run-time error. (This run-time error may not cause program termination, but rather some program-specific error that potentially may be quite subtle.) C generally does no array bounds checking at compile time or at run time, although some compilers may provide this as an option. Consider the example in Figure 6.3. In this example, the array subscript 10 is not in the range allocated for the array A. (The indices for array A range from 0 to 9.) This will not produce a syntax error in C. Most compilers will allocate space for array B in memory locations that immediately follow those of A. Thus, A[10] will often correspond to B[0], A[11] to B[1], and so on. In the example in Figure 6.3, the number 127 will be printed out by most compilers.

This method of referencing arrays is not recommended practice as it is abstruse and not portable. A compiler is not obligated to allocate space for array B immediately after array A. Syntax checking programs like lint will often produce a warning for this kind of array references. However, if the array index is an expression whose value is not known until run time, no static syntax checking can reveal the error.

Multidimensional Arrays

Arrays of multiple dimensions are permitted in C. A two-dimensional table of test scores could be declared as shown in Figure 6.4.

It represents an array of 80 integers arranged in a two-dimensional table of 20 rows and 4 columns. (This data might be interpreted as the test scores for 20 students on each of four tests.)

```
int A[10];
int B[10];

A[10]=127;
printf("%d \n",B[0]);
```

Figure 6.3. Example of a misuse of arrays

In referring to the data in a two-dimensional array, the first index is considered the row and the second index is considered the column. *Multidimensional* arrays in C are always stored in row-major order. This means that, in order to examine the array elements in the order in which they are stored in memory, one must go across each row from the lowest numbered row to the highest. In more general terms, one must vary the right-most array index most rapidly. With an array declaration of "double D[2][3]," the elements would be stored in memory in the order shown in Figure 6.5.

The first row is stored in order, followed by the second row. This can be generalized to many dimensions by following the rule of varying the right most index most rapidly, the second from the right next most rapidly, and so on.

Refer again to the declaration "double D[2][3];." With this method of array storage, D[1] represents the second row of the D array, and, therefore, is an array of three doubles. That is, D[1] is a shorthand notation to represent all members of the array that are in row one (1).

As with most other computer languages, arrays are most useful for applying a uniform process to each element of the array. This is often accomplished by means of a "for" loop, as in Figure 6.6.

```
int tests[20][4];
```

Figure 6.4. Declaration of a two-dimensional array

```
D[0][0] D[0][1] D[0][2] D[1][0] D[1][1] D[1][2]
```

Figure 6.5. Internal order of array members

```
#include <stdio.h>

int test[20][4];
int i, j;
extern int getint( void ); /* Inputs an integer from the keyboard */

for ( i = 0; i < 20; i++ )
{
    printf ( "\n Enter the scores for student number %d: ", i);
    for ( j=0; j<4; j++ )
    {
        test[i][j] = getint();
    }
}
```

Figure 6.6. Processing array members

The function getint() is an assumed function that reads an integer from the keyboard and returns that value. This is the same function that was defined and used in Program 4.1 of Chapter 4.

Array Initialization

To initialize an array, the array name in the declaration is followed by a list of values that are to be assigned to the array elements. This list has to be arranged in row-major order. To denote that this is a list, this group of values is enclosed in brackets. For example, consider Figure 6.7. This initialization assigns the character 'C' to message[0], the space character to message [1], and so on. It is possible to have fewer items in the list than array elements. In this situation, the remaining right-most array elements are not given any value. If there are more initializers than array elements, a syntax error results.

For multidimensional arrays, initializations can take two general forms. The first is to list the initial values in one long list in row-major order. An alternative is to group the values by rows. Two initializations with identical results are given in Figure 6.8.

With these definitions, A[0,0,0] = B[0,0,0] both having the value 1, A[1,1,2] = B[1,1,2] having the value 19, and so forth. All the values of A match the corresponding values of B.

```
char message[10] = {'C',' ','c','o','m','p','i','l','e','r'};
```

Figure 6.7. Initialization of an array

```
int A[2][3][4] =
                {1,2,3,4,5,6,7,8,9,10,11,12,13,14,
                 15,16,17,18,19,20,21,22,23,24 };

int B[2][3][4] =
        {
            {
                {1,2,3,4}, {5,6,7,8}, {9,10,11,12}
            }
            {
                {13,14,15,16}, {17,18,19,20},
                {21,22,23,24}
            }
        };
```

Figure 6.8. Initializing multiple-dimensional arrays

Character Arrays and Strings

As defined in Section 2.8, a string literal in a C program is defined as a sequence of characters or valid escape sequences enclosed by a pair of double quotes. The string

```
"C Compiler\n"
```

is a valid string constant that will be represented in memory by 12 times the size of memory occupied by one character. The last memory location in the sequence will contain the null byte '\0', which is added by the language translator. In C, a sequence of characters that is terminated with a null character is called a *string*.

An alternative definition of a string in C is as a character array terminated by a null byte. As a convention, when using character arrays, a null byte should be appended to the sequence to make it a string. To follow this convention, the string "C Compiler\n" could have been defined as an array using the code

```
char message[12] = {'C',' ','c','o','m','p','i','l','e','r','\n','\0'};
```

or more easily as

```
char message[12] = "C Compiler\n";
```

The second method is appropriate since a string literal is, by definition, an array of characters terminated by a null byte. This example can be simplified one step further. The size of the array can be determined by the compiler from the length of the initializer, in the following method:

```
char message[] = "C compiler\n";
```

The only cases in which an array can be defined without an explicit definition of its size are the following:

1. With an initializer that implicitly determines the size.
2. As a formal parameter.
3. In a referencing declaration where the size is given elsewhere in a defining definition.

Declaration of arrays without explicitly stating the number of members is not restricted to character arrays. Figure 6.9 illustrates the initialization of an integer array.

```
int test[] = { 100, 100, 100, 100 };
```

Figure 6.9. Numeric array declaration with initialization

This declaration causes test to be defined as an integer array of four members, each of which is initialized to 100.

A commonly used and valuable data structure is a two-dimensional array of characters, for example, char class[100][25]. This can be used to store a list of names. We can consider it to be a two-dimensional array of characters, or a one-dimensional array of 100 strings. Each string has a maximum length of 25. The reference class[6] refers to the seventh row of 25 characters, which is the seventh name in the list. (Actually, only 24 characters can be stored if we want each row to be a string. The last byte is needed for the '\0'.)

In general, if we follow the convention of calling the first index the row and the second index the column, then we can refer to any row of a two-dimensional array by using only one subscript following the array name. There is no corresponding notation for referencing an entire column of an array in C. This difference between rows and columns of arrays is based upon the fact that arrays in C are stored in *row-major order*. As discussed previously, this means that the elements of a row are stored in contiguous (consecutive) memory locations. The elements of a column of an array are not located together. Recovering the elements of a row is the same process of indexing as through any other array. This is not true for columns.

There is a powerful group of string functions that are provided in a library by all ANSI compliant compilers. Prototype function declarations for these appear in the header file string.h. These functions will be described in detail in Chapter 8. In this chapter, we briefly discuss three of the most useful. The function strcmp() can be used to compare two strings. It requires two string variables or string literals as parameters. It then compares these strings character by character until a difference is found. At that point, the function determines which of these two characters is larger. The result of that comparison becomes the result of the function. If the variables name1 and name2 are character arrays in which strings have been stored, then "strcmp(name1, name2)" will return a positive integer if the contents of name1 are alphabetically greater than those of name2; will return zero if the two parameters are exactly equal; and will produce a negative value if name1 is alphabetically less than name2. Notice that the expression "name1 < name2" does not compare the strings, but compares the memory addresses that are represented by these array names.

The strcpy() function is used to copy the characters in one string to those in another array of characters. This function requires two string parameters. The result of the function is to copy the string in the second parameter to the first parameter. With the arrays used in the previous paragraph, the function call "strcpy(name1, name2)" has the result of copying the string in name2 to be the value of the string name1. The first parameter must be large enough to hold the entire string in the second parameter.

The strcat() function has the task of concatenating two strings. It also requires two parameters. A copy of the string represented by the second parameter is appended to the end of the string represented by the first parameter. The programmer must be sure that the first string was declared with enough space to hold the entire concatenated string.

Each of these functions uses the fact that strings terminate with a null byte to determine when to stop their processing. If the parameters passed do not have this property, the behavior of the function is undefined. It may cause an extremely long loop that terminates only when the processor happens to find a null byte in memory or gets a memory addressing error.

Another function that proves useful in examples that input integer is atoi(). This function is also provided in the standard library. Its prototype declaration is in the header file stdlib.h. This function converts a string given as a parameter to an integer. Thus, the function call

```
i = atoi( "1234" );
```

where i has type in converts the string "1234" to the integer 1234, which becomes the value of i.

Program 6.1 illustrates the use of strings and the string functions. This program inputs a list of names. These names arc then sorted using the insertion sort algorithm. The sorted list is written to the standard output device (generally the terminal).

```
#include <string.h>
#include <stdio.h>

#define MAX_NAMES 10
#define MAX_SIZE 15

void input_list( int n,
        char name_list[MAX_NAMES][2][MAX_SIZE]);
void insertion_sort( int n,
        char name_list[MAX_NAMES][2][MAX_SIZE]);
void print_list( int n,
        char name_list[MAX_NAMES][2][MAX_SIZE]);
int getint( void );


main()
{
    char name_list[MAX_NAMES][2][MAX_SIZE];
    int n, i;

    printf( "Please input the number of names: ");
    n = getint();
    while ( n > MAX_NAMES )
```

Program 6.1. Sorting with strings (continues)

```
        {
                printf("ERROR! The number of names must be no ");
                printf( " greater than %d \n", MAX_NAMES );
                printf( "Please re-enter!\n");
                n = getint();
        } /* end while */

        input_list( n, name_list );

        insertion_sort( n, name_list );

        print_list( n, name_list );

        exit( 0 );
} /* end main */

void input_list( int n,
          char name_list[MAX_NAMES][2][MAX_SIZE])
{
        int i;

        printf("Enter the names, first name on one line,");
        printf(" last name on the next.\n");
        for( i=0; i<n; i++ )
        {
                gets(name_list[i][1]);
                gets(name_list[i][2]);
        }
} /* end input_list */

void insertion_sort( int n,
          char name_list[MAX_NAMES][2][MAX_SIZE] )
{

        int i, j, k;
        char temp1[MAX_SIZE], temp2[MAX_SIZE];

        for ( i=1; i<n; i++)
        {
                for (j=0; j<i; j++)
                {
                        if ((strcmp(name_list[j][2],name_list[i][2])>0 ) ||
                          ( (strcmp(name_list[j][2],name_list[i][2])==0) &&
                          (strcmp(name_list[j][1],name_list[i][1])>0)))
                        {
                                strcpy( temp1, name_list[i][1]);
                                strcpy( temp2, name_list[i][2]);
```

Program 6.1. (continued)

```
                        for ( k=i; k>j; k-- )
                        {
                                strcpy( name_list[k][1],
                                        name_list[k-1][1]);
                                strcpy( name_list[k][2],
                                        name_list[k-1][2]);

                        } /* end for k */

                        strcpy( name_list[j][1], temp1 );
                        strcpy( name_list[j][2], temp2 );

                } /* end if */
            } /* end for j */
        } /* end for i */

} /* end insertion_sort() */

void print_list( int n,
            char name_list[MAX_NAMES][2][MAX_SIZE] )
{
    char name[2*MAX_SIZE + 1];
                /* enough space for both names and  */
                /* one space between them.          */
    int i;

    printf( "The sorted names are : \n");
    for( i=0; i<n; i++)
    {
            strcpy( name, name_list[i][1] );
            /* append a space to the first name */
            strcat( name, " " );

             /* append the last name to the first name. */
            strcat( name, name_list[i][2] );

            printf( " %d. %s \n", i+1, name );

    } /* end for */

} /* end print_list() */

int getint( void )
{
    char digit_array[10];
    int answer, error, i;
```

Program 6.1. (continued)

```
    error = 1;
    while (error)
    {
        error = 0;
        i = 0;
        gets(digit_array);

        /* as a string, the contents of digit_aray[i] */
        /* are terminated with a null byte.           */
        while ( (i < 10)&& (digit_array[i] != '\0') )
        {
            if ( ( digit_array[i] < '0') ||
                 (digit_array[i] > '9' ) )
            {
                error = 1;
                printf( "ERROR! Non-digit entered.");
                printf( " Please re-enter.\n");
                break;
            }
            i++;

        } /* end while */
    } /* end while */

    answer = atoi( digit_array );

    return( answer );
} /* end getint() */
```

Program 6.1. (continued)

The array name_list is a three-dimensional array that stores up to 100 first and last names. The first names are stored in column 1 and the last names are stored in column 2 for each person's entry. These are stored in separate entries as the sort's comparison needs to examine the last names first, but the names are to be printed out with the first name first and the surname last. In the input function, the array reference name_list[i][1] refers to a character array (string) of up to MAX_SIZE-1 characters. It stores the first name for the ith person.

The strcmp() function is used to compare the names. The last names are compared first. If these are identical, then the first names are compared. In the function, print_list() uses the strcat() function to concatenate the first and last names into one name array. This has the advantage of placing the two names next to each other with only one intervening space.

6.3 POINTERS

Pointer Definition, Declaration, and Use

The use of *pointer* data types in C provides the possibility of quite dynamic and flexible data structures. A pointer in C is a variable—that is, a memory location—that can hold the address of another memory location. This provides a level of indirection analogous to that of indirect addressing in most assembly languages. Indirect addressing allows a variable to hold the address, or location, of a second variable, and to use that address "indirectly" to access the value of the second. C extends this assembly language concept by requiring identification of the type of the value to which the pointer variable points. In the simple example of Figure 6.10, the variable x is defined to be a pointer to an integer.

The * punctuator symbol in the declaration denotes a pointer. This causes the compiler to allocate enough memory for one address, and to record that the data stored at that address should be interpreted as an integer.

The amount of memory allocated for a pointer by a particular compiler is invariant with respect to the type of data to which it points. (The one exception to this is that a pointer to a function may have a different size.) A pointer to an array of 100 doubles occupies exactly the same amount of memory as a pointer to a single character. Figure 6.11 illustrates the declarations of these two types of pointers.

The amount of space allocated for these two variables, double_array_ptr and ch_ptr, is identical. Notice that double_array_ptr is not an array, but is a pointer to an array. (The amount of space in bytes allocated for one pointer depends upon the instruction set of the underlying execution environment. If the execution environment has to produce addresses for 64K bytes of memory, pointers would have a minimum length of 16 bits; to address 1 megabyte of memory requires a minimum of 20 bits.)

As demonstrated in Figure 6.10, a pointer variable is declared by the use of an asterisk between the type and the identifier name. The complete syntax appears as follows:

```
storage_class type_specifier * declarator;
```

```
int *x;
```

Figure 6.10. Declaration of a pointer to an integer

```
double (*double_array_ptr)[100];
char *ch_ptr;
```

Figure 6.11. Declaration of pointer variables

Pointer Operators and Pointer Usage

Pointer variables that have static duration are implicitly assigned the value of a null pointer unless there is an explicit initialization. Automatic pointer variables that are not explicitly initialized have an undetermined value. A null pointer value is a special value that is interpreted to mean that the pointer does not point to any object. The value NULL is defined in the standard header file stddef.h and others.

In any case, it is necessary to initialize a pointer through declaration or assignment to point to a memory object to be manipulated. A common error of novice programmers is to assume that the declaration of a pointer to an object creates an instance of that object. It does not. One method of making such an assignment to a pointer is through use of the *address operator* &. This is a unary operator which, when used in the context "&x," gives the address of x. Notice that x here is usually not a pointer variable. This is illustrated in Figure 6.12.

In this example, ptr is assigned the address of the variable x. This is a valid assignment since x has type int and ptr is a pointer to an int. The memory map in Figure 6.12 demonstrates one possible content of primary memory after execution of this code. The fact that the variable x and the variable ptr are in adjacent memory locations is not required, but is typical of many compilers. Most compilers allocate memory in adjacent memory locations for variables that are declared together.

This address operator can be used with any variable except one with storage class register or with a bit field. (Bit fields and the register storage class are discussed in Chapter 9.) The address operator & has as high a precedence level as the other unary operators, and associates right to left.

```
int *ptr;
int x;

x = 5;
ptr = &x;
```

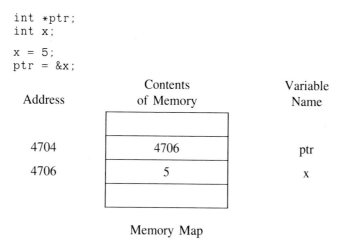

Memory Map

Figure 6.12. Using the address operator

Another method of assigning a value to a pointer variable is to assign an integer constant cast to the proper type. This is extremely useful for systems programming in order to monitor or change the contents of particular memory addresses that have special purposes. For example, this technique can be used to change the value of interrupt vectors or to monitor some operating system parameter.

To assign a constant to a pointer variable, the constant should be cast to a pointer of the proper type using the cast operator, as illustrated in Figure 6.12. Pointers are not the same as integers. In fact, they may, on a particular computer, require more bits than an integer; another execution environment may require fewer bits than an integer. The cast (int *) means "pointer to an integer."

A pointer with constant values is a powerful tool that should be utilized only when the architecture of the machine is well understood and when its use is required. The general applications programmer should avoid the use of constants for pointer values as they produce code that is difficult to modify and is not portable.

Complementary to the address operator is the unary *indirection operator* "*", sometimes called the dereferencing operator. When applied to a pointer-valued expression, this operator produces the value stored in the memory address contained in that pointer location. In the context of the definitions and assignments of Figure 6.12, the expression *ptr means to retrieve the value of the integer *to which the address stored in ptr points*. Since the variable x was assigned the value 5, and since ptr was assigned the address of variable x, the expression "*ptr" has a value 5 also. In fact, until the content of the variable ptr is changed, any modification to the value of the variable x will be reflected in "*ptr," and vice versa, as these two refer to the same memory location.

The indirection operator is also used to change the value of an object to which a pointer points. Consider the example and memory map in Figure 6.14. In this

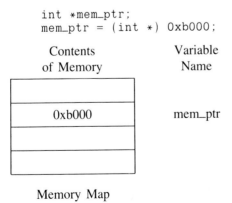

```
int *mem_ptr;
mem_ptr = (int *) 0xb000;
```

Contents   Variable
of Memory   Name

| 0xb000 | mem_ptr |

Memory Map

Figure 6.13. Initializing pointers with a constant

```
int *px;
int y   ;

px = &y;
*px = 10;
```

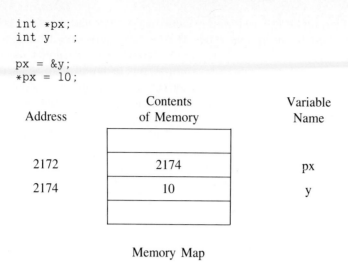

Memory Map

Figure 6.14. Use of the indirection operator

code, the address of y (2174) is stored in variable px. Then the value of y is changed to 10 because the expression "*px = 10" causes 10 to be assigned to the location to which the value of px is pointing, that is, to location 2174.

As with other variables, pointer variables can be initialized as part of the definition. Obviously, the value of this initializer must be a valid address. This can be accomplished by means of the address operator. See Figure 6.15. In this situation, px is declared to be a pointer to an integer, and is initialized to point to the integer variable x. That is, px contains the address of the integer x, or 2102.

```
int x;
int *px = &x;
```

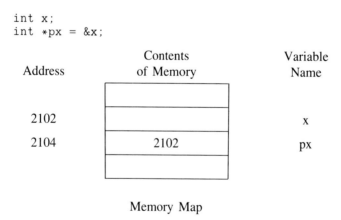

Memory Map

Figure 6.15. Pointer initialization in declarations

Parameter Passing with Pointers

Having introduced pointers, we now warn the programmer that the examples of the use of pointers given to this point, although accurate, are generally to be avoided. The real value and the primary uses of pointers in C are threefold.

1. To address and increment through data structures like arrays.
2. To construct dynamic data structures, for example, queues and stacks whose size and memory requirements vary at run time (as discussed in Chapter 11).
3. To have the effect of passing function parameters by reference rather than by value.

This third usage is the subject of this section. C supports only one method of *parameter passing—by value*. Passage by value has the restriction that the actual parameter is not altered by changes to the corresponding formal parameter. To permit a change to a formal parameter in order to modify the corresponding actual parameter, many other programming languages provide a mechanism for parameter passing called "parameter passing by reference," in which the actual parameter and the corresponding formal parameter refer to the same memory location. (In Pascal, these are referred to as "var" parameters.) This mechanism can be simulated in C by passing a pointer as the parameter's value.

Call by reference can be implemented in C as illustrated in the function swap() that exchanges the values of its two parameters. (See Program 6.2) When swap() is called, the variable a will contain the value &x (the address of x) and b will contain &y (the address of y). The statement "temp = *a;" retrieves the value to which a points and assigns it to temp; "*a = *b;" obtains the value to which b points and assigns it to the location to which a points; and "*b = temp;" assigns the value of temp to the location to which b points. Notice that the contents of the actual parameters, &x and &y, are not changed; they still contain the same address. But each actual parameter has access to any changes in the memory locations to which it points.

To recapitulate, parameter passing "by reference" in C is simulated by the use of an address for the actual parameter. The corresponding formal parameter is likewise a pointer. Since the contents of the actual parameter are copied to the formal parameter, both pointers contain the same address, and thus refer to the same object. Any changes to that object or value are reflected in the calling function.

This technique to share values and objects among functions is used extensively in C. You should be aware of this technique when using many of the standard functions that are provided by C. Any function that requires a parameter that is used to return a value to the caller, such as input routines, uses a pointer to return the modified value. Many of these functions are discussed in Chapter 8.

```
void swap( float *, float * );

main()
{
    float x, y;

    x = 12.78;
    y = 758.99921;
    printf( "Before swap: x = %f y = %f\n", x, y );
    swap( &x, &y );
    printf( "After swap: x = %f y = %f\n", x, y );
    exit(0);
}

/* Swap the value of two floating point objects */
void swap( float *a, float *b )
{
    float temp;

    temp = *a;
    *a = *b;
    *b = temp;
    return;
}
```

Program 6.2. Passing parameters by reference

Arrays as Pointers

In the programming language C, pointers and arrays are intimately related. The value of an array name is, in fact, a pointer to that array. In particular, the name is the address of the first element of the array. This differs from most other types in C. If x is an integer variable, its address is retrieved by use of the address operator, &x. However, if A is an array (e.g., int A[30]), then the address of the array A is referenced by the symbol A, not by &A. (This same address can also be referenced by the expression &A[0].)

This equivalence between arrays and pointers has several interesting implications. One is that, since the value of the array name is a pointer to the first member of the array, an array can be used as a function parameter that acts as a parameter passed by reference. This is illustrated in Program 6.3.

In this example, zero_array() will be called with parameters consisting of a pointer to a char and the number of members in that array. The formal parameters of zero_array() are declared accordingly. Notice that the number of members of the array is not required in the declaration of a_line[] in the function since the corresponding actual parameter, line, has space allocated. The function zero_

```
#define MAX_LINE 80

char line[MAX_LINE];

main()
{
    int i;
    void zero_array( char *, int );

    zero_array( line, MAX_LINE );

    /* This loop will print out MAX_LINE zeros */
    for( i=0; i<MAX_LINE; i++ )
    {
        printf("line[%d] = %d\n", i, line[i] );
    } /* end for */

    exit(0);
}

/* Initialize a char array to nulls */
void zero_array( char a_line[], int size)
{
    int i;
    for ( i=0; i < size; i++ )
    {
        a_line[i] = '\0';
    }
}
```

Program 6.3. An array as a function parameter

array() operates on the actual parameter by means of the pointer a_line to the actual array.

Additionally, since an array name is actually a pointer to the first member of the array, the corresponding formal parameter could have been declared as a pointer to the proper type. The parameter a_line in Program 6.3 could have been declared as "char * a_line". An analogous situation exists for an external pointer reference to an array defined elsewhere. Program 6.4 illustrates this situation.

The fundamental difference between an array and a pointer definition is that an array definition requires that a specific number of memory locations be allocated for that array. Notice the way that pointer parameter types are declared in the prototype. The prototype

```
void zero_array( char *, int );
```

means that zero_array() expects a pointer to a character as the first parameter and an int as the second.

```
#define MAX_LINE 80

char line[MAX_LINE];

main()
{
    int i;
    void zero_array( char   *, int );

    zero_array( line, MAX_LINE );

    /* This loop will print out \max-line zeros. */

    for( i=0; i<MAX_LINE; i++ )
    {
        printf("line[%d] = %d\n", i, line[i] );
    } /* end for */

    exit(0);
}

/* Initialize a char array to nulls */
void zero_array( char   * a_line, int size)
{
    int i;
    for ( i=0; i < size; i++ )
    {
        a_line[i] = '\0';
    }

    return;
}
```

Program 6.4. An array as a function parameter

A pointer definition allocates only enough space for the pointer itself. If a pointer variable is used as an array in the absence of a corresponding array definition—that is, in the absence of a corresponding actual array parameter or external array definition—the array will most likely reference memory locations that either are unallocated or have been allocated for another purpose. The compiler will permit such usage, but the program will not function as desired during execution. The errors produced may be quite subtle and difficult to trace. Consider Program 6.5.

The example in Program 6.5 is the same as that in the previous two programs with the exception of the manner in which the array line is declared in the main program. This is not a syntax error, but is the potential source of abstruse logic errors. The memory locations accessed in this for loop for the array a_line may be

```
/* improper usage example */
#define MAX_LINE 80

char  * line;        /* line is declared here, but space */
                     /* for the array is not allocated.  */
main()
{
    int i;
    void zero_array( char[], int);

    zero_array( line, MAX_LINE );
    for( i=0; i<MAX_LINE; i++ )
    {
        printf("line[%d] = %d\n", i, line[i] );
    } /* end for */

    exit(0);

}

/* Initialize a char array to nulls */
void zero_array( char a_line[], int size)
{
    int i;
    for ( i=0; i < size; i++ )
    {
        a_line[i] = '\0';
    }
}
```

Program 6.5. Example of a misuse of arrays

used for some other purpose. This loop may corrupt some other variables or data structures in the program.

Since an array name is a reference to an address, the statement

```
array1 < array2
```

will not compare the contents of the two arrays; it will compare their starting addresses. The assignment statement

```
array1 = array2
```

is invalid as the name of an array is not an lvalue.

Pointer Arithmetic and Comparison

There is a group of arithmetic and relational operators that are valid when applied to pointers. Before introducing these, it is useful to reexamine the use of the sizeof unary operator. This operator is used to determine the number of bytes that an object or type occupies in memory. Its syntax is

SIZE OF EXPRESSION

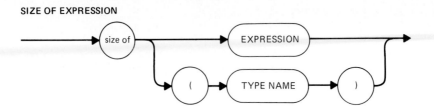

where "expression" is a variable or expression and "type_name" is a type keyword. The number of bytes used by a particular type is implementation defined.

For Figure 6.16, assume that an integer is represented in 4 bytes. The variable x
will have a value of 4, y will have the value 80, and z will have the value 20.

Notice that even though A represents the address of the array, when an array
name is used in the sizeof operator, the value is the number of bytes in the entire
array.

Now let us return to the topic of interest of this section: *pointer arithmetic*. The
arithmetic operators that are permitted on pointers are these:

1. Adding a pointer and an integer.
2. Incrementing (++) or decrementing (−−) a pointer.
3. Subtracting a pointer and an integer.
4. Subtracting two pointers.

What actually happens with these operations is not what initially may be expected, but is extremely useful. Adding the integer 1 to a pointer variable
increments the address stored in that pointer by the size of the type associated with
the pointer. Thus, if pi is a pointer to an integer, and if an integer occupies 4
bytes, then "pi = pi + 1" or "pi++" adds four to the address that is stored in
variable pi. The same operation can be performed via the sizeof operator, albeit
less easily. The two columns of code in Figure 6.17 produce the same result in px.
Notice the convenience of the use of pointer arithmetic. (This example assumes
that a pointer and an int are the same size. This is not always true.)

```
int A[5][4];
int x,y,z;

x = sizeof (int);
y = sizeof (A);
z = sizeof (A) / sizeof ( A[0]);
```

Figure 6.16. The sizeof operator

```
int x;                          int x, temp;
int * px = &x;                  int * px = &x;

++px;                           temp = (int) px;
                                temp = temp + sizeof(*px);
                                px = (* int) temp;
```

Figure 6.17. Using pointer arithmetic

These two portions of code have the same effect. In the second example, it was necessary to copy the address stored in px into the integer variable temp by means of a cast. (Pointer casts are explained more fully in Section 6.6) The addition was then performed using the sizeof operator to determine the size of the object to which px points. The result was converted from integer form back into a pointer via another cast. If the statement "px = px + sizeof (*px)" had been used instead of copying to an integer variable, the contents of the variable px would have been incremented by the square of the sizeof (*px) because of the special meaning of addition with a pointer.

A more useful example of the use of pointer and integer addition arises in the domain of arrays. The equivalence of an array name and a pointer to the first element of the array permits the definition of the array reference operator [] in terms of pointer indirection and pointer arithmetic. Given an array A, the definition of the [] operator is that A[i] is identical to (*(A+i)). Recall Program 6.4 in which an array was passed to a function and then accessed. This function could be rewritten using a pointer instead of using the array referencing operator as in Program 6.6.

In this example, the statement

```
*a_line++ = '\0';
```

means that the null is assigned to the object to which a_line points. The pointer is then incremented by the size of a char so that a_line points to the next element of the array. (Notice that the postfix increment operator has a higher precedence than the indirection operator *. Thus, the value incremented is the address in the pointer variable a_line, rather than the object to which a_line points. Since it is a postfix increment operator, this incrementation does not occur until after the value is retrieved for use in the indirection and assignment.)

As a further example, consider a function to copy strings. Figure 6.18 illustrates such a function. This function assumes that the actual parameters corresponding to the formal parameters from and to have been properly defined to allocate sufficient space. Also, from is assumed to contain a string, that is, to be terminated by a null byte.

This loop is functionally equivalent to the function in Figure 6.19, which references the array elements through an index. This same function might even

```
#define MAX_LINE 80

char line[MAX_LINE];

main()
{
    int i;
    void zero_array( char *, int  );

    zero_array( line, MAX_LINE );

    /* This loop will print out MAX_LINE zeros. */

    for( i=0; i<MAX_LINE; i++ )
    {
        printf("line[%d] = %d\n", i, line[i] );
    } /* end for */

    exit(0);

}

/* Initialize a char array to nulls */

void zero_array( char *a_line, int size )
{
    int i;

    for ( i = 0; i < size; i++)
    {
        *a_line++ = '\0';
    }
}
```

Program 6.6. Passing arrays to functions

```
strcpy( char *from, char *to)
{
    while (*from != '\0')
    {
        *to++ = *from++;
    }
    *to = '\0';
}
```

Figure 6.18. Using pointers to copy arrays

```
strcpy( char * from, char * to)
                        /* This could also be specified as      */
                        /* "strcpy( char from[], char to[])"    */
{
    int i;
    i = 0;
    while (from[i] != '\0')
    {
            to[i] = from[i];
            i++;
    }
    to[i] = '\0';
}
```

Figure 6.19. Using array references to copy arrays

appear in the cryptic form shown in Figure 6.20 if written by more experienced C programmers. This loop terminates when the null byte (i.e., 0) is reached, since zero is interpreted as false in C. When this loop termination occurs, the variables to and from contain the address of the word of memory just beyond that of the null byte in this string.

As discussed in a previous chapter, this cryptic form is not the most readable and understandable. Notice that since the increment operator ++ has a higher precedence than the indirection operator *, the *address* in to and that in from are incremented, not the contents of memory to which they point. Since the increment operator used is the postfix version, the incrementing of the addresses occurs after these addresses have been used to retrieve their contents for copying. The length of this explanation is indicative of the complexity of the expression. From a software engineering point of view, either of the previous, more explicit forms is preferred. Some compilers may produce more efficient machine code from this cryptic version, although an optimizing compiler can produce efficient machine code from any of these expressions.

Pointers may be initialized to point to a string literal at the time of declaration. For example, the declaration

```
char *command = "copy file1 file2";
```

allocates space for the string literal and initializes the variable command with its

```
strcpy( char * from, char * to )
{
        while ( *to++ = *from++ );
}
```

Figure 6.20. Using pointer to copy strings

address. (This same task can be accomplished at run time by a simple assignment statement.)

Pointer subtraction is a legitimate operation, as illustrated in Program 6.7. The "for loop" in the function example_function() will loop 1,000 times as the variable n will be assigned the value 999.

Notice that the result of the pointer subtraction ptr2 - ptr1 is an integer that is the number of array elements from ptr1 to ptr2. It is not the difference in the two memory addresses stored in ptr1 and ptr2. Instead, it is the difference of the memory addresses divided by the size of the base type (int in this case).

A topic related to pointer arithmetic is *pointer comparison*. Pointer values may also be compared using the relational operator. The programmer should remember that the quantities being compared are addresses and not the values pointed to by those addresses. This technique is useful when the pointers are referring to various portions of the same object, for example, to separate elements of a single array or structure. Examine the function specified in Figure 6.21. This function gives the string pointed to by to, a reversed copy of the string pointed

```
void example_function( int * ,int * );


main()
{
    int example_array[1000];

    example_function( &example_array[0],
                          &example_array[999] );

    exit(0);
}

void example_function( int * ptr1, int * ptr2 )
{
    int i, n;

    n = ptr2 - ptr1;

    printf( "n= %d\n", n );
    for ( i = 0; i < n+1 ; i++ )
    {
        /* loop body */
    }
    return;
}
```

Program 6.7. Pointer subtraction

```
reverse_str( char * from, char * to)
{
    char * ptr = from;

    while( *ptr != '\0' )    /* move ptr to the end of */
    {                        /* the "from" string.     */
        ptr++;
    }

    while ( ptr != from )    /* compares two pointers */
    {
        *to++ = *--ptr;
    }

    *to = '\0';

    return;
}
```

Figure 6.21. Pointer comparison

to by from. The comparison "ptr != from" in the second while loop compares the address in ptr with that in from. It does not compare the characters pointed to by ptr and from.

   Data elements that compose an array are guaranteed to be stored in consecutive memory locations. The order in memory of two separate objects is not specified, and may vary depending on patterns of memory usage. That is, if an array A is declared just before array B, the memory locations for A are not guaranteed to have lower addresses than those for B. Therefore, two pointers that point to different objects generally should not be compared.

6.4   ARRAY, POINTERS, AND FUNCTIONS IN COMBINATION

Combinations of Pointers and Array

The array, function, and pointer declarations can be combined to form various composite, or derived, types. The first declaration given in Figure 6.22 is equivalent to the parenthesized version "int *(array_ptr[5]);." It defines an array of five pointers to integers.

```
int *array_ptr1[5];
int (*array_ptr2)[5];
```

Figure 6.22. Arrays and pointers

The second declaration in the example in Figure 6.22 defines a pointer to an array of five integers.

There is a slight but important difference in the syntax of these two; and a more dramatic semantic difference caused by the relative order of binding of the indirection operator (*) and the array referencing operator ([]). Binding order is the relative time at which punctuators such as [], (), or * are applied in a declaration. Punctuators in a declaration bind in the same order as their corresponding operators would be executed in an expression when following the precedence rules. As the array referencing operator [] has a higher precedence than the indirection operator *, parentheses are necessary in the second example of Figure 6.22 to modify the default binding order. The subexpression (*array_ptr2) denotes a pointer. The fact that this is followed by [5] means that this is a pointer to an array of five elements whose base type is an integer. In the first example, the [5] binds first to array_ptr1, producing an array. Next is the *, which means that this is an array of pointers. Last is the base type. This gives an array of pointers to ints.

To illustrate the difference, consider the size of the variables array_ptr1 and array_ptr2 from the examples above. The first, array_ptr1, is an array of five pointers to integers. If pointers occupy 4 bytes each, then this array variable array_ptr1 requires the allocation of 20 bytes of memory. The second variable, array_ptr2, is a pointer to an array. As such, it occupies only the amount of space required for one pointer, typically 4 bytes. The variable array_ptr2 is not an array.

As demonstrated here, parsing these combinations of pointers and arrays can be quite complicated. Further examples are given in the section Parsing Examples.

To illustrate the utility of an array of pointers, consider the following scenario. A program is being developed that accepts and performs five user commands. The function under consideration will accept the input string representing a command as a parameter and will return one for true if the input is valid, and zero for false if the input is not valid. The valid keywords will be stored in an array. A possible declaration and a possible initialization of this array are shown in Figure 6.23.

This declaration produces a two-dimensional array of 35 characters. The initializations are given as values for each of the five rows. Therefore, the first four elements of the first row have the following values:

```
keywords[0][0] = 'a'
keywords[0][1] = 'd'
keywords[0][2] = 'd'
keywords[0][3] = '\0'
```

```
char keywords[5][7] =
    {
      "add",
      "delete",
      "modify",
      "list",
      "quit"
    };
```

Figure 6.23. An array of strings

The remaining three array locations in that row are not initialized. There are
wasted memory locations in this array structure. However, they will cause no
problems as the string functions that can be used to process this data look for the
null byte. The unused array locations will never be examined by these functions.
    This two-dimensional array could then be searched as shown in Figure 6.24.

```
#define SUCCESS 1
#define FAILURE 0

char keywords[5][7] =
{
    "add",
    "delete",
    "modify",
    "list",
    "quit"
};

int validate ( char * str )
/* str points to a user command string */
{
    int i;

    for ( i = 0; i < 5; i++)
    {
        if ( strcmp( str, keywords[i] ) == 0 )
        {
            return SUCCESS;
        }
    }
    return FAILURE;
}
```

Figure 6.24. A function to validate user command input

The strcmp function used here is the standard C function used to compare two strings that was discussed earlier. (Aggregate data types cannot be compared by use of the relational operators.) It requires two strings as parameters. If the first is lexicographically (i.e., alphabetically) less than the second, the function returns a negative value. If the two strings are identical, it returns 0; if the first is greater than the second, it returns a positive value.

Notice that, since keywords is a two-dimensional array, keywords[i] refers to one complete row of seven characters. This array could alternatively be defined as an array of pointers. A hypothetical memory map for this data structure is shown in Figure 6.25.

```
char * keywords[] =
{
    "add",
    "delete",
    "modify",
    "list",
    "quit"
};
```

Figure 6.25. Array of pointers in memory

In this method, the initializers specify the size of the array. This allows the definition to be more easily modified. If the list of keywords is modified in any way, the compiler will be able to determine the necessary sizes. This also represents a slightly more compact storage representation. In this method, the keywords are stored as consecutive strings with no intervening bytes of memory. The declaration as a two-dimensional array, as in the example of Figure 6.24, requires space for seven characters for each of the five keywords. This results in a few bytes of wasted space. (This is not a compelling reason to choose either method. The ease of modification is a more significant criterion.) With this definition as an array of pointers, the function to validate the string is slightly modified.

Notice the use of the #define preprocessor directive in Figure 6.26, which defines an identifier that can be evaluated by the compiler to determine the number of elements in the array. This adds to the modifiability and portability.

Another alternative for the implementation of this function is to use a sentinel to terminate the array of keywords. One appropriate choice for this sentinel is the

```c
#define NUM_KEYWORDS ( sizeof(keywords)/ sizeof( char * ) )
#define SUCCESS 1
#define FAILURE 0

char * keywords[] =
{
    "add",
    "delete",
    "modify",
    "list",
    "quit"
};

int validate( char * str )
{
    int i;

    for ( i = 0; i < NUM_KEYWORDS; i++)
    {
        if ( strcmp( str, keywords[i] ) == 0 )
        {
            return SUCCESS;
        }
    }
    return FAILURE;
}
```

Figure 6.26. A function to validate user command input (version 2)

empty string '''', that is, the null byte. Another possibility is a pointer with a value of zero, as seen in Figure 6.27. Notice that the pointer (char *)0 was used for comparison to maintain consistent types.

Program 6.8 demonstrates another algorithm that uses the close relationship between pointers and arrays. The main program inputs up to 15 names of ten characters each. The user enters a return by itself on a line to indicate that all names have been entered. These names are stored in the array names. The array pointers is initialized to point to the corresponding entries in the names array. That is, pointers[0] points to names[0], pointers[1] points to names[1], and so on. The bubble() function uses the bubble sort algorithm to sort the names. The interesting point about this function is that it moves the pointers in the array pointers and does not change the names array. When the sorting function is finished, the main program prints out the names in the original order by printing the array names; the sorted names are printed out by printing the strings to which the pointers in the array pointers point. There are not two copies of the names, but

```
#define SUCCESS 1
#define FAILURE 0

char * keywords[] =
{
    "add",
    "delete",
    "modify",
    "list",
    "quit",
    0
};

int validate( char * str )
{
    int i;

    for (i=0; keywords[i] != (char *) 0 ; i++)
    {
         if ( strcmp( str, keywords[i] ) == 0 )
         {
              return SUCCESS;
         }
    }
    return FAILURE;
}
```

Figure 6.27. A function to validate user command input (version 3)

```
#include <stdio.h>
#define MAX_NAMES 10
#define NAME_SIZE 15
#define TRUE 1
#define FALSE 0

typedef  int  boolean;

main()
{
    char * pointers[MAX_NAMES];
    char names[MAX_NAMES][NAME_SIZE];
    boolean more = TRUE;
    int count =0;
    int i;

    void bubble( char *p[], int n );

    /*get names to sort */

    printf( "Enter the names, one per line. ");
    printf( " Enter a maximum of %d names \n", MAX_NAMES );
    printf( "Enter a return, i.e. an empty line, ");
    printf("to signal that you are finished. \n");

    while (more && (count < MAX_NAMES))
    {
        puts("Enter Name: ");
        gets( names[count] );
        if ( names[count][0] == '\0')
        {
            more = FALSE;
        } /* end if */
        else
        {
            count++;
        } /* end else */
    } /* end while */

    /* initialize pointer array to point to names */
    for ( i=0; i<count; i++ )
    {
        pointers[i] = names[i];
    } /* end for */

    bubble( pointers, count );
```

Program 6.8. Name sorting by moving pointers (continues)

```
    printf( "Original Order \n");
    for ( i=0; i<count; i++ )
    {
        printf( "%s\n", names[i] );
    } /* end if */

    printf( "Sorted Order \n");
    for ( i=0; i<count; i++ )
    {
        printf( "%s\n", pointers[i] );
    } /* end if */

    exit(0);
} /* end main */

void bubble( char * pointers[], int count)
{
    int i, j;
    char *temp;

/* Sort names by exchanging the pointers to the names instead of the n
themselves */

    for ( i=count-1; i>0; i-- )
    {
        for ( j=0; j<i; j++ )
        {
            if ( strcmp( pointers[j], pointers[j+1] ) > 0 )
            {
                temp = pointers[j];
                pointers[j] = pointers[j+1];
                pointers[j+1] = temp;
            } /* end if */
        } /* end for j */
    } /* end for i */

    return;

} /* end  bubble */
```

Program 6.8. (continued)

there are two access paths to each name. One path is through the names array and
the other is via the pointers array.

This technique is useful from the viewpoint of efficiency as pointers can be
moved more quickly than can strings. The technique is even more beneficial if the
base type of the array is larger.

Functions and Pointers

The utility of pointers as parameters to functions has been demonstrated in the discussion of simulating parameter passing "by reference." It is also convenient to allow a function to return a pointer. This technique is often used when returning a string of characters.

As demonstrated in previous chapters, the definition of a function permits the declaration of the type of the value to be returned. To return a pointer, the asterisk symbol is used with the type specifier as shown in Figure 6.28.

This declaration states that the function strcat() will return a pointer to a character.

To call this function and to use its return value properly, at least one of the following conditions has to be satisfied.

1. The function's defining declaration has to occur in the same file as the function call, and prior to that call.
2. A prototype declaration must appear in the same file as the call and before that call. This declaration may be coded in the source file or in an included header file.

(These points are true of functions in general, not just those that return a pointer.)

A referencing declaration is a declaration of the function's name and the type it returns; a defining declaration of the function gives the body of that function in addition to the parameters. For an external function returning a pointer to a char value, the required prototype declaration would be "extern char *." Notice that in a referencing declaration, the body of the function is not specified. (The parameter types may or may not be specified, according to whether prototype declarations are in use. It is generally better to include the parameter types as the compiler can use them to do additional type checking.)

If one of these conditions is not satisfied, when the compiler encounters a call

```
/* Concatenate string s2 to s1, returning the pointer to the
resulting string (s1). */

char * strcat( char * s1, char * s2)
{
    /* Body omitted here.
    It should concatenate the strings. */

    return s1; /* Return the pointer. */
}
```

Figure 6.28. A function that returns a pointer

to a function such as strcat() before it encounters the defining declaration, it assumes that the value returned has type int. This may cause an improper return of the value to the caller.

To illustrate proper parsing of the declaration of the above function, recall that the function call operator has a higher precedence than the indirection operator *. Thus, in a declaration, the () binds tighter than the *, leading to the following interpretation of that declaration.

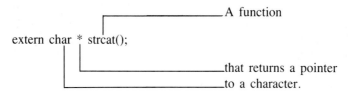

To declare a pointer to a function that returns an integer, parentheses are used to overcome the default binding of the punctuators: "extern int (*functptr)();." A pointer to a function is a difficult concept to grasp. If a function is considered to be an object in memory that contains the set of instructions for that function, then a pointer to the function is the address of the first instruction in this set of instructions. (The perspicacious reader will observe that a function is more than a set of instructions in memory as the execution of a function also involves the manipulation of data, that is, the parameters and local variables.) Consider the example in Figure 6.29, which shows the prototype declaration of the header of the qsort() function that is included by the standard in the header file stdlib.h.

Notice the parameter (*compar)(). This parameter is a pointer to a function that is used by the quicksort function to compare the size of two of the objects to be sorted. This qsort function is designed to sort an array of any base type for which a comparison function can be defined. This results in a very useful generic sort function. It is further examined in Chapter 8.

Parsing Examples

The various combinations of arrays, pointers, and functions can produce many, very obscure, complex declarations and expressions. These are best avoided when possible because of their complexity and the misunderstandings that can accompany their use. We will discuss a few slightly more complicated examples. These examples should not be considered an endorsement of their use.

```
#include <stdlib.h>
qsort( void *base, size_t nmemb, size_t size, int (*compar)(void*, void*));
```

Figure 6.29. The qsort function with a pointer to a function

One common declaration has the form

```
char **ch_ptr;
```

This declares ch_ptr to be a pointer to a pointer to a character. Another functionally equivalent declaration is

```
char *ch_ptr[];
```

These are equivalent because an array name is a pointer. Either of these can be, and often is, used as a formal parameter corresponding to an actual parameter that is a two-dimensional array. The two-dimensional array argument defines the space for the array. The pointer ch_ptr is used to access the elements of that array.

Conversely, if a variable is declared as a two-dimensional array, it can be referenced by means of pointers. Thus, with the definition

```
char carray[5][10];
```

the references "ch = **carray," where ch has a type char gives the first element of the first row of that array. It is equivalent to "ch = carray[0][0];."

The combination

```
int *funct()
```

means that funct is a function that returns a pointer to a character. This is the same as

```
int *(funct())
```

since the function punctuator binds more tightly than the pointer punctuator *. When parenthesized as

```
int (*funct)();
```

the result is the declaration of a pointer to a function that returns an integer. This is a valuable, albeit lesser used declaration.

Table 6.1 gives some declarations with their interpretations. Deriving these can become a puzzle, which some people enjoy solving. The fact that they often require intense concentration to decipher is sufficient warning as to their use.

Declaring Array and Pointer Parameters in Function Prototypes

The parameter list for function prototypes can be given in two general styles. In one style, the parameter type and identifier are both specified. In the second style, only a list of parameter types is given. The following two delcarations, one in each style, are equivalent.

Table 6.1. Cryptic Combinations of Arrays, Pointers, and Functions

`int(*funct)( void )`	A pointer to a function that returns an int.
`int (*funct)( float)`	A pointer to a function that returns an int and requires a float parameter.
`char *(*cfunct)( void)`	A pointer to a function that returns a pointer to a char.
`char *(*cfunct)( int*)`	A pointer to a function that returns a pointer to a char and that has a pointer to an integer as a parameter.
`int **iarray[5]`	An array of pointers to pointers to ints.
`int (**iarray)[5]`	A pointer to a pointer to an array of five integers. This could be used as a formal parameter corresponding to a three-dimensional array.
`int ***iptr`	A pointer to a pointer to a pointer to an integer. It can be used with a three-dimensional array as the previous.

```
float average( float scores[100], int num );
float average( float [100], int );
```

In the first style, the formal parameter identifier in the prototype does not have to be identical to the formal parameter identifier in the function definition, although they should have the same type. Thus, the defining declaration for the function whose prototype appears above could begin as follows.

```
float average( float grades[100], int num_of_students )
{
        /*Body of function here.*/
}
```

Since the identifier is merely a placeholder in the prototype, it is often omitted and the second style is used. Table 6.2 gives a group of function prototypes in this style with an explanation of their meaning.

The order of binding of the various punctuators remains the same as if the parameter identifiers were present. The array declarator [] binds before the pointer punctuator *, unless parentheses are used to modify this order. In Table 6.2, the second parameter to function f3() is an array of 10 pointers. However, in function f4(), the second parameter is a pointer to an array of 10 floats.

Table 6.2 also illustrates that array parameters can be declared with or without an indication of the size. If the size is given, then the actual array parameter corresponding to it should have the same size.

Table 6.2. Array and Pointer Parameters in Function Prototypes

`int f1(int, float);`	A function that requires two parameters, an int and a float, and that returns an int.
`int f2(int [], float *);`	A function that requires two parameters, an array of ints and a pointer to a float, and that returns an int.
`double f3(int [10], float *[10]);`	A function that requires two parameters, an array of 10 ints and an array of pointers to float, and that returns a double.
`long int f4(int (*)[], float (*)[10]);`	A function that requires two parameters, a pointer to an array of int and a pointer to an array of 10 floats, and that returns a long int.
`int f5(int (*)());`	A function that returns an int, and that requires one parameter, a pointer to a function that returns an int.
`int f6(int *());`	A function that returns an int, and that requires one parameter, which is a function that returns a pointer to an int.

6.5   COMMAND-LINE ARGUMENTS

One common use of array pointers in C is for *command-line arguments*. When a program is invoked in a hosted environment, initial data (arguments) can be provided to that program from the command line. (A particular C implementation does not have to be hosted; but if it is, the host environment has to provide this ability in order to meet the standard.)

One useful example program has the function of typing the contents of a text file on the terminal, that is, on the standard output device. If this program were called type, then it could be invoked via the command line

```
type outfile
```

where outfile is the name of the file to be output.

To use command-line arguments, the C program has to be written with two arguments to the function main. The first of these, often called *argc* for argument count, is an integer that gives a count of the number of arguments; the second, traditionally called *argv* for argument vector, is an array of pointers to the strings that are the actual arguments. The value of argv[0] is always the name of the program. Then argv[1] through argv[argc-1] are the arguments to that program.

```
main( int argc, char * argv[] );
{
    if (argc != 2)
    {
        printf( "Incorrect form: type filename\n" );
    }
    else
    {

            /* the code to print the file goes here */
    }
    exit();
}
```

Program 6.9. Declaring command-line arguments

The standard specifies that argv[argc] will be a null pointer. Since every program to be executed in this manner has a name, argc has to be at least one. The program described begins as shown in Program 6.9.

This program cannot be completed until a discussion of file input and output is presented. In this example, notice that the number of elements in the array argv[] was not specified. This specification was not necessary as this is a formal parameter. The actual parameters are given on the command line itself, which is entered by the user. The hosting environment has allocated sufficient memory for these, and then initializes argv[] with pointers to those strings. Since the number of elements is not specified, the pointer to the array argv[], which is declared above as "argv[]," could have also been declared as a "pointer to a pointer": **argv.

To illustrate further the use of command-line arguments, consider Program 6.10 which reverses the words on the command line. Thus, if the command is entered as

```
reverse this string
```

this program will echo back

```
string this
```

(This program may not have any importance in the realm of useful programs, but it does illustrate the use of arguments on the command line and arrays of pointers.) Notice that this program works regardless of the number of strings that compose the argument list. Also, the initialization expression in the for loop

```
main( int argc, char * argv[] )
{
    for ( ; argc > 1; argc-- )
    {
        printf( "%s ", argv[argc-1] );
    }
    exit(0);
}
```

Program 6.10. Using the values of argc and argv

is the null (empty) statement. It is not necessary as the hosting environment gives
argc the appropriate value.

6.6 CASTING POINTERS

C is generally flexible about the conversion of a value of one type to a different
type. (We asserted in Section 4.13 that implicit conversions should be avoided in
favor of explicit casts.) One area in which the ANSI C specification requires the
enforcement of types—that is, does not permit general implicit conversions—is
among the pointer types. The only implicit conversions permitted are to or from a
pointer and a void type. (The void type is discussed in the next section.) All other
conversions require a cast. Explicit conversions among pointers to any object are
permitted with a few implementation-defined interpretations. (These interpretations involve the alignment of various objects of different sizes. Some
compilers require the addresses of certain objects to begin on an even-numbered
address, or to have some other similar property). The example from Figure 6.13,
repeated here, demonstrates the use of a pointer cast to cast an integer constant to
a pointer.

```
int *mem_ptr;
mem_ptr = (int*) 0xb000;
```

Another possible implementation-defined problem lies in the conversion between
a pointer and an integer. Such conversions are permitted in either direction. But if
the integer type is not large enough to contain the value of the address in the
pointer, the result is defined by the implementation.

   The most common use of pointer casts is in the dynamic allocation of memory.
Functions that allocate memory often return a pointer to a character array of the
required length. If this memory is to be used for some other type of object, the
pointer has to be cast to reflect the type of this structure. These dynamic memory
allocation functions will be further explained and demonstrated in Chapter 11.

6.7 VOID TYPE AND POINTERS

The type void discussed in Chapter 4 has a special significance with respect to pointers. A pointer to a void is a generic pointer in that such a pointer can point to any object. All other pointers are declared as pointers to a particular type. However, a pointer to a void cannot be dereferenced using the indirection operator as the compiler does not know how to interpret the memory locations to which it points. Thus, a type conversion of the void pointer is required. Type coercions (i.e., casts, to void *) are also permitted. Void type pointers are often used in the declaration of function formal parameters when pointers of more than one type are acceptable.

6.8 PORTABILITY AND SOFTWARE ENGINEERING ISSUES

This chapter has explained the method used by C to pass parameters "by reference." This method is to pass the address of the parameter rather than the parameter's value. It is important to realize that the normal technique of passing parameters by value has an important software engineering role. Since actual parameters passed by value are not modified by changes to their corresponding formal parameters, they are isolated from mistakes in the function. This is an important form of information hiding that not only makes the program more understandable, but also can make the debugging task easier. The called function and the calling function are less tightly coupled—or connected together—by value parameters than they are by reference parameters. Errors in the called function are less likely to propagate to the calling function.

The use of initializations as part of the declaration, although often very clear, can sometimes lead to misunderstandings. A particular case in which such initializations may be problematic is the use of variables to initialize other variables. Another potential problem is the confusion that can arise between the initialization of static and automatic variables. Static variables are initialized only once, when they are first created. They are then extant for the life of the program. The value of a static variable during execution is always the last value that was assigned to it. Automatic variables are created each time that the function in which they reside is entered. Furthermore, an initialization of dynamic duration variables recurs each time that the variable is recreated. Consider Program 6.11.

The dynamic duration variable fraction seems at first glance to be always initialized to the value 12/5 since x is initialized to 12 and y to 5. This is not true. The confusion arises because the variables x and y have static storage duration whereas fraction has dynamic. Thus, x and y are initialized only one time, whereas fraction is reinitialized each time that the function sample_function() is called. If the values of x or y are modified before the function sample_function()

```
static float x = 12.0;
static float y = 5.0;

sample_function(void)
{
    auto float fraction = x/y;
    printf( "The fraction is: %f", fraction );
}

main()
{
    sample_function();
    x = 10.0;
    y = 25.0;
    sample_function();

    exit(0);
}
```

Program 6.11. Initializations of automatic and static variables

is called, their new values will be used to initialize fraction. In the second call to sample_function(), the variable fraction is initialized to 10.0/25.0. The programmer should be aware of the trade-offs in the use of static and automatic initialization.

Another example of the flexibility of C arises from the equivalence of arrays and pointers. Because of this equivalence, and the fact that multidimensional arrays are stored in row-major order, it is possible of pass a single-dimensional array to a function requiring a multidimensional array, or vice versa. Consider the example in Program 6.12.

In this example, the elements of these two arrays are matched in the following way:

```
single[0]<=>multi[0][0]
single[1]<=>multi[0][1]
single[2]<=>multi[0][2]
single[3]<=>multi[0][3]
single[4]<=>multi[0][4]
single[5]<=>multi[1][0]
...,
single[9]<=>multi[1][4]
```

We mention this equivalence to caution against its use. As a rule, such correspondences are confusing. (That is not to say that they should never be used, but only when their use actually adds to the understandability of the code by reducing the complexity.) This equivalence is often used to increase the execution effi-

```
int single[10]={0,1,2,3,4,5,6,7,8,9};

main()
{

    funct( single );

}

funct( int multi [2][5] )
{
    int i, j;

    for( i=0; i<2; i++)
    {
        for(j=0; j<5;j++)
        {
            printf( "%d\n", multi[i][j] );
        }
    }
}
```

Program 6.12. The equivalence of single- and multidimensional arrays

ciency since accessing arrays, particularly multidimensional arrays, is generally slower than using pointers. This concern about "micro" optimization often has less effect than more global optimization performed by choosing an efficient algorithm.

When initializing multidimensional arrays, it is most understandable to group the initializer values by rows rather than to specify them in one list. The examples of Figure 6.8 illustrate this difference. The second example is preferable to the first.

Another note of caution in the use of multidimensional arrays is appropriate here. It is important to use the correct syntax for the declaration and use of multidimensional arrays. For example, A[2][5] is the correct format whereas A[2,5] is not. (This second format may prove tempting to Pascal programmers as it is valid in that language.) This problem is made more insidious by the fact that this is not a syntax error. Most C compilers understand the reference A[2,5] to be a use of the comma operator with a single-dimensional array. The comma operator was described in Chapter 4. It is sufficient here to understand that the comma operator allows two expressions to be specified where one is normally required, and that the value of a comma operator expression is that of the right-hand expression. Thus, the reference A[2,5] is actually a reference to A[5], as the value of the comma expression 2,5 is 5. This obviously is not what was intended.

The programmer should be careful about attempting to extend every concept that works for single-dimensional arrays to multiple-dimensional arrays. Even though a single-dimensional array parameter in a function can be declared without a reference to the size, the same is not true of multiple-dimensional arrays. If a function declarator begins with the heading "bad_function(char sample_array[ ][ ])," the function will not be able accurately to decode a reference to a member of that array such as sample_array[2][3]. The problem is that the length of rows is not known. Without this knowledge, the address of an element in that row cannot be determined. It is acceptable to use sample_array[2][ ] since the compiler knows the length of each row. This is all the information that is necessary as arrays are stored in a row-major order.

When using library functions such as the I/O or string functions, the programmer should always include the associated header files that contain the proper declarations of these functions. Failure to declare functions will result in the return value defaulting to int. This can be particularly disastrous if the function actually returns a type that requires more bits, for example, a long int. The result can be an obscure error causing a loss of data that can give completely incorrect answers.

There is a definite portability advantage in letting the compiler determine the size of an array from the initializer values. This assumes that the array will never have to be any larger than the size given by the initializers. Similarly, using a pointer or specifying an array with no size (e.g., A[]) for formal parameters can make a function more portable. The corresponding actual parameters must be declared with a large enough size to reserve sufficient memory space.

This chapter has discussed the assignments of constants to pointers as a method of specifying a specific memory address for system programming. This is a very powerful technique for accessing the underlying hardware, but it is dangerous for applications programmers. The use of constants for addresses is completely nonportable.

Programmers often make the assumption that a pointer is the same size as an integer, and store pointers into integer variables. This is not a safe assumption and should be avoided. Such a conversion can result in the loss of data so that the pointer values are not preserved. Even though such conversions work with one compiler, they may not on another. This leads to portability problems. To the reader of a program, this type of conversion makes the program difficult to understand.

When referencing the size of objects and arrays, the sizeof operator will provide a more portable implementation than would a hard coded value. The sizeof operator can be used to determine the number of members of an array in a portable way, as illustrated in the section Pointer Arithmetic and Comparison.

The use of pointer arithmetic has similar advantages. Regardless of the underlying hardware word size or the compiler in use, pointer arithmetic increments or decrements the value of a pointer by the appropriate amount to reflect the size of the object to which it points. Portability is enhanced.

The C programming language has a wide variety of operators, functions, data types, and other constructs that can be used in many flexible ways to serve a great variety of purposes. But their misuse can result in nonportable or difficult-to-understand, if not incorrect, code. The C programmer must learn to apply these in a disciplined manner.

6.9 SUMMARY

This chapter has presented details of some of the most pragmatic data structures in the C language. The array is the first of the aggregate data types of C to be presented. Arrays provide the ability to group homogeneous data into meaningful collections that can then be manipulated as a group or as independent elements. The syntax of the declaration and of the use of arrays of both single and multiple dimensions was discussed.

A data type that is closely associated with arrays in C is the pointer type. The value of a pointer variable is a memory address. Thus, a pointer variable "points" to another memory location. In this chapter, we have discussed the declaration of pointer variables by means of the * symbol and the use of pointer variables to store values by means of the indirection operator, which also uses the * symbol. The address operator & retrieves the address of an lvalue.

The relationship between pointers and arrays in C is fundamental. It is based on the fact that the name of any array is actually a pointer to that array. This relationship is the source of great power in data manipulation. At the same time, it can also serve as a source of great confusion if the relationship is not mastered early. The relationships between arrays and pointers were further explained by an examination of order of binding of the referencing punctuators. In particular, it was noted that the punctuators *, (), and [] bind in declarations in the order that the corresponding operators would execute according to the C precedence rules.

Pointer arithmetic was introduced. Arithmetic performed with a pointer operand results in the value being scaled according to the size of the object to which it points.

This chapter concluded with an examination of some of the software engineering and portability considerations of arrays and pointers.

Keywords

address operator	argc
aggregate type	argv

array   multidimensional
base type   parameter passing
by reference   pointer
by value   pointer arithmetic
command-line argument   pointer comparison
derived type   row-major order
indirection operator   simple types
initialization   string
member   vector

References

Draft American National Standard x3.159–198x, Programming Language C. This is the ultimate authority on questions of syntax and semantic of the C language. Copies may be obtained from Global Engineering Documents, Inc., 2805 McGaw, Irvine, CA 92714.

Jaeschke, R. 1988. Exploring the subtle side of the 'sizeof'. *C Users J.* 46–8. InfoPro Systems.

Jaeschke, R. 1988. For certain uses typedef is far superior to define. *C Users J.* 34–6. InfoPro Systems.

Plauger, P. J. 1988. Types play central role in new standard C. *C Users J.* 17–21. InfoPro Systems.

Singh, B., and T. L. Naps. 1985. *Introduction to Data Structures.* St. Paul, Minn.: West Publishing. This book discusses array and structure declaration and usage in general.

Wirth, N. 1986. *Algorithms and Data Structures.* Englewood Cliffs, N.J.: Prentice-Hall. This book discusses array and structure declaration and usage in general.

Discussion Questions

1. Why did the designers of C choose to pass all parameters by value?

2. What are the differences between the initialization of static variables and of automatic variables?

3. What are the differences between initialization in the declaration and initialization by means of an assignment statement? Is one method more efficient than the other?

4. Explain the phrase "row-major order" for storing elements of an array. Does this order seem more intuitive than "column-major order"?

5. Could general-purpose programming languages such as C get along without aggregate data types such as arrays?

6. Explain the differences between the declaration and initialization on the left and the declaration and assignment statements on the right.

```
char *title[] =                         char title[4][20];
{
    "Instructor",                       strcmp(title[0], "Instructor");
    "Assistant Professor",              strcmp(title[1], "Assistant Professor");
    "Associate Professor",              strcmp(title[2], "Associate Professor");
    "Professor"                         strcmp(title[3], "Professor");
}
```

7. Why is there no difference in the size of a pointer variable that points to an integer and the size of one that points to an array of 1,000 integers?

8. When command-line arguments are used, why is the char *argv[] declared without a length? Does space not need to be allocated for this array variable?

9. Are there any differences in the results of the declarations "char * a," "char a[100]," and "char *a[100]"? If there are, what are the differences? If there are no differences, explain why they are the same.

10. Are there any differences in the results of the formal parameter declarations "char **a," "char a[ ][ ]," and "char * a[ ]." If there are, what are the differences? If there are no differences, explain why they are the same.

11. In the section Pointer Arithmetic and Comparison, the assertion was made that the statement "px = px + sizeof(*px)" would result in incrementing the value of px by the square of *px because of the special meaning of addition with pointers. (The declaration of px was "int * px.") Explain this increment value.

12. Explain the fact that A[i] is identical to *(A+i) where A is an array and i is an integer.

Exercises

1. Give the declaration for each of the following arrays that has exactly the number of elements indicated.
   a. An array called SS_Numbers of 7000 unsigned integers.
   b. An array called Address to hold an address of up to 35 characters.
   c. An array called Class_Role to hold 45 names of 35 characters each.

    d. An array of integers called Enrollment to contain the enrollment in each of 20 classes in 30 departments on three campuses.

2. For each of the following variables, give a declaration that initializes the variable to that value.
   a. The int i to value 1809.
   b. The float f to the value 8.27.
   c. The char array A to the string "Alan Turing."
   d. The int array grades to the values 95, 56, 77, 95, 86, 81 in that order.
   e. The two-dimensional array streets to the names "Main," "High," "Wall," "Fifth Avenue," "Ventura," "Pennsylvania."

3. Consider the following array declaration

   ```
   int B[10][30];
   ```

   Which of the following array references is syntactically valid? For the invalid ones, explain what is wrong.
   a. B[0][0]
   b. B[10][30]
   c. B[7][10]
   d. B[7,10]
   e. B[7]

4. With the declaration C[5][3], what is the order in which the elements of array C are stored in the computer's memory?

5. Write a program fragment consisting of a for loop that will input the values of the array class_names that have been declared as "char class_names [100][35]." Input one name per line.

6. How many characters are represented by the string "Computer Science"?

7. If pointer and integer variables require 4 bytes of memory, doubles require 8 bytes, and char variables require 1, how much space is occupied by each of the following variables?

   ```
   int i;
   int * ip;
   char c;
   char * cp;
   char ch_array[10][20];
   char * names[10][20];
   char * (names_ptr[10][20]);
   ```

8. Given the declarations and initializations

```
int x = 2;
int y = 3;
int z[3] = {9, 8, 7};
int *ptrx = &x;
int *ptry = &y;
```

what is the value of each of the following expressions?
a. z[0] = x;
b. *ptrx
c. *ptrrx == *ptry
d. ptrx
e. *ptrx + *ptry
f. ptrx++
g. z
h. *(z+1)
i. z[2] == *(z+2)
j. sizeof(ptrx)
k. sizeof(*ptrx)
l. sizeof(z)
m. &x

9. Given the declarations

```
float * fp;
float f;
```

a. Give an assignment statement that will make f and *fp refer to the same memory location.
b. Now write an assignment statement that gives f the value 1809.1988 without using the variable name f.

10. Suppose that a pointer variable occupies 4 bytes. With declaration "int *pi, *pj;" suppose that pi is assigned the decimal value 756. (Notice that this is the address to which pi points, not the contents of that location.) After the following statement, what values will pi and pj contain?

```
pj = pi++;
```

11. Consider the following declarations:

```
float F[512];
float *f1_ptr, * f2_ptr;
int i;
```

With these declarations, is the following program segment syntactically correct? If so, what does it print out? If not, what is the error?

```
fl_ptr = F;
f2_ptr = &F[511];
i = (int) (f2_ptr - f2_ptr) + 1;
printf( "The array F has %d elements. \n");
```

12. Write a function that will take a string as a parameter and will return the length of that string. Use array indexing to refer to elements of the array in the function body.

13. Write the function described in Exercise 12 except that the elements of the string should be referenced by pointers and pointer arithmetic in the function body.

14. Write a function to exchange or swap the values of its two string parameters. Suppose that the first parameter points to the string "abc" and the second parameter points to the string "defg" before the call to the function. After the call, the first parameter should have the value "defg" and the second should have the value "abc".

15. Program 6.10 reverses the order of words given on a command line. Modify this program to reverse the characters of the command line.

16. Write a function that will input a sequence of words from the terminal, capitalize the first letter in each word, and then write these words back to the terminal. You may assume that the input has a maximum length of ten lines, each of which may be up to 80 characters long.

Programming Problems

1. Write a program that will print the contents of a file to the terminal screen. Use a command-line argument to specify the file. Check the command-line parameters for errors, so that precisely one file name is entered in addition to the program name.

2. Write a program that will concatenate the contents of a group of files. Use command-line arguments to specify the files. The program should work for any number of files. These files are to be specified in the order that the concatenation is to occur. The last file given is to be the source of the concatenation. (In UNIX, the operating system command to do this is called "cat.")

3. A teacher often needs help in maintaining grade records for a class. Write a C program that will allow a teacher to enter the students' names and their scores on each of three tests, seven computer program assignments, and a final examination. Sort the names and corresponding grades into alphabetic order by last name. Find the class average on each test, including the final examination. For each student, determine a final average by means of the following weighting scheme:

Tests	35%
Computer programs	40%
Final examination	25%

    Print out a grade book consisting of one row for each student's name, test scores, program grades, final examination grade, and final average. At the bottom of the columns for the tests and final examination, print the class average.

4. Using a curve to determine letter grades for a test assumes that the grades approximate a normal distribution. That assumption means that grades near the mean are given the grade C, those a little above the mean are assigned a B, those a little below are given a D, and those significantly above or below the mean are assigned an A or F, respectively. More precisely, it is determined by the following:

A	More than one and a half standard deviations above the mean.
B	Between a half and one and a half standard deviations above the mean.
C	Within a half of a standard deviation above or below the mean.
D	Between a half and one and a half standard deviations below the mean.
F	More than one and a half standard deviations below the mean.

    Thus, if the mean of the test scores is 75 and the standard deviation is 10, the C's range from 70 to 80, B's from 80 to 90, D's from 60 to 70, A's above 90, and F's below 60.

    Write a C program that will allow a teacher to input the names and test scores for a class, will find the average and the standard deviation, and will print out a list of each student's name, the corresponding test score, and the letter grade on the test.

    The standard deviation is defined as the sum of the squares of the deviation of each score from the mean divided by the number of scores. Thus, if M is the mean (average) of the test scores, x_i represents the ith test score, and N is the number of scores, the following formula gives the standard deviation:

$$\text{SQRT} \left(\frac{(x_1 - M)^2 + (x_2 - M)^2 + (x_3 - M)^2 + \cdots + (x_N - M)^2}{N} \right)$$

The output from this program should consist of the grading scale; a list of students' names, test scores, and letter grades; and the class mean and standard deviation.

5. Words are anagrams if some rearrangement of the letters of one will produce the other. For example, the following words are all anagrams of each other: rats, star, tars. Write a C program that will determine the number of pairs of anagrams that appear in an input list of words (up to ten characters each). The program should allow up to 20 words—that is, character sequences—to be input, one per line.

6. Write a collection of C functions to perform matrix arithmetic. These operations should include adding two matrices and subtracting two matrices. (These operations are performed by adding or subtracting corresponding elements.) Other functions are a test for equality between two arrays, and raising an array in a integer power.

   Write a C testing program that presents the user with a menu of these functions. Use this to test these matrix functions thoroughly.

7. Gaussian elimination is a method for solving a system of simultaneous linear equations by representing them as a matrix. (A solution is a choice of values for the variables that will make all of the equations true.) That is, the set of equations given here has the solution $x = 1$, $y = 2$, $z = -2$.

$$2x + 3y + 4z = 0$$
$$x + y + z = 1$$
$$x - 3y + z = -7$$

   This set of equations can be represented by the matrix:

   ```
   2    3   4    0
   1    1   1    1
   1   -3   1   -7
   ```

   This is called the augmented matrix of coefficients. The method of Gaussian elimination consists of rules for transforming the augmented matrix of coefficient into an upper triangular matrix that has all zeros under the diagonal. These rules are that any row can be replaced by the sum (or difference) of any other two rows, and that any row can be multiplied by a constant. The method of Gaussian elimination describes an order of applying these rules to obtain a triangular matrix. The general method is to "eliminate" the first column under the diagonal (i.e., elements $A_{1,2}$ to $A_{1,n}$ for a matrix A representing n equations), then to eliminate the second column under the diagonal (elements $A_{2,3}$ to $A_{2,n}$), and so on. This continues until an upper triangular matrix is produced. To eliminate (i.e., to convert to zero), the coefficient $A_{i,j}$, it is sufficient to multiply row i by the value $A_{i,j}/A_{i,i}$ and then add this row to row j. This process is illustrated and annotated below:

2	3	4	0
1	1	1	1
1	−3	1	−7

2	3	4	0	Multiple row 1 by −1/2 and add to row 2.
0	1/2	−1	1	
1	−3	1	−7	

2	3	4	0	Multiple row 1 by −1/2 and add to row 3.
0	1/2	−1	1	
0	−9/2	−1	−7	

2	3	4	0	Multiple row 2 by −(−9/2)/(1/2) and add to
0	1/2	−1	1	row 3.
0	0	8	−16	

Once this form has been reached, a method called backward substitution will reveal the solution. The last row represents the equation "$8z = -16$," which can easily be seen to have the solution "$z = -2$." With this value for z, the second row can be seen to represent the equation "$(1/2)y - (1)(-2) = 1$," which has the solution "$y = 2$." A similar substitution for z and y into the equation represented by the first row will give the solution "$x = 1$."

Write a C program that will first input the value of n, the number of equations, then will input the n + 1 coefficients that represent each of the n equations. The program should then use the method of Gaussian elimination to find the solution of these equations. (A set of n equations in n unknowns does not always have a unique answer. Sometimes, there are multiple solutions, and other times, no solution. Both of these situations can be detected by the presence of zeros on the diagonal. If this occurs, your program should print an appropriate error message.)

8. Games are often used for purposes other than entertainment. One such game is the game of Life, which was invented by John H. Conway as a genetic model of the laws of birth, death, and survival in a constrained environment. (This was described in an article in the October 1970 issue of the *Scientific American*, page 120.) The playing board consists of a square configuration of squares. The number can be a parameter of your program. Typical sizes are five by five and eight by eight. Each square either is empty or contains a single organism. The fate of a particular square is governed by the following rules:

    a. An organism will be born in an empty location that has exactly three neighbors.

    b. An existing organism will die if it has four or more neighbors (from overcrowding), or if it has fewer than two neighbors (from loneliness). If an organism has either two or three neighbors, it will survive for another generation.

Write a C program that will input an initial configuration of organisms on the game board and the number of generations to be processed. Then print out the board's configuration after each generation.

9. One of the primary objectives of any program that requires extensive interaction with a user is rigor. It should not be possible for the user to cause the program to terminate abnormally by anything that is input. A frequent source of problems is the input of numeric data. If a letter or punctuation symbol is accidently or mistakenly typed when the program is expecting integer or float data, the program will abnormally terminate.

Write two C functions, one for integer and one for float data, that will input a number as a string of characters. Then convert that string to the appropriate numeric format. Issue polite error messages in the case of error, and permit the user another chance.

10. Tic-tac-toe is a well-known game in which the goal is to place your mark in three positions in a row (horizontally, vertically, or diagonally) before your opponent can do the same with his or her mark. This game has a solution in that it is always possible to achieve a tie, that is, to avoid losing. The game board can be represented by a three-by-three array of zeros and ones (or X's and O's.) Write a C program that allows two users to play this game by indicating a pair of integers to represent each play.

A more complicated version of this program is to allow the computer to make the moves for one player. An even more complicated version can be obtained by changing to three dimensions. The game board can then be represented by a set of three arrays, each of which is three by three. Can you find an algorithm that will always achieve a tie in this case? (The game can be made even more challenging by increasing the size of the array to four by four and requiring four matches in a row to win.) Be warned that increasing beyond two dimensions makes the algorithm to solve this problem quite difficult.

11. Implement and test the code for Exercises 12, 13, 14, and 16.

12. Consider the following function description:

```
#define FORWARD 1
#define BACKWARD 0
```

```
typedef int boolean;

char *findit(boolean whichway, char*s, int c)
```

This function is to search the string s for the first occurrence of the character c. If whichway == FORWARD, it searches from left to right; if whichway == BACKWARD, it searches from right to left. It returns either a pointer to the first occurrence of c in s or (char*) NULL if c is not found. Implement this function along with a driver function that allows the user to enter a string to be searched, a character to locate, and the direction of the search. After a string is entered, display "Not Found" or the character number in s where c is located. Use pointer arithmetic to compute the character number by using the string address and the value returned from findit().

7 Structures, Unions, and Strings

One of the strengths of the C programming language is the diversity of data structures that are available in the language syntax. Chapter 6 presented arrays and pointers. This discussion of data structures is continued here with the presentation of structures and unions. Structures are aggregate types that group heterogeneous data. They are contrasted with arrays, which are collections of homogeneous data. Unions provide a method of prescribing different data types for overlapping portions of memory.

7.1 SYNTAX AND SEMANTICS OF STRUCTURES

Introduction to Terminology and Concepts

The first topic of this chapter is another category of aggregate types, the *structure*. A structure is a heterogeneous, aggregate data type. (In some other programming languages, such as Pascal, the equivalent type is called a "record.") The use of a structure allows the C programmer to group together logically related information even though the components have different types.

   The constituent elements of a structure are called *members*. In the declaration of a structure, each member is given a name. The entire structure is also given a name. To refer to a particular member of the structure requires a combination of the structure's name and that of the member. Another name, the *tag,* can be associated with the structure. The tag is the name of the newly created structure template itself rather than the data structure. Thus, the tag is the name of the template that is used as a pattern to create the structure. This tag can then be used to create many instances of that structure without repeating the detailed member-by-member declaration.

Structure Declaration

A structure declaration is introduced by the keyword *struct*. This is optionally followed by the tag name. The list of pairs of member types and names follows in a bracketed list. This list is optionally followed by this particular structure's name. This syntax is seen explicitly in the Figure 7.1.

The example in Figure 7.2 is the declaration of a structure called part_ description, which consists of three members: an integer for the part number, an integer for the part quantity, and a float for the price.

The name PART_DESC_RECORD is the tag, and is used to define another instance of the structure called another_part. This second structure also has three members with the same member names as in the first structure. These members are distinguished by the name of the structure of which they are a part.

STRUCT SPECIFIER

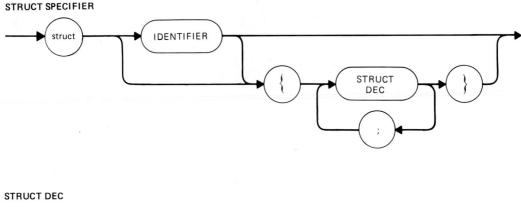

STRUCT DEC

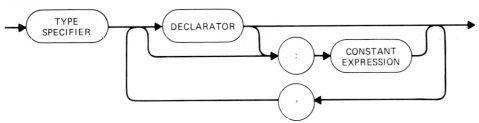

Figure 7.1. Structure syntax diagram

```
struct   PART_DESC_RECORD
{
     int part_no;
     int quantity;
     float price;
} part_description;

struct PART_DESC_RECORD another_part;
```

Figure 7.2. Declaration of structures

```
struct   PART_DESC_RECORD
{
    int part_no;
    int quantity;
    float price;
 };

struct PART_DESC_RECORD part_description;

struct PART_DESC_RECORD another_part;
```

Figure 7.3. Use of a structure tag for declaration

The same purpose can be accomplished with the declarations given in Figure 7.3.

In this case, the template for the record is described separately from the declarations of the two structures. A third alternative method is presented in Figure 7.4.

The primary difference between the example in Figure 7.4 and the previous two examples is that a tag was not used in this latest sample declaration. This has no impact upon the two structures being declared, but limits the use of this structure type. There can be no other structures that have the same type as these two. The tag not only has the advantage of specifying the structure only once, but also allows other structures to have the same type as these.

A structure can be named with a typedef class specifier. Remember that a typedef declaration does not create a new type but gives another name for that type. This is particularly useful with complicated structures. Figure 7.5 shows yet another declaration of the part description structure to demonstrate the use of the typedef.

This illustration demonstrates two methods of defining the typedef identifier. The method on the right defines a structure tag first, then uses that tag in the declaration of the type. The left method avoids the use of the structure tag.

Notice that the use of the type name created with the typedef is quite similar to


```
struct
{
    int part_no;
    int quantity;
    float price;
} part_description, another_part;
```

Figure 7.4. Declaration of a structure

```
typedef struct                    struct PART_DESC_RECORD
{                                 {
    int part_no;                      int part_no;
    int quantity;                     int quantity;
    float price;                      float price;
} PART_TYPE;                      };

PART_TYPE part_description,       typedef struct PART_DESC_RECORD
          another_part;                          PART_TYPE;

                                  PART_TYPE part_description,
                                            another_part;
```

Figure 7.5. Declaration of a structure with a typedef

the use of the structure tag. The difference is that the use of the tag must be preceded by the keyword struct; this is absent when the typedef name is used.

Referencing Structure Members

To access a particular member of a structure, the structure's name is modified by the *dot operator* followed by the member's name. (This method of qualification differs from that of an element of an array in which an index is used in a subscript operator.) To access the second member of the structure part_description, the expression to be used is part_description.quantity. The period is called the dot operator. This operator has the highest precedence in C along with ( ) and [ ]. This qualified name identifies an integer variable to be treated like any other integer variable. (That is, a value can be assigned to that variable. It can be used in an expression, or it can be used as an integer parameter to a function.) It is, in fact, an lvalue. Figure 7.6 contains valid uses of the structures and members as declared in Figure 7.5.

It is often useful to define a pointer to a structure. This is illustrated in Figure 7.7. In this code, both a pointer, part_ptr, and an instance of the structure, part_rec, are declared. Before part_ptr can be used to reference a structure, it must be assigned a value. That is, it must be made to point to an instance of a PART_DESC_RECORD structure. One method of giving part_ptr a value is the statement

```
part_ptr = &part_rec;
```

The name of a structure differs from the name of an array in that the structure's name is *not* a pointer to the structure whereas the array name is a pointer to the

```
struct
{
    int part_no;
    int quantity;
    float price;
} part_description, another_part;


part_description.quantity = 12;
another_part.price = 75.34;
another_part.quantity = 17;
another_part.part_no = 12345;
printf( "The total value of part number %d is $%f \n",
        another_part.part_no,
        another_part.quantity * another_part.price );
```

Figure 7.6. The use of structures and their members

```
struct   PART_DESC_RECORD
{
    int part_no;
    int quantity;
    float price;
}

struct PART_DESC_RECORD * part_ptr, part_rec;
```

Figure 7.7. Use of pointers to structure members

array. Thus, the address operator & is needed to obtain the address of part_rec. (Another general method of giving a value to a pointer to a structure is through dynamic memory allocation. This is discussed in Chapter 11.)

There are two ways to refer to a member of a structure using a pointer. One way is

```
(*part_ptr).quantity = 10;
```

This assigns the value 10 to the quantity member of the structure to which part_ptr points. The parentheses are required because the dot operator (.) has higher precedence than the indirection operator (*). This combination is used so often that a more convenient notation has been specified—the *arrow operator*, whose token −> is a combination of the minus and greater-than symbols. The precedence of the arrow operator is the same as that of the dot operator. The use of the arrow operator is demonstrated in the statement:

```
part_ptr->quantity = 10;
```

To reiterate, the dot operator and the arrow operator are in the highest precedence class in C, that is, no operator has a higher precedence. The other operators in this class are the referencing operators for functions ( ) and for arrays[]. These operators all associate from left to right. This associativity gives the natural order of evaluation for various combinations of structures, arrays, functions, and pointers.

Name Spaces

As illustrated in Figures 7.2 through 7.5, the same member name can be used in two (or more) records. The use of the unique structure name with the dot or arrow operator sufficiently qualifies the name. The use of an identifier for more than one purpose is called name *overloading*. The C programming language defines four *name spaces*. Within each of these name spaces, a name must be unique; but the same identifier can appear in two or more separate name spaces. The compiler can differentiate between them by the context of their use.

The four name spaces defined by the C language and visible to a standard C compiler are the following:

1. Statement labels (discussed in Chapter 12).
2. Tags of structures, unions (discussed later in this chapter), and enumerations (discussed in Chapter 9.)
3. Members of structures, unions, and enumerations.
4. All other identifiers.

Thus, each structure tag must be unique among the set of all tags. Within a particular structure, all the member names must be unique. Furthermore, all other identifiers, such as variable names and function names, must be unique among themselves. However, a structure member in one structure can have the same name as a member of another structure; an integer variable can have the same name as a structure member, a label, and the tag of a structure. There is no conflict among the spaces.

It is important to note here that, although there is no conflict among name spaces in C, it is generally a better style, from a software engineering perspective, to avoid more than one use of the same name. Although the compiler can differentiate among these, the human reader may be confused. Such confusion should be avoided.

Structure Assignment and Initialization

One of the most potent aspects of the aggregate data types is the capability of accessing the entire aggregation rather than merely its individual parts. (The ability to access the components is, of course, vital also.) An illustration of this is that one structure can be assigned to another structure of the same type in one simple statement. For example, in the statement

```
*part_ptr=part_rec;
```

the entire contents of part_rec are copied to the address in part_ptr.

In the context of the example in Figure 7.7, the example of Figure 7.8 is syntactically correct, and results in the structure on the left-hand side of the assignment operator having the same value as that on the right. (One restriction is that the structures involved in the assignment must have the same type. It is not sufficient for the corresponding members to have the same type. This is discussed further in Section 7.4.)

This single statement is semantically equivalent to a sequence of assignment statements that individually copy the members of one structure to those of the other.

Structures can be initialized as part of the definition. The values to be assigned are prescribed in a list that is enclosed in brackets. They are separated by commas, and must be given in the order in which the corresponding members are given. The type of the value must be compatible with the member to which it corresponds. If there are fewer initializers in the initialization list than there are elements in the structure, the remaining elements may or may not be initialized according to whether they have static duration (initialized to zero) or dynamic duration (not initialized).

```
struct PART_DESC_RECORD part_description, another_part;
part_description = another_part;
```

Figure 7.8. Structure assignment

```
struct weather
{
    int high_temp, low_temp; /* in degrees Fahrenheit          */
    float pressure;
    char wind_dir;          /* wind direction, 'N' = north,    */
                            /* 'S' = south, 'E' = east,        */
                            /* 'W' = west                      */
    int wind_speed;         /* wind speed in MPH               */
} today = { 75, 57, 30.25, 'N', 2 };

struct weather yesterday = { 82, 59, 30.1, 'W', 5 };
```

Figure 7.9. Structure initialization

In C, there must be an object—that is, a structure—to be initialized. Therefore, an initialization of a template definition with no structure declaration cannot occur. For example, in Figure 7.3, the template with the tag PART_DESC_ RECORD cannot be initialized, although the two structures, part_description and another_part, can be.

Structures can also be used as the return value of functions. Program 7.1 performs a binary search of an array of structures, returning the required structure as the value of the bsearch() function.

```c
#include <stdio.h>
#include <string.h>
#define MAX_BOOKS 1000;

typedef char string[50];
typedef struct
{
   string book_title;
   string author;
   long int catalog_no;
   int date_published;
} book_rec;

book_rec bibliography[] =
{
   { "An Introduction to Operating Systems", "Deitel", 837153L, 1984 },
   { "Fundamentals of Computer Algorithms", "Horowitz and Sahni",
                  7814735L, 1984},
   { "The Unix Programming Environment", "Kernighan and Pike",           }
                  8362851L, 1984 },
   {"Elements of the Theory of Computation", "Lewis and Papadimitriou",
                  8021293, 1981 },
   { "Programming Languages: Design and Implementation", "Pratt",
                  834567L, 1984 },
   { "Algorithms", "Sedgewick", 8736435, 1988 },
   { "Algortihms and Data Structures", "Wirth", 8561628, 1986 }
};

main()
{
   book_rec bsearch(book_rec *, string, int, int);
   book_rec book;
   int no_books, answer;
   string author_to_find;

   no_books = sizeof(bibliography) / sizeof(book_rec);
```

Program 7.1. A binary search returning a structure (continues)

```
answer = 'y';
while (answer == 'y')
{
  printf("Enter book author: ");
  gets(author_to_find);

  book = bsearch(bibliography,author_to_find,0,no_books-1);

    if (book.catalog_no == 0)
    {
      printf("No book found for author %s\n",author_to_find);
    }
    else
    {
      printf("Author: %s\n",book.author);
      printf("Title:  %s\n",book.book_title);
    }
    printf("Do you want to retrieve another book (y or n)? ");
    answer = getchar(); getchar();
  }
  exit(0);
}

book_rec bsearch(book_rec bibliography[],
          string author_to_find, int low, int high)
{
  int mid, result;
  book_rec book;

  mid = (low + high)/2;

  if (low > high)
  {
    book.catalog_no = 0;
    return(book);          /* In this case, book has fields which are
               /* uninitialized, but these are not referenced
               /* in the main program. The fact that the catelog_no
               /* field is 0 is used as a flag. */
  }
  result = strcmp(bibliography[mid].author,author_to_find);
  if (result == 0)
  {
    return(bibliography[mid]);
  }
  if (result < 0)
  {
    book = bsearch(bibliography,author_to_find,mid+1,high);
    return(book);
```

Program 7.1. (continued)

```
   }
   else /* result > 0 */
   {
     book = bsearch(bibliography,author_to_find,low,mid-1);
     return(book);
   }
}
```

Program 7.1. (continued)

The following are some comments about Program 7.1. Notice that the bibliography array is an array of structures and is in order by author's name. This ordering is critical to the correct operation of the binary search algorithm. Also, notice that the bsearch( ) function takes a pointer to an array as its first parameter and that it returns a structure. This function could have been written to return a pointer to that structure. Program 7.1 uses the gets( ) function, which is provided in C's standard I/O library with its prototype declaration appearing in "stdio.h." This function is discussed more completely in Chapter 8. Briefly, its purpose here is to read a string from the standard input until it comes to a new-line character.

This program has been simplified to illustrate the topics of this chapter. In particular, the bibliographic information is limited to seven books. For this to be more realistic, this information should include many more books and should be stored as a file. File input and output are two of the topics of Chapter 8.

Differences Between Structures and Arrays

As a review, consider the fundamental differences between arrays and structures.

1. A structure is heterogeneous; an array is homogeneous.
2. An array's name is a pointer to the array; a structure's name is not.
3. The components of an array (elements) do not have individual identifiers; the components of a structure (members) each has its own name.
4. An element of an array is accessed by means of a subscripted array reference operator; the member of a structure is accessed by the dot or arrow operator.
5. Structures of the same type can be copied using the assignment operator. Arrays cannot.

The next section examines some of the typical uses of structures and their combinations with other data types.

7.2 USAGE OF STRUCTURES

Combinations of Structures and Arrays

One of the more powerful combinations of data structures in C is the use of structures or arrays as members of another structure, and structures as the base type of an array. Consider the example in Figure 7.10 in which a structure uses another structure and an array as members, and which declares an array of structures.

This sample declaration creates an array called company that contains 1,000 elements. Each element is a structure with the tag employee_record. Thus, company[765] is one element of the array and has type struct employee_record. Each employee record has four separate members. The syntax of a reference to the emp_id field of the element of the company array with the index 765 is company[765].emp_id.

Each employee record in the company array has one aggregate field called name and another called address. The composite name company[765].name[0] is a reference to the single character that represents the first character of that employee's name. To refer to the city in which a particular employee resides requires the use of the dot operator twice in the following manner: company[765].address.city. The array index has to immediately follow the array name; the dot operator and the member name have to immediately follow the name of the structure. (Notice that company[765] is the name of a structure, as is company[765].address.) To specify the second letter of the city of the employee

```
struct address_record
{
    char street[30];
    char city[30];
    char state[3];
    int zip;
};

struct employee_record
{
    int emp_id;
    char name[20];
    struct address_record address;
    float salary;
};
struct employee_record company[1000];
```

Figure 7.10. Arrays as structure members

with index 765, use the composite name company[765].address.city[2]. As the array reference operator [ ] has the same precedence level as the record member referencing (dot) operator and as these associate left to right, the expression company[765].address.city is equivalent to the parenthesized version ((company[765]).address).city.

The example in Figure 7.10 is repeated in Figure 7.11 with the use of typedef's.

It is clear that such a combination of arrays and structures provides a useful synergism that neither could provide alone. Arrays alone fall short as they do not allow distinct data types for elements; structures are limited as they do not provide indexing, which is an easy method of repetition of a data grouping.

Pointers to Structures and Structure Parameters

As discussed and illustrated previously, pointers to structures are legitimate and are often quite propitious. Consider the declarations and assignment statement in Figure 7.12.

In this context, emp_ptr contains the address of the first byte of an emp_rec structure. A reference to this employee's street address has the form: emp_ptr–> address.street or (*emp_ptr).address.street. Notice that in both cases the dot

```
typedef char nametype[30];
typedef char statetype[3];

typedef struct
{
    nametype street;
    nametype city;
    statetype state;
    int zip;
} address_record;

typedef struct
{
    int emp_id;
    nametype name;
    address_record address;
    float salary;
} employee_record;

employee_record company[100];
```

Figure 7.11. Using typedefs to declare structures with array members

```
struct address_record
{
    char street[30];
    char city[20];
    char state[3];
    int zip;
};

struct employee_record
{
    int emp_id;
    char name[20];
    struct address_record address;
    float salary;
};

struct employee_record * emp_ptr;
struct employee_record  emp_rec;

emp_ptr = &emp_rec;
```

Figure 7.12. Pointers to structures

operator is used between address and street as address is a structure, not a pointer to a structure.

One of the more common uses of pointers to structures is in passing parameters by reference to a function. Standard C permits the use of both structures and pointers to structures as parameters. The use of a structure as a parameter results in the production of a local copy of that structure for use by the called function. That is, the structure is passed by value, and the actual parameter is unchanged. To simulate parameter passing by reference, pass a pointer to the structure. (The address operator & is used with a structure to pass the address of the structure as a parameter.) Often the use of a pointer to a structure is more efficient than passing the entire structure, since, in the latter case, the compiler causes a copy of the structure to be produced. Program 7.2 illustrates this point.

A member of a structure can be used as a function's actual parameter, provided that the corresponding formal parameter has a compatible type. This corresponding formal parameter will not itself be a member of a structure.

Structures and I/O

When a member of a structure has a simple data type (character, integer, or float types), its value can be input or output by use of the standard I/O functions

```c
struct address_record
{
    char street[30];
    char city[20];
    char state[3];
    int zip;
};

struct employee_record
{
    int emp_id;
    char name[20];
    struct address_record address;
    float salary;
};

struct employee_record emp_rec =
{
    123,
    "John Doe",
    {
        "915 Elm St.",
        "New York",
        "NY",
        10101
    },
    12500.00
};

main()
{
    void display1( struct employee_record * );
    void display2( struct employee_record );

    display1( &emp_rec);
    display2( emp_rec );
    exit(0);
}

/* passing a pointer */
void display1( struct employee_record * emp_ptr )
{
    printf( "id = %d\n", emp_ptr -> emp_id );
    printf( "name = %s\n", emp_ptr -> name );
     printf( " address = %s \n %s \n %s %d \nSalary = $%8.2f \n",
    emp_ptr -> address.street,
```

Program 7.2. Two methods of passing record parameter (continues)

```
        emp_ptr -> address.city,
        emp_ptr -> address.state,
        emp_ptr -> address.zip,
        emp_ptr -> salary);
}
/* passing entire structure */
void display2( struct employee_record emp )
{
    printf( "id = %d\n", emp.emp_id );
    printf( "name = %s\n", emp.name );
    printf( " address = %s \n %s \n %s %d \nSalary = $%8.2f \n",
            emp.address.street,
            emp.address.city,
            emp.address.state,
            emp.address.zip,
            emp.salary);
```

Program 7.2. (continued)

provided in the C library. A more efficient form of I/O is possible in which an entire structure is written to, or read from, a file. This is known as direct I/O and is discussed in Chapter 8.

7.3   UNIONS

Definition and Motivation

Another method of grouping related information is the *union* data type. The syntactic differences between unions and structures are minimal. A union is composed of a group of members of heterogeneous types. The important semantic difference is that these members occupy the same memory locations. That is, rather than allocating space for each member individually, the compiler merely allocates enough space for the largest of the members. Consequently, only one member of a union can be safely accessed at one time. The C programmer should be warned that the inappropriate use of unions can lead to cryptic, difficult-to-understand code. (The union will be discussed here so that the discussion of data structures in C is complete.) Unions can generally be avoided for most applications. They are most useful for systems programming in which it is important to access the underlying execution environment. The union can also be used by the general applications programmer to provide a generic data structure which can encapsulate information about an object when the type of that information varies from time to time.

Upon initial consideration, the value of unions may not be apparent. However, there are occasions when some data items are logically related, but only appear independently. A typical example is that of a geometric object. It may be a square, a triangle, a rectangle, or a trapezoid, but it can be only one of these at a time. Each of these kinds of objects has different characteristics. To describe a square, a data structure needs to record only the length of a side; for a triangle, the height and base (or the length of three sides, or two sides and an angle, or two angles and a side); for a rectangle, the length of the sides; for a trapezoid, the length of a side and the height. Thus, the number, type, and names of the members depend upon the kind of geometric object. A structure could be defined to describe this situation, but only a subset of the members would be used at any one time. A union provides a more appropriate form for the description of this structure. (The syntax for a union to describe this data structure will be presented in the next section.)

Declaration of Unions

A union declaration is introduced by the reserved word *union*. As with a structure, this is optionally followed by the tag name. The list of member types and names follows in a bracketed list. This list is optionally followed by this particular union's name. This syntax is seen explicitly in Figure 7.13.

This syntax is identical to that of a structure except for the use of the reserved word "union" in place of "struct." In an analogous manner, the use of the tag name assigns a name to the template for that particular union declaration. That tag name can be used to define several union data structures with the same member names. The use of a name following the list of members results in the allocation

UNION SPECIFIER

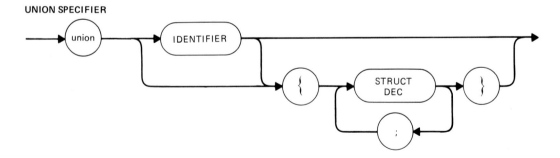

Figure 7.13. Syntax diagram for union declaration

of the appropriate memory space. (Remember that only enough space is allocated to store the largest member of that union.) The example in Figure 7.14 illustrates these concepts.

This creates a template for a union data structure called FLOAT_INT_CHAR, two instances of that union called value and another_value, and a pointer to a union of that type with the name value_ptr. In both value and another_value, enough space is allocated for the largest of the three members of the union. This same space can be accessed three ways; as a float, as an int, and as a char. The members all access the same storage, or part of it.

Pascal programmers will recognize the similarity between C's unions and Pascal's variant records. The variant record of Pascal also permits the declaration of multiple fields that share memory locations. The primary difference, outside of obvious syntactic differences, is that, in Pascal, a tag field is required to differentiate among the variant choices.

Referencing Members of a Union

The same methods that are used to access the members of a structure are used to access those of union: the dot operator and the arrow operator. In the context of the declarations in Figure 7.14, the float field of the union called value could be accessed by

```
value.fvalue = 12.456;
```

After such an assignment, the reference value.ivalue will fetch part or all of the bits that represent the value 12.456. The result is implementation dependent. (Generally, it is the value achieved by interpreting the bits representing the floating-point value as an integer with part possibly truncated.)

```
union FLOAT_INT_CHAR
{
    float fvalue;
    int ivalue;
    char cvalue;
}   value;

union FLOAT_INT_CHAR another_value;

union FLOAT_INT_CHAR * value_ptr;
```

Figure 7.14. Declaration of a union

The assignment

```
value_ptr = &value;
```

causes the pointer variable value_ptr to point to the union value. Subsequently, the references

```
value_ptr -> fvalue
value.fvalue
```

refer to the same member and have the same value.

Unions can be initialized as a part of the declaration. The syntax is similar to that of structure initialization with the exception that only one value is given as unions really only represent a single value. Only the first element can be initialized in this manner. In Figure 7.15, the field fvalue is initialized to 12.345.

Usage Examples

Program 7.3 motivates and explains the utility of the union data structure. As is typical, this example involves a combination of structures, arrays, and unions.

```
union FLOAT_INT_CHAR
{
    float fvalue;
    int ivalue;
    char cvalue;
}  value = { 12.345 };
```

Figure 7.15. Initialization of a union

```
#include <stdio.h>
#include <string.h>

const float PI = 3.14159;
const int TRUE = 1;
const int FALSE = 0;

typedef int boolean;

main()
{
```

Program 7.3. Use of unions (continues)

```
typedef struct
{
     float side;    /* the length of a side */
} square_type;

typedef struct
{
     float radius;    /* the length of the radius */
} circle_type;

typedef struct
{
     float base;
     float height;
}parallelogram_type;

typedef struct
{

     float base;       /* the length of base the triangle.*/
     float height;     /* the height of the triangle. */
} triangle_type;

typedef union
{
     square_type square;
     circle_type circle;
     parallelogram_type parallelogram;
     triangle_type triangle;
} geometric_shapes;

typedef struct
{
     float area;
     geometric_shapes shape;
} object_type;

object_type object;

char kind[14];
float area;
char temp[10];
boolean more, error;
```

Program 7.3. (continued)

```
more = TRUE;
do
{
    error = FALSE;
    printf( "What kind of object?\n");
    printf( "Enter 'none' to quit.\n");
    kind = gets();

    if ( strcmp( kind, "square") == 0 )
    {
        printf( "Enter the length of a side: " );
        temp = gets();
        object.shape.square.side = atof( temp );
        object.area = object.shape.square.side *
            object.shape.square.side;
    }
    else if ( strcmp( kind, "circle") == 0 )
    {
        printf( "Enter the radius of the circle: " );
        temp = gets();
        object.shape.circle.radius = atof(temp);
        object.area = object.shape.circle.radius *
            object.shape.circle.radius * PI;
    }
    else if ( strcmp( kind, "parallelogram") == 0 )
    {
        printf( "Enter the base and the height of the");
        printf( " parallelogram on separate lines.\n" );
        temp = gets();
        object.shape.parallelogram.base = atof(temp);
        temp = gets();
        object.shape.parallelogram.height = atof(temp);
        object.area = object.shape.parallelogram.base *
            object.shape.parallelogram.height;
    }
    else if ( strcmp( kind, "triangle") == 0 )
    {
        printf( "Enter the length of the base and height");
        printf( " on separate lines.\n");
        temp = gets();
        object.shape.triangle.base = atof(temp);
        temp = gets();
        object.shape.triangle.height = atof(temp);

        object.area = 0.5 * object.shape.triangle.base *
                object.shape.triangle.height;
```

Program 7.3. (continued)

```
}else if ( strcmp( kind, "none") == 0 )
{
     more = FALSE;
}
else
{
     printf( "Error. No object by that name.\n");
     printf( "Please re-enter.\n");
     error = TRUE;
}
if ( !error && more )
{
     printf( "Area = %f\n", object.area );
}

     } while (error || more);


     exit(0);
}
```

Program 7.3. (continued)

This program uses the gets( ) function, which was also used in Program 7.1. In addition, the function atof( ) is used here to convert a string of characters that represent a floating-point number to a float. This function is included as part of the standard C libraries, and is discussed more completely in Chapter 8.

Notice the union type geometric_shapes. This union has four members, all of which utilize the same storage area. An object of type geometric_shapes will be allocated the number of bytes required by the largest of the members.

7.4 PORTABILITY AND SOFTWARE ENGINEERING ISSUES

The capability of organizing logically related data of various types into one aggregate collection in the form of structures and unions is a powerful mechanism. This abstraction of structures and unions has been extended in the C standard by the ability to assign, to pass as parameters, and to return as function values, in addition to initializing structures and unions. These are valuable abstraction techniques and should be used where possible. However, the programmer should be aware that many older, nonstandard C compilers do not support these operations upon structure and unions. Many of these compilers do not allow a structure to be assigned to another structure, but require a member-by-member assignment. Likewise, they forbid the use of structures as a parameter, permitting only a pointer to a structure to be so used. These older compilers permit the return of a pointer to a structure or union, but not the structure or union itself.

In this chapter, we discuss the various name spaces provided in C. Although it is true that the same name can be used as an identifier for several different purposes as long as those names are in different name spaces, the use of one name for more than one purpose is a poor style that should be avoided. Even though the compiler may be able to differentiate among the various uses, a programmer or reader of the program will have much more difficulty. A better style is to use a unique name for each identifier.

One of the strengths of C is that it provides operators that allow the programmer to access the underlying bit strings that are used to represent data. This can be particularly useful in systems programming or in situations in which the use of memory has to be optimized. (This is considered a strength for systems programming, but the creation of programs that depend upon the execution environment is dangerous and is considered a poor style for the general applications programmer. These techniques should be avoided unless required by the nature of the program.) Unions can be used in such an endeavor by permitting the same data to be viewed in different ways through the various field names. Care should be taken in doing this because most compilers have rules about variable alignment and length. These rules vary from compiler to compiler. A given compiler may require that all variables begin at an even address (a full-word boundary); another may not have this restriction. To achieve these constraints, the lengths of a union may be padded, or various fields may not be aligned as intuition would imply. Thus, accessing the value of a union through one member after assigning the value through a separate member may give unexpected results, and different results with different compilers. The inherent portability problems of such uses of the union are apparent. Some of these problems can be avoided by using the "sizeof" operator to determine the amount of storage that a particular component requires. Casting may also work although some types cannot be cast to each other.

A source of complication in the use of structures is the combination of the unary operators, for example, *, ++, --, with the structure reference operators . and ->. The referencing operators have the highest precedence, with left-to-right associativity; all the unary operators are at the next lower precedence levels and associate right to left. Even with this knowledge of the precedence and associativity, some confusing constructs can be created. The example of Figure 7.16, which is paraphrased from Kernighan and Ritchie, (1978, p. 123), illustrates some of the difficulty.

With these declarations, novices have a tendency to use the expression "*ptr.i" instead of "ptr->i" or "(*ptr).i." The first expression is syntactically incorrect since, because of the precedence, this is equivalent to *(ptr.i).

```
struct int_list
{
    int i;
    int *j;
};

struct int_list node;
struct int_list * ptr;
```

Figure 7.16. A record and a pointer to a record

There are many more combinations that can be quite cryptic and difficult to understand. The expression "++node.i" increments i, not node; "++ptr–>i" increments i, not ptr. This can be seen from the relative precedence. Parentheses change the order so that "(++ptr)–>i" increments ptr before accessing the component i. The expression "ptr–>i++" increments i. The expression "*ptr–>j" fetches the integer to which j points. That is, the referencing operator –> is executed before the indirection operator * because the referencing operator has the highest precedence. To extend this example farther, the expression "*ptr–>j++" increments j after accessing the integer to which it points; "(*ptr–>j)++" increments the integer to which j points; "*ptr++–>y" increments ptr after accessing the integer to which j points. These are confusing combinations that require some thought to decipher. A better approach from a software engineering point of view is to separate these into two or more expressions or to use extra parentheses to clarify the order. For example, the expression "*ptr–>j++" could be broken into two expressions. The first, "*(ptr–>j)," accesses the integer to which j points; the second, "(ptr–>j)++," increments j. (The parenthesis here are not necessary in either expression.) The general rule in programming is that clarity is more important than conciseness. (Another issue that has to be addressed at times is that of efficiency of operations. However, conciseness of expression does not always correspond to efficiency of operations. Efficiency is often a factor of the compiler and the manner in which the object code is generated.)

For an assignment to be made between two variables, those variables must have the same or compatible types. With the simple types such as int, char, float, or double, the meaning of same type is obvious. If i has type int, then j has the same type as i if, and only if, it has type int also. (The meaning of "compatible types" is slightly more complex. This was discussed in detail in Chapter 4.) The definition of when two structures have the same type may not be as clear to the novice. In particular, two structures or unions have the same type if one of the following situations is true.

1. Both are declared in the same statement, that is, in the list (separated by commas) following a structure declaration.

```
struct
{
    int field1;
    float field2;
    char *field[25];
} s1;

struct
{
    int field1;
    float field2;
    char *field[25];
} s2;
```

Figure 7.17. Two structures with different types

2. They are declared with the same structure or union tag.
3. They are declared with the same type name, which was created by a typedef.

For arrays, the conditions are analogous except that condition 2 has no analog as there is no tag for an array.

One implication of this definition is that two *anonymous structures* that have the same member types in the same order, or even the same member names and types in the same order, are not identical types. (An anonymous structure is one that is declared without any tag or without a typedef name.) Thus, in Figure 7.17, the two structures do not have the same type. Thus, the assignment

```
al = a2; /*illegal assignment*/
```

would be illegal.

In Chapter 5, the differences between typedef and #define were introduced. The differences between these two are most apparent when they are used with structures. As a review, remember that #define is a preprocessor directive, and typedef is a keyword of the C language. The typedef creates a new name for an existing type, whereas the preprocessor replaces the identifier created by the #define directive with the corresponding string. The compiler is unaware of the existence of the #define identifier, but assigns a special meaning to typedef names. Because of these differences, their uses overlap, but are not identical, as will be discussed next.

Both the typedef and the #define can be used to create new names for a type, and then to declare a variable with that name. The examples in Figure 7.18 illustrate the manner in which each accomplishes this task. The example on the right is given as a demonstration of the capabilities of #define. The reader is advised to use the typedef form.

```
typedef struct                          #define phone_dir_type struct \
{                                       { \
    char name[25];                          char name[25];\
    char phone_no[10];                      char phone_no[10];\
} phone_dir_type;                       }

phone_dir_type phone_dir;               phone_dir_type phone_dir;
```

Figure 7.18. Typedef and #define used to declare a structure

There are some obvious syntactic differences. (Remember that the #define requires a back slash (\) at the end of a line that is to be continued. Also, the #define does not end with a semicolon as it is not a C statement.) The typedef method is generally preferred from a software engineering perspective. The use of #define requires the programmer and a reader of the program to understand the syntax rules of the preprocessor as well as those of C. In fact, there are situations in which the typedef is the only method of accomplishing a particular declaration, and others in which the #define is the only method. Figure 7.19 illustrates two situations in which the typedef is the only method to use.

All the assignments in the left example of Figure 7.19 are valid. The assignment "dir3 = dir1;" in the right example is not valid as dir3 and dir1 have different types. Their types are different because, after the preprocessor replaces the identifier phone_dir_type with the corresponding structure, these two are declared with separate anonymous structure definitions. The identifiers dir1 and dir2 have the same type as they are declared in the same statement.

The identifiers name1 and name2 in the right example present another problem. These identifiers are declared in the same statement, avoiding the pre-

```
typedef char *name_type;              #define name_type char *
typedef struct                        #define phone_dir_type struct\
{                                     { \
    char name[25];                        char name[25];\
    char phone_no[10];                    char phone_no[10];\
} phone_dir_type;                     }

phone_dir_type dir1, dir2;            phone_dir_type dir1, dir2;
phone_dir_type dir3;                  phone_dir_type dir3;
name_type name1, name2;              name_type name1, name2;

dir2 = dir1;  /* same types */       dir2 = dir1;    /*same type */
dir3 = dir1;  /* same types */       dir3 = dir1;    /* Error! */
name1=name2;  /* same types */       name1 = name2; /* Error! */
```

Figure 7.19. Declaration in which typedef works but #define fails

vious problem. In this situation, the preprocessor replacement yields the declaration

```
char *name1, name2;
```

This gives name1 the type "char *" whereas name2 has the type "char." The typedef does not have this problem as it creates a new type name for "char *." In the left example, both name1 and name 2 have the type "char *." A related problem is that the expression "sizeof (phone_dir_type)" causes a syntax error if the right-hand definition is used, but is correct if the left-hand definition is used.

There are some situations in which the #define can be used and the typedef cannot. In particular, #define allows arguments, as illustrated in Chapter 5. In general, typedef should be used whenever a name for a type is being created; the #define is most useful for general string processing when the string involved is not a type.

Let us reemphasize a point that was made earlier in the chapter. There can be some confusion between the use of a typedef name and a tag from a structure or union. They can be used in analogous manners and for similar purposes. Consider the example in Figure 7.20.

The primary difference is that, in a declaration, a structure tag has to be preceded by the reserved word "struct" whereas the typedef name does not. Neither has a clear advantage in understandability or portability. Some programmers prefer the use of the structure tag since the keyword "struct" is explicitly given. This clearly and explicity documents that the object being declared is a structure. This information is more hidden with the typedef name. Hiding information is a valuable technique in handling complexity. It is often useful to hide the implementation details of an object by using a typedef.

7.5 SUMMARY

Chapter 7 introduces the syntax and semantics of C's heterogeneous aggregate data object type, structures. A structure is aggregate because it is a named collection of several data items; it is heterogeneous since the data items in each such collection can have differing types. The individual components of a structure are called members; the name of a template describing a structure is a tag. This

```
typedef struct {float f; int i;} STRUCT_NAME;
STRUCT_NAME s1;

struct STRUCT_TAG {float f; int i;};
struct STRUCT_TAG s2;
```

Figure 7.20. Typedef versus structure tag

tag can be used in the declaration of multiple structures with the same member names.

The name of a structure serves as an abstraction of that aggregation. Such a structure name can be used as an actual parameter to a function resulting in all the members of the structure being transmitted to the function; two structures declared with the same "struct" statement or with the same tag can be directly assigned to each other. A structure can be initialized as part of its declaration by listing the values in the same order as given in the declaration.

The individual members of a structure can be accessed by means of the dot operator. The result is a composite name consisting of the structure name followed by a dot and then the member name. This composite name is then an identifier of the member and can be used in the same manner as any other identifier of similar type. If an identifier is a pointer to a structure, then the arrow operator should be used as a shorthand to access a member. These two operators are at the highest level of precedence in C.

The second major topic of this chapter was the declaration and use of unions. A union is composed of a group of data elements that occupy the same set of memory locations. A union is most appropriate when a particular logical grouping of data consists of separate types of data, only one of which is in use at a particular time or when the same area of storage must be accessed in two different ways. A union is declared with a syntax similar to that of a structure, except for use of the reserved word "union" rather than "struct." Members of a union are accessed by the same syntax as are members of a structure.

This chapter concluded with an examination of some of the portability and software engineering considerations of the use of structures and unions.

Keywords

anonymous structures	overloading
arrow operator	struct
dot operator	structure
indirection operator	tag
member	union
name space	

References

Cooper, D., and M. Clancy. 1985. *Oh! Pascal!* (2nd ed.) New York: W. W. Norton. This book about Pascal contains a good discussion about Pascal's record variant, which is similar to C's union.

Draft American National Standard x3.159–198x, Programming Language C. This is the ultimate authority on questions of syntax and semantic of the C language. Copies may be obtained from Global Engineering Documents, Inc., 2805 McGaw, Irvine, CA 92714.

Harbison, S. P., and G. L. Steele. 1984. *C Reference Manual,* Englewood Cliffs, N.J.: Prentice-Hall. This book contains a good discussion of name spaces.

Jaeschke, R. 1988. For Certain Uses typedef is Far Superior to #define. C *Users J.* 34–36. InfoPro Systems.

Jensen, K., and N. Wirth. 1974. *Pascal User Manual and Report* (2nd ed.). New York: Springer-Verlag. This book is the a reference manual for the language Pascal written by the designer of the language. It includes a description of the syntax of the record variant, which is similar to C's union.

Kernighan, B., and D. Ritchie. 1978. *The C programming language,* Englewood Cliffs, N.J.: Prentice-Hall.

Discussion Questions

1. What are the software engineering ramifications of using the same name for two members in two separate structures? In general, what are the implications of name overloading? When is it helpful? When is it detrimental?

2. Explain the significance of the four spaces in C. In how many different ways can the same name be used in one function of a C program?

3. What are the advantages of structures over arrays? What are the advantages of arrays over structures?

4. What is the difference between the scope of an identifier and the name space of an identifier?

5. What is the difference between the name of a structure and a structure tag?

6. Under what circumstances is it better to initialize a structure in the declaration than in an assignment statement?

7. What are the advantages of the equivalence of pointers and arrays.

8. Why is the name of an array in C equivalent to a pointer to the array whereas a structure's name is not a pointer?

9. Discuss the use of typedefs versus #defines. How are typedefs superior to #defines for naming types?

Exercises

1. Give the C declarations for a data structure template for a symbol table for a single function in a compiler. This symbol table should be large enough to describe 200 identifiers. Each identifier should be represented by the identifier's name (maximum 30 characters), an integer memory address, and the identifier's type. The types should include int, char, float, and arrays.

2. Create an instance of the data structure in the previous exercise by use of that structure's tag.

3. Refer to the following declarations in answering these questions.

```
struct address_rec
{
    char street[30];
    char city[30];
    char state[3];
    int zip;
};

struct emp_rec
{
    char name[30];
    float salary;
    struct address_rec address;
    int id_no;
}employee;
struct emp_rec company[1000];
struct emp_rec * emp_ptr;
```

For each of the following, tell the type of each variable. If an identifier is not a syntactically valid variable, write "invalid."

Identifier	Type
a. employee	_____
b. emp_rec	_____
c. employee.salary	_____
d. employee.name	_____
e. employee.address.street	_____
f. company.name[7]	_____
g. company[7].name	_____
h. company[1].address.street	_____
i. emp_ptr –> name	_____
j. *emp_ptr.name	_____
k. *(emp_ptr.name)	_____

4. Suppose that the following declarations are given in the context of the declarations of the previous problem.

```
struct emp_rec emp1, emp2;
```

In the most succinct way possible, copy all the values that are held in the members of emp1 to the corresponding members of structure emp2.

5. Give a declaration that initializes the structure employee of Exercise 3.

6. Consider the following declarations.

```
int A[100];
struct s
{
    int i1, i2;
    float f;
    char ch1, ch2;
}st1, * st2;

union u
{
    int i1, i2;
    float f;
    char ch1, ch2;
}un1;

struct s B[20];
```

Suppose that integer and character variables occupy 2 bytes on a particular computer, that floats occupy 4 bytes, and that pointers occupy 2 bytes. How much memory is occupied by each of the following variables? (Assume no padding inside the structures and unions.)

```
A        _____
A[1]     _____
st1      _____
st2      _____
un1      _____
B        _____
```

7. Give the declarations for a structure to describe a professor's grade book. This grade book is to contain each student's name and the student's grades on two midterm examinations, a final examination, 12 homework assignments, and seven computer programs. Store the homework grades and the computer programs in arrays for easy processing. There are no more than 50 students in the class. The examination scores should be represented as floating-point fields; the others as integer fields.

8. Give the declarations for a union that will be used to summarize sports statistics for an individual. For a basketball player, the structure should

contain members for the player's number of free throws attempted, number of free throws made, number of field goals attempted, number of field goals made, number of rebounds, number of steals, and number of assists. For a baseball player, the data to be stored includes the number of times at bat, the number of hits, the number of walks, and the number of runs batted in. For a hockey player, record the number of shots, the number of goals, the number of assists, and the number of minutes penalized.

9. Write a declaration for a union embedded in a structure. The structure describes each employee in a company. For each employee, the following data is required: name, employee identification number, address, telephone number, and work category (hourly or salaried). For hourly employees, additional information is needed about rate of pay, current work station (an integer id), seniority level (number of months of employment here), and the number of days worked in this pay period. For salaried employees, the data needed is the monthly salary, the number of years of education, and job classification (line management, middle management, or executive management).

Programming Problems

1. Write a function that will input the value of the fields for the data for one employee as described in Exercise 9.

2. Write a program to be used by a teacher to determine the final grade average for a class of students. The grade categories for each student are those described in Exercise 7. The final grade percentage should be determined by using the following weights.

Mid-term tests	40%
Final exam	25%
Homework	10%
Computer programs	25%

The program should input the scores from each student by means of a function with the prototype:

```
void get_scores(struct scores *);
```

Use the above weights to determine the student's final percentage. The program should also calculate the class average.

3. Various computer architectures place the bits representing various data into a memory word in varying orders. Some place the byte containing the least significant bits in the right-hand position and others in the left-hand position of

a computer word. Write a C program to determine the order that your compiler uses. One method of doing this, if your computer has a 16-bit word, is to use a union that has an integer for one member and two characters for its second member. Then place a value such as the hexadecimal number 2F, and print out the values of the two characters in hexadecimal. The order in which these values appear will reveal the order in which they were stored in memory. (A similar procedure will work if the word size of your computer is different from 16 bits.)

4. Write a C program to perform fractional arithmetic. This program should allow fractional expressions involving fractions combined with arithmetic operators. For example, the user may input the following:

    2/5 + 6/7

    2/3 / 1/2

    12/5 * 4/3

With this input, the program should print out

    44/35

    4/3

    48/15

The program should read each line and perform the indicated operation and write out the correct fractional answer. These operations should be performed by using integer arithmetic rather than converting to real data. (Notice that the division symbol is used in two ways: as the separator between the numerator and denominator, and also as the division operator.)

Use a structure such as the following to hold the information about each fraction.

```
struct FRACTION
{
    int numerator;
    int denominator
};
```

Write functions for addition, multiplication, and division that each accepts two FRACTIONS as parameters and returns a FRACTION.

5. Write a program consisting of a collection of functions to perform arithmetic operations upon complex numbers and a driver program to test them. These include operations to add, subtract, multiply, and divide two complex numbers. Division of complex numbers is achieved by multiplying by the con-

jugate of the denominator divided by itself. That is, the division $(a + bi)/$ $(c + di)$ is calculated by the following formula:

$$\frac{a + bi}{c + di*} \quad \frac{c - di}{c - di} = \frac{a*c + b*d + (b*c)i - (a*d)i}{c^2 + d^2}$$

There should also be a function to find the absolute value of a complex number. [For the complex number $a + bi$, this is defined to be sqrt($a^2 + b^2$).] Represent each complex number as a structure. Each function should accept an instance of this structure as a parameter.

6. Symbolic differentiation is the process of manipulating the symbols that represent a mathematical function to produce the symbols (the equation) for the function that is the derivative of the original. For polynomials, this is a relatively straightforward procedure based upon these two facts:
   a. The derivative of a sum is the sum of the derivatives, that is, $d(f + g)/dx = df/dx + dg/dx$.
   b. The derivative of a term ax^n is nax^{n-1}.
   Use these facts to write a program that will symbolically differentiate any polynomial of a degree less than or equal to 100. Represent each term of the polynomial as a structure with one member for the coefficient and one for the exponent. The polynomial can then be represented as an array of such members.

7. In graphic applications, it is often useful to know whether two lines intersect. Write a program that will allow the user to describe up to seven lines by giving their two end points. Then report which pairs of lines intersect. For ease in description, allow the user to name each line. (The user may choose such names as "l1" or "l2," or more informative names, such as "side1.") Sorting the lines into horizontal (or vertical) order by their left end point may simplify the algorithm. Represent each line as a structure with members for the name of the line and for each of its end points.

8. You are to simulate the playing of several card games of Clock-Patience. Each preshuffled deck of 52 cards is represented as follows:

   Thirteen cards per line of input.
   Four consecutive lines of input represent one deck.
   Each card is represented by face name and suit where face names are A, 2, 3, 4, 5, 6, 7, 8, 9, T, J, Q, K, and the four suits are S, H, D, C (e.g., AS = ace of spades, 5H = five of hearts, TD = ten of diamonds, and JC = jack of clubs).

   Represent each card as a structure and the deck as an array of card structures.

Deal the cards, one at a time, face down, in a clockwise fashion so they would cover the numbers of a standard analog clock. Begin the deal at one o'clock and proceed to 12 o'clock, then place one card in the center of the clock. Continue to deal in this fashion from the preshuffled deck until all 52 cards are distributed face down.

After all 52 cards have been dealt, begin the game by drawing the top card from the central pile. Place this card face up under the pile that corresponds to its face value on the clock. For example, an ace is placed under the pile at the one o'clock position and the next card is taken from the top of his pile. A jack is placed at 11 o'clock, a queen at 12 o'clock, and a king under the center pile. Whenever you place a card face up on the bottom of a pile, you must remove the top card of that pile and use it as your next card. The game continues in this way until you turn up the fourth king.

For each game your program completes, output the order in which the piles were completed. The output line will contain the symbols for the names of the piles, ordered by the time at which all four of a kind appeared in the pile. Do not place any spaces between the symbols. After each game, skip one blank line, and proceed to simulate the next game. The last line of input will contain a period (.) in the first column.

Sample input:

```
JS7C2H9DQDTD8H6CKD8C3C3D5S
AD4CACQH9C5H8DTC7H2C3SJCKH
9H5C2S4H4S6STS4DKS7D8SQC6H
AHJH3H6D5D2DKCJDTH9SASQS7S
6H7STS4D7CKS9D4S3H5C3D4CAH
2CQD9S4H2H3SKH5SQHJD7D8C7H
KD6C6S2DJSTCJHKC5HTHTD8S9C
8DJC6D8HQC2S5D9HACQSAS3CAD
```

Corresponding output:

```
5QAJ349K
JQ82A6K
```

(This program specification appeared as Problem 1 in the 1984 East Central Region Scholastic Programming Contest.)

9. Write a program that will shuffle a deck of cards. (This program could be used to produce the input for the previous problem.) The output from this program should be a sequence of pairs of characters to represent the deck of 52 cards. Specifically, the output from this program should be in the same form as the input to the previous problem. Again, represent each card as a structure and the deck as an array of card structures. (See Chapter 10 for a

discussion of rand(), the random number generator whose header is specified in the file stdlib.h.)

10. Consider the Cartesian coordinate system consisting of only the nonnegative integers on the plane. Define a *window* W on the plane to be the rectangle whose lower left corner and upper right corners are given by the points (x_{min}, y_{min}) and (x_{max}, y_{max}), respectively. Given the line segment L that connects the points $P_1 = (x_1, y_1)$ and $P_2 = (x_2, y_2)$, determine either
    a. the end points $p_1 = (u_1, v_1)$ and $p_2 = (u_2, v_2)$ of the largest subsegment l (possibly of length zero) of L that lies *on* or within the window W, or
    b. that no segment of L lies *on* or within W.
    Write a program that reads the window W and the line segment L from standard input, and writes W, L, and l to the standard output.
    The input file consists of lines of integers in the form

   $$x_{min}\ x_{max}\ y_{min}\ y_{max}\ x_1\ y_1\ x_2\ y_2$$

    where each integer is right-justified in a column of width eight starting in column one and no integer is more than seven digits.
    For each input line, the program should produce three lines of output conforming exactly to one of the two forms:
    a. If some subsegment of L does lie on or within W, then the three lines should be

   $$x_{min}\ x_{max}\ y_{min}\ y_{max}\ x_1\ y_1\ x_2\ y_2$$

   $$u_1\ \ v_1\ \ u_2\ \ v_2$$
   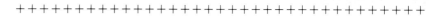

    b. Otherwise, the lines should be:

   $$x_{min}\ x_{max}\ y_{min}\ y_{max}\ x_1\ y_1\ x_2\ y_2$$

No intersection

   ++

Each integer output should appear right-justified and blank-padded on eight column boundaries (i.e., x_{min} is in columns 1–8, x_{max} is in columns 9–16, etc.). The third line contains 64 +'s.

Sample input:
```
    1000    2000    1000    2000    1200    1200    1800    1800
    1000    2000    1000    2000       0       0    3000    3000
    1000    2000    1000    2000       0       0    1000    3000
    1000    2000    1000    2000       0       0    2000    2000
```

Corresponding output:
```
1000  2000  1000  2000  1200  1200  1800  1800
1200  1200  1800  1800
+++++++++++++++++++++++++++++++++++++++++++++++++++
1000  2000  1000  2000     0     0  3000  3000
1000  1000  2000  2000
+++++++++++++++++++++++++++++++++++++++++++++++++++
1000  2000  1000  2000     0     0  1000  3000
No intersection.
+++++++++++++++++++++++++++++++++++++++++++++++++++
1000  2000  1000  2000     0     0  2000  2000
1000  1000  2000  2000
+++++++++++++++++++++++++++++++++++++++++++++++++++
```

Use structures to represent each line, and to represent the window.
(This program specification appeared as Problem 1 in the 1986 East Central
Region Scholastic Programming Contest.)

8 Standard I/O Library

The standard C library contains many functions for performing input and output, both to the screen or keyboard and to files. This chapter will review library usage, and then present many of the commonly used I/O functions. This discussion will include a review of files, file access, and file organization. Next, the various I/O functions are presented according to the following categories: file access, character and line I/O, formatted I/O, direct I/O, file positioning, operations on files, and error handling. The discussion concludes with a discussion of some implementation-specific details of I/O followed by the portability and software engineering sections.

8.1 STANDARD LIBRARIES

In earlier chapters, we noted that the C language designers chose to exclude most data structure operators (such as string operators), all I/O operators, and many of the more complex mathematical operators (such as exponentiation) from the definition of the C language. Instead, these and other capabilities are implemented either as functions that are called from C programs or as macros defined in header files.

An extensive complement of functions designed to fulfill the foregoing needs has been specified by many compiler vendors and in the C language standard. These functions are collected into related sets called libraries. A library, then, is a file consisting of a collection of object modules. Library files are created and maintained by utility programs called library managers. The UNIX program *ar* is an example of a library manager.

Previous chapters have introduced I/O and string functions. This chapter will complete the discussion of the standard I/O library. Subsequent chapters will address the remaining standard libraries.

8.2 HEADER FILES

Library function prototypes and macros associated with function usage are declared in header files that are supplied with each library. For example, the file string.h that was introduced in Chapter 6 supplies the external declarations for the string library functions. Header files also contain #define symbols and macros to go along with a library. Thus, the library header files contain (1) prototype function declarations that specify return type and number of arguments for each function and/or (2) preprocessor directives that create functionlike and objectlike macros that are related to the proper usage of the library functions.

The header file to be used with the I/O library is named stdio.h.

The inclusion of library header files in a programmer's source file is not enforced by the compiler but is strongly encouraged. The header file will supply the proper prototype declarations and preprocessor directives for use of the library. We note here that not all I/O "functions" are implemented as true functions, but instead some may be implemented as functionlike macros. For example, the I/O routine getchar() is often coded in stdio.h as a macro using the #define preprocessor directive. A common example is

```
#define getchar() getc(stdin)   /* example from stdio.h */
```

If stdio.h is included in a source file and the programmer also writes a function prototype declaration for getchar(), such as

```
extern int getchar( void );
```

then a syntax error will be produced by the compiler.

8.3 LINKING THE STANDARD I/O LIBRARY

When using the standard I/O library, it is usually not necessary to specify explicitly the name of this library to the linkage editor. Most C programming environments automatically search this library. There are some PC-based C compilers that require that you specify the name of the standard I/O library when the linkage editor is executed. The documentation supplied with each compiler provides the necessary details for linking.

8.4 FILES AND FILE ACCESS

Streams

The input and output functions allow data to be transferred between a program and external devices in the form of *streams* of bytes. A stream is an ordered sequence of bytes that either originates from (input) or is destined for (output) some device such as a terminal, printer, disk or tape file, or some other peripheral. The host operating system and the C library I/O functions map the diverse physical data representations used by these devices into a logical data stream.

File Access

A file is a named, ordered sequence of bytes stored on a disk or tape device. The contents of a file can be accessed either sequentially or directly. Sequential access refers to the process of serially reading data from start to end in a file. For example, to read byte 10 using sequential access, one would first have to read bytes 1 through 9. Direct access provides a means to go directly to byte 10, for example, without first reading the preceding bytes.

Whether one is doing sequential or direct access, the I/O functions must keep track of the current "position" or byte number within the file so that the next I/O operation is performed in the proper place within the file. C associates an internal file pointer with each open file that "points" to the next byte to be read from a file (for input) or the next available position in the file for writing (for output). For example, if a file is opened for reading, the file pointer is initially set to offset 0 from the start of the file. If 1 byte was read from the file, then the file pointer would be advanced to point to the next byte in the file. For output operations, if a new file is opened and a byte written, then the file pointer would point to offset 1, the second (yet to be written) byte, into the file. Although the file pointer cannot be directly modified, it can be examined and set through the use of the file position functions, to be discussed in this chapter.

File Organization

The bytes in a file can be organized into logically related groups called records. For example, a file that consists of people's names could be organized into fixed-length records 30 bytes long. If ten names were stored in the file, then the file would consist of ten records or 300 bytes of data.

Records can be subdivided into fields. Using the above example, a name record might consist of a ten-character first name field and a 20-character last name field. A more complicated record format might even call for fields of variable length, and thus variable-length records.

When using the I/O functions, it is up to the programmer to map the stream of bytes that compose the file into logical entities such as records and fields. This will be demonstrated in Sections 8.8 and 8.9.

Text and Binary Files

The process of mapping the physical data from a device to the stream of bytes seen by the C program may result in a discrepancy between the data received or written by a C program and that stored on the physical device. This is often the case with text data. A file of text data is usually composed of lines, each of which is composed of printable characters. A problem with this definition is the specification of a line-termination character. C considers lines to be terminated by a new-line character. In contrast, MS-DOS views lines as being terminated by a carriage-return, line-feed pair. Thus, if we are running a C program in an MS-DOS environment, we have a discrepancy between the internal C representation of a line and the external operating system's representation.

The standard C I/O functions allow the programmer to read files in a host OS-independent way, called *text mode,* or in a host dependent manner called *binary mode*. This distinction did not exist on many pre-ANSI compilers such as UNIX-based compilers. If the reader is using a pre-ANSI compiler, these different modes may not be available.

Text mode affords a mapping that provides a consistent translation between the physical representation of lines in the host environment and the C language line conventions (i.e., lines terminated by a new line). This mapping implies that there may not be a one-to-one correspondence between the data that is written or read by the program and that on the physical device. For example, the string "this is a line\n" contains 15 characters, but writing this line to a MS-DOS file in text mode would result in the transmission of 16 characters. When the line is read back into the C program, only 15 characters will be transferred into memory.

In contrast, binary mode guarantees that data read from a stream will correspond to that previously written.

Text mode is used when processing files that consist of printable characters. Binary mode should be used when a file will contain nonprintable data such as numeric values (integers, floats, etc.) in their internal representation (i.e., binary) formats. Binary mode files should also be used when the file is to be accessed directly. Direct access is further considered in Section 8.9.

To use a file in C, the programmer must first gain access to the desired file. This is done using the file-access functions, which are the topic of the next section.

8.5   FILE-ACCESS FUNCTIONS

Files must be opened in order to perform I/O. Opening is the process of requesting services and resources from the host environment that support input and output operations. In C, fopen() provides this service. The syntax of the call is shown in Figure 8.1.

```
FILE *fopen ( char *file_specification, char *mode);
```

Returns a pointer to an object of type FILE, or null
pointer in case of failure. The macro NULL in stdio.h can
be used to represent a null pointer.

Figure 8.1. fopen() function

The string to which file_specification points gives the name of the desired file.
When executed, fopen() makes the necessary requests of the host operating
system to locate the named file. It also associates an instance of a data structure of
type FILE that keeps information about the file, including the internal file pointer
from which (or to which) the next I/O operation will read (or write) data.

The mode parameter is a pointer to a string that specifies the I/O operations that
will be performed on the file. Table 8.1 shows the modes that are specified in the
ANSI standard.

The modes that contain the '+' symbol indicate update mode. This mode
allows a file to be both read and written (without closing and reopening), thus
supporting "update in place" algorithms.

There is a limit to the maximum number of files that may be opened simultaneously. This is usually a function of both the particular C language implementation and the host operating system. In the case of the C language, the

Table 8.1. fopen() Modes

Mode	Description
"r"	Open a text file for reading.
"w"	Create a text file for writing, destroy existing data.
"a"	Open a text file (or create) for writing at the end.
"rb"	Open a binary file for reading.
"wb"	Create a binary file for writing, destroy existing data.
"ab"	Open a binary file (or create) for writing at the end.
"r+"	Open a text file for reading and writing.
"w+"	Open a text file for reading and writing, destroy existing data.
"a+"	Open a text file (or create) for read/write, write at the end.
"r+b" or "rb+"	Open a binary file for reading and writing.
"w+b" or "wb+"	Open a binary file for reading and writing, destroy existing data.
"a+b" or "ab+"	Open a binary file (or create) for read/write, write at the end.

Note: The b (binary) modes are not available on many pre-ANSI compilers.

```
int fclose( FILE *stream);
```

Returns zero if successful; nonzero otherwise.

Figure 8.2. fclose() function

```
int feof(FILE *stream)
```

Returns nonzero (true) if the EOF indicator is set for the stream; otherwise, feof() returns zero (false).

Figure 8.3. feof() function

#define OPEN_MAX (coded in stdio.h) specifies the maximum number of files that can be opened simultaneously. (For pre-ANSI C compilers, OPEN_MAX may be called by a different name.)

Hosted versions of the C language automatically open three streams at program start-up: *standard input, standard output,* and *standard error.* The names of these pointers as declared in stdio.h are *stdin, stdout,* and *stderr,* respectively. Stdin and stdout are used by functions that do not accept a file pointer parameter in the call. Examples that we have used include printf(), scanf(), and getchar(). The standard input is usually the keyboard and the standard output is usually the screen. The standard error, stderr, is used to output diagnostic messages to the user. Some implementations also open other streams such as *stdprn,* the standard printer.

Once I/O to a file is completed, the programmer should "close" the file using the fclose() function, illustrated in Figure 8.2.

The parameter stream must have been previously assigned a pointer of type FILE by a call to fopen(). fclose() causes any buffered data to be written and frees resources in the host environment for use with subsequent fopen() requests. (Discussed in Section 8.11 Buffering of I/O.)

The programmer does not need explicitly to close the standard input, output, and error streams. This is handled by the execution environment.

A function that can be used to check for EOF for files that have been opened for input is feof(). Its prototype is illustrated in Figure 8.3.

The use of feof() will be illustrated in Programs 8.3 and 8.5, after we consider some of the I/O functions.

8.6   CHARACTER AND LINE I/O

The simplest and most versatile form of I/O is character I/O. The functions in this category support transfer of 1 or more bytes of data. We begin by considering those that transfer a single byte of data.

Single Character I/O

Character I/O functions and macros are presented in Table 8.2.

The functions fgetc(), getc(), and getchar() return the next character (if any) from the input stream if successful, or EOF if unsuccessful. fputc(), putc(), and putchar() return the character that was written if successful, EOF otherwise. Likewise, ungetc() returns the pushed character if successful, EOF otherwise.

Notice that getc() and putc() are functionally identical to fgetc() and fputc() but that the implementation of each pair differs; the former pair being macros, the latter functions. The reason for the macro versions is to permit runtime performance optimization. Due to buffering of input and output, the functions fputc() and fgetc() simply retrieve or insert a character into a primary memory buffer in most cases. This requires a relatively small amount of code—perhaps a single line of C code. The overhead of a function call can add substantial overhead to these operations. The macro versions avoid this overhead.

Notice also that the character I/O functions return a value of type int. For end-of-file or I/O errors, this value is a negative integer: EOF (defined in stdio.h). It would be incorrect to treat the return value as a type of char because this negative return value, when stored in a character variable, and later compared to the negative integer EOF, may never result in equality. This potential error is illustrated in Figure 8.4.

Given the incorrect declarations in Figure 8.4, when the int value EOF is returned by getchar(), it will be truncated to a char. Then, for the comparison to EOF, it will be widened back to an int. If the widening does not extend the sign (this is implementation dependent) then the widened value will never equal EOF. Always treat the value returned from the character I/O functions as type int.

Consider Program 8.1. This program reads a file of text and creates a new file containing an encrypted version of the input. Character I/O is used to read and write the two files whose names are specified on the command line.

Table 8.2. Character I/O Functions

int fgetc(FILE *stream)	Get the next character (if present) from the input stream.
int getc(FILE *stream)	A (possibly) macro implementation of fgetc().
int getchar()	getc(stdin);
int fputc(int c, FILE *stream)	Write the character specified by c to the output stream.
int putc(int c, FILE *stream)	A (possibly) macro implementation of fputc().
int putchar(int c)	putc(stdout, c);
int ungetc(int c, FILE *stream)	Push the character c back into the input stream. The character will be input by the next input function call. The character is not actually written into the file, but kept in a buffer. Pushing back more than one character without intervening input operations is not guaranteed to work.

```
        extern char getchar(void)
        char ch;

        while ((ch = getchar()) != EOF)
        {
            /* potential infinite loop */
        }
```

Figure 8.4. Incorrect declaration of getchar() return type

```
#include "stdio.h"

/*
 *  Encryption program:  crypt file1 file2
 *  Encrypt file1, writing the cipher text into file2.
 */

#define crypt( c ) (((c) + 2) % 128)

main( int argc, char *argv[] )
{
    FILE *ip, *op;   /* input and output file pointers */
    int c;           /* input character */

    if (argc != 3)
    {
        printf("crypt file1 file2");
        exit(1);
    }
    if ((ip = fopen(argv[1], "r")) == NULL)
    {
        printf("Cannot open file %s\n",argv[1]);
        exit(2);
    }
    if ((op = fopen(argv[2], "wb")) == NULL)
    {
        printf ("Cannot open file %s\n",argv[2]);
        exit(3);
    }
    while ((c = fgetc( ip )) != EOF)
    {
        fputc( crypt(c), op );
    }
    fclose( ip );
    fclose( op );
    exit(0);
}
```

Program 8.1. File encryption

This program will accept two command-line arguments: a file to encrypt and an output file to hold the cipher text. The program reads the input file one character at a time and encrypts each character. This is done by adding two to each character code (e.g., "a" becomes "c," "l" becomes "3"), with the provision the resulting codes will be in the range 0–127. Once a character is encrypted, it is written to the output file.

Line I/O

The line I/O functions are used to read or write a string of characters up to a new line—hence, the name line I/O. These functions are used with text files. Table 8.3 lists the line I/O functions.

Consider Program 8.2, which is a revision of Program 8.1 using fgets() and fputs(). Program 8.2 is invoked from the command line using two arguments: an input file name to encrypt and an output file name to hold the encrypted file. The program reads the first file a line at a time, encrypts each line (held in the array line), and outputs the encrypted line to the output file. Notice that fgets() returns a NULL pointer on EOF or if an error is encountered. Also notice that the encryption algorithm was modified to avoid inserting a premature null byte into the output line.

Notice that Program 8.1 is more general than Program 8.2 as the first version is not limited by the length of a line.

Table 8.3. Line I/O Functions

```
char *fgets(char *s, int n, FILE *stream)
```
Reads at most n - 1 characters from the stream into the array pointed to by s, or reads up to the next new-line or EOF (whichever comes first). If read, a new-line is retained. A null byte is appended to the data. On EOF, a NULL pointer is returned. If successful, fgets() returns the value of the parameter s.

```
char *gets(char *s)
```
Reads characters from stdin into the array pointed to by s until a new-line or end-of-file is encountered. If read, a new-line is discarded. A null byte is appended to the data. On EOF, a NULL pointer is returned. If successful, gets() returns the value of the parameter s.

```
int fputs(char *s, FILE *stream)
```
Writes to the indicated stream the string to which s points. The terminating null byte is not written. If successful, it returns zero; nonzero for an error.

```
int puts(char *s)
```
Writes to stdout the string to which s points. The null byte is not written, but a new-line [or host-dependent line-terminator character(s)] is written in its place. It returns zero for success and nonzero for an error.

8.7 FORMATTED I/O

Formatted I/O operations provide the facility to convert between internal data representation and characters (ASCII or EBCDIC, depending on the execution environment). The printf() function is a member of the formatted I/O family. This family includes input, output, and internal memory conversion functions.

```c
#include <stdio.h>
#include <ctype.h>

/*
 *  Encryption program:  crypt file1 file2
 *  encrypt file1, writing the text into file2.
 */
#define MAX_LINE 80

main( int argc, char *argv[] )
{
    FILE *ip, *op;          /* input and output file pointers */
    char line[MAX_LINE];    /* line to be encrypted */
    void crypt( char * );

    if (argc != 3)
    {
      printf("crypt file1 file2\n");
      exit(-1);
    }
    if  ((ip = fopen(argv[1], "r")) == NULL)
    {
      printf("Cannot open file %s\n",argv[1]);
      exit(-2);
    }
    if ((op = fopen(argv[2], "w")) == NULL)
    {
      printf("Cannot open file %s\n",argv[2]);
      exit();
    }
    while (fgets(line, (sizeof(line) - 1), ip) != NULL)
    {
      crypt( line );
      fputs(line, op);
    }
    fclose( ip );
```

Program 8.2. Encryption program using fgets() and fputs() (continues)

```
    fclose( op );
}

/*  Encrypt a string of characters */

void crypt( char *sp )
{
    int c;  /* character to encrypt */

    for( c = *sp;  c != '\0'; sp++, c = *sp)
    {
      *sp = (c + 2) % 127 + 1;
    }
    return;
}
```

Program 8.2. (continued)

The formatted I/O functions all have one parameter in common: a format control string. The format control string is used to specify the operation of the formatted I/O function. This string can specify how data is to be converted between internal memory and external representation (e.g., binary to character) and it can specify other characters to be input or output. In the call

```
        printf("The value is %d\n",int_value);
```

the string "The value is %d\n" is an example of a format control string.

Format control strings can be composed of both ordinary characters other than % and conversion specifications that are introduced by the character %. In the printf() example above, %d is a conversion specification and the remainder of the format string is composed of ordinary characters.

In the remainder of this section, we will examine the three sets of formatted I/O functions: input, output, and memory conversion. We will also examine the permissible format control strings for each of these functions.

Formatted Output

The printf() function, a member of this set of functions, is an instance of the more general fprintf() function. The prototype for fprintf() is illustrated in Figure 8.5.

```
int fprintf(FILE *stream, char *format, ...);
```
        Returns the number of characters output or a negative value for an error.

Figure 8.5. fprintf() function

[The function printf() is a call to fprintf() with the stream set to standard output.]

The ellipses (. . .) indicate a list of zero or more arguments. There should be one argument for each conversion specification in the format control string. The function fprintf() outputs to the stream to which the parameter stream points under the control of the format string. For each conversion specification in the format, a corresponding argument value from the optional list is converted to external format and transmitted to the output stream.

The syntax diagram in Figure 8.6 describes the fprintf() format control string. Figure 8.7 presents examples of fprintf calls using various conversion specifications.

FPRINT FORMAT CONTROL STRING

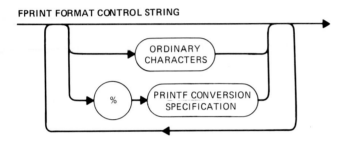

FPRINT CONVERSION SPECIFICATION

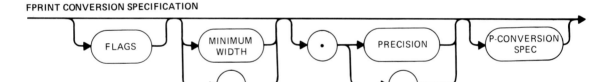

Ordinary characters are simply output as they are encountered.

Width—minimum size of the output field. If the converted value has fewer characters, it will be right-justified with spaces for padding (or left-justified if the - flag is used). Padding character is the space unless (1) the width starts with zero, in which case zeros are used for padding; or (2) a precision is specified, in which case, zeros are used.

Precision for integers: minimum number of digits to output
       for e, E, f (doubles): number of digits after the decimal point
       for g, G (double): maximum number of significant digits
       for s (string): maximum number of characters to output

Figure 8.6.   fprintf() format control string (continues)

FLAGS

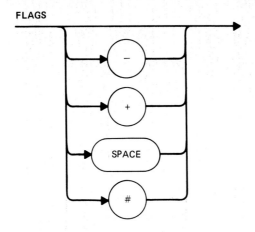

Flags   –   Use left justification
        +   Always begin with a + or – sign (default is – only)
        space   Add a leading space to the result

        #   Alternate form of conversions as follows:
        o   Begin output with a zero
        x   Begin output with 0x
        X   Begin output with 0X
        e, F, f, g, G Always include a decimal point
        g, G   Include trailing zeros

INTEGER SPEC

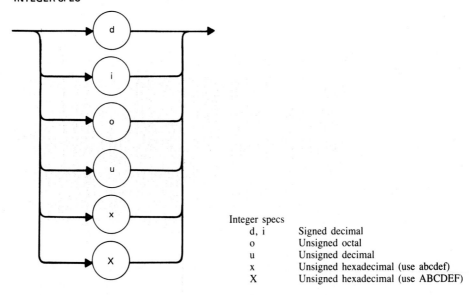

Integer specs
    d, i   Signed decimal
    o   Unsigned octal
    u   Unsigned decimal
    x   Unsigned hexadecimal (use abcdef)
    X   Unsigned hexadecimal (use ABCDEF)

Figure 8.6. (continued)

DOUBLE SPEC

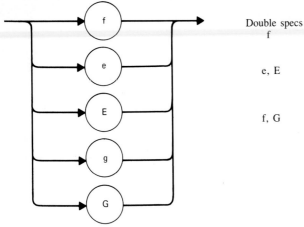

Double specs

f   Use format [–]###.### where the precision spec indicates the number of digits after the decimal. The default precision is six.

e, E   Use scientific notation style, [–]#.###+ or –e## where the precision specifies the number of digits after the decimal. e causes the letter e to introduce the exponent, E uses the letter E. The default precision is six.

f, G   Use either the f spec or e (or E if G is used). e is used if the exponent is less than –4 or greater than the value of the precision spec.

P-CONVERSION SPEC

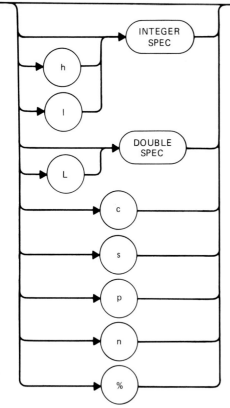

h   The integer argument is a short or unsigned short int.

l   The integer argument is a long int or unsigned long int.

L   The double argument is a long double.

Other specs

c   A char argument is output as a character

s   The argument is a pointer to a string. Characters are output up to the null or the specified precision

p   The argument is a pointer. It is output in an implementation specific manner. U or u is often used if p is not supported in pre-ANSI implementations.

n   Causes no output or conversion. The argument is a pointer to an integer into which is written the number of characters output so far by this printf() call.

%   Output a %. Causes no conversion.

Figure 8.6. (continued)

fprintf() call	Resulting Output
`fprintf(fp,"*%d*\n",123);`	`*123*`
`fprintf(fp,"*%10d*\n",123);`	`*         123*`
`fprintf(fp,"*%-10.5i*\n",123);`	`*00123       *`
`fprintf(fp,"*%x*\n",123);`	`*7b*`
`fprintf(fp,"*%ld*\n",64000L);`	`*64000*`
`fprintf(fp,"*%c*\n",'x');`	`*x*`
`fprintf(fp,"*%5c*\n",'x');`	`*    x*`
`fprintf(fp,"*%s*\n","field");`	`*field*`
`fprintf(fp,"*%10s*\n","field");`	`*     field*`
`fprintf(fp,"*%10.3s*\n","field");`	`*       fie*`
`fprintf(fp,"*%f*\n",123.45);`	`*123.450000*`
`fprintf(fp,"*%10.3f*\n",123.45);`	`*   123.450*`
`fprintf(fp,"*%e*\n",123.45);`	`*1.234500e+002*`
`fprintf(fp,"*%g*\n",1.00053);`	`*1.00053*`

Figure 8.7. Using fprintf()

Formatted Input

The fscanf() function is the input version of fprintf(). It is used to read characters from a stream, convert them to internal representation, and assign those values to parameters. The format control string specifies the conversions to be performed. The prototype for fscanf() is shown in Figure 8.8.

The ellipses indicate that zero or more parameters can follow the format string. These parameters *must be pointers*, because scanf() returns the values that it reads from the input stream into locations specified in the call. As was discussed in Section 6.3, in order to return values through parameters, we must simulate call-by-reference. For example, the fscanf() call

```
fscanf(iptr, "%d", &int_value)
```

would input characters representing a decimal integer value, convert those characters to internal representation, and store the resulting value in the variable int_value. fscanf() thus needs the address of int_value, not its value. A common

```
int fscanf(FILE *stream, char *format, ...);
```

Returns the number of input values assigned, or EOF in case of failure or end-of-file.

Figure 8.8. fprintf() function

error is to call fscanf() with arguments that are not pointers! In the absence of a function prototype declaration for fscanf(), this would not cause a syntax error but would cause an execution-time error.

The function scanf() is an instance of fscanf() that reads from the standard input device. The call

```
scanf("%d", &int_value)
```

would read base-10 digits from the stream stdin, convert these characters into the binary representation of the integer, and store the value in the variable int_value.

The format for the fscanf() format control string is presented in Figure 8.9.

FSCANF FORMAT CONTROL STRING

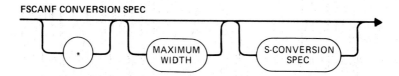

White space   White space in the control string instructs fscanf() to read and discard white space up to the first non-white-space character. Newlines are considered to be white space. Thus, fscanf() will skip blank lines to find its input.

Non-white-space   Characters other than white-space and the % must match the next input character in the stream, otherwise fscanf() terminates and returns to the caller.

FSCANF CONVERSION SPEC

fscanf conversion spec

  Conversion specs are processed by first skipping leading white-space characters (except for the [, c, and n specs). Next, characters that match the spec are processed. If the non-white-space character does not match the spec, processing terminates and fscanf() returns to the caller. Matching characters are processed until either the width is exhausted or until a character that does not match the spec is encountered.

  *   Indicates that the next input value is to be read but its value is skipped (i.e., not returned to the caller). Example: %*d would skip the next integer value in the stream.

  Width   The maximum input field width to be processed.

Figure 8.9. fscanf() format control string (continues)

INTEGER SPEC

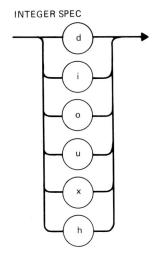

Integer specs

d,i   Input must be an optionally signed decimal integer and receiving parameter must be a pointer to an integer.

o   Input must be an optionally signed octal integer.

u   Input must be an unsigned decimal integer.

x   Input must be an optionally signed hexadecimal integer.

n   Does not read any input, but stores the number of characters read so far by this call to scanf() into the corresponding parameter.

h   May precede the above integer specs. Indicates that the receiving parameter is a short int (default is int).

l   May precede the above integer specs. Indicates that the receiving object type is long (default is int).

L   Same as l.

FLOAT/DOUBLE SPEC

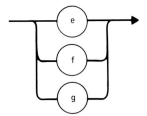

float/double specs

e, f, g   Input must be a floating-point number. A sign may be used.

l   May precede the above float/double specs. Indicates that the receiving parameter is type double (default is float).

L   May precede the above float/double specs. Indicates that the receiving parameter is type long double.

Figure 8.9. (continued)

SCANSET

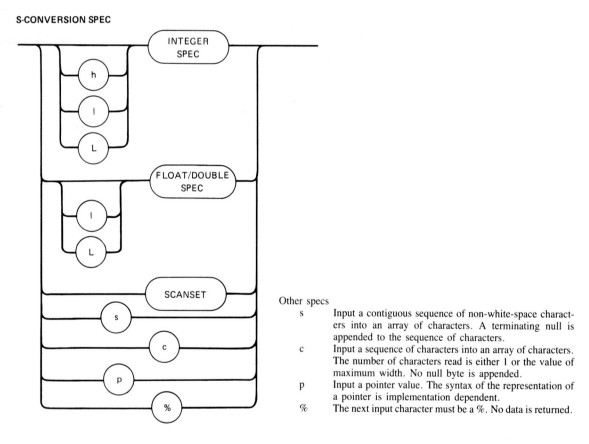

Scanset   The scanset represents a set of possible characters that are to be read into an array of characters. For
           example, [abc] indicates that any sequence of the characters a, b, or c is to be read. The circumflex (^)
           indicates not all of the characters in the scanset. For example, [^abc] would indicate that valid
           characters are all possible characters except a, b, and c.

S-CONVERSION SPEC

Other specs

s   Input a contiguous sequence of non-white-space charact-
        ers into an array of characters. A terminating null is
        appended to the sequence of characters.

c   Input a sequence of characters into an array of characters.
        The number of characters read is either 1 or the value of
        maximum width. No null byte is appended.

p   Input a pointer value. The syntax of the representation of
        a pointer is implementation dependent.

%   The next input character must be a %. No data is returned.

Figure 8.9. (continued)

Figure 8.10 presents some example fscanf() calls and input values. When the format control string contains ordinary characters, these should match the input. For the input line

    It is hot

the fscanf() call

    fscanf(ip,"%s is %s",w1,w2)

would result in the assignment of "It" to the array pointed to by w1 and "hot" to the array addressed by w2. Given the same call and the input line

    It was hot

the w1 array would contain "It," but the input would terminate at "was" because this is a mismatch with the control string. (The w2 array would not be given a value from the call.)

Notice the conversion specification in Figure 8.9 called *scanset*. The scanset specification will control the reading of a specific set of characters into a string. For example, given the input line

    5540099Avery

the fscanf() call

    fscanf(ip,"%[1234567890]%s",w1,w2)

would input the string "5540099" into the w1 array and "Avery" into array w2. The scanset specification %[1234567890] indicates that only characters that match those in the brackets will be input. The fscanf() call

    fscanf(ip,"%[^n]",line)

will read any character into line up to a new-line since the circumflex \n indicates any character except new line.

Input	Parameter Type	Call	Value Assigned to Parameter
25	int ivalue	fscanf(ip,"%d",&ivalue)	25
26.95	float fvalue	facsnf(ip,"%f",&fvalue)	26.95
64000	long lvalue	fscanf(ip,"%ld",&lvalue)	64,000
junk 62	int ivalue	fscanf(ip,%*s%d",&ivalue)	62
abc	char c1,c2,c3	fscanf(ip,"%c%c%c",&c1,&c2,&c3)	c1 = a,c2 = b, c3 = c
Computer	char line[10]	fscanf(ip,"%s",line)	Computer\0
Computer	char line[10]	fscanf(ip,"%5s",line)	Compu\0

Figure 8.10. Using fscanf()

When successful, the functions fscanf() and scanf() return the number of successfully processed fields. If fscanf() or scanf() encounter an input field that does not match the respective conversion specification the scanning operation terminates and the function returns the number of successfully processed fields to that point. The file pointer is still positioned to the start of this last field, thus allowing the field to be rescanned by another call to fscanf() with a more appropriate conversion specification. This fact can be used for error recovery. As an example of this capability, consider the problem of reading a file of records with the following format:

```
name-1 score1 score2 score3 ... scoreN
name-2 score1 ... scoreM
        .
        .
        .
name-X score1 ... scoreQ
```

Each name has an associated list of integral scores, but the number of scores for each name may vary. Program 8.3 uses fscanf() to read each record and compute the average score for each individual. Notice that the call fscanf("%d",&score) is utilized to read the scores. When this call fails to return a value of one, we know that the next name in the file has been encountered. This name can be rescanned using the %s conversion specification.

```c
#include <stdio.h>

main(int argc, char *argv[])
{
    FILE *ip;
    int count, total, score;
    char name[20];

    if (argc != 2)
    {
        printf("Command format is:  avg input-file\n");
        exit(1);
    }

    /* open the input file */
    if ((ip = fopen(argv[1],"r")) == NULL)
    {
        printf("Cannot open input file %s\n",argv[1]);
        exit(2);
    }
```

Program 8.3. Recovering from fscanf() input errors (continues)

```
   while (!feof( ip ))
   {
       /* Read in person's name */
       if (fscanf(ip,"%20s",name) != 1)
       {
         printf("Each line must start with a name\n");
         fclose(ip);
         exit(3);
       }
       /* Read and sum integers until another name is encountered */
       for (total = count = 0; fscanf(ip,"%d",&score) == 1; count++)
       {
         total += score;
       }
       printf("average for %s is %d\n",name,total/count);
   }
   fclose(ip);
   exit(0);
}
```

Program 8.3. (continued)

Internal Memory Conversion

There are two functions that are equivalent to fprintf() and fscanf() except that their output and input, respectively, come from or go to an array in memory instead of a stream. The prototypes for these two functions are presented in Figure 8.11.

Like fprintf(), the operation of sprintf() is controlled by the format control string. Ordinary characters that appear in the control string are stored in the target

```
int sprintf(char *array, char *format, ...)
```

Converts values from the ... list of parameters into characters and stores these characters into the array. Returns the number of characters stored into the array, excluding the terminating null byte.

```
int sscanf(char *array, char *format, ...)
```

Converts characters from the array to internal format and assigns these values to the locations specified in the ... list. Returns EOF if a conversion failure occurs. Otherwise, it returns the number of input items assigned.

Figure 8.11. sprintf() and scanf() functions

array. For any conversion specifications in the control string, corresponding values from the optional parameter list are converted and stored in the array. A null byte is appended to the end of the array of characters.

For sscanf(), the input characters come from the array, are converted according to the control string, and stored to the indicated addresses specified in the optional parameter list.

Program 8.4 illustrates a call to both sprintf() and sscanf(). The output from Program 8.4 is shown in Figure 8.12.

```
#include <stdio.h>
#include <string.h>

main()
{
   int in_int, out_int;
   float in_float, out_float;
   char convert_line[50], out_str[10];
   char *in_str = "test";

   in_int = 10;
   in_float = 3.14;

   sprintf(convert_line, "converted values = %d %f %s\n",
           in_int, in_float, in_str );
   printf("%s", convert_line);

   sscanf(convert_line, "%*s %*s = %d %f %s",
           &out_int, &out_float, out_str );
   printf("out_int = %d, out_float = %f, out_str = %s\n",
           out_int, out_float, out_str);
   exit(0);
}
```

Program 8.4. Using sprintf() and sscanf()

```
converted values = 10 3.140000 test
out_int = 10, out_float = 3.140000, out_str = test
```

Figure 8.12. Output from Program 8.4

Notice that the two %*s conversion specifiers were used in the call to sscanf() to skip the words "converted" and "values" that were stored in the array in_str by the call to sprintf().

8.8 DIRECT I/O

The two functions in this category, fread() and fwrite(), will read or write one or more blocks of data. The prototypes for these two functions are illustrated in Table 8.4.

These two functions will read or write *nblks* of data that are each *size* bytes in length from or to the specified stream. For fread(), the source of the data is the array to which ptr points. For fwrite(), the destination of the data is the array to which ptr points. In other words, fread() and fwrite() will transfer (size * nblks) bytes of data. Notice that the file pointer is the last parameter whereas in previous I/O functions it was the first.

The function fread() returns the number of records successfully read, which is usually equal to the value of the third parameter. The return value will be less than the value of that parameter if end of file is encountered.

The function fwrite() returns the number of records successfully written.

The type of the value returned is size_t. This special type is the type of the sizeof operators. It is defined in many of the standard header files, including stdio.h. For pre-ANSI compilers, fread() and fwrite() will return an integer or some variation of an integer (such as unsigned or long).

Direct I/O functions are useful for reading and writing records from (or to) a file. For example, suppose that we had a parts master file consisting of a record for each part described by the structure in Figure 8.13. One could read and write a record of type MASTER_REC using the following calls:

```
fread(&part_description, sizeof part_description, 1, fp)
fwrite(&part_description, sizeof part_description, 1, fp)
```

Table 8.4. Direct I/O Functions

```
size_t fread(void *ptr, unsigned int size, unsigned int nblks,
                 FILE *stream);
size_t fwrite(void *ptr, unsigned int size, unsigned int nblks,
                 FILE *stream);
```

```
struct PART_DESC_RECORD
{
        int        part_no;
        int        quantity;
        float      price;
};

typedef struct PART_DESC_RECORD MASTER_REC;

MASTER_REC part_description;
```

Figure 8.13. Part record description

The fread() call would transfer (sizeof part_description) bytes from the file indicated by fp into the structure part_description. In similar fashion, the fwrite() call would transfer the same number of bytes to the file indicated by fp from the structure. More than one record could be transferred if a value greater than one were used for the third argument in the above calls, but this would require an array of structures in which to read (or from which to write) the records.

As an example of the usage of fread(), suppose the data for a parts inventory has been stored in a text file. The format of each of the records is

Columns 1–2   Part number
Columns 3–5   Quantity on hand
Columns 6–11   Price

The data file is illustrated in Figure 8.14.

We wish to create a master file containing the data of Figure 8.14 where each record in the master file will be stored as a MASTER_REC type structure (see Figure 8.13). Thus, we need to read the fixed-field input text file and write a file

```
01100125.00
02050075.00
03112007.50
04060012.50
05102017.50
06015150.00
07023023.00
08350001.25
09300002.45
10083275.00
```

Figure 8.14. Hypothetical inventory data using fixed-length fields

of structures. Program 8.5 illustrates such a program, together with an appropriate header file to describe the master file. This code illustrates the use of fscanf(), fprintf(), and fwrite().

Notice that the input file is opened for reading in text mode whereas the output file is opened for writing in binary mode. Binary mode is used because the output is not text, but the binary representation of the various numeric values in the inventory records. We noted above that some pre-ANSI fopen() functions do not distinguish between text and binary modes. In this case, read and write modes are all that are needed.

The functions fread() and fwrite() and the inventory file created by Program 8.5 are further discussed in the next section.

```
contents of master.h:

struct PART_DESC_RECORD
{
  int   part_no;
  int   quantity;
  float price;
};

typedef struct PART_DESC_RECORD MASTER_REC;

#define MAX_RECORDS 10

contents of mkmaster.c

#include <stdio.h>
#include "master.h"

/*
 *  This program creates the parts master file.  The input
 *  is read from a fixed format ASCII file that was keyed to disk.
 *  The output is written as C structures to the master file.
 */
main()
{
  int i = 0;
  MASTER_REC master_rec;
  FILE *in, *out;
```

Program 8.5. Reading text files and writing structures (continues)

```
    if ((in = fopen("master.dat", "r")) == NULL)
{
      fprintf(stderr, "Cannot open master input file\n");
      exit(1);
    }
    if ((out = fopen("parts.mast", "wb")) == NULL)
    {
        fprintf(stderr, "Cannot open master output file\n");
        fclose(in);
        exit(2);
    }
    while (!feof(in))
    {
        i++;
        if (fscanf(in, "%2d%3d%6f", &master_rec.part_no,
            &master_rec.quantity, &master_rec.price) == 3)
        {
          fwrite( &master_rec, sizeof master_rec, 1, out);
        }
        else
        {
          printf(stderr,"Invalid data at record %d\n",i);
          printf(stderr,"Attempting to continue processing\n");
        }
    }
    fprintf(stdout, "%d Records processed\n", i);
    fclose(in);
    fclose(out);
    exit(0);
}
```

Program 8.5. (continued)

8.9 FILE POSITIONING

It is sometimes convenient directly to access a particular set of bytes in a file, without first reading all preceding bytes. This is accomplished by using a *direct* (or *random*) *access* method. As the C I/O functions view a file as a stream of bytes, the method of providing direct access to a file is to provide functions that will position the internal file pointer to a particular byte within the file. Once positioned, the next I/O operation will read or write data beginning with the designated byte. The file-positioning functions are described in Table 8.5.

As an example of direct access, consider the problem of maintaining the inventory master file created by Program 8.5 in the last section. Assume that each month a set of transactions is generated that represent updates to be applied to the master file. For example, two simple transactions might be to (1) change the

Table 8.5. File Positioning Functions

```
int fseek(FILE *stream, long int offset, int whence)
```

Sets the file position indicator for the file designated by stream. For *binary mode* files, the offset can be either relative to the current position or an offset from the start or end of the file. The meaning of the offset is determined by the value of the whence parameter. The possible values for this parameter are #defined in stdio.h using the names shown below.

whence == SEEK_SET from the beginning of the file
whence == SEEK_CUR from the current position in the file
whence == SEEK_END from the end of the file

For text mode files, the offset is either zero or a value returned by the ftell() function.

Notice that binary mode files afford more flexibility in setting the internal file pointer as compared with text mode files. This is due to the possible discrepancy between internal and external representation of text mode files (see Section 8.4). This discrepancy does not exist for binary mode files. fseek() returns nonzero in case of failure.

```
long int ftell(FILE *stream)
```

Returns the current position of the internal file pointer.
Values returned from ftell() can be used in calls to fseek().
ftell() returns -1L in case of failure.

---

quantity for a part and (2) change the price for a part. Transaction records could be stored in a text file using variable-length fields, each delimited by white space. Figure 8.15 illustrates the record format.

Two example records are illustrated below:

```
6 p 66.66      /* change price for part number 6 */
4 q 55         /* change quantity for part number 4 */
```

We will assume that we can have up to MAX_RECORDS number of records in the transaction file and that the record for part_no 1 is stored in the first record of the file, the record for part_no 2 is in the second record, and so on, and the record for part_no MAX_RECORDS in the last record. In this way, we can use the part number from each transaction record as the key directly to locate a record in the master file. This also corresponds to the order of the records in the master file created by Program 8.5.

Notice that we do not require that the transaction records be ordered by part number. Also, there may be zero or more transactions for each master file record.

```
part number <space> transaction code <space> new value
```

Part number	Integer between 1 and 10.
Transaction code	A single character:
	p => update price or q => update quantity.
New value	Either a floating-point value (new price)
	or an integer (new quantity).

Figure 8.15. Transaction file record format

For each transaction record, we need to be able directly to position the internal file pointer in order to read and rewrite records in the master file.

The fseek() function can be used to position, or *seek,* the desired master file record. To use fseek(), we must know the byte number within the file at which the desired record begins. Like array elements, the individual bytes in a file are considered to be offsets into the file. Thus, record 1 begins at byte offset 0 in the file. What is the offset for record 2? It must begin at byte offset sizeof(MASTER_REC), since the first record would occupy byte offset 0 through byte offset sizeof(MASTER_REC) – 1. In general, record number N would begin at offset (N – 1)*sizeof(a master record). To update the master file, we use the following algorithm:

1. fscanf() a transaction record.
2. Using fseek(), position to the master file record indicated by the part_no from the transaction record.
3. fread() the master file record.
4. Change the quantity or the price in the master record.
5. Using fseek(), reposition in the master file to the start of the master record.
6. fwrite() the new master record to the master file.

Notice step 5. It is necessary to reposition to the start of the record to be updated, because after the fread() in step 3, the internal file pointer for the master file will be positioned to the next record past the one to be updated. In essence, we must back up the file pointer in order to fwrite() the update record into the proper position.

Program 8.6 presents an update program that performs the algorithm described above.

```
#include <stdio.h>
#include "master.h"

MASTER_REC master_rec;
```

Program 8.6. Master file update program (continues)

```
main()
{
    FILE *mptr, *tptr;
    MASTER_REC master_rec;
    int trans_part;        /* part number from a transaction record */
    char trans_code;       /* transaction code from a trans. record */
    int trans_qty;         /* transaction quantity */
    float trans_price;     /* transaction price */
    long start_byte;       /* first byte of a master record */
    int count = 0;         /* number of records processed */
    if ((mptr = fopen("parts.mast", "rb+")) == NULL)
    {
        fprintf(stderr,"Cannot open master file\n");
        exit(1);
    }
    if ((tptr = fopen("parts.dat", "r")) == NULL)
    {
        fprintf(stderr,"Cannot open transaction file\n");
        exit(2);
    }
    /* process transaction records */
    while (fscanf(tptr,"%d %c",&trans_part,&trans_code) == 2)
    {
        /* compute the first byte of the desired master record */
        start_byte = (long)(trans_part - 1) *
                    (long)(sizeof master_rec);

        /* seek to the record number in the transaction record */
        if ((fseek(mptr, start_byte, SEEK_SET) == 0) &&
            (fread(&master_rec, sizeof master_rec, 1, mptr) == 1))
        {
            switch (trans_code)
            {
            case 'q': /* update quantity on hand */
                fscanf(tptr,"%d",&trans_qty);
                master_rec.quantity = trans_qty;
                break;
            case 'p': /* update price */
                fscanf(tptr,"%f",&trans_price);
                master_rec.price = trans_price;
                break;
            default:
                printf("invalid code in transaction\n");
                break;
            }
            /* seek back to the record and update it */
            if (fseek(mptr, start_byte, SEEK_SET) != 0)
```

Program 8.6. (continued)

```
      {
        printf("Error seeking back\n");
        exit(3);
      }
      if (fwrite(&master_rec, sizeof master_rec, 1, mptr) != 1)
      {
        printf("Error updating master\n");
        exit(4);
      }
      count++;
    }
    else
    {
      fprintf(stderr,"Error reading master file\n");
      exit(5);
    }
  }
}
fclose(mptr);
fclose(tptr);
fprintf(stdout,"%d records processed\n",count);
exit(0);
}
```

Program 8.6. (continued)

Take note of the code to compute the starting byte offset for a given record and the call to fseek() as follows:

```
/* compute the first byte of the desired master record */
start_byte = (long)(trans_rec.part_no - 1) *
             (long)(sizeof master_rec);

/* seek to the record number in the transaction record */
if ((fseek(mptr, start_byte, SEEK_SET) == 0) &&
    (fread(&master_rec, sizeof master_rec, 1, mptr) == 1))
{
    . . .
}
```

The offset parameter in the fseek() call must have type long int. As the starting byte position could exceed the size of an integer, it is good coding practice to perform the computation of the starting byte using long arithmetic, as was done in the code above. The SEEK_SET parameter in fseek() indicates that the offset parameter is relative to the start of the file. Notice also that the fread() will not be executed if fseek() fails, because of the "short-circuit" property of the && operator.

The reader might question the need for using direct access in the above application. After all, why not sort the transaction file in order of part_ no, make a single sequential pass through both files, and create a second, updated master file? This approach could be more efficient if a large percentage of the master file were to be updated or if the master file was small, as in the above example. However, for a large file with a relatively low percentage of updates, the direct access method would prove more efficient and would not require the creation of a second copy of the large master file.

8.10   OPERATIONS ON FILES

Several functions are provided to create, rename, and remove (delete) files. These functions are outlined in Table 8.6.

These functions are useful for applications that require the use of "work" files. For example, a text editor could create a temporary file to hold a copy of the text

Table 8.6. Operations on Files

```
int remove(char *filename)
```

Deletes the specified file name. Returns zero if successful, nonzero otherwise.

```
int rename(char *old, char *new)
```

Renames the file specified by the string old to the name specified in the string new. Returns zero for success, nonzero for failure.

```
FILE *tmpfile()
```

Creates and opens for update a temporary file that will be automatically deleted when it is closed or the program terminates. Returns a pointer to the stream for the file if successful or a null pointer in case of failure.

```
char *tmpnam(char *array)
```

Generates a file name that is different from any existing files. Generates a different name each time it is called. Two returns are possible: If the array pointer is a null, then tmpnam() returns a pointer to an object in memory containing the new name. If array is not null, the name is returned to that array. The array should be declared as char array[L_tmpnam]. L_tmpnam is defined in stdio.h.

during the edit session. Upon successful completion of the session, the temporary file could be copied over the original file, and then the temporary file would be removed.

8.11 ERROR HANDLING

Error Indicators

Each open stream has associated with it an error indicator and an EOF indicator. These indicators are initially "cleared" (set to zero) after a successful open, and will be "set" by subsequent I/O calls upon detection of an error (for the error indicator) or end-of-file (for the EOF indicator). Several functions are provided that will test, clear, and retrieve the value of the error indicator. These functions are presented in Table 8.7.

Program 8.7 illustrates the operation of ferror() and clearerr(). The program opens a file for writing, attempts to read the file, and in the process tests and clears the error indicator.

The output from Program 8.7 is illustrated in the following.

```
error indicator off
error indicator is on
error indicator is off
```

Table 8.7. Error-Handling Functions

```
void clearerr(FILE *stream)
```

Clears the value of the error indicator for the stream to the value initially set by a successful open().

```
int ferror(FILE *stream)
```

Returns nonzero (true) if the error indicator for stream is set; otherwise it returns zero (false).

```
void perror(const char *s)
```

Using the current value in errno, maps this error code to an error message string. It writes the string to the standard error stream. If the parameter s is not null, then the error message is prepended with the string to which s points, followed by a colon.

```
#include <stdio.h>

main()
{
      FILE *fp;
      int c;

      fp = fopen("dummy", "w");
      if ( !ferror(fp) )
      {
          printf("error indicator off\n");
      }
      /* Attempt to read a file open for writing */
      c = fgetc(fp);
      if ( ferror(fp) )
      {
          printf("error indicator is on\n");
      }
      clearerr(fp);
      if ( !ferror(fp) )
      {
          printf("error indicator is off\n");
      }
      fclose(fp);
      exit(0);

}
```

Program 8.7. Use of error-handling functions

Notice that the error indicator was set by the incorrect getc() call and cleared by the call to clearerr().

Buffering of I/O

The input and output functions presented in this chapter are typically implemented using *buffering*. Buffered I/O works by transferring blocks of data between primary memory in the computer and the I/O device. For example, on input the user must type an entire line before the data is made available to the C program. The line is stored in a buffer, and when the return is entered, the data is made available to the program. Calls to getchar() simply retrieve characters from the buffer. For disk input, an entire block of characters may be read into a buffer when the first fread() is executed, and subsequent calls to fread() may retrieve data from the buffer. For output, data is also buffered. This means that calls to putchar() or fwrite(), for example, may not immediately result in data being displayed or written to the I/O device. The data may be deposited into a buffer and held until the buffer is full, and then written to the device. Buffering provides for optimization of device I/O operations and for keyboard input, it allows the user to backspace to correct errors.

Buffering is usually transparent to the programmer. However, when an execution exception occurs, buffering sometimes becomes noticeable. For example, a program might crash after execution of a printf() call, but no output is seen on the screen. This is so because the output was held in the buffer. Writes to a disk file may not be completed if the program (or the computer system) crashes before a complete block was produced. Another place where buffering is noticeable is in keyboard input. Sometimes buffered keyboard input is not desirable. For example, when writing an interactive video game or a menu system, it is best to have the program react to a single keystroke and not require that a return be entered each time.

The C library provides several functions that can be utilized to control buffering. These are listed in Table 8.8.

The function setbuf() is supplied for compatibility with pre-ANSI compilers. setvbuf() can be used to specify nonbuffered I/O for applications such as the menu or video game discussed above. It can also be used to cause buffering to be done in user-space instead of system-space, if this is necessary for performance reasons.

The function fflush() can be called at critical points in a program to guarantee that output is physically delivered to the device. For example, fflush() is useful to make sure that output is displayed to a user before a particular operation or to assure that critical data base updates are written to disk.

Output written to the standard error stream, stderr, is always unbuffered by default.

8.12 PORTABILITY AND SOFTWARE ENGINEERING ISSUES

In a hosted operating system environment, many of the C I/O functions ultimately will make I/O requests to the host operating system. Operating system constraints can raise a number of portability issues that are discussed in the following.

The number of concurrently open streams is a function of both the C implementation and the host operating system. Each C implementation defines a fixed number of FILE structures. Since one FILE structure is allocated per open stream, the number of available file structures imposes one limit on the number of currently open streams. Operating systems also allocate resources for each open file. The maximum number of open files per user is usually determined at the time the operating system is booted or generated. For C programs that utilize a large number of open files, the C programmer will have to be concerned about these constraints.

Table 8.8. Functions to control buffering

```
void setbuf(FILE *stream, char *buf)
```

The following calls are equivalent.
   setbuf(stream, NULL) setvbuf(stream, NULL, _IONBF, 0);
   setbuf(stream, buf)   setvbuf(stream, buf, _IOFBF, BUFSIZ);
setbuf() returns no value. See setvbuf() for details.

```
int setvbuf(FILE *stream, char *buf, int mode, size_t size);
```

setvbuf() must be called after a file has been opened but prior to performance of any I/O
  operations on the file. It is used to specify the desired type of buffering, using the
  following macros for the *mode* parameter (macros are defined in stdio.h):

     _IOFBF Full buffering. Fill the entire buffer when possible.
     _IOLBF Uses line buffering. Buffers are flushed when new-lines are read or
             written.
     _IONBF No buffering.

If the parameter *buf* is not null, then the array to which it points may be used as the buffer
  instead of the system supplied buffer. The parameter *size* gives the size of this buffer.

    setvbuf() returns zero if successful, nonzero for failure.

```
int fflush(FILE *stream)
```

Causes any buffered data to be written to the stream. Returns nonzero if a write error
  occurs.

Section 8.4 described the differences that are encountered in the representation
of text files on different operating systems. The C I/O routines attempt to mask
these differences (as in line-termination characters). However, writing of
nonprintable characters to text files can result in the transfer of data that cannot
later be read. For example, outputting a control-z to a text file on a UNIX system
causes no problem and that byte can be read later. However, writing a control-z to
a MS-DOS text file will later be interpreted as an EOF, and thus will not be read
back in.

Many pre-ANSI versions of C support a lower level of I/O functions called
system-level I/O. The system-level I/O functions are used as primitives for the file
I/O functions described in this chapter. System-level functions include open(),

close(), read(), write(), and seek(). The reader should refer to his or her C library documentation for a description of these functions.

It is recommended practice to check the return value of all I/O function calls. When writing programs that open files for writing, it is sometimes tempting to assume that fopen() calls and fwrite() calls will never fail. An occasional system or media error, however, could cause even these functions to fail. If the return values are not checked in order to produce reasonable diagnostic messages for the user, the user is left with few clues as to why the program is not working properly. The functions ferror() and perror() can be used to check for and process errors.

Hosted environments that support I/O redirection make it easy to write software tools called filters. A filter is a program that accepts its input from the standard input, performs some processing on the input, and sends the processed data to the standard output. An example of a filter is a sort program. I/O redirection allows the programmer to change the source of the standard input and/or the target of the standard output, without the knowledge of the program. In UNIX and MS-DOS systems, the command

```
sort < file_name
```

would redirect the contents of file_name to the standard input of the sort program. The command

```
sort > file_name
```

would redirect the standard output of the sort program into file_name. The command

```
sort < file_namel > file_name2
```

would redirect both the standard input and output. Finally, I/O redirection usually supports piping that allows filters to be connected together. The command

```
sort < file_name | print
```

would result in a sorting of the contents of file_name and the redirection of the output of sort into the standard input of the print command. Filters like sort and print simply read input from the stream stdin and write output to the stream stdout. The run-time environment takes care of redirecting the assignment of these streams to files or pipes. Single-function filter programs have been used in systems such as UNIX to create a collection of software development tools.

The programmer must verify that library function names, parameters, and return values are in compliance with the standard when porting pre-ANSI programs to the ANSI environment. Several functions, such as fputs(), puts(), fprintf(), printf(), and fflush() have return values which differ between many pre-ANSI and ANSI compliant compilers. Some functions have different parameters. For example the conversion specifiers %i, %p, and %n are new in the

ANSI specification. The fopen() modes that specify binary file I/O are nonexistent or specified differently on pre-ANSI systems. A few functions have been renamed and/or added by the specification. For example, the standard function remove() is called unlink() on many pre-ANSI systems and the functions tempfile() and tmpnam() are new.

8.13   SUMMARY

In C, I/O is carried out by functions (and a few macros) that are stored in the standard I/O library. The header file stdio.h should be included in modules that utilize the standard I/O functions.

The I/O functions read and write *streams* of data. A stream is an ordered sequence of bytes. In most hosted environments, three streams are opened automatically at program start-up time. These are the standard input (stdin), standard output (stdout), and standard error (stderr) streams.

A good variety of I/O functions are contained in the library. Table 8.9 presents a summary of the functions described in this chapter.

Table 8.9. Standard I/O Function Summary

`FILE *fopen(char *file_spec, char *mode)`	Gain access to a file.
`int fclose(FILE *stream)`	Close the stream.
`int fgetc(FILE *stream)` `int getc(FILE *stream)`	Read a character.
`int getchar()`	Read a character from stdin.
`int fputc(int c, FILE *stream)` `int putc(int c, FILE *stream)`	Write a character.
`int putchar (int c)`	Write a character to stdout.
`char *fgets(char *array, int n, FILE *stream)`	Read a line.
`char *gets(char *array)`	Read a line from stdin.

(continued)

Table 8.9. (continued)

`int fputs(char *array, FILE *stream)`	Write a line.
`int fputs(char *array)`	Write a line to stdout.
`int ungetc(int c, FILE *stream)`	Put a character back into the input stream.
`size_t fread(void *array, unsigned int size,` `        unsigned int nblks, FILE *stream)`	Read nblk blocks of size bytes into array.
`size_t fwrite(void *array, unsigned int size,` `        unsigned int nblks, FILE *stream)`	Write nblk blocks of size bytes from array.
`int fseek(FILE *stream, long int offset,` `        int whence)`	Set the internal file pointer for stream.
`long int ftell(FILE *stream)`	Get the current value of the internal file pointer.
`int fprintf(FILE *stream, char *format, ...)`	Formatted output.
`int fscanf(FILE *stream, char *format, ...)`	Formatted input.
`int sprintf(char *array, char *format, ...)`	In-memory conversion to characters.
`int sscanf(char *array, char *format, ...)`	In-memory conversion of values.
`void clearerr(FILE *stream)`	Clear the file error indicator.
`int feof(FILE *stream)`	Test the end-of-file indicator.
`int ferror(FILE *stream)`	Test the file error indicator.
`int perror(const char *s)`	Map errno to an error message.

(continued)

Table 8.9. (continued)

`void setbuf(FILE *stream, char *buf)`	Set buffering mode.
`int setvbuf(FILE *stream, char *buf,` `        int mode, size_t size)`	Set buffering mode.
`int fflush(FILE *stream)`	Causes any buffered data to be written to the stream.
`int remove(char *filename)`	Delete the specified file name.
`int rename(char *old, char *new)`	Renames a file.
`FILE *tmpfile()`	Creates and opens a temporary file.
`char *tmpnam(char *array)`	Generates a file name that is different from any existing files.

The C I/O functions support two varieties of files: binary and text. Text files are useful for storing printable text. Binary files are best for storing values in their internal formats and other nonprintable values. Binary files are also best for files that will be accessed using direct access functions such as fseek().

Keywords

access method
binary mode file
buffered I/O
character I/O
conversion specification
direct I/O
fields
FILE pointer
file position
filters

format control string
formatted I/O
line I/O
records
standard error
standard input
standard output
streams
text mode files
update mode

References

Draft American National Standard X3.159-198x, Programming Language C, 1987. Copies may be obtained from Global Engineering Documents, Inc., 2805 Irvine, CA 92714 (1-800-854-7179).

Horspool, R. N. 1986. *C Programming in the Berkeley UNIX Environment*. Scarborough, Ont.: Prentice-Hall, Page 109 discusses fflush().

Stevens, A. 1987. C as a Data Definition and Manipulation Language. *C Users J*. 3(2): 13–23. Info-Pro Systems, Denville, N.J.

Vernon, V. 1987. The Human Interface Data Input and Validation Using C, *C Users J*. 3(2): 36–44. Info-Pro Systems, Denville, N.J.

Discussion Questions

1. Discuss the contents of stdio.h. Examine the declaration of the I/O functions. Locate I/O "functions" that are implemented as macros.

2. Most operating systems perform buffering on I/O. For example, when performing input operations, an entire line (for terminals) or an entire block (for disk files) may be read into an internal memory buffer, even though the programmer requested only a single byte. Subsequent I/O operations may retrieve the bytes from the buffer. For output, data may be inserted into a buffer and, at a later time, transmitted to the output device. What might be the advantages of buffering I/O? For output operations, what might be a disadvantage?

3. On multiprogramming operating systems, it is conceivable that a single file may be opened and read or written by more than a single program. What might be the consequences of multiple updates to a file? What would be needed in order to make such access possible?

4. Discuss the implementation of variable-length records in a file. What sort of information would be needed in order to store and later retrieve variable-length records? What would be the implications for file update algorithms if variable-length records were used?

5. In the text, we discussed the idea of connecting filters using I/O redirection to form more powerful programs. For example, the command

   ```
   sort | print
   ```

   was discussed. I/O redirection redirects stdin and stdout, but not stedrr. Why should stderr not be redirected the same as stdout?

6. Program 8.6 in this chapter made the assumption that the part number for each part record corresponds to the record number in the file for each part. In general, record keys such as part number cannot be mapped directly to a

record number in a one-to-one fashion. For example, given a person's Social Security number as key, a file would require 999,999,999 records in order to use the one-to-one mapping between keys and records. Discuss alternative ways of mapping record keys to record numbers for cases such as the Social Security number key.

Exercises

1. Below is a list of I/O and file operations. To the right of each operation, list the standard I/O function (or functions) used to carry out the operation.

Operation	Function
Close a file and free the FILE information.	fclose()
Position the internal file pointer.	_____
Open a file and allocate FILE information.	_____
Input a line from a text file.	_____
Input a block of characters from a file.	_____
Write a line to a file.	_____
Write a single character to a file.	_____
Write a block of characters to a file.	_____
Return a character to the input stream.	_____
Get the value of the internal file pointer.	_____
Input characters and convert to internal representation.	_____
Convert from internal representation to characters and output values.	_____
Convert from internal representation to characters and store the characters into an array.	_____
Convert values stored in an array of characters to internal values and assign the values to variables in memory.	_____

2. Identify the purpose of the following fopen() mode parameters.

Parameter	Purpose
"rb"	
"r"	
"wb"	
"w"	
"ab"	
"a"	
"r+"	
"w+"	
"rb+"	
"wb+"	

3. The function getchar() reads from the stream _____. The function putchar() writes to the stream _____.

4. Suppose that a record contains the following information:
   3-digit part number
   23-character part description
   6-character price
   Write a structure declaration to describe this record. Allow room for a null byte where appropriate.

5. For the record described in Exercise 4, write an expression that will determine the value of the offset parameter for a call to fseek(). For example, if the variable record_no contains a record number in the range of 1–N, write an expression that will give the offset of the first byte of the given record number.

6. The optional list of parameters in the fprintf() call are values to be output, whereas the optional list in fscanf() are pointers. Why is this distinction necessary?

7. List the fprintf() conversion specification that would be used to output a value of each of the types listed below.

Type	fprintf() conversion spec
Signed decimal integer	_____
Unsigned decimal integer	_____
Unsigned octal integer	_____
Unsigned hex integer	_____
Double, use ###.### format	_____
Output a character	_____
Output a string	_____

8. The fscanf() conversion specs %d, %x, and %o are all used to input integers. Explain the differences in meaning among these three conversion specs.

Programming Problems

1. Using the character I/O functions, write implementations of the fread() and fwrite(). Then use fread() and fwrite() to implement the character I/O functions getchar() and putchar().

2. Write a program that will read the cipher text produced by Program 8.1 and provide clear text. Send the output to the standard output stream. Your program should use character I/O functions.

3. Write a program that will read the cipher text produced by Program 8.2. Can you use the line I/O functions to read the encrypted file? Output the results to the standard output.

4. Consider the following input data:

001Pressure switch	015.90
002Ram	034.00
003Check valve	022.15
004Gauge	115.50
005Pump	251.25
006Hydraulic motor	331.10
007Electric motor	127.00
008Strainer	015.25
009Tank	780.00
010Filter	062.40
011U-tube	110.00
012Union tee	012.00
013Union straight	010.00
014Double-rod cylinder	043.50
015Piston motor	625.00
016Pneumatic silencer	039.75
017Fluidic indicator	042.00
018Temperature switch	127.00
019Probe	080.50
020Servo	110.00

Enter this data into a text file using an editor. Write a C program that will read the text file and produce a master parts file that has the following format.

3-digit part number
23-character description
6-digit floating point price
4-digit integer giving the quantity on hand

Code a structure to represent the records and write the records using the structure. Initialize the quantity on hand to zero. Write another C program that will read the master file and produce a report showing the information in the file. Your report should include a title and column headings.

5. Modify Program 8.6 so that it uses the transaction records described in Figure 8.14 to update the master file in Problem 4. Produce a file of test transactions, and use the report generator program from Problem 4 to verify that your program is operating correctly.

6. Suppose that the part numbers for the master file described in Problem 4 are given by the data shown below.

101Pressure switch	015.90
802Ram	034.00
740Check valve	022.15
220Gauge	115.50
110Pump	251.25
301Hydraulic motor	331.10
222Electric motor	127.00
203Strainer	015.25
430Tank	780.00
343Filter	062.40
111U-tube	110.00
012Union tee	012.00
442Union straight	010.00
510Double-rod cylinder	043.50
487Piston motor	625.00
605Pneumatic silencer	039.75
733Fluidic indicator	042.00
055Temperature switch	127.00
193Probe	080.50
551Servo	110.00

Write programs to build a master file using the record structure described in Problem 4, generate a report, and update the file using transaction records similar to those in Figure 8.14. You may not allocate 999 records to the master file, but you may allocate between 20 and 100 records to the file. You should develop an algorithm to map the record keys shown to a record number in the master file. Develop a set of test transactions to test your update program.

7. Modify Program 7.1 so that it reads a file of book information from a text file and builds the bibliography from that data. Design the input file and use fscanf() or another input function to read it. Read the data, build the bibliography, and test it by attempting to retrieve information from the bibliography.

8. Write a mailing-list processing program. The program will be a menu-driven system that will allow the user to add new mailing addresses, erase addresses, find a subset or all addresses according to particular keys, save and load addresses to and from disk, display addresses on the screen, and output mailing label information to a disk file for later printing. The system should maintain the addresses in ascending order by last name, so that at any instant information will be displayed in sorted order.

Address information should be stored in the program using an array of structures. Each structure should contain the following information:

Last name	15 printable characters
First name	20 printable characters
Street1	30 printable characters
Street2	30 printable characters
City	20 printable characters
State	2-character abbreviation
Zip	99999 (old) zip code format

The program should allow storage of up to 100 address records.

The menu should support the following commands: Add address, Erase address, Find addresses, Save addresses to disk, Load addresses from disk, Display currently selected addresses, Print labels for currently selected addresses (to disk), Quit address processing. Choices from the menu should be selectable using the first letter of each of the menu picks: A/a, E/e, F/f, S/s, L/l, D/d, P/p, Q/q.

The following are some specifics about each command:

Add	Prompts the user for each field. Following entry of the information, the user should be asked to confirm that the information is correct so that erroneous addresses are not entered into the list. Add will then insert the new record into the list such that the records are maintained in ascending order by last name.
Erase	Prompts for last name. Displays the first match and prompts for delete confirmation. If positive confirmation is given, the address is deleted and the command is done. If the negative confirmation is given, the search continues to the next match or to the end of the list. After a deletion, the list should be compressed.
Find	Selects either all or a subset of records from the list for use by display and print. Each find overwrites any previous "find list." Find will prompt the user for the selection key, which is either last name, Zip code, or all.
Save	Prompts the user for a file name and then writes all addresses into the specified file.
Load	Prompts the user for a file name and then loads the addresses from the specified file.
Display	Displays all addresses selected by the last Find command.
Print	Prompts the user for a file name and then "prints" formatted labels into the file. Labels should be formatted and output so that each address is printed using four lines of output with three or four blank lines separating each label. The second street address line should be skipped if it does not contain information. First and last names should be concatenated with a space between

them. City and state are separated with a comma, followed by three spaces and the Zip code. Examples are shown below:

William French   Mike Mitchell
Blackburn Hall   305 Main St.
State University   Ohio Ave, OH   44550
Columbus, OH   42200

Quit   Leaves the address processing system.

The system should be written using at least two separately compiled modules. These modules are described below.

Module 1: List Processing Module

This module "hides" two list data structures and provides all operations on the lists. The lists are declared as static in this module. The lists are designated as list 1 and list 2. The module has the following functions:

```
int intaddr(int list)
```

Initializes list 0 or list 1. Returns 1 or 0 (checks for valid list values). 0 indicates failure, 1 indicates success.

```
int addaddr(struct ADDR *ap, int list)
```

Adds an address to list 0 or 1. Returns 1 or 0. Checks for valid list parameter values and room in the list.

```
int deladdr(int rec, int list)
```

Deletes record number rec from the specified list. Checks for valid parameters, returning 0 or 1 accordingly.

```
int getaddr(struct ADDR *ap, int rec, int list)
```

Stores the address specified by rec from list into the address structure indicated by ap. Returns 0 or 1 if the parameters are correct.

```
int getqty(int list)
```

Returns the number of records in list 0 or 1. Returns 0 if an invalid value of list is passed.

Code the address structure (ADDR), function prototype declarations, and the size of all arrays using macros in the header file list.h. list.h must not include declarations of actual data.

Module 2: Command Module

This module includes the functions main(), add(), erase(), find(), store(), load(), display(), and plabel(). These functions control the processing of a menu selection except for plabel(). plabel() is used by the other functions to output a formatted label to the screen or to the "print" file. The prototype for plabel() is

```
void plabel(struct ADDR *ap, FILE *fp)
```

fp is either a file pointer for an open file or the standard output stream *stdout*.

The command module functions use the list module functions to carry out their operations. For example, the pseudocode for the find command might be

```
intaddr(1);  /* initialize list 1 -- holds selected records */

n = getqty(0);

/* For each record in list 0, see if it meets the
 * selection criterion. If it does, add it to list 1.
 */
for (i = n; i < n; i++)
{
  getaddr( &address, i, 0);
  if (address meets the criterion)
  {
      addaddr( &address, 1);
  }
}
```

An advantage of this design is that the list data structure can be changed, and as long as the prototype of the list functions remains the same, the command module will remain unchanged. For example, linked lists or files can be used to store the lists and the command module functions will remain unaffected.

9. Suppose that a file exists that has records with the following format and data:

```
Course name     Enrollment and instructor for each section

SAN151 30 Smith 27 Sanders 23 Williams
SAN174 22 Jenkins 32 Walters 29 Jennings 24 Denning
       19 Jones 34 Sanders 22 Foster
SAN281 19 Fisher
SAN373 31 Foster 23 Gupta
SAN475 25 Smith 18 Wilson 22 Jennings 19 Jaworski
```

Write a program that will read a file of data as shown above and compute and output the average section enrollment for each course. Use fscanf() to read the data file. Notice that there are a variable number of sections per course and that data for a course may span lines.

9

Miscellaneous Operators, Types, and Statements

This chapter consists of a collection of less-used but valuable concepts in the C programming language. These concepts fall primarily into the category of additional types and new operators. In particular, the subjects of this chapter are (1) bit fields and bitwise operators, (2) additional types, and (3) the null statement.

Bit fields give a method of referring to one or a small number of bits as a part of a structure. Bitwise operators are a collection of operators that can be applied to bit fields as well as to other integer variables. These operators differ from other integer operators in that they operate on 1 bit at a time. These operators are the bitwise AND, OR, XOR, the complement operator, the shift operators, and the assignment operators.

The additional types discussed in this chapter are enumerated constants, the constant, volatile, and noalias type qualifiers, and the register storage class specifier. The specific purpose of each will be discussed in that section.

The last syntactic element to be discussed in this chapter is the null statement. The null statement is the statement in C that specifies an empty statement. Uses of this statement will be illustrated.

This chapter concludes with comments relating to software engineering and portability considerations.

9.1 BIT FIELDS AND BITWISE OPERATORS

C allows much greater access to the execution environment than do most high-level languages. This is a great benefit to systems programmer who must be concerned about an efficient mapping of an algorithm to the execution environment. This section presents a type that allows access to, and a group of operators that permit manipulation of, individual bits (binary digits). Most high-level languages choose to give the programmer only a more abstract view of the computer's memory by hiding the implementation of the bits. In permitting access to bits, C makes it possible to efficiently perform bit operations that generally require the use of assembly language. However, this flexibility introduces the possibility of misuse by general applications programmers. It is quite easy to

318

create programs that are not portable because of dependence upon features of the underlying execution environment.

Bit Fields

Bit fields allow the programmer to give a name (as part of a structure) to a single bit or a short sequence of bits. Programmers often perceive that this can permit a level of storage efficiency that is not possible in many other high-level programming languages. (This perception is not always accurate. Optimizing compilers often do a better job of producing efficient programs than the programmer.) For example, if a group of boolean flags are needed, they can all be packed into a single word of memory. The value of each bit can be individually set or tested as needed. The same purpose can be accomplished less efficiently by using a separate integer for each boolean flag.

A bit field is declared as a member of a structure or union. It is syntactically differentiated from other kinds of fields by the presence of a colon and a field width. (See Figure 9.1.)

The type of a bit field must be one of the integral types (int, unsigned int, or signed int). Unsigned int is recommended. The field width specifies the number of bits in the field. This width must be a nonnegative integer constant and it cannot be greater than the number of bits in an ordinary object of the same type. This maximum is implementation dependent, and generally is determined by the word size of the underlying hardware. If an int variable normally occupies 16 bits, then an int bit field can be at most 16 bits long.

The example in Figure 9.1 illustrates the use of bit fields as boolean variables. To reference the value of a particular bit field, the usual structure member reference notation is used: symbol_table_entry[i].is_extern. This example also demonstrates that bit fields and normal fields may be mixed in one structure. Now consider Figure 9.2, which is a refinement of Figure 9.1.

The typedef boolean has been added to Figure 9.2 as a means of self-documentation. One of these fields could be referenced in the following manner:

```
struct SYMBOLS
{
    unsigned int is_reserved_word : 1;
    unsigned int is_variable : 1;
    unsigned int is_extern : 1;
    unsigned int is_static : 1;
    char * token;
} symbol_table_entry[100];
```

Figure 9.1. Declaration of bit fields

```
#define TRUE 1
#define FALSE 0

typedef unsigned int boolean;

struct SYMBOLS
{
    boolean is_keyword : 1;
    boolean is_variable : 1;
    boolean is_extern : 1;
    boolean is_static : 1;
    char * token;
} symbol_table_entry[1000];
```

Figure 9.2. Boolean bit fields

```
symbol_table[707].is_extern = TRUE;
if (symbol_table[123].is_variable == FALSE)
{
    /*if body*/
}
```

This is an excellent use of the bit fields that does not suffer from portability problems and adds some storage efficiency. (Any compiler, regardless of the word size, will be able to refer to 1 bit. Since there is no interaction among the various boolean bit fields, the mapping of this structure into the execution environment will not affect the use of these fields. With larger bit fields, implementation details can produce portability problems.)

Recall that the members of the structures in Figures 9.1 and 9.2 contain a mixture of bit- and nonbit-field members. The allocation of these members to storage is implementation dependent because nonbit fields often require alignment on a byte or word boundary. This is a requirement of many execution machines. If we assume that the member token in Figure 9.2 requires word alignment and that it requires one word of storage, then an instance of the SYMBOLS structure will require two words of memory, one for the packed bit fields and one for the pointer. This leaves unallocated bits in the first word. These unused bits are collectively referred to as a "hole."

The unit of storage to which bit fields are allocated is implementation dependent. Bit fields may be packed, for example, into a byte or a word. A word is the most common unit. In that case, each bit field will be packed into a word, but if there is insufficient space in a word for the next bit field, the remaining bits of that word are skipped and the next field is allocated to the next word of memory. Consider Figure 9.3.

Assume that a word is 16 bits. In Figure 9.3, field1 is allocated to 9 bits of a

```
struct
{
    int field1 :  9;
    int field2 : 11;
} struct_with_holes;
```

Figure 9.3. Holes in a structure

word of memory, but field2 cannot be packed into that same word. This bit field is allocated to a second word, leaving a 7-bit "hole" in the first word.

An unnamed bit field with a width of 0 indicates that the remainder of the current unit of memory should be unused. The next field is to begin in a new memory boundary. This allows the programmer to control the placement of bits and "holes" in a structure. See Figure 9.4.

The example of Figure 9.4 differs from that of Figure 9.1 in that the unnamed field forces the next bit field, is_external, to be allocated in another word of memory. The remainder of the first word is unused. (There is no good reason to waste this space in this case. This example is just used to indicate the syntax and semantics of a zero-width field.) This type of alignment is most useful to map a bit field to a particular portion of a memory word. For example, a system program may need to manipulate a particular bit of an interrupt vector or status register.

Bit fields can be assigned a value as in "symbol_table_entry[1].is_external = TRUE," but bit fields are not lvalues. This means that the address operator cannot be applied to a bit field. This makes sense as most computers have an address for each word, or perhaps each byte, of memory, but not for each bit of memory.

The code in Figure 9.5 demonstrates a use of bit fields to hold a character and attribute information about the display of that character. The character to be displayed is stored in the member char_info.ch. The member char_info.blink is a 1-bit field to denote whether or not that character is to blink when displayed. The member char_info.background is a 3-bit field that is used to specify one


```
struct
{
    unsigned int is_reserved_word : 1;
    unsigned int is_variable      : 1;
    unsigned int                  : 0;
    unsigned int is_extern        : 1;
    unsigned int is_static        : 1;
    char * token;
} symbol_table_entry[100];
```

Figure 9.4. Bit fields for alignment

```
struct
{
    unsigned int blink          : 1;
    unsigned int background     : 3;
    unsigned int intensity      : 1;
    unsigned int foreground     : 3;
    unsigned int   ch           : 8;
} char_info;
```

Figure 9.5. Bit fields for character attributes

of eight colors to be used for the background for that character. The field char_info.foreground is a similar 3-bit field that specifies the color for the character itself. The 1-bit field char_info.intensity determines whether the character is to be displayed in normal or high intensity.

Bitwise Operators

The purpose of the *bitwise operators* is to manipulate individual bits of memory. They are permitted only on the integer types, including bit fields. The value of one particular bit can be set to a specific value (0 or 1), or examined to determine its value.

First we discuss the *bitwise AND (&), OR (|), and EXCLUSIVE OR (^)*. These should not be confused with the logical AND (&&) and OR (| |) operators that treat the value of a variable as a single operand, rather than operating upon individual bits.

The bitwise AND operator performs an AND operation upon each bit of its right operand with the corresponding bit of the left operand. Thus, if the int variable x has the value 796 that has the binary representation 0000001100011100_2 on a machine with a 16-bit word size, and if y has the value 279 that has the binary representation 0000000100010111_2, then the expression "x & y" has the value 276, or 0000000100010100_2 in binary. This value has a one in each position in which both of the operands have a one, and a zero elsewhere.

The bitwise OR performs analogously. The expression "x | y" has the value 799, which is 0000001100011111_2 in binary, if x and y have the values specified in the previous paragraph. That is, the value of this expression is achieved by putting a one in each location in which either x or y, or both, have a one, with zeros elsewhere. The exclusive or differs in that a one is produced in a given position if either operand has a one in that position, but not both. Therefore, in the above context, "x ^ y" has the value 523 or binary 0000001000001011_2.

The AND operator is useful for "testing" for the presence of one bits or for setting bits to zero. This process of setting to zero is called "masking." As a more practical example, consider the situation in which characters are represented by the ASCII coding scheme, and are transmitted with an odd parity bit as the eighth (left-most) bit. In the internal processing, this parity bit needs to be removed. If the character is stored in variable c, the bit is masked by the statement

```
c = c&'\x7f';
```

as the hexadecimal constant 7f has the binary representation 01111111. If c has the value 'M', which is binary 11001101 in ASCII with odd parity, the above statement produces 01001101, which is ASCII for 'M' with no parity.

The OR operator, sometimes called inclusive or, is useful for setting bits, that is, for forcing a particular bit to be one. As a practical example, remember that the difference between the ASCII representation for uppercase and lowercase characters is that the sixth bit is one for the lowercase characters and zero for the uppercase. Thus, the ASCII code for 'A' is 01000001_2, whereas that for 'a' is 01100001_2. If the character variable contains any character, the statement "c=c | 32" converts that character to the corresponding lowercase character. (Note that $32 = 00100000_2$.) This statement works correctly no matter what character (uppercase or lowercase) c contained before this statement. To convert from lowercase to uppercase, use the AND operator a = a & '\xDF'. These statements should be well commented to explain their purpose, and to reveal the reason for the number 32.

Two other useful bitwise operators are the left and right *shift operators*. The left shift operator shifts the bit string of the left operator to the left. The right operand specifies the number of positions to shift. The token for this left shift operator is <<. If the int variable i has the value $796 = 0000001100011100_2$, then i = i << 4 gives the value $0011000111000000_2 = 12736$. The bits shifted into the left by the left shift operator are always zero. The right operand, which specifies the number of positions to shift, should always be an integer expression with a nonnegative value. The interpretation for negative shift values is implementation dependent. (Notice that shifting to the left multiplies the operand by 2 for each bit position shifted. This is a faster method of multiplication by a power of 2 than the use of the multiplication operator *, although some execution environments may implement the multiplication operator by shifting.)

The right shift operator >> is analogous to the left shift with a change in direction of the shift. If the operand to be shifted is an unsigned integer, the bits shifted in on the left are zeros. As an example, suppose that the unsigned int variable x has the value $671 = 0000001010011111_2$ on a machine with a 16-bit word size. The result of the expression x = x >> 3 is to give x the value $83 = 0000000001010011_2$. Note that this is the integer answer that is achieved by dividing 671 by $8 = 2^3$.

If the operand is signed, the result of a right shift is implementation dependent. The implementation may shift in zeros on the left as with unsigned; some implementations may choose to drag the sign. Thus, if the operand has a negative value, that is, a left bit of one, ones may be shifted into the left. This is useful in that it maintains a negative value when shifting a negative integer to the right. Consider the situation in which the signed int variable x has the value –671. In a two's complement notation, which many computers use, this has the binary representation 1111110101100001_2. The initial (left-most) one indicates that this is a negative number. The result of the statement x = x >> 3 depends on the compiler. In some systems, this will result in giving x the binary number $1111111110101100_2 = -84$, in others, the result will be $0001111110101100_2 = 8108$. (Notice that the first method produces the integer answer that would result from dividing –671 by 8.) The programmer should be careful in using signed integers for shift operands to check the appropriate compiler manuals before employing this operand.

Another bitwise operator is the one's *complement operator,* which is a unary operator that converts each one to a zero, and each zero to a one. If the int variable x has the value $671 = 0000001010011111_2$, then the expression ~x has the value 1111110101100000_2, which is –672 in two's complement arithmetic.

The example in Figure 9.6, which was adapted from Kernighan and Richie, (p. 45), gives a function that returns the n bits starting at bit position pos. It assumes that the bits are numbered from the right starting at zero. These bits are returned as the right-most bits of the unsigned int return value.

The function call "determine_bits (i, 7, 4)" returns bits 4, 5, 6, and 7 as the right-most bits of the return value. The return value has zeros elsewhere.

Consider the expression ~0<<n. The first part, ~0, produces a word with all one bits. This is then shifted left n bits. Since the bits shifted into this word are zeros, this expression has zeros in the n right-most bit positions with ones in the

```
unsigned int determine_bits( unsigned int i, unsigned int pos,
                                unsigned int  n )
{
    unsigned int answer, mask;
    if ( ( pos < n ) || ( pos > 8 * sizeof( unsigned int ) ) )
    {
        /* error */
        return ( -1 );
    }
    else
    {
        mask = ~( ~0 << n );
        answer = ( i >> ( pos + 1 -n ) ) & mask;
        return ( answer );
    }
} /* end determine_bits */
```

Figure 9.6. The determine_bits() function

remainder of the word. The statement "mask = ~(~0<<n);" gives mask the complement of this, that is, ones in the n right-most bit positions with zeros in the remainder of the word. The expression i >> (pos + 1 –n) shifts the desired bits to the right side of the word. When this is combined with mask by means of the bitwise AND, the n right-most bits are left unchanged, and the remainder of the bits are cleared to zero.

These bitwise operators can be used in conjunction with the assignment operator to produce compact operators when the target of the assignment is identical to the left operand of the bitwise operator. These operators are &=, |=, ^=, ~=, <<=, and >>=. The semantics of all can be illustrated by an example involving one of these. The statement "x &= y;" where x and y are both int variables, is equivalent to "x = x & y."

Each of the operators in this section can be applied to any integer variable or bit field. When used in combination with bit fields, these operators can provide a powerful mechanism for the efficient manipulation of small pieces of data.

The precedence table presented as Table 9.1 gives the precedence of all the operators in C. In particular, it indicates the relative precedence of the bitwise operators that have been introduced in this chapter.

Table 9.1. Precedence Table

Operator	Operator Precedence (Listed from Highest to Lowest Precedence)	Associativity
Reference	() [] . ->	Left to right
Postfix	++ --	
Unary	! ~ - ++ -- (type) * & sizeof	Right to left
Multiplicative	* / %	Left to right
Additive	+ -	Left to right
Bitwise shift	<< >>	Left to right
Relational	< <= > >=	Left to right
Equality	== !=	Left to right
Bitwise AND	&	Left to right
Bitwise XOR	^	Left to right
Bitwise OR	|	Left to right
Logical AND	&&	Left to right
Logical OR	||	Left to right
Ternary	? :	Right to left
Assignment	= += -= *= /= %= >>= <<= &= ^= |=	Right to left
Comma	,	Left to right

To illustrate some of these operators, consider the problem of writing a function to convert uppercase alphabetic characters to lowercase. Most execution environments use the ASCII coding of characters. This was briefly examined earlier in this section. (We will consider the EBCDIC coding scheme next.). An examination of the ASCII codes will show that the code for each lowercase character is 32 more than the code for the corresponding uppercase letter. For example, uppercase 'A' has the code 65 whereas lowercase 'A' has code 97. Assuming that each ASCII code is represented in 1 byte, the difference in the codes is that the lowercase has bit 5 set to one whereas the uppercase has that bit off (0). (The numbering of bits begins at 0 for the least-significant bit and proceeds to 7 for the most significant.) Figure 9.7 illustrates this for a few characters.

The function to switch from upper- to lowercase must change bit 5. The function in Figure 9.8 sets this flag by means of the bitwise OR operator and a mask with value 32.

Giving mask the value 32 actually gives it the binary value 0010000_2. When this is OR'ed with the value of ch, the one in bit position 5 of mask changes the value of bit position 5 in ch to one. The remainder of the bits in ch are left unchanged because of the zeros in mask.

This conversion task for EBCDIC characters is slightly different. For this coding scheme, the difference between the codes for uppercase and those for lowercase is 64. Also, the lowercase characters have a numerically smaller code than those of the uppercase characters. The code for lowercase 'a' is $129 = 10000001_2$, and that for uppercase 'A' is $193 = 11000001_2$. The difference in the binary codes is that the lowercase characters have a zero in bit position 6 and the uppercase characters have a one in that location. The function shown in Figure

Character	ASCII Code
'A'	01000001_2
'a'	01100001_2
'B'	01000010_2
'b'	01100010_2
'J'	01001011_2
'j'	01101011_2
'Z'	01011010_2
'z'	01111010_2

⬆——— bit 5

Figure 9.7. Comparison of uppercase and lowercase ASCII codes

```
char to_lower( char ch ) /* ASCII */
{
    #define MASK   32

    if ( ( ch >='A' ) && ( ch <= 'Z' ) )
    {
         ch = ch | MASK;
    }
    return( ch );
}
```

Figure 9.8. Changing ASCII uppercase to lowercase

9.9 performs this conversion for EBCDIC by means of a mask and the bitwise AND operator.

   Program 9.1 combines these two functions with conditional compilation to produce a program that can be used for either ASCII or EBCDIC coding schemes.

   Notice that, in this program, the bitwise operator used is the EXCLUSIVE OR. Consider the sample conversions in Figure 9.10 to convince yourself that this works in both cases.


```
#include <stdio.h>

main()
{
    char to_lower( char );
    char str[80];
    int i;
    char ch;

    gets(str);

    i = 0;
    while (str[i] != '\0' )
    {
         ch = to_lower( str[i] );
         putchar( ch );
         i++;
    }
    putchar('\n');
```

Program 9.1. Conversion from uppercase to lowercase (continues)

```
            exit(0);
    } /* end main */

    char to_lower( char ch )
    {
        #ifdef ASCII
        char mask = 32;
        #else
        char mask = 64;
        #endif

        if ( ( ch >='A' ) && ( ch <= 'Z' ) )
        {
            ch = ch ^ mask;
        }
        return( ch );
    }
```

Program 9.1. (continued)

```
char to_lower( char ch ) /* EBCDIC */
{
    #define MASK   64

    if ( ( ch >='A' ) && ( ch <= 'Z' ) )
    {
        ch = ch & ~MASK;
    }
    return( ch );
}
```

Figure 9.9. Changing EBCDIC uppercase to lowercase

ASCII Conversion		EBCDIC Conversion	
01000001	'A'	11000001	'A'
^00100000	32	^01000000	64
01100001	'a'	10000001	'a'

Figure 9.10. Sample conversions using Program 9.1

9.2 ADDITIONAL TYPES

In this section, we introduce several new types. The first type, enumerated constants, provides a method of giving a name to an integer constant. This is a valuable technique for adding understandability to a C program. The register keyword is a storage class specifier that also conveys some information to the compiler about the use of the object. The last three new types—const, volatile, and noalias—are more accurately described as type qualifiers. The use of these types in a declaration also provides some information to the compiler about certain properties of an object. Each will be discussed in turn.

Enumerated Constants

Programs often involve the manipulation of a relatively small set of discrete values. Consider the case of writing a lexical analyzer. A lexical analyzer is a portion of a compiler that categorizes each unit (i.e., token) of the program as to its purpose. A programmer may have to categorize the use of a token as a variable, a reserved word, a constant, or a delimiter; in writing a compiler, a programmer may have to specify the type of an identifier; in writing a payroll program, a programmer may have to typify each employee as salaried or hourly. In each case, there are a finite number of discrete values that describe some property or quality. In traditional programming languages, these values are coded with integers or characters. For example, 0 or 'S' may be used to represent salaried and 1 or 'H' to represent hourly.

C provided the capability of naming these constant values. Instead of using 0 and 1 or 'S' and 'H' to represent salaried and hourly, the programmer can use the names salaried and hourly to represent these values. That is, the programmer can create a new type by specifying the values to be used. As a consequence, the program is much more understandable. Instead of the program being sprinkled with special numbers or characters that are used to code other meanings, the C program can contain meaningful names to represent them. These values are called *enumerated constants*. C allows a programmer to create an enumerated type that represents a set of these enumerated constant values, and to declare variables of this type.

The syntax of the creation of an enumerated type and the declaration of variables of this type are given in the syntax diagram of Figure 9.11.

In the following example, the identifier languages is the name of this enumerated type. The list that follows that name specifies the enumerated values. The variables mastered and unknown can then have any of the listed enumerated constants as their values. For example, the assignment "mastered = ADA" is valid.

These values are represented internally as integers. By default, the values associated with these enumerated constants start with 0 for the left-most value, and increase by 1 for each subsequent value. In Figure 9.12, the enumerated constant C is represented by 0, Pascal by 1, Ada by 2, and so on. This default can be changed by assigning any particular value another integer value in the declaration. Figure 9.13 illustrates this.

ENUM SPECIFIER

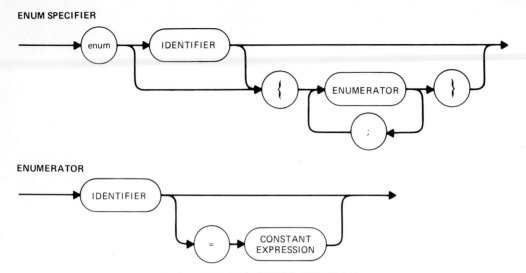

Figure 9.11. Syntax diagram for enumerations

In Figure 9.13, blue is represented by the integer 0, green by 7, yellow by 8, red by 9, white by 10, purple by 0, and pink by 1. Notice that there can be several enumerated constants with the same integer value.

Enumerated constants can be considered to be a value of a new type. Another view is that each is the name for an integer constant. As such, these enumerated constants can be used anywhere that an integer is valid. In particular, enumerated constants can be used in arithmetic expressions. For example, if i is an integer, the expression i = blue + 1; is syntactically valid, although this is generally a misuse of enumerated constants. Furthermore, the value of an enumerated constant cannot be modified; such constants are constant, not variable.

An enumerated type can be assigned any storage class except register. (See the next section.) The name space of enumerated constants is the same as that of the tags of structures and unions.

```
enum languages { C, Pascal, Ada, FORTRAN, COBOL, Modula_2 }
mastered;

languages unknown;
```

Figure 9.12. An example of enumerated constants

```
enum colors {blue, green=7, yellow, red, white, purple=0, pink};
```

Figure 9.13. Enumerated constants given specific values

```
register int i;
register float f;
```

Figure 9.14. Register declarations

Register Storage Class Specifier

The *register* storage class specifier is a promise by the programmer that the address of the object will not be used. That is, this object will never be used as an operand to the address operator &. (A syntax error is produced if the address of a register class variable is taken.) With this information, the compiler is able more aggressively to optimize storage representation of this object. Sometimes such an object is placed in one of the machine's fast registers. The use of the register keyword effectively results in a dynamic storage duration with the suggestion that the value of this variable be stored in one of the machine registers. The suggestion of storing the value in a register can often speed the execution of the program. Access to such machine registers is much faster than to primary memory. The example in Figure 9.14 illustrates register declarations.

This storage in a register is merely a suggestion to the compiler. The types that are permitted to be stored in registers and the number of variables that are effective are implementation dependent. The number of registers that can be used in this manner depends upon the underlying hardware, but it is always a relatively small number. If too many active variables carry this specification simultaneously, not all may actually be stored in registers. Those that are not stored in registers are allocated memory as normal automatic variables. Furthermore, registers have a finite length, generally one or two words. If a particular variable type requires more storage than can be accommodated by a register, the register specifier is not permitted.

Constant Type Qualifier

C allows the programmer to specify names for constant values or to indicate that particular formal function parameters are not to be modified. An identifier is declared as a *constant* by using the constant type qualifier *const* in its declaration. The example in Figure 9.15 demonstrates some simple uses of constants.

A *constant* is similar to a variable in that it is the name of a storage location. It differs from a variable in that its value cannot be modified during program execution. Therefore, the use of the *constant type qualifier* is actually a promise by the programmer that the value of that object will not be modified during program execution. Furthermore, the compiler will enforce this.

```
const int true = 1;
const int false = 0;
const float pi = 3.1415;
const struct coordinates
{
    float x;
    float y;
} origin = { 0.0, 0.0 };
```

Figure 9.15. Use of constant declarations

A value may be given to a constant via an initialization as part of the declaration, as shown in Figure 9.15. (This type of initialization occurs during compilation, rather than during program execution.) The constant identifier can then be used as any other constant in the program.

The use of well-chosen constant names can add greatly to the readability and understandability of a program. Rather than using special numbers throughout a program, meaningful constant names can better communicate their purposes.

As can be seen in the examples of Figure 9.15, constant names can be given to complex data structures in addition to simple integer and float values. When used in this manner, the constant property is associated with the identifier origin, but not with the tag coordinate. That is, the declaration

```
struct coordinate pt1;
```

does not make pt1 a constant.

A type name for a constant can be created by means of the typedef modifier; see Program 9.2.

This set of declarations creates a constant origin and a variable point1 with the same type. The identifier point1 is a variable, not a constant, as it was declared with the structure tag.

Constants can be used with pointers in some interesting, and sometimes confusing, combinations. In Figure 9.16, the first declaration gives a pointer variable var_ptr_to_const, which points to a constant. This means that var_ptr_to_const can be assigned a new address, but the value it points to cannot change.

The second declaration gives a constant pointer to a variable. The address cannot be modified, although the location to which it points can be changed. The third declaration gives a pointer object in which both the address and the character to which it points are constant. The assignments that are marked as illegal in Figure 9.16 will produce compilation errors.

A common use of constants is as formal parameters of functions. If a parameter should not be permitted to change, declaring it with the type qualifier const will guarantee that property. The corresponding actual parameter does not

```
typedef const struct pt_tag
{
    float x;
    float y;
} point;

point origin = {0.0, 0.0};
struct pt_tag  point1= {1.0,2.0};

main()
{
    origin.x = 1.0; /* invalid assignment since origin is a const */
    point1.x = 3.0; /* valid assignment since point1 is not const */
}
```

Program 9.2. Typedef for a constant

```
void cfunc( char * ptr )
{
    const char * var_ptr_to_const;
    char * const const_ptr_to_var;
    const char * const const_ptr_to_const;

    var_ptr_to_const = ptr;        /* legal assignment of addresses */
    *var_ptr_to_const = *ptr;      /* illegal assignment since the  */
                                   /* char to which it points is a  */
                                   /* constant.                     */
    const_ptr_to_var = ptr;        /* illegal assignment since the  */
                                   /* address is a constant         */
    *const_ptr_to_var = *ptr;      /*legal assignment               */
    const_ptr_to_const = ptr;      /* illegal assignment of address */
    *const_ptr_to_const = *ptr;    /* illegal assignment of value   */
}
```

Figure 9.16. Constants and pointers

have to be a constant. When its formal parameter is constant, the actual parameter will not be modifiable within the function. This is particularly useful in passing string literals or other arrays. Arrays (and strings) are always passed as a pointer. This is actually C's method of parameter passing by reference. Passing a parameter by reference permits modification of the passed value. With arrays, there is no alternative; they must be passed by reference even when they are not to be modified. Declaring the corresponding formal parameter as a constant can solve this dilemma.

Many of the functions provided in C's standard libraries use the constant declaration for formal parameters for this very purpose. The function prototype for strcat() is the following:

```
char *strcat(char *s1, const char *s2);
```

This function, as you will recall, has the task of concatenating the string to which s2 points to that to which s1 points. As a result, s1 has the new, concatenated string. But s2 should remain unchanged. The const type qualifier assures this. The string to which s2 points cannot be modified in the body of the strcat() function.

Volatile Type Qualifier

The *volatile type modifier* is used to indicate that the value of an identifier may change in ways that are not apparent to the compiler. For example, registers used for memory-mapped I/O, variables shared with other processes (e.g. a semaphore) or variables used for interrupt vectors may be modified by sources outside the program. In a multiprogramming system in which several programs are executing concurrently, any shared variables should be declared as volatile.

This volatile modifier restricts the compiler from performing certain optimizations on that identifier. For example, if a variable is not modified by any statement in a program, some compilers may place that variable in a read-only section of memory. The volatile modifier informs the compiler that this optimization is not appropriate in this situation.

The syntax of the volatile type modifier is to precede the declaration with the reserved word *volatile* (Figure 9.17).

Even though there may be no obvious modifications to the object in this program, the value of a volatile type object may not be stable. This is the reason for the choice of the term "volatile."

Like the modifier const, volatile can be used with a pointer. It has the same combinations as const, giving a volatile pointer to a stable object, a stable pointer to a volatile object, and a volatile pointer to a volatile object. Volatile can also be

```
volatile unsigned int i;
volatile struct
{
    /* Appropriate structure members declared here. */
} volatile_struct;
```

Figure 9.17. Declarations using volatile

```
volatile int s1, s2;                    volatile int s1, s2;

/* producer */                          /*consumer */
const int true = 1;                     const int true = 1;
main()                                  main()
{                                       {
    void p(volatile int i);                 void p(volatile int i);
    void v(volatile int i);                 void v(volatile int i);

    do                                      do
    {                                       {
        /* produce resource */                  p(s1);
        p(s1);                                  /* consume resource */
        v(s2);                                  v(s2);
    } while ( true );                       } while ( true );
    exit(0);                                exit(0);
}                                       }
```

Program 9.3. Use of volatile types for process synchronization

used with const, as in "volatile const int interrupt_vector," to declare an object that should not be modified by the program in which it is declared, but may be modified by some outside process or device.

Program 9.3 illustrates a hypothetical use of a volatile type as semaphores to control the production and consumption of some resource.

These two programs are assumed to operate concurrently. (This is a nonportable section of code which depends upon the underlying execution environment.) The semaphore variables s1 and s2 synchronize access to the resource. This assures that there is no attempt to consume the resource before it has been produced. The functions p() and v() are implementation-dependent functions that are responsible for making processes wait or letting waiting processes proceed. A discussion of these functions is beyond the scope of this book. There are references at the end of the chapter for those interested in pursuing this topic.

Noalias Type Qualifier

Noalias is a type qualifier that allows the compiler to optimize an object more aggressively. It specifies to the compiler that this object is the only access path that will ever exist to this object. It is most helpful with pointers. This type qualifier is a promise by the programmer that another pointer will never provide access to the object to which this variable points. (See Figure 9.18)

This type modifier was introduced primarily so that C compilers could be written for vector processors, or for other situations in which the same kind of

```
noalias char * ch;
noalias double darray[1000];
```

Figure 9.18. Declarations using noalias

```
void vector_add( const float *V1,        void vector_add(
       const float *V2,                    const noalias float *V1,
       float *V3,                           const noalias float *V2,
       int vector_length )                  noalias float *V3,
                                            int vector_length )
{                                        {
   int i;                                   int i;

   for (i=0;i<vector_length;i++)            for (i=0;i<vector_length;i++)
   {                                        {
      V3[i] = V1[i] + V2[i];                   V3[i] = V1[i] + V2[i];
   } /* end for */                          } /* end for */
   return;                                  return;
} /* end vector_add()*/                   } /* end vector_add() */
```

Figure 9.19. Vector addition to illustrate volatile

optimization as used by vector processors is desired. A vector processor is a
multiprocessor that can simultaneously apply the same operation to multiple
pieces of data. The function in Figure 9.19 illustrates a situation in which the
noalias type qualifier can allow the processor to make some optimizations.

In the left example of Figure 9.19, the translator cannot be sure that the vectors
V1 and V2 do not overlap V3. If these do overlap, the additions will have to
proceed as indicated in the loop as earlier additions may affect the values to be
used in later additions. In the right-hand example, the noalias type modifier
assures the translator that there is no overlap. Consequently, this function can be
optimized to take advantage of the vector nature of the underlying execution
environment. All the additions can occur simultaneously.

The next sections will introduce an element of C that provides some convenience in programming, especially in loops. This is the null statement.

9.3   THE NULL STATEMENT

The *null statement* is a valid C statement that specifies no operation. It can be
used anywhere in a C program by writing a semicolon. It is generally used as a

place holder inside another syntactic unit. For example, the initialization portion of a "for" loop can be skipped by use of the null statement. In the example in Figure 9.20 the initialization and modification portions of a "for" loop are skipped by means of the null statement.

The examples in Figure 9.21 demonstrate some other typical uses of the null statement.

The null statement can lead to some errors that are difficult to find. If a semicolon is placed after the right parenthesis in a "while," then the intended body is not executed. Figure 9.22 illustrates this problem.

In Figure 9.22, the semicolon after the right parenthesis specifies a null statement that is taken to be the body of the loop. Since the loop control variable is not modified in that body, an infinite loop results. A similar problem can occur with a "for" loop in which the empty body is executed several times, followed by one execution of the intended body.

```
int ch;

for ( ; ch = getchar() != '\n'; )
{
    /* body of loop */
}
```

Figure 9.20. The null statement in a for loop

```
/* read to end of line */
while (getchar() != '\n');
                                              null statement

/* sum the first n integers */
for (sum = 1, i=2, i<n; sum + = i);
                                              null statement
                                              comma statement
```

Figure 9.21. Examples of the null statement

```
while( !feof( fp )); /*incorrect use of null statement*/
{
    /* process data */
}
```

Figure 9.22. Example of incorrect use of null statement

9.4 SOFTWARE ENGINEERING AND PORTABILITY ISSUES

A major software engineering goal is understandability of programs. One mechanism that C provides to add understandability and readability to software is the use of constant identifiers and enumerated types. Meaningful names for number, character, and string constants are more understandable than multiple occurrences of these special numbers, characters, or strings. In addition, constant identifiers ease program maintenance. If a value of a constant that is used in various places needs to be changed, it should be given a name, and that name should be used in its place. Then only the value used to initialize the constant identifier has to be altered if the value needs to be changed. The implications for changes necessary for portability are apparent. The C programmer should be aware that the const, volatile, and noalias type qualifiers have appeared as a result of the standardization effort. They do not appear in most pre-ANSI standard compilers.

Identifiers for constants can also be created by use of the #define preprocessor directive. The differences between the use of the #define and const are similar to those between #define and typedef, which were discussed in Chapter 7. The const type qualifier creates an identifier that is known to the compiler. The #define creates an identifier that is replaced by its value before the compiler is invoked. The #define is a more general-purpose string manipulator, but the const is generally preferred for software engineering reasons. The case of the #define requires the programmer and the reader of the program to understand the syntactic rules of the preprocessor in addition to those of C. The #define is notorious for the introduction of errors which are difficult to find. The C compiler is not aware of the presence of the #define. Thus, errors in the #define are reported by the C compiler at the statement which uses the defined identifier. The source of the error is thus difficult to locate.

In using an on-line debugger, the use of const establishes an identifier about which the debugger is aware. This is not true for an identifier created by a #define.

If a type is declared as constant, in a typedef or structure declaration, each use of that type to create an object produces an object which cannot be modified. The #define can be used to create a type declaration, but the resulting type does not produce a constant object.

Constants can be declared inside a function. This produces an identifier whose scope is limited to that function. The ability to hide information inside functions is an important technique in handling the complexity of large programs. The only way to accomplish this with a #define is to use the #undef preprocessor command at the end of the function.

As was mentioned previously, the declaration of formal function parameters as constants when they are not to be modified is very beneficial. This guarantees that the actual parameter will not be modified inadvertently (which is particularly a problem when the actual parameter is an array). In addition, the use of the type qualifier const gives the reader of the program additional information about the intended use of this parameter. Notice that this is not possible with the pre-processor commands.

Bit fields and the bitwise operators can add efficiency to a program. However, their undisciplined use can also lead to portability problems. In fact, an optimizing compiler can often produce more efficient code than can a human. The general applications programmer should be careful in the use of bitwise operators and bit fields. The guiding principles are to strive for understandability and portability.

The use of enumerated constants has similar advantages over #define. The enum also has the advantage that the integers can be automatically assigned to identifiers by the compiler. The programmer does not have to keep track of these.

The order in which bits are physically stored in a word of memory is implementation dependent. That is, some compilers may map the first bit field of a structure to the left-most portion of the memory word; others may map the same field to the right-most portion of the memory word. This will be of concern only if the programmer is representing a group of bits to be used by the hardware, operating system, or other system software which uses a particular ordering of bits. In this case, the documentation for the compiler should be consulted to determine the placement of bit fields. Consider, again, Figure 9.5, which is repeated in the following.

```
struct
{
    unsigned int blink: 1;
    unsigned int background : 3;
    unsigned int intensity : 1;
    unsigned int foreground : 3;
    unsigned int ch : 8;
} char_info;
```

Compiler X might allocate these fields in the following manner.

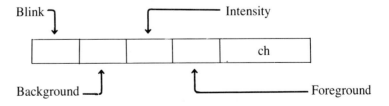

Compiler Y for the same machine might allocate these same fields as shown in the following.

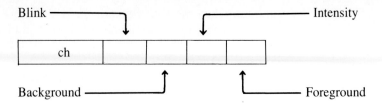

If the former is the intended result, then the structure members for Figure 9.5 would have to be reordered for use with compiler Y. The ordering of bit fields *cannot* be assumed to be portable. Programmers should avoid writing code that depends upon the order of allocation of bit fields.

A third problem with bit fields is in alignment. The ways that bit fields are aligned with respect to memory boundaries and the size of holes cannot be assumed to be portable.

Another portability problem is in the use of bitwise right shift with unsigned operands. The propagation of the sign is implementation dependent. Some compilers shift in ones on the left if the sign is negative; others shift in zeros.

9.5 SUMMARY

This chapter described a set of types, operators, and statements that are useful for some specific tasks, such as systems programming and some which are useful for all C programmers. The first topic addressed was the bit field type. A bit field is a member of a structure that is a fixed number of bits. Such a bit field is a technique for using a computer's memory more efficiently.

The next topic in this chapter was the set of bitwise operators. These are operators that manipulate the individual bits of their operands. This set consists of bitwise AND (&), OR (|), EXCLUSIVE OR (^), the left (<<) and right (>>) shift operators, and the bitwise complement operator(~).

The register type specifier can be considered to be a suggestion to the compiler that this variable be stored in one of the computer's register. Storage in a register allows the program faster access to a variables value, and a thoughtful use of register type specifiers can substantially increase the execution efficiency of a program.

Enumerated constants and constant type modifiers provide two methods of giving meaningful names to special numbers, characters, or strings which are important in all C programs. Other types described in this chapter are the volatile and noalias type qualifiers. These are used to convey information about the use of objects from the programmer to the compiler. A compiler can use this information to optimize or avoid optimization of the storage representation of the objects.

A discussion of the null statement, and software engineering and portability considerations conclude this chapter.

Keywords

bit fields	enumerated constant
bitwise AND &	noalias
bitwise exclusive OR ^	noalias type qualifier
bitwise operator	null statement
bitwise OR		register
complement operator ~	shift operators <<, >>
const	volatile
constant	volatile type qualifier
constant type qualifier	

References

Deitel, H. M. 1984. *An Introduction to Operating Systems,* Reading, Mass.: Addison-Wesley. This book includes a discussion of process synchronization in general, and semaphores in particular.

Draft American National Standard x3.159–198x, Programming Language C. This is the ultimate authority on questions of syntax and semantic of the C language. Copies may be obtained from Global Engineering Documents, Inc., 2805 McGaw, Irvine, CA 92714.

Kernighan, Brian, and Dennis Ritchie, 1978. *The C Programming Language,* Englewood Cliffs, N.J.: Prentice-Hall.

Plauger, P. J. 1988. Touching memory: Standard C Makes the Art More Precise. *C Users J.* 6, (4). 25–32.

Plum, T. 1988. X3J11 Approves Revised Draft for Second Public Review, *C Users J.* 6, (2). 51–52.

Stroustrup, B. 1986. *The C++ Programming Language,* Reading, Mass.: Addison-Wesley. The type qualifier const is a recent addition to C. The syntax and semantics for const are those used in the similar language C++. This book describes C++, including const.

Tanenbaum, A. S. 1987. *Operating Systems, Design and Implementation,* Englewood Cliffs, N.J.: Prentice-Hall. This book includes a discussion of process synchronization in general, and semaphores in particular.

Discussion Questions

1. How can you determine if the use of the variable "i" when declared as "register int i;" makes a program faster than when declared by "int i;"?

2. Under what circumstances would you expect a register declaration to make a difference in program efficiency?

3. What are the differences among the following three groups of syntactic units in C?
   a. Enumerated constants.
   b. Identifiers given values by a #DEFINE preprocessor directive.
   c. Identifiers defined with the "const" type modifier.

4. C is sometimes called a "high-level assembly language." What features of this chapter would give credence to that nomenclature?

5. Are both the bitwise AND and the logical AND operators necessary in C, or can one be implemented by using the other? What about bitwise OR and logical OR?

6. In this chapter, the comma operator was introduced. How many other uses are there for a comma in C other than as the comma operator? How can these other uses be differentiated from the comma operator?

7. Discuss the concept of alignment of objects in memory. How does alignment produce "holes" in structures?

Exercises

1. Write a C program that will input values into the bit fields specified in Figure 9.5.

2. Give a declaration for an enumerated constant that represents the shapes circle, triangle, square, pentagon, hexagon. Let triangle be represented by the constant 3, square by 4, pentagon by 5, hexagon by 6, and circle by zero.

3. Write a function that will accept an enumerated constant as described in Exercise 2 and will return the integer associated with that constant. (This corresponds to the ord function of Pascal.)

4. Write a function that accepts an integer value and returns the enumerated constant that corresponds to that integer as described in Exercise 2. (This is the inverse of the function in Exercise 3.)

5. Give the constant declarations for the following constants:
   a. A 10-by-10 int array called "zero" whose values are all 0.
   b. A float constant called "e" whose value is an approximation to the Euler's number of mathematics (2.718281828459045).

6. Complete the following table by filling in the blanks with the correct binary strings. (Assume an 8-bit word size.)

x	y	x & y	x | y	x ^ y	~ x
01101001	11000111	_____	_____	_____	_____
10001110	_____	10000110	_____	_____	_____
_____	11110000	_____	_____	_____	10001101

7. Write a C statement that will do each of the following. Give your assumptions about the size of int and the order of bits in a word in your execution environment.
   a. Set the fifth bit of the int variable x.
   b. Clear the tenth bit of the int variable y.
   c. Test the seventh bit of the int variable z.

8. Write a C statement to:
   a. Shift the value in the int variable x three places to the right.
   b. Shift the value in the int variable y seven places to the left.

9. If the int variable z contains the value −707, what value will each of the following variables be assigned? (Test your answers on the computer. Most computers represent negative integers in two's complement form.)
   a. y = x << 2;
   b. z = x >> 4; (with no sign extension)
   c. w = x >> 4; (with sign extension)

10. Code a function with the prototype "complement_bits(unsigned int, unsigned int pos, unsigned int n)" that gives the complement of just those n bits of variable i starting at position pos.

11. Demonstrate that your compiler produces holes in its alignment process by declaring a structure with bit fields, then using the sizeof operator to determine the amount of space occupied by that structure.

12. Consider the following structures:

```
struct
{
    unsigned int f1 : 1;
    unsigned int f2 : 3;
    unsigned int f3 : 2;
    int f4;
}s1;

struct
{
    unsigned int f1 : 8;
    unsigned int f2 : 9;
    unsigned int f3 : 8;
}s2;
```

Assume that an integer requires a 16-bit word for storage. Assume that bits are allocated to words. What is the size in bytes of s1? Of s2?

13. Explain in words the meaning of the following declarations.
    a. const int *ptr;
    b. int * const ptr;
    c. const int *const ptr;
    d. float * volatile fptr;
    e. volatile float *fptr;

14. Which of the four statements in the function below are valid?

```
int afunct( const int *p1, int *const p2, int *)
{
    *p1 = x;          /* statement #1 */
    p1 = &x;          /* statement #2 */
    *p2 = x;          /* statement #3 */
    p2 = &x;          /* statement #4 */
}
```

Programming Problems

1. Write a C program that will input the type of shape (triangle, circle, square, rectangle, trapezoid), will prompt for the appropriate dimension (e.g., radius for a circle; length of a side for a square; length and width for a rectangle; etc.), and will produce and output the area and perimeter (circumference) of that shape. Store the information about the shape in a union as in Program 7.3. Use enumerated constants for the kind of object.

2. Write a C function that will multiply any number by any power of two and a driver to test it. This program should do the multiplication by shifting. The power of two should be a positive integer. You may wish to compare the efficiency of multiplication by shifting versus ordinary multiplication by coding the function both ways and timing each for a significant number of multiplies. See the time() function in Chapter 10 for a function that will do this timing.

3. Extend the function in the previous problem by permitting the power to be negative. This effectively allows for division. The answer to the division should be a structure that includes the entire number, including the fractional portion.

4. Extend the function described in Problem 2 to allow multiplication by any integer, rather than just by powers of two. Use shifting and addition, but do not use the multiplication operator.

5. A set is a data structure that some other languages provide, but which is missing from C. A set is defined to be an unordered collection of elements. The operations that can be performed on sets are union, intersection, difference, and comparisons (subset, superset, membership). Create a program that will allow a young student of mathematics better to understand the set concept and associated operations.

    First choose a universal set of elements. (A good choice would be the integers 1 to 16.) Inform the user of your program that he or she will be allowed to specify the elements from the universal set that are to be included in each of three sets, called A, B, and C. Having initialized the sets, the user should then be encouraged to type in any valid combination of sets and set operators. For example:

    A + B   represents the union of A and B.
    A * B   represents their intersection.
    A − B   represents their difference.

After each such expression, your program should report the contents of that expression. Further expressions to be permitted are assignments, like:

    C := A + B   which gives C the value of A union B.

Other valid operations are "<" for "is a subset of ?," ">" for "is a superset of?," "=" for "are equal?," and "in" for "is an element of?." The program's response to each of these should be true or false. (Notice that "<," ">," and "=" require two sets as operands, whereas "in" requires an element and a set as in "1 in A.")

    Code each operation as a separate function. The formal parameters that are not supposed to change should be declared as const.

Represent each of these sets by an integer or a structure consisting of a sequence of bit fields. The value of the ith bit or the ith bit field indicates the presence or absence of element i in the set. That is, the value 00001011 can be interpreted to mean that the corresponding set contains the elements 1, 2, and 4. Use the bit operations to perform the required operations.

6. The game Master Mind is a guessing game in which one player chooses four colors from a set of six. (Repetitions are permitted.) The other player then attempts to guess those four colors in order. After each guess, the first player responds by informing the second player about how many colors were exactly correct (the correct color in the correct position) and how many were the correct color but in an incorrect position.

   Write a C program in which the computer picks the colors and reports the number of colors correct. The user attempts to guess and the computer reports on the progress. In playing the game, the player should not be required to type in the entire color names, but rather the first letter of each color. For example, "OGBG" is interpreted to mean "orange, green, blue, and green." At the beginning of the game, the user should be presented with the game's instructions, if needed.

   To select the four colors, a random number generator is used. [The C ANSI standard prescribes that the random number function rand() be included in the standard library and its header in the header file stdlib.h.] Such a random number generator is actually a "pseudorandom number generator" in that the number generated is determined by the seed. The seed is a static local variable that is modified at each execution of the function, and is used to generate the pseudorandom number. This ensures that the number generated varies from call to call. To improve the unpredictability of this generator, the player should use the time of day as the seed. The ANSI standard specifies a group of such functions whose headers are included in the file time.h. These functions are discussed in Chapter 10.

   The colors in this program should be represented by an enumerated type.

7. Many people write checks for all their bills and balance their checking accounts once a month. Write a C program to improve this process, and also to enable a user to keep better track of expenses. This program should be designed to be run at the end of the month to help balance a checking account and to keep track of money spent in each of several budget categories.

   The budget categories to be included are the following:

   Housing
   Utilities
   Automobile
   Gasoline

Food
Savings
Entertainment
Charitable contributions
Miscellaneous

The first item to be input is the beginning balance. Next is the information about checks and deposits. This check information is to be input from the terminal in any order (that is, not in order by check number or date). The information on each check is the check number, the amount of the check, the budget category, and the date.

The output should consist of the checks listed in order by check number, followed by the deposits, the total of the checks, the total of the deposits, the beginning balance, and the ending balance. Then print out the amount spent in each budget category.

The information for each check or deposit is to be input on one line in the following order:

One letter for the budget category
Amount
Date (month, day, year in the formal mm/dd/yy, e.g., 01/15/88)
Check number (none for deposits)

Do not require the user to input a check number for a deposit. Use a structure to represent each check or deposit. Use an enumerated type for the budget categories. This program should work for up to 150 checks and deposits per month. The number of checks is not known in advance. Use a sentinel to end input.

10 Support Libraries

C programming environments are supplied with a wealth of support functions. Previous chapters have presented some of these functions. The I/O functions were discussed in several chapters, most thoroughly in Chapter 8. The string manipulation functions were introduced in Chapter 6. In this chapter, we will examine many of the functions commonly referred to as string, utility, or mathematics functions.

The functions will be presented in the following categories: string and character manipulation, string conversion, random number generation, mathematical functions, operating system communication functions, sorting and searching functions, date and time functions, debugging aids, and locale-specific behavior.

A group of useful functions for dynamic memory management and exceptional control flow will be presented in Chapters 11 and 12 respectively.

Recall that libraries are associated with header files that contain the appropriate function declarations and associated macros. For example, the files string.h and stdio.h are used with the string and I/O libraries. In similar fashion, the functions discussed in this chapter should be used in conjunction with the appropriate header files. The standard headers are

```
assert.h    math.h      stdio.h
ctype.h     setjmp.h    stdlib.h
float.h     signal.h    string.h
limits.h    stdarg.h    time.h
locale.h    stddef.h    errno.h
```

The appropriate header file will be specified for each function discussed in this and subsequent chapters.

In ANSI-conforming C compilers, one header file, stdlib.h, contains the declarations of most of the functions to be discussed in this chapter. Many current nonstandard C compilers are not supplied with this header file. In this case, the reader should refer to his or her local library documentation to determine the appropriate file to include when using the functions to be discussed here.

Several special types and macros are common to many of the header files, and are also included in the file stddef.h. They are

```
ptrdiff_t    An integer type representing the difference
             between two pointers

size_t       The type of the sizeof operator and the type
             used by several of the standard library
             functions.
```

348

The common macros are

`NULL`	`A null pointer constant`
`errno`	`A modifiable object in memory that has type volatile int. This object is initialized to zero at program start-up, and is set to a nonzero error code to indicate errors by several library functions.`
`offsetof (type, id)`	`An integer constant expression with type size_t that is the offset in bytes into the structure type of the member id.`

In the course of presenting each of the library functions, we will discuss the ways that the above types and macros are utilized.

The first group of functions to be discussed are those used for string and character manipulation.

10.1 STRING AND CHARACTER MANIPULATION

Character Manipulation

There are several macros (or functions) declared in the header file ctype.h that are useful for *testing* and *manipulating characters*. These can be divided into two groups: macros that test various attributes of characters and macros that change the case of characters.

The character testing group consists of 11 macros with descriptive names. In each case, the macro requires one integer parameter (the character to be tested) and returns an integer. The integer returned is to be interpreted as a boolean value (true or false). A nonzero integer implies that the character parameter satisfies the test of the macro; a zero answer means that it failed the test. Table 10.1 presents the character testing macros.

Table 10.1. Character Testing Macros (or Functions)

Function Name	Value Returned
`#include <ctype.h>`	
`int isalnum(int c)`	Nonzero if c is the code for an alphanumeric character.
`int isalpha(int c)`	Nonzero if c is the code for an alphabetic character.

Table 10.1. continued

Function Name	Value Returned
int iscntrl(int c)	Nonzero if c is the code for a control character (any nonprinting character).
int isdigit(int c)	Nonzero if c is the code for a decimal digit.
int isgraph(int c)	Nonzero if c is the code for a graphic character (any printing character other than space).
int islower(int c)	Nonzero if c is the code for a lowercase alphabetic character.
int isprint(int c)	Nonzero if c is the code for a printing character (any character that is not a control character).
int ispunct(int c)	Nonzero if c is the code for any nonalphanumeric, printing character.
int isspace(int c)	Nonzero if c is the code for a white-space character.
int isupper(int c)	Nonzero if c is the code for an uppercase alphabetic character.
int isxdigit(int c)	Nonzero if c is the code for a hexadecimal digit (0–9, A–F, or a–f).

The remaining group of character macros is composed of a macro to convert a lowercase character to the corresponding uppercase letter and another to do the opposite conversion. These are shown below.

```
int tolower(int)    Maps only uppercase characters to lowercase;
                    otherwise returns the parameter unchanged.
int toupper(int)    Maps only lowercase characters to uppercase;
                    otherwise returns the parameter unchanged.
```

As a simple example, recall the algorithm for inputting digits that represent an integer and converting that character representation to type int. The code is shown below.

```
char string[20], *sp;
int value = 0;

puts("Enter a digit");
gets(string);
```

```
for (sp = string; *sp >= '0' && *sp <= '9'; sp++)
{
    value = value * 10 + (*sp - '0');
}
```

The for loop shown above could be recoded using isdigit() as follows:

```
for (sp = string; isdigit(*sp); sp++)
{
    . . .
}
```

As a further example, recall our code to convert from lower- to uppercase, which is reproduced below.

```
int ch;

ch = getchar():
if (ch >= 'a' and ch <= 'z')
{
    ch = ch - 'a' + 'A';
}
```

The if statement recoded using the character conversion functions is

```
if (islower(ch))
{
    ch = toupper(ch);
}
```

In fact, since toupper() only maps lowercase characters, the if statement is redundant, and the code could be further collapsed to

```
ch = touper(ch);
```

Notice that the expression

```
toupper(ch)
```

does not modify the parameter *ch*. The parameter is examined, and the converted character is the return value of the macro, so an assignment operator is required to update the value of the variable ch.

String Manipulation

The header file string.h declares several functions that are useful in manipulating arrays of characters or arrays of generic objects. These functions can be grouped into the categories of copy functions, concatenation functions, comparison functions, searching functions, and miscellaneous functions. Within each of the categories there are many functions, so it is not reasonable to explain all of them in detail. In this chapter, we will present the most commonly used functions, with

Table 10.2. String Copy Functions

```
#include <string.h>

void *memcpy(void *target, const void *source, size_t n)
void *memmove(void *target, const void *source, size_t n)
```

memcpy() and memove() copy n characters from the object to which *source* points to that to which *target* points. The results of memcpy() are implementation dependent if the objects overlap, whereas memove() is guaranteed to work even if they overlap. Both functions return the value of target.

```
char *strcpy(char *target, const char *source)
char *strncpy(char *target, const char *source, size_t n)
```

Copy characters from the *source* to the *target*. strcpy() copies until a null byte is found in the source string. strncpy() copies at most n characters. If the source is shorter than n characters, strncpy() appends null bytes into the target until n characters have been copied. The results are implementation dependent if the source and target overlap.

some examples. All of the functions are listed in Appendix A. The interested reader should refer to local compiler documentation for descriptions of functions that are not completely described in this text.

We will begin the discussion with a presentation of the *string copy functions*, which are presented in Table 10.2.

The memcpy() and memove() functions should be used if objects other than arrays of characters and string literals are to be copied. The functions strcpy() and strncpy() should be used for character arrays. The function strncpy() is recommended because strcpy() may cause a run-time error if a bogus source string is passed that is not properly null terminated. Strncpy() should be called, with the third parameter being the size in bytes of the target array.

Most C libraries have strcpy() and strncpy(), but older nonstandard compilers may not have memcpy() and memmove().

The next category of string functions are the *concatenation functions*. These are detailed in Table 10.3.

Table 10.3. String Concatenation Functions

```
#include <string.h>

char *strcat(char *target, const char *source)
char *strncat(char *target, const char *source, size_t n)
```

Table 10.4. Comparison Functions

```
#include <string.h>

int memcmp(const void *s1, const void *s2, size_t n);
int strcmp(const char *s1, const char *s2);
int strncmp(const char *s1, const char *2, size_t n);
```

Both functions concatenate the *source* string onto the end of the *target* string. The null byte at the end of the original target string is overwritten with the first character of the source, and the new, concatenated string is null terminated. The function strcat() will copy characters until a null byte is found in the source. The function strncat() will copy at most n bytes. The target is always null terminated. Both functions return a pointer to the concatenated string.

The *comparison functions* are illustrated in Table 10.4. The comparison functions compare the string to which *s1* points with that to which *s2* points. All three functions return an integral value that is either less than, equal to, or greater than zero. Negative means that string s1 is less than s2, zero means the two are equal, and positive means that s1 is greater than s2. The functions memcmp() and strncmp() compare at most n bytes. A null byte terminates the comparison for strcmp(). If a null is encountered before n bytes are compared, the comparison for strncmp() terminates.

The comparison is done byte by byte. Strings are equal if all compared bytes are equal in value. String *s1* is less than string *s2* if either (1) the contents of the strings are equal up to some character, and at the first character position that is different, the character from *s1* is less than the character from *s2;* or (2) the string to which *s1* points is shorter than the string to which *s2* points, and the two strings have identical bytes up to the end of s1. The greater-than comparison is analogous.

When comparing characters, one must know the value of the character codes to determine the result of a comparison. For ASCII, the following results hold true:

```
'a' > 'A'
'A' < 'Z'
'a' < 'z'
'0' < '1'
'0' < 'A'
```

The complete ASCII and EBCDIC code charts are listed in Appendix B.

The function memcmp() should be used when the values to be compared are not characters (such as an array of ints). Strcmp() or strncmp() should be used when

Table 10.5. String Searching Functions

```
#include <string.h>

/* String and Memory-Character Search */
void *memchr(const void *s, int c, size_t n)
char *strchr(char *s, int c)
char *strrchr(char *s, int c);
```

Locate the first (or last) occurrence of *c* in the string to which *s* points. The function memchr() converts *c* to an unsigned int and compares at most n bytes. The functions strchr() and strrchr() compare until a match is found or until the null byte in the search string is found. Strchr() finds and returns a pointer to the first occurrence of *c* in *s;* strrchr() finds and returns a pointer to the last occurrence. A NULL pointer is returned if *c* is not found in the search string. Strchr() or strrchr() should be used when searching character strings. Memchr() can be used when searching other array types.

the two strings are arrays of characters or string literals, with strncmp() the recommended function.

String searching functions can be used to locate characters or substrings within another string. Table 10.5 presents the commonly used string searching functions.

Figure 10.1 illustrates a simple usage of these two functions.

The most powerful of the searching functions is strtok(). Its prototype is shown in Table 10.6.

```
#include <stdio.h>
#include <string.h>

char *str = "The string to be searched.";

main()
{
    printf("%s\n",strchr(str,'s'));
    printf("%s\n",strrchr(str,'s'));
}
```

The output is:

```
string to be searched.
searched.
```

Figure 10.1. Using strchr() and strrchr()

Table 10.6. Strtok() Function

```
#include <string.h>

/* String-Token */
char *strtok(char *s, const char *delimit)
```

The function strtok() is called repeatedly to break the string to which *s* points into a sequence of tokens (substrings) that are delimited by characters from the string to which *delimit* points. The first call to strtok() searches *s* for a character not found in *delimit*. If no such character is found, a null pointer is returned. If such a character is found, then this is the start of the first token. Strtok() then searches from there for a character that is contained in *delimit* (a delimiter character). If it is found, it is overwritten in *s* with a null. If not found, the token extends to the end of the string *s*. A subsequent call to strtok(), with NULL for the first parameter starts searching from the end of the last token (strtok(), saves this value between calls). The value returned is a pointer to the first character of the token or a null pointer if there is no token.

Consider Program 10.1, which illustrates the use of strtok().

```
#include <stdio.h>
#include <string.h>

char *str =               /* string to be parsed */
     "main() { int a; a = 0; a++; printf(\"%d\",a);}";

char *delimit = "{;}"; /* C delimiters */

main()
{
     char *token;
     int i = 0;

     token = strtok(str, delimit);

     while (token != NULL)
     {
          printf("token #%d is %s\n",i,token);
          i++;
          token = strtok(NULL, delimit);
     }
     exit(0);
}
```

Program 10.1. Using strtok() to parse a string

Table 10.7. Miscellaneous String Functions

```
#include <string.h>

void *memset(void *s, int c, size_t n)
```

Copies the value of *c*, converted to an unsigned int type, into each of the first *n* characters of the string to which *s* points. Returns the pointer *s*.

```
size_t strlen(const char *s)
```

Returns the number of characters in the string to which *s* points. The count includes all characters up to but does not include the terminating null byte.

The tokens displayed by this program are "main()," "int a," "a = 0," "a++," and "printf("%d",a)." After the while loop terminates, the original string will have been modified such that nulls have replaced the delimiter characters.

Additional searching functions are listed in Appendix A.

The final group of string functions to be discussed are the miscellaneous category. These are listed in Table 10.7.

The function memset() is used to copy a certain value into all or part of an array. Consider Program 10.2, which illustrates these two functions.

This program will initialize the array line to 80 blanks using memset(). Next, a null byte is added to the line to make it a proper string. Finally, strlen() is used to count the number of non null bytes in line (79). Notice that strlen() and sizeof do not always give the same value when used with an array. Sizeof is always the total

```
#include <stdio.h>
#include <string.h>

main()
{
  char line[80];

  memset(line, ' ', sizeof(line));

  line[79] = '\0';

  printf("number of bytes in line = %d\n",strlen(line));
}
```

Program 10.2. Using memset() and strlen()

number of bytes allocated to the array; strlen() is the actual number of nonnull bytes in the array, which is not a constant value.

This concludes the discussion of the string and character manipulation functions. Next, we will examine functions used to convert the string representation of numbers to numeric types.

10.2   STRING CONVERSION

Data representing numeric values is often read into a C program in the form of character strings. In order to perform arithmetic computations upon such data, it must first be converted into the proper internal representation for an arithmetic value. For example, the characters could be converted to the internal representation for an int or double. Chapter 8 presented the function sscanf() that provides this facility. This function is very general. If a string representing a number has been input and it is required that it be converted to internal representation, a set of simple utility functions is provided as an alternative to sscanf(). These are atof(), atoi(), and atol().

The *string conversion utility functions* are declared in the header file stdlib.h. The names of the functions were conceived years ago when C was running exclusively on machines that utilize the ASCII character code. Thus, atof() means ASCII-to-float, atoi() means ASCII-to-integer, and atol() means ASCII-to-long. Today, of course, C is running on non-ASCII machines as well. Thus, for an execution environment that uses ASCII, the names are still appropriate, but for an environment not using ASCII, the names are not appropriate.

Table 10.8 presents the prototype declaration for the conversion functions.

Table 10.8. Base-10 String Conversion Functions

```
#include <stdlib.h>

double atof(char *sptr);     /* ASCII-to-float */
```

Converts the string to which *sptr* points to double representation and returns this value. Returns zero if no conversion could be performed.

```
int atoi(char *sptr)         /* ASCII-to-integer */
```

Converts the string to which *sptr* points to int representation and returns this value. Returns zero if no conversion could be performed.

```
long int atol(char *sptr)    /* ASCII-to-long */
```

Converts the string to which *sptr* points to long int representation and returns this value. Returns zero if no conversion could be performed.

```
#include <stdio.h>

#ifdef ANSI
#include <stdlib.h> /* Contains conversion function
                      * declarations. */
#else
  extern int    atoi();
  extern long   atol();
  extern double atof();
#endif

main()
{
  long a_long;
  int  an_int;
  double d1, d2;

  an_int = atoi("  256 is the max");
  a_long = atol(" -64000 is the minimum");
  d1 = atof("  1.004e14");
  d2 = atof("-5.03443");
  printf("i1 = %d\nl1 = %ld\nd1 = %g\nd2 = %g\n",
                  an_int,a_long,d1,d2);
}
```

Program 10.3. Using string conversion functions

The string in each of the conversion functions may contain leading white space. The first non-white-space character should be either a sign or the first character of the number. Finally, the number can be followed by one or more characters that are not a part of the number. The conversion terminates at the first non-numeric character. This final portion of the string will be ignored. Program 10.3 illustrates the usage of these functions.

The output from Program 10.3 is illustrated in Figure 10.2.

Notice that the code was written to be used with either ANSI-compliant or older model C compilers through the use of conditional compilation. Also notice that

```
i1 = 256
l1 = -64000
d1 = 1.004e+014
d2 = -5.03443
```

Figure 10.2. Output from Program 10.3

Table 10.9. String Conversion, Other Bases

```
#include <stdlib.h>

/* String-to-long */
long int strtol(char *sptr, char **endptr, int base)

/* String-to-unsigned-long */
unsigned long int strtoul(char *sptr, char **endptr, int base)
```

Both strtol() and strtoul() convert the digits in the string addressed by *sptr* to long and unsigned long representations respectively. The parameter *base* is a value between 2 and 36 that represents the radix of the digit string. The letters from a (or A) through z (or Z) are used for digits between 10 and 35. The parameter *endptr* is used to hold a pointer that points to any text after from the *sptr* string that follows the values converted (see Figure 10.3).

the %g specifier is used to output the doubles d1 and d2. The %g specifier is converted to %f or %e, depending upon the value that is output. [See the discussion of fprintf() in Chapter 8 for more details.]

For conversion of integers in base systems other than base-10, two additional functions are available, see Table 10.9.

For strtol() and strtoul(), the source string, addressed by sptr, may contain three parts: (1) initial white space, (2) an optional sign and digits that represent an integer, and (3) a final string of other nondigit characters. The leading white space is ignored. The converted integer is returned as the value of the function, and a pointer to the start of the final string is returned in endptr. The functions return zero if no conversion could be performed. Consider the code fragment illustrated in Figure 10.3.

```
#ifdef ANSI
#include <stdlib.h>
#else
   extern long int strtol();
#endif
long int x;
char *endptr;

x = strtol("  9F7B60 is the max", &endptr, 16);
printf("In decimal, x = %ld, final string = %s\n",x,endptr);
```

Figure 10.3. Using strtol()

The above call to strtol() would result in x being assigned the integer represented by hex 9F7B60, and endptr would be set to point to the string following the last digit of that number. The output from the printf() call in Figure 10.3 is

In decimal, x = 10451808, final string = is the max

The functions in the next category are useful for generating random numbers.

10.3 RANDOM NUMBER GENERATION

A sequence of pseudorandom numbers can be generated using srand() and rand(). *Random numbers* are generated by performing some arithmetic operations upon a value called the seed. The seed is initially set by calling srand(). The rand() function uses the seed to generate a random number, and then replaces the seed with that random number. The next call to rand() then has a new seed on which to operate. Thus, the same sequence of random numbers will be generated for a given seed, and hence the name "pseudorandom" numbers. The C language standard presents the code in Program 10.4 as an example of the implementation of srand() and rand().

Notice that the computation of *next* eventually will cause overflow. C will simply truncate any values that cannot fit into the variable. Notice also that *next* has static duration so that its value will be retained across calls to rand().

Both srand() and rand() are declared in stdlib.h. The declarations and descriptions of srand() and rand() are summarized in Table 10.10.

In order to obtain a different sequence of random numbers each time a program is executed, a different seed value must be used for each execution. One way to do this is to use the current time of day as a seed. The time() function (discussed later in this chapter) will fetch this time. This is illustrated in Program 10.5.

```
static unsigned long int next = 1;

int rand(void)
{
   next = next * 1103515245 + 12345;
   return (unsigned int)(next/65536) % RAND_MAX;
}

void srand(unsigned int seed)
{
   next = seed;
}
```

Program 10.4. Implementation of srand() and rand()

Table 10.10. Random Number Generation Functions

```
#include <stdlib.h>
void srand(unsigned int seed);     /* Seed-random */
```
Causes the next random number produced by rand() to be computed using the value in seed.

```
int rand(void)                          /* Random */
```
Generates a pseudorandom number between 0 and RAND_MAX (inclusive) based upon the last random number so generated. The first random number generated is based upon the value of the seed set by srand(). If srand() has not been called, a seed of 1 is used. RAND_MAX is defined in stdlib.h.

Program 10.5 uses the random number functions to simulate rolling of a die. The random number generator functions produce a value between 0 and RAND_ MAX. For our simulation, we desire to map this random number into an integer between 0 and 5, representing one of the six sides of the die. Thus, we could use the expression

```
(rand() % 6)
```

to put the random number into the desired range.

The program allows the user to enter the number of rolls desired, and then proceeds to count the number of times that each face turns up.

```
#include <stdio.h>
#include <time.h>

#ifdef ANSI
#include <stdlib.h>
#else
#define RAND_MAX 0X7fffffff
#endif

main()
{
   unsigned int seed;
   int face, rolls, count, results[6];
   char line[20];

   seed = (unsigned int) time( NULL );

   srand(seed);
```

Program 10.5. Random number generation (continues)

```
        puts("Enter number of rolls");
        gets(line);
        rolls = atoi(line);

        for (count = 0; count < rolls; count++)
        {
            face = rand() % 6;
            results[face]++;
        }
        for (face = 0; face < 6; face++)
        {
            printf("for side %d = %d\n",face,results[face]);
        }
        exit(0);
    }
```

Program 10.5. (continued)

The output from Program 10.5 for 50, 1000, and 2000 rolls is shown in Figure 10.4. Note that if you run this same program, you are likely to get different answers unless you run it at precisely the same time of the day that we did.

For 50 rolls:

    for side 0 = 11
    for side 1 = 7
    for side 2 = 5
    for side 3 = 10
    for side 4 = 9
    for side 5 = 8

For 1000 rolls:

    for side 0 = 176
    for side 1 = 161
    for side 2 = 161
    for side 3 = 172
    for side 4 = 167
    for side 5 = 163

For 2000 rolls:

    for side 0 = 299
    for side 1 = 355
    for side 2 = 352
    for side 3 = 322
    for side 4 = 333
    for side 5 = 339

Figure 10.4. Output from Program 10.5

Notice in Program 10.5 that the value returned from time() was cast to the type (unsigned int) expected by srand().

For C implementations that do not supply stdlib.h and the macro RAND_MAX, one should #define RAND_MAX to the largest possible value returned by rand(). For our example, on a DEC Vax, the following macro can be utilized.

```
#define RAND_MAX 0X7fffffff
```

Many simulations require a random number in the range of (0,1). To use the rand() function for these applications, simply divide by RAND_MAX as shown in the expression below.

```
u = (float)rand() / (float)RAND_MAX
```

The next group of functions to be discussed are the mathematical library functions.

10.4   MATHEMATICAL FUNCTIONS

There are two categories of *mathematical functions:* those that accept and return double-precision values and those that accept and return integer values. We will first discuss the double-precision-valued functions.

Double-Precision-Valued Functions

The double-precision-valued functions are declared in the header file math.h. Also defined in math.h are three macros with type double: EDOM, ERANGE, and HUGE_VAL. EDOM is an acronym for *Error DOMain*; ERANGE is an acronym for *Error RANGE;* HUGE_VAL is a positive double expression that is not necessarily representable as a float. If the value of an input parameter for a math function exceeds its allowable range, the value returned is implementation dependent, but the object *errno* (defined in a math.h) will be set to EDOM. If the result of the function cannot be represented by a double-typed value (as a result of overflow, for example), HUGE_VAL is returned by the function and errno is set to ERANGE. Note that errno is set to zero when the program starts, but is not reset to zero by each individual library function. To use errno, the programmer should set it to zero before calling a math function, and then test the value of errno after the function returns. The recommended way to check for errors from the math functions is to check the value of errno.

The file float.h contains the definition of various constants that describe implementation limits upon float and double values.

For the purpose of presentation, the double-precision-valued functions can be grouped into the following categories.

Exponential and logarithmic functions
Hyperbolic functions
Nearest integer, absolute value, and remainder functions
Power and square root functions
Trigonometric functions

The functions that are most likely to be used are presented. Others are listed in Appendix A.

Table 10.11. Mathematical Function Overview

#include <math.h>

Exponential and logarithmic functions.

double exp(double x)	Computes the exponential of x with the base e.
double log(double x)	Determines the natural logarithm of x.
double log10(double x)	Determines the base-10 logarithm of x.

Hyperbolic functions. The input to these functions is in radians.

double cosh(double x)	Returns the hyperbolic cosine of x.
double sinh(double x)	Returns the hyperbolic sine of x.
double tanh(double x)	Returns the hyperbolic tangent of x.

Nearest integer, absolute value, and remainder.

double ceil(double x)	Returns the smallest integer not less than x.
double fabs(double x)	Returns the absolute value of x.
double floor(double x)	Returns the largest integer not greater than x.
double fmod(double x, double y)	Returns the remainder of x / y, where the remainder is computed as $x - i * y$ for some integer i where i is the largest integer such that $|remainder| < |y|$.

Power and square root functions.

double pow(double x, double y)	Returns x raised to the y power. A domain error (EDOM) occurs if x is zero and y is less than or equal to zero, or if x is negative and y is not an integer.
double sqrt(double x)	Returns the nonnegative square root of x. A domain error (EDOM) occurs if x is negative.

Trigonometric functions. The value returned from the trigonometric functions is measured in radians.

(continued)

Table 10.11. continued

double acos(double x)	Returns the arc cosine of x for x in the range of [−1,1]. The result is in the range [0,π].
double asin(double x)	Returns the principal value of the arc sine of x, where x is in the range [−1,1]. The result is in the range [−π/2,π/2].
double atan(double x)	Returns the principal value of the arc tangent of x. The result is in the range (−π/2,π/2).
double atan2(double y, double x)	Returns the principal value of the arc tangent of y/x using the signs of both y and x to determine the quadrant of the return value. The result is in the range (−π,π].
double cos(double x)	Returns the cosine of x where x is measured in radians.
double sin(double x)	Returns the sine of x, where x is measured in radians.
double tan(double x)	Returns the tangent of x, where x is measured in radians.

In order to use a math function, many C compilers require that the math library be specified on the C compiler command line (or in a make file). For example, UNIX C compilers may require the command line option -lm to instruct the linker to search the math library.

A few simple examples of math library functions follow.

Figure 10.5 illustrates the values of some of the commonly used mathematical functions for a particular parameter value.

It was noted in Table 10.11 that many of the trigonometric functions accept (or produce) values that are measured in radians. Program 10.6 accepts a measure from the user in degrees, converts degrees to radians, and outputs the value of the sine and cosine of that angle.

```
ceil(4.2) == 5.0
ceil(−4.2) == −4.0
fabs(4.2) == 4.2
fabs(−4.2) == 4.2
floor(4.2) == 4.0
floor(−4.2) == −5.0
pow(3.0,2.0) == 9.0
```

Figure 10.5. Commonly used function values

```
#include <stdio.h>
#include <math.h>

#ifdef ANSI
#include <stdlib.h>
#else
  extern double atof();
#endif

const double pi = 3.1415;

main()
{
    double degrees, radians;
    char angle[20];

    puts("Input angle in degrees");
    gets(angle);
    degrees = atof(angle);
    radians = degrees * (pi/180);
    printf("cosine \t sine\n");
    printf("%4.2f \t %4.2f\n",cos(radians),sin(radians));
    exit(0);
}
```

Program 10.6. Converting degrees to radians

Integer Valued Functions

The functions in this category all accept integer or long int values and return int or long int results. The functions are declared in stdlib.h. The ranges of values for the integer types are specified in limits.h. See Table 10.12 for a description of the integer math functions.

Table 10.12. Integer Valued Functions

```
#include <stdlib.h>
```

`int abs(int i);`   Returns the absolute value of i.

`div_t div(int numerator, int denominator)`

Computes numerator/denominator, and returns the quotient and remainder in a structure of type div_t (declared in stdlib.h), where div_t is defined as follows:

Table 10.12. continued

```
typedef struct
{
   int quot;    /* quotient */
   int rem;     /* remainder */
} div_t;
```

long int labs(long int i)   Returns the absolute value of i, where both
                               the return value and i have type long int.

ldiv_t ldiv(long int numerator, int denominator)

Computes numerator/denominator, and returns the quotient and remainder in a
structure of type ldiv_t, where ldiv_t is defined as follows:

```
typedef struct
{
   long quot;    /* quotient */
   long rem;     /* remainder */
} ldiv_t;
```

10.5 DATE AND TIME FUNCTIONS

Time is recorded and stored internally in arithmetically encoded formats. Two
times are kept: the calendar time and processing time. The calendar time is a
representation of the current date and time. The processing time is the amount of
processor time utilized by a program during execution. The internal representations of these times are implementation dependent. However, encodings that are
often used are (1) the number of elapsed seconds from a reference date for
calendar time and (2) the number of elapsed fractions of a second from start-up for
program execution time. The former type is defined as time_t and the latter
clock_t in the header file time.h. The macro CLK_TCK in time.h specifies the
number per second of the type clock_t. That is, the resolution of the clock is such
that it ticks CLK_TCK times per second [clock()/CLK_TCK has the unit
seconds].
  Two categories of functions are provided in the date and time library.

1. Functions that fetch and manipulate calendar and processor time in the
   encoded formats.
2. Functions that convert the encoded calendar time into date and time,
   including hours, minutes, seconds, year, month, day, and so on.

The header file time.h declares these functions. We will now examine the first category of functions.

Encoded Time Manipulation Functions

Table 10.13 presents the functions and associated types that manipulate the time in its encoded formats.

It is often claimed that integer arithmetic is more efficient than floating-point arithmetic on computers. Program 10.7 uses the clock() function to instrument a simple program to compare the time taken to execute floating-point and integer arithmetic operations.

Table 10.13. Encoded Time Functions

```
#include <time.h>

clock_t clock(void)
```

Returns the amount of processor time used by the program since its invocation. The value (clock_t) (–1) is returned if the time is not available.

```
time_t time(time_t *timer)
```

Returns the current encoded calendar time. The parameter can be either a NULL or a pointer to a variable of type time_t. If this parameter is not NULL, the encoded time is also stored at the given location. The value (time_t)(–1) is returned if the time cannot be determined.

```
double difftime(time_t time1, time_t time0)
```

Returns the value (*time*1-*time*0) in seconds. *time*0 and *time*1 are encoded calendar times returned by time() or mktime().

```
#include <stdio.h>

#ifdef ANSI
#include <time.h>
#else
  typedef long clock_t;
  typedef long time_t;
```

Program 10.7. Using the clock() function (continues)

```
  extern clock_t clock();
#endif

static double d1, d2 = 1233.2, d3 = 223.4;
static int i1, i2 = 1223, i3 = 893;

static const max_iterations = 10000;

main()
{
    clock_t start_time, mid_time, end_time;
    register int i;

    start_time = clock();

    for (i = 0;  i < max_iterations;  i++)
    {
      d1 = d2 / d3;
      d2++;  d3++;
    }

    mid_time = clock();

    for (i = 0; i < max_iterations;  i++)
    {
      i1 = i2 / i3;
      i2++;  i3++;
    }

    end_time = clock();

    printf("Time for doubles = %ld, time for integers = %ld\n",
           mid_time-start_time, end_time-mid_time);
    exit(0);
}
```

Program 10.7. (continued)

The output from Program 10.7 for one machine is shown below.

Time for doubles = 99996, time for integers = 33332

The results seem to substantiate the claim, showing that the floating-point operations require three times as much time as the integer operations on the particular machine used for this example.

The time() function is most often used in one of two ways. The first is simply to fetch the encoded calendar time and store that value for later reference. For example, one could store the last modification date for a record in a file. The second use of time() is to fetch the calendar time and the convert it to a format suitable for human consumption. To accomplish this, one of the following time conversion functions can be used.

Time Conversion Functions

The time conversion functions are used to convert between the encoded version of the calendar time and various human-readable versions of the time. These functions use the structure *tm* that is declared in time.h. It is illustrated in Figure 10.6.

The flag tm_isdst in Figure 10.6 is positive if daylight savings time is in effect, zero if it is not, and negative if this information is not available. The use of this structure is illustrated in Program 10.8 and in Table 10.14, which presents the time conversion functions.

```
struct tm {
    int tm_sec;         /* seconds after the minute - [0,59] */
    int tm_min;         /* minutes after the hour - [0,59] */
    int tm_hour;        /* hours since midnight - [0,23] */
    int tm_mday;        /* day of the month - [1,31] */
    int tm_mon;         /* months since January - [0,11] */
    int tm_year;        /* years since 1900 */
    int tm_wday;        /* days since Sunday - [0,6] */
    int tm_yday;        /* days since January 1 - [0,365] */
    int tm_isdst;       /* daylight savings time flag */
};
```

Figure 10.6. Broken-down calendar time structure

Table 10.14. Time Conversion Functions

```
#include <time.h>

struct tm *localtime(time_t *timeptr)
```

Accepts a pointer to an encoded time and returns a pointer to a structure containing the broken-down time that corresponds to the given encoded time value. The returned pointer points to a single static structure so that if localtime() is called again, the same pointer is returned that points to the updated structure.

```
char *asctime(struct tm *timeptr)
```

(continued)

Table 10.14. continued

Accepts a pointer to the tm structure containing a date and time and then returns a pointer to a string with the form:

Mon Jan 01 08:30:23 1988\n

The values in the string are determined by the values in the structure pointed to by timeptr.

```
struct tm *gmtime(time_t *timeptr)
```

Like localtime(), but converts the encoded time to the broken-down format expressed in Greenwich Mean Time.

```
time_t mktime(struct tm *timeptr)
```

Accepts a pointer to a broken-down time structure and returns the corresponding encoded calendar time.

Program 10.8 illustrates the use of time() to fetch the encoded time, of localtime() to convert the encoded time into the broken-down time structure, and, finally, of asctime() to convert the broken-down time into the standard time string.

```
#include <stdio.h>
#ifdef ANSI
#include <time.h>
#else
  typedef long time_t;
  extern time_t time();
#endif

main()
{
    struct tm *broken_down_time;
    time_t current_time;

    current_time = time(NULL);

    broken_down_time = localtime(&current_time);

    printf("time %d - %d - %d\n",broken_down_time->tm_mon+1,
      broken_down_time->tm_mday, broken_down_time->tm_year+1900);

    printf("%s\n",asctime(broken_down_time));
    exit(0);
}
```

Program 10.8. Using the time conversion functions

The output from Program 10.8 is illustrated below.

```
time 3 - 16 - 1988
Wed Mar 16 13:56:59 1988
```

Notice that the month number in the time structure is in the range [0,11] and that the year is the number of years since 1900. This necessitates the addition of 1 and 1900, respectively, to these structure members.

10.6   SEARCHING AND SORTING FUNCTIONS

The searching and sorting functions are declared in stdlib.h. Two functions are provided: (1) binary search and (2) a sort function. Both functions are discussed below.

Binary Search

Binary search is a fast method for locating an element an ordered (sorted) array. The element to be located is called the *key*. Consider the list shown below.

−244 −203 −102 −44 −2 5 52 75 105 211 455

Suppose that we want to determine whether the key value 211 is in the list. If we began at the start of the list (at left), then ten comparisons would be required to find the value. Binary search takes advantage of the fact the list is ordered, and begins its search in the middle of the list. In our example, 211 would be compared with 5 (the middle value), and thus it is immediately apparent in which half of the list the desired element must lie. The next step in the search is to discard the unneeded half, split the remaining half, and again compare. Thus, the key would be compared with 105, and again half of the elements in the list can be discarded. Binary search would locate the value in three or four comparisons as compared with the ten required by the sequential search. On the average, sequential search would require on the order of N/2 comparisons whereas binary search will require on the order of $\log_2(N)$ comparisons, where N is the length of the list. For a small list, the difference in execution time is not an issue but for larger arrays the savings in time can be substantial.

The generalized binary search function provided in the C library is illustrated in Table 10.15.

Table 10.15. Binary Search Function

```
#include <stdlib.h>

void *bsearch(void *key, void *base,
              size_t nmemb, size_t size,
              int (*compar)(void *p1, void *p2))
```

Returns a pointer to the matching member of the array or NULL if no match is found.

Key is a pointer to the value to be located.

Base is a pointer to the start of the array to be searched. The array must be in ascending order.

Nmemb is the number of elements in the array.

Size is the size in bytes of each array element.

Compar() is a pointer to a function that will compare two of the array elements. Compar() returns negative if *p1 < *p2, zero if *p1 = = *p2, and positive if *p1 > *p2. (The expressions *p1 and *p2 are used loosely here to indicate the objects to which p1 and p2 point.)

The user of bsearch() must supply a pointer to his or her own comparison function that compares elements of the array. Given the comparison function and the size of each item in the array, the bsearch() function can work with items of any type. We will illustrate the use of this function in Sorting.

Sorting

A sorting function is provided that will sort an array of elements stored in internal memory. Like bsearch(), the sort function is generalized so that it can sort items of any type. Table 10.16 illustrates the calling sequence.

Table 10.16. Sort Function

```
#include <stdlib.h>

/* quick-sort */
void qsort(void *base, size_t nmemb, size_t size,
           int (*compar)(void *p1, void *p2))
```

qsort() does not return a value.

Base is a pointer to the start of the array to be sorted.   *continues*

Table 10.16. continued

Nmemb is the number of elements in the array.
Size is the size in bytes of each array element.
Compar() is a pointer to a function that will compare two array elements.
Compar() returns negative if *p1 < *p2, zero if *p1 == *p2, and positive if
    *p1 > *p2. (The expressions *p1 and *p2 are used loosely here to indicate the
    objects to which p1 and p2 point.)

Program 10.9 illustrates a very simple usage of both bsearch() and qsort().
More complex applications are left as programming problems. In this program, an
unordered list of integers is first sorted using qsort(), and then that list is searched
for a particular element using bsearch().

```c
#include <stdio.h>
#include <stdlib.h>

int list[] = {5, -102, 75, -44, 455, -203, -244, 211,
          105, -2, 52 };

main()
{
  extern int test_int(int *x, int *y);   /* comparison function */
  int key_value, i, item_number;
  size_t list_size = sizeof(list)/sizeof(list[0]);
  int *keyptr;

  qsort(list, list_size, sizeof(list[0]), test_int);
  printf("array has been sorted, new order is:\n");
  for (i = 0; i < list_size; i++)
  {
    printf("element %d = %d\n",i,list[i]);
  }

  printf("searching for item %d\n",key_value = 211);
  keyptr = (int *)bsearch(&key_value, list, list_size,
            sizeof(list[0]), test_int);
  item_number = (int)(keyptr - list);
  printf("Key located at element %d\n",item_number);
}

/*  Compare two integers.  Returns negative if *x > *y,
 *  zero if *x == *y, and positive if *x > *y.
 */
```

Program 10.9. Sort and search an array of integers (continues)

```
int test_int(int *x, int *y)
{
    return(*x - *y);
}
```

Program 10.9. (continued)

The output from Program 10.9 is illustrated in Figure 10.7.

```
array has been sorted, new order is:
element 0 = -244
element 1 = -203
element 2 = -102
element 3 = -44
element 4 = -2
element 5 = 5
element 6 = 52
element 7 = 75
element 8 = 105
element 9 = 211
element 10 = 455
searching for item 211
Key located at element 9
```

Figure 10.7. Output from Program 10.6

10.7 COMMUNICATING WITH THE HOST OPERATING SYSTEM

Functions in this category are declared in stdlib.h. These functions allow information to be passed between the host operating system and the C program.

Examining the Environment

Both the UNIX and MS-DOS operating systems provide an "environment" consisting of "variables" and associated values. For example, the UNIX command

```
     C-shell (csh)          Bourne-shell (bsh)

  setenv TERM vt100, or      TERM=vt100
  setenv TERM=vt100          export TERM
```

creates the *environment variable* TERM and the associated value vt100, which is stored in the environment. The MS-DOS command PATH=c:\dos;c:\tools creates an environment variable named PATH with associated value c:\dos;c:\tools. UNIX also has a PATH environment variable. In both UNIX and MS-DOS, the value of an environment variable is simply a string of characters. The environment can be accessed from within a C program by using the getenv() call illustrated below:

```
#include <stdlib.h>

/* get-environment */
char *getenv(char *name)
```

Returns a pointer to the beginning of a string containing the value of the name pointed to by the *name* parameter. If no match is found, NULL is returned.

Program 10.10 illustrates a simple program that can be used to determine the values of both TERM and PATH from the environment.

The output of this program for one of the author's environments is illustrated below.

```
Your terminal type is vt100
Your path is .:/usr/users/troy/bin:/usr/ucb:/bin:/usr/bin:/
usr/local
```

```
#include <stdio.h>

#ifdef ANSI
#include <stdlib.h>
#else
    extern char *getenv();
#endif

main()
{
  char *cptr;

  if ((cptr = getenv("TERM")) != NULL)
  {
    printf("Your terminal type is %s\n",cptr);
  }
  if ((cptr = getenv("PATH")) != NULL)
  {
    printf("Your path is %s\n",cptr);
  }
  exit(0);
}
```

Program 10.10. Examining the environment

Notice that the value for TERM in this example is vt100 and the value for PATH is the string of directory names.

Many environments support an alternative way to examine the host environment. In these systems, a third parameter is passed to the main() function that has a pointer to each environment string. This argument is illustrated below.

```
main(int argc, char *argv[], char *envp[])
{
}
```

This is a nonstandard feature. Interested readers are referred to their local system documentation.

Executing an Operating System Command

Another function that allows communication with the host environment is the system() function, used to send a command to the host operating system's command processor, or shell. The prototype for the function is shown below.

```
#include <stdlib.h>

int system(char *command)
```

> Passes the string addressed by *command* to the host command processor. If *command* is NULL, system() returns nonzero if the command processor exists, and zero otherwise. (Figure 10.9 in Section 10.8 illustrates the zero return.)

Program 10.11 illustrates a rudimentary restricted command processor. It displays a simple menu showing a restricted set of operations from which a user may choose, and uses the system() function to map the menu choices into the commands of the host operating system.

```
#include <stdio.h>
#include <stdlib.h>

/* restricted command processor */
main()
{
    int menu(void), cmd;
    char *getfile(void);
    char oscommand[30];
```

Program 10.11. Using the system() functions (continues)

```
        while ((cmd = menu()) != 4)
        {
          switch(cmd)
          {
            case 1: system("ls -l");
                   break;
            case 2: strcpy(oscommand,"cat");
                   strcat(oscommand,getfile());
                   system(oscommand);
                   break;
            case 3: strcpy(oscommand,"rm");
                   strcat(oscommand,getfile());
                   system(oscommand);
                   break;
            case 4: system("logout");
                   break;
            default: puts("Enter 1, 2, 3, or 4\n");
          }
        }
}

/* display menu and return selection */
int menu(void)
{
    char choice[20];

    system("clear");
    puts("1 - show directory");
    puts("2 - display a file");
    puts("3 - delete a file");
    puts("4 - stop working");
    puts("Enter 1,2,3, or 4");
    gets(choice);
    return(atoi(choice));
}

/* prompt for and accept a file name */
char *getfile(void)
{
    static char file[20];

    puts("Enter file name: ");
    gets(file);
    return(file);
}
```

Program 10.11. (continued)

The host operating system under which Program 10.11 was tested also had a command called *clear* that erases the user's terminal screen before the menu is displayed for each iteration.

Exiting Program Execution

The function exit() can be used at program termination to return a value to the host operating system. The prototype declaration is shown below.

```
include <stdlib.h>

void exit(int status);
```

When called, exit() causes all open I/O streams to be flushed and closed. Any temporary files created by tmpfile() are deleted. If the value of status is zero, then a value indicating successful termination is returned to the host operating system. If the value of status is nonzero, an implementation-defined value indicating unsuccessful termination is returned.

The facility to return a value to the host operating system is most useful when a series of programs is utilized in a command file (also called a batch or script file) of operating system commands where continuation of the sequence of commands is dependent of successful completion of prior commands. To support this, many host operating systems have an environment variable that is set to the exit status of the last program. For example, the UNIX C shell has the $status variable and MS-DOS has the ERRORLEVEL parameter. The variables can be examined using command language (shell) commands, affording the opportunity conditionally to control program execution from the command file. For example, the left column below shows a UNIX C shell command and the right column illustrates an MS-DOS command that examines the exit() status returned by myprog.

```
myprog                              myprog
if ($status == 1) ...               If errorlevel 1 ...
```

It is possible to specify a set of functions that are to be executed automatically upon successful program termination. The function atexit() stores a list of functions that are to be automatically executed "at exit" time. For example, the code fragment

```
#include <stdlib.h>

extern void clsall(void);
extern void clrline(void);

atexit(clsall);
atexit(clrline);
```

would "register" the addresses of clsall() and clrline() to be executed when the program successfully terminates (i.e., when exit() is called). Functions that are registered are executed in LIFO (last-in, first-out) order, so in the above example, clrline() would be executed before clsall(). Up to 32 functions can be registered. The atexit() function does not exist on most pre-ANSI compilers, although many UNIX systems have a similar function called onexit().

To terminate a program immediately and indicate abnormal termination, the abort() function can be called. This function neither accepts nor returns an argument, may not flush or close open I/O streams, and sends an implementation-defined value to the host operating system that indicates unsuccessful program termination. The abort() function is also called by the assert macro that is described in the next section.

10.8   DEBUGGING AIDS

The header file assert.h defines or uses two macros (assert() and NDEBUG) that are useful for debugging. The macro assert() can be implemented as shown in Figure 10.8. It is found in the header file assert.h.

The assert() macro is invoked with one argument. If the argument is zero, assert() generates a message to the standard error stream (stderr) stating the value of the expression, the source file name containing the assert call, and the source line number of the call. The macro then calls abort(), which terminates execution of the program. Notice that the action of the assert macro can be disabled by defining the macro NDEBUG (no debug).

Recall Program 10.11, the restricted command processor. The system() call is used to pass a command to the host operating system's command processor. If system() is called with a NULL argument, e.g. system (NULL), then 0 is returned if a command processor does not exist; otherwise nonzero is returned. If no command processor exists, Program 10.11 is inoperable. We could thus use the assert macro to test for the existence of a command processor as shown in the code fragment in Figure 10.9.

```
#ifndef NDEBUG
#define assert(exp) { \
    if (!(exp)) { \
        fprintf(stderr, Assertion failed %s, file %s, line %d\n", \
            #exp, __FILE__, __LINE__); \
        abort(); \
        } \
    }
#else
#define assert(exp)
#endif
```

Figure 10.8. Implementation of assert macro

```
#include <stdio.h>
#include <stdlib.h>
#include <assert.h>

/* restricted command processor */
main()
{
    int menu(void), cmd;
    char *getfile(void);
    char oscommand[30];

    assert(system(NULL));
    while ((cmd = menu()) != 4)
    {
      ...
    }
}
```

Figure 10.9. Using the assert macro

If there is no command processor available, system() will return zero and the
program will output the message

```
Assertion failed: system(NULL), file c:\bin\smallsh.c, line 15
```

and the program will terminate. (The path c:\bin\smallsh.c is the path name for the
source file in this example.) If a command processor is available, the program will
behave as before.

The action of the assert macro can be completely disabled by compiling the
program with the NDEBUG macro defined prior to inclusion of assert.h. The
simplest way to do this is to specify the definition of the macro on the compile
command line. This can be done in a UNIX environment by using the –DNDEBUG
flag with the compile command.

10.9   LOCALE-SPECIFIC BEHAVIOR

With the introduction of ANSI C, the C I/O and string conversion functions have
been adapted, and some new functions have been introduced, so that C programs
are able to produce results adapted to nationalities, cultures, and languages other
than English. These results are called *locale-specific behavior*. Examples include:

  1. The alphabet. Many languages use characters in addition to the Latin alphabet
     or other non-Latin symbols. The I/O, character manipulation, and conversion

functions should be adaptable to support for other alphabets and associated collating sequence.

2. The collating (sorting) sequence of symbols in the alphabet. Most European languages use a code like ASCII in which some of the ASCII punctuation codes are used for alphabetic characters. The ordering of these codes is not alphabetic. The function strcoll() has been introduced that can map a string to a format compatible to locale-specific comparison using strcmp() and memcmp().

3. Decimal point usage. Several European countries use a comma or a centered dot as opposed to the U.S. period. Formatted I/O functions [like printf()] can be adapted to produce locale-specific results.

4. Date and time. The string produced by the asctime() function for date and time is not appropriate for many countries. The function strftime() can be used to produce a result adapted to the locale.

The function setlocale() and the file <locale.h>, can be used to change or query a program's locale. The interested reader is referred to his or her local documentation if the need arises to change the locale-specific behavior of any of the above-mentioned functions. See also Appendix A.

10.10 PORTABILITY AND SOFTWARE ENGINEERING ISSUES

A major source of portability problems for pre-ANSI standard compilers is variation between implementations of the library functions. Since the library functions are not a part of the language, compiler vendors have exercised considerable freedom in both the determination of what functions to implement and how to implement them. These variations are an obvious source of portability problems.

ANSI-compliant compilers will go a long way toward solving this problem as the standard specifies a required set of functions and associated header files. Programmers should be certain to include the relevant header files to obtain the standard function prototype and macro declarations. Many vendors will supply functions in addition to those specified in the standard. Programming for maximum portability calls for localization of such nonstandard functions within modules or conditionally compiled code so that these functions can be easily located during the porting process.

If a nonstandard compiler is used, the programmer either should include the relevant header file that contains the function declarations, or if header files are not provided, be certain properly to declare the return value type of each function that is used. This is critical for the math and date/time functions. If the functions are not explicitly declared, C will assume that the return type is an integer, which is usually not the case for math and date/time functions. For example, a simple expression such as

```
x = sqrt(y)
```

will function incorrectly if sqrt() is not declared as type double. It is equally important to be sure that function parameters have the proper types if a non-ANSI compiler is utilized. With ANSI-compliant compilers that have function prototype declarations in the header files, the compiler will check for proper parameter types. Without prototype declarations and in the absence of other compile time analyzers such as lint, no parameter checking is performed by the compiler. Thus, for example, if sqrt() is called with an integer parameter, incorrect results will be returned (in the absence of prototypes).

Functions that interact with the host operating system are obvious sources for portability problems. Uses of functions like abort(), exit(), getenv(), and system() involve implementation-specified behavior. Such behavior should be carefully documented. For example, programs that utilize the system() function will not operate on a host operating system without a command processor. Since command processors vary with host systems, the argument to the system() function will vary. For example, listing a directory on MS-DOS could be done with the call system ("dir"), but on UNIX the proper call is system("ls –l"). Programs that depend upon the definition of a particular environment [using getenv()] will be host system dependent. In addition, one implementation may even allow a program to modify the environment, whereas others may not.

The setlocale() function can be called at run time to allow adaption of a program to other languages without recompiling or relinking. The run-time selectability of the locale provides a simple adaptation of a program for use internationally.

10.11   SUMMARY

This chapter has presented many of the functions and header files associated with the string, mathematics, utility, and date/time libraries. Table 10.17 summarizes the functions that were discussed.

Table 10.17. String, Mathematical, Utility, Date/Time, and Debugging Functions

Character manipulation, <ctype.h>:

```
int isalnum(int c)
int isalpha(int c)
int iscntrl(int c)
int isdigit(int c)
```
                                                                    continues

Table 10.17. continued

```
int isgraph(int c)
int islower(int c)
int isprint(int c)
int ispunct(int c)
int isspace(int c)
int isupper(int c)
int isxdigit(int c)
int tolower(int c)
int toupper(int c)
```

String manipulation, <string.h>:

```
void *memcpy(void *target, const void *source, size_t n)
void *memmove(void *target, const void *source, size_t n)
char *strcpy(char *target, const char *source)
char *strncpy(char *target, const char *source, size_t n)
char strcat(char *target, const char *source)
char strncat(char *target, const char *source, size_t n)
int memcmp(const void *sl, const void *s2, size_t n)
int strcmp(const char *sl, const char *s2)
int strncmp(const char *sl, const char *s2, size_t n)
void *memchr(const void *s, int c, size_t n)
char *strchr(char *s, int c)
char *strrchr(char *s, int c)
char *strtok(char *s, const char *delimit)
void *memset(void *s, int c, size_t n)
size_t strlen(const char *s)
```

String conversion, <stdlib.h>:

```
double    atof(char *string)
int       atoi(char *string)
long int  atol(char *string)
long int  strtol(char *string, char **endptr, int base)
unsigned long strtoul(char *string, char **endptr, int base)
```

Random number generation, <stdlib.h>:

```
void    srand(unsigned int seed)
int     rand(void)
```

Mathematics, double-valued functions <math.h> and <float.h>:

```
double acos(double x)
double asin(double x)
double atan(double x)
double atan2(double y, double x)
double cos(double x)
double sin(double x)
```

continued

Table 10.17. continued

```
double  tan(double x)
double  cosh(double x)
double  sinh(double x)
double  tanh(double x)
double  exp(double x)
double  log(double x)
double  log10(double x)
double  pow(double x, double y)
double  sqrt(double x)
double  ceil(double x)
double  fabs(double x)
double  floor(double x)
double  fmod(double x, double y)
```

Mathematics, integer-valued function <stdlib.h> and <limits.h>:

```
int       abs(int i)
div_t     div(int numer, int denom)
long int  labs(long int i)
ldiv_t    ldiv(long int numer, long int denom)
```

Date and time, <time.h>:

```
clock_t   clock(void)
double    difftime(time_t time1, time_t time0)
time_t    mktime(struct tm *timeptr)
time_t    time(time_t *timeptr)
char      *asctime(struct tm *timeptr)
struct tm *gmtime(time_t *timeptr)
struct tm *localtime(time_t *timeptr)
```

Sorting and searching, <stdlib.h>:

```
void *bsearch(void *key, void *base,
        size_t nmemb, size_t size,
        int (*compar)(void *p1, *p2))
void qsort(void *base, size_t nmemb, size_t size,
        int (*compar)(void *p1, void *p2))
```

Communicating with the host OS, <stdlib.h>:

```
void      abort(void)
int       atexit(void (*func)(void))
void      exit(int status)
char      *getenv(char *name)
int       system(char *string)
```

continued

Table 10.17. continued

Debugging aids, <assert.h>:

```
    void assert(int expression)
    NDEBUG
    (both are macros)
```

Locale-specific Behavior, <locale.h>:

```
    char *setlocale(int category, const char *locale)
```

This table does not describe every function specified in standard C. Appendix A contains such a list.

Keywords

character manipulation
clock_t
communication with host operating
    system
data and time functions
debugging aids
environment variable
errno

locale-specific behavior
mathematical functions
random numbers
searching and sorting functions
size_t
string conversion functions
string manipulation functions
time_t

References

Draft American National Standard x3.159–198x, Programming Language C. Copies may be obtained from Global Engineering Documents, Inc., 2805 McGaw, Irvine, CA 92714.

Harbison, S. P, and G. L. Steele. 1984. *A C Reference Manual,* Englewood Cliffs, N.J.: Prentice-Hall.

Discussion Questions

1. Discuss the importance of passing parameters of the proper type to functions, especially the math functions because their parameter types are usually doubles. If function prototypes are supported, the compiler will perform the proper type conversions. If prototypes are not supported (or not used), the

programmer must be sure that parameters have the proper types, or the proper casts are utilized. The same is true of return values for functions.

2. The functions qsort() and bsearch() can operate on any contiguously allocated list in memory. For example, these functions can work with integer arrays, double arrays, or arrays of structures. Discuss the way in which bsearch() can determine where each list element begins (for comparison). Discuss how qsort() might move elements within the array to produce the reordered array.

3. Qsort() and bsearch() can be used to sort more complex data types, such as structures. Discuss how the comparison function would be declared to utilize structures as arguments.

4. The random number generation functions rand() and srand() are called "pseudorandom number generators." Discuss the reason why these functions are not true random number generators.

5. Discuss the facilities in your operating system for defining and examining the environment.

6. Discuss the use of environment variables. For example, consider the way PATH and HOME (home directory) could be accessed and used by a C program.

Exercises

1. Describe how the assert macro could be used in a program to validate the range of a subscript's value that is used for an array reference. Given the array int array[MAX] and the subscript i, write an instance of the assert macro that will validate the value of i.

2. Obtain a listing of math.h. What functions are declared in that file that were not presented in this chapter? Are any of the functions missing from math.h?

3. Obtain a listing of time.h. Is the type time_t declared in your implementation? If so, state the declaration. If not, what is the type returned from time()?

4. List the operating system commands on your system to:
   a. Give an environment variable a value.
   b. Change the value.
   c. Display the entire environment (all variables and values).

5. Write an operating system command file for your system that will execute two programs. The first should be executed unconditionally, but the second should be executed only if the first exits with a value of 1. You may use operating system utilities, or you may write two of your own programs that set the exit status.

6. Code the following macros using correct C language statements:
   a. `tobinary(int c)` converts the character digit represented by c to the int binary equivalent.
   b. `issign(int c)`   1 if c is a '+' or '-' sign, 0 otherwise.
   c. `isoctal(int c)`   1 if c is a valid base-8 digit, 0 otherwise (c is a character code).

7. Write an erroneous code segment that could be used to demonstrate the superiority of strncpy() over strcpy().

8. Write a function that accepts a string and a character and returns the number of times the character occurs in the string. Your function should use strchr().

9. Give the value for the following function calls:
   a. ceil(101.1)
   b. ceil(−1.2)
   c. floor(101.1)
   d. floor(−1.2)
   e. pow(2.0,4.0)
   f. fabs(−33.2)

10. Suppose that it is desirable to enter the local telephone directory into a file and write a C program that will accept a phone number, search the directory using bsearch(), and return the name and address associated with the phone number. Can the data from the phone directory be stored in the file in the same order as found in the book and searched using bsearch()? Explain your answer.

Programming Problems

1. For a given year, y, the date of Easter can be computed as follows.
   a. Subtract 1900 from y and let the result be called r.
   b. Divide r by 19. Let a be the remainder.
   c. Divide $(7a + 1)$ by 19. Ignore the remainder. Let the quotient be b.
   d. Divide $(11a + 4 − b)$ by 29. Let m be the remainder.
   e. Divide r by 4. Ignore the remainder. Let q be the quotient.

f. Divide $(r + q + 31 - m)$ by 7, call w the remainder.

g. The date of Easter is $25 - m - w$. Call this result d. If d is positive, then the month is April. If d is nonpositive, then the month is March, and the date is $31 + d$.

Write a C program that accepts a year and displays the date of Easter, in the form month, day, year. Allow the user to enter years until a year of 0 is entered.

2. A simple sorting algorithm, called bubble sort, sorts a list by comparing adjacent pairs of elements in the list, and if the elements are out of order, exchanging them. Bubble sort makes repeated passes through the list until no more exchanges are necessary. In the first pass, the comparison begins with elements 1 and 2, next 2 and 3, etc., until elements $n - 1$ and n are compared. For ascending (sorted from smallest to largest) sort, this will "bubble" the largest element to the nth position in the list. Next, element 1 and 2, 2 and 3, etc., through $n - 2$ and $n - 1$ are compared. Each pass reduces the number of comparisons by one, until the list is sorted. For this problem, do the following three steps:

a. Code a bubble sort function that will sort an array of integers. The function should accept a pointer to the array and the number of elements in the array and then sort the array into ascending order. Instrument the function so that it counts the number of array element comparisons and outputs the number of comparisons and the number of elements in the array.

b. Code another function that uses qsort() to sort the same array that is described in part a. Refer to Program 10.9. Instrument the comparison function so that it counts the number of comparisons used by the C library qsort() function. Use a static variable for the counter.

c. Write a driver program that generates an array of 5000 random numbers using srand() and rand(). The driver should sort the array using qsort() and your bubble sort functions. Evaluate the relative efficiency of the two sorting algorithms by examining the number of comparisons and run time required by each sort algorithm.

3. A game played with two coins is called odds and evens. When the two coins are tossed, the result is odds if only one head or one tail shows. The result is even if the coin faces are the same. Write a program using random number generation that simulates this game. Allow the user to enter the number of tosses desired, and have the program count and display the total number of odds and the number of evens.

4. T. A. Chance lives in Las Vegas. Each day, while waiting for the bus, he plays a game of "three difference." In this game, the player repeatedly flips a coin

until the difference between the number of heads tossed and the number of tails tossed is equal to three. The player pays $1 for each flip of the coin, but receives $8 at the end of each game completed. Each day, Mr. Chance sets aside $10 for playing this game and plays until either (a) he loses all of the money he set aside for the day or (b) one game is completed. Write a program to simulate the daily winnings obtained by T. A. Chance for a specified number of days playing the game. Also compute the average daily winnings.

5. Write a program to simulate the game of Bingo. Write the program so that it reads Bingo cards from a file. For example, a Bingo card might be represented as:

```
 5  10   3  13   6
29  16  21  25  23
37  42  35  33  41
51  48  58  59  46
74  66  72  64  75
```

The program should read in a card and then simulate a game by generating the called numbers using srand() and rand(). The program should display the initial card, and each "called" number. When a called number is found to be on the card, display the card with an asterisk beside each "covered" number. For example, at some point in the simulation, the card might look like:

```
 5  *10   3  13    6
29   16  21  25   23
37   42 *35  33  *41
51   48  58  59   46
74   66  72  64  *75
```

Play the game until a win is detected. A winning card is one with all of one row, column, or diagonal covered. At this point, output the message "Bingo!" and the winning card with asterisks. The program should then read another card from the file and begin the play again. Read and play games until EOF is detected in the file.

6. The following are the results of the Indianapolis 500 race for certain early years. The time is the elapsed time and the speed is the average speed.

Year	Driver	Time	Speed
1911	Ray Harroun	6:42:08	74.59
1912	Joe Dawson	6:21:06	78.72
1913	Jules Goux	6:35:05	75.93
1914	Rene Thomas	6:03:45	82.47

continued

Year	Driver	Time	Speed
1915	Ralph DePalma	5:33:55	89.94
1916	Dario Resta	5:34:17	84.00
1919	Howdy Wilcox	5:40:42	88.05
1920	Gaston Chevrolet	5:38:32	88.62
1921	Tommy Milton	5:34:44	89.62
1922	Jimmy Murphy	5:17:30	94.48
1923	Tommy Milton	5:29:50	90.95
1924	L. L. Corum and Joe Boyer	5:05:23	98.23
1925	Peter DePaolo	4:56:39	101.13
1926	Frank Lockart	4:10:14	95.90
1927	George Souders	5:07:33	97.545
1928	Louis Meyer	5:01:33	99.482
1929	Ray Keech	5:07:25	97.585
1930	Billy Arnold	4:58:39	100.448
1931	Louis Schneider	5:10:27	96.629

Write one or both of the following programs that use this data.

a. Write a program that will read this data into an array of structures. The structure should hold the race date, driver's name, and time and speed information. Use qsort() to sort the array into ascending order by race speed, and then output the results in the format shown above but in order of speed. The comparison function that you write should use as parameters pointers to the structure that is used to hold the race data.

b. Write a program that will read the race data into an array of structures. The structure should hold the data as shown above (year, driver, time, and speed). The program should then allow the user to enter a year and then display the race information for that year. Use bsearch() to locate the proper structure in the array, and output an appropriate message for years that are not available.

7. Code and test the macros described in Exercise 6. Write an interactive driver program to test your code.

8. Write an interactive program that allows the user to query the environment. For example, if the user entered TERM, the program would output the string associated with that environment variable, or a message indicating that that variable is not used in the environment. Allow the user to exit the program with a "q" for quit.

9. Code and test the function described in Exercise 8. Write a driver program to test your function.

10. Write a program that reads the standard input and counts the number of words. Words are delimited by a space, comma, hyphen, semicolon, colon, or new-line. Your program should use the strtok() function and it should output its count to the standard output.

11. Write a desk clock program to help you to remember the time. The program should clear the screen, and display the date and time in the center of the screen. The display could be

Tuesday, May 1, 1988

10:56 AM

The program should update the time every second, so that you are right on time.

11 Dynamic Aspects of C Programming

The major topics of this chapter concern various aspects of C programming that are dynamic in nature. First, the concept of dynamic action is explained. Next, the primary category of C's dynamic capabilities are explained. These are the dynamic memory management functions malloc(), calloc(), realloc(), and free(). These functions provide the ability to allocate and free memory locations for variables in a program at run time. Several examples are presented to illustrate these functions.

Finally, this chapter discusses the techniques, types, macros, and functions provided to allow the definition of functions with a variable number of arguments. These are the type va_list, and the functions (or macros) va_start(), va_arg(), and va_end().

The chapter concludes with a discussion of software engineering and portability considerations.

11.1 INTRODUCTION

The adjective *dynamic* is used in computer science to describe the behavior of events that occur during program execution such as assigning values to variables. This is contrasted with the term *static,* which describes operations that are completed before the program is executed. (Static here should not be confused with the C keyword static; it is being used here in a more general sense.) Compilation is a static process; the tool lint (a syntax checker), which is provided by the UNIX operating system, is a static tool. An input statement like scanf() makes dynamic assignment of values to variables.

Dynamic behaviors have the advantage of flexibility. Decisions are deferred until the program is executed. If all assignments had to be static—that is, if assignment statements were restricted to the use of constants and no input statements were permitted—programs would be much less flexible. Dynamic behavior can also produce greater efficiency of resource usage. A file is often more useful than an array because an array has to have a static declaration of its

393

length, whereas a file's length can vary at run time. (Files also have the advantage of being more permanent than arrays.)

There are disadvantages to the use of dynamic properties. A compiler or other static tools are often incapable of detecting errors in the use of dynamic objects. These errors may only occur in certain circumstances during run time, and run-time errors are difficult to correct. This difficulty results from the fact that the static tools (compiler, lint, etc) cannot simulate run-time conditions, and the fact that the errors often produce strange results, the sources of which are difficult to locate.

The primary example of dynamic behavior described in this chapter is the dynamic allocation of memory. ANSI standard C and most other pre-ANSI standard versions provide functions that allocate and free (deallocate) memory during the execution of a program. The determination of the amount of memory to allocate is ordinarily accomplished before the program begins to execute. For example, in an array declaration like "int array[1000]" the compiler can determine exactly how many bytes of memory are needed for this array. This is a static process. If this is a static array (using the C keyword static), then the actual memory locations for this array are allocated when the program is loaded into memory and remains there until the program terminates. If this is an automatic array, then space is allocated when the block in which it is declared is entered. This allocation occurs at run time and is, therefore, considered dynamic. The problem with both of these examples of memory allocation is that they require the programmer to determine the maximum size of each data structure during the program's design. This technique has three disadvantages: (1) The programmer may have been incorrect in the estimate of maximum size, in which case the program will fail when that maximum is exceeded. (2) The program makes inefficient use of available memory when the maximum size is not used. (3) If the size of an object needs to be increased, the program has to be recompiled with a change in the declaration.

The dynamic memory management functions are useful since the programmer often does not know how much memory will be required for an object until run time. These functions permit the programmer to calculate and request the amount of memory that is needed for an object constructed during program execution. Consider the memory requirements for a general-purpose spreadsheet program. Users create spreadsheets of many different sizes, and run spreadsheets on many different sizes of machines. One solution is to declare the spreadsheet data structure to be the largest that will fit into memory. However, this maximum will depend upon the execution environment. With dynamic memory management, the spreadsheet program can determine the amount of memory available on that machine at run time, and then allocate precisely that amount. An even better solution is initially to allocate a small amount of space, and then to allocate more space as the user's needs expand. C's dynamic memory management functions can fulfill the requirements of each of these solutions. The next section will provide an explanation of the syntax and semantics of each of these functions.

11.2 DYNAMIC MEMORY MANAGEMENT

Purpose

As introduced in the previous section, the dynamic memory allocation and deallocation functions of C allow the programmer to defer allocation of memory to data structures until run time; and to return that memory to the system when no longer needed. Using these functions, a programmer can produce data structures whose size and shape change during program execution. For instance, the programmer can dynamically produce an array, a search-tree data structure, a linked list, or a queue. After discussing these functions, we will illustrate such data structures in some examples.

Standard Memory Allocation/Deallocation Functions

Four memory management functions are specified in the ANSI standard. (Most pre-ANSI standard C compilers contain these functions also.) The prototypes of these functions are presented in Figure 11.1.

The prototype header declarations of these functions are given in the header file *stdlib.h*. Thus, this header file should be included in any file that accesses these functions.

The function *malloc()*, for "memory allocate," allocates the number of bytes of memory specified in the parameter size. The value returned by this function is a pointer to the beginning of this newly allocated space. This value, which is specified as a pointer to type void, should be cast to the appropriate pointer type.

```
#include<stdlib.h>

void *malloc(size_t size);
void *calloc(size_t num_mem, size_t size);
void *realloc(void * ptr, size_t size);
void free(void * ptr)
```

Figure 11.1. Memory allocation and deallocation functions

```
char *carray1;
char *carray2;
float *farray;
size_t n;

carray1 = (char *) malloc( 100 );
carray2 = (char *) malloc( 100 * sizeof( char ) );

puts("Enter number of floats:");
scanf( "%u", &n );
farray = (float *) malloc( n * sizeof( float ) );
```

Figure 11.2. Examples of malloc()

If the size is zero, or if the space specified cannot be allocated, the function returns a null pointer. This newly allocated space is not initialized.

The examples in Figure 11.2 illustrate three uses of the malloc() function. In the first use, 100 bytes of memory are allocated for carray1. The second example is an improvement as it clearly allocates sufficient space for 100 characters in this character array. If a character is represented in 1 byte, these two are equivalent. However, the second example is more portable than the first.

The third use of malloc() in Figure 11.2 illustrates the dynamic nature of this function. The amount of space allocated cannot be determined until the value of the variable n is read during program execution.

In each use of this function in Figure 11.2, notice that malloc() returns a pointer to the newly allocated space, which is then cast to the appropriate type.

Program 11.1 gives a more complete demonstration of a use of malloc().

The function calloc(size_t num_mem, size_t size), for "clear and allocate," is similar to malloc() in that it also allocates memory. The primary differences are the method of determining the amount of space to allocate and the fact that calloc() initializes (clears) the memory. This function allocates space for num_mem objects, each of which is size bytes. In other words, calloc() allocates num_mem * size bytes of memory.

The other difference between these two functions is that calloc() initializes the newly allocated memory locations. Each bit is set to zero. Note that this may not be the representation for a floating-point zero or a null pointer constant. Do not assume that this initial value can be used in floating-point arithmetic or pointer operations.

The calloc() function, like malloc(), returns a pointer to the beginning of the newly allocated space. If the allocation fails, or if either num_mem or size is zero, then a null pointer is returned.

The examples in Figure 11.3 are the calloc() equivalent of those in Figure 11.2.

The realloc(void *ptr, size_t size) function is used to change the amount of

```
#include <stdio.h>
#include <stdlib.h>

main()
{
    char * string;
    unsigned int n;
    printf(" Enter size: ");
    scanf( "%u",&n );

    /* allocate space, including space for the null byte */
    string = malloc( (n+1)*sizeof( char ) );

    printf("Enter up to %u characters: \n", n);
    scanf( "%s", string );

    /* remainder of program to manipulate this string. */

    printf( "The input string is: %s\n", string );
    exit(0);
} /* end main */
```

Program 11.1. Use of malloc()

```
    char *carray1;
    char *carray2;
    float *farray;
    unsigned int n;

    carray1 = (char *) calloc( 100, 1 );
    carray2 = (char *) calloc( 100, sizeof( char ) );

    puts("Enter number of floats:");
    scanf( "%u", &n );
    farray = (float *) calloc( n, sizeof( float ) );
```

Figure 11.3. Examples of calloc()

storage that is allocated for a particular object. (Normally, this is used to increase the amount of storage required, but could be used to decrease the number of bytes of memory used.) This function changes the size of the object to which ptr, the first parameter, points. The memory allocated contains size bytes of memory, where size is the second parameter to realloc(). This operation does not guarantee that the same memory locations will be used, but does guarantee that the contents of the object will not be changed up to the smaller of the old and new sizes. If ptr is a null pointer, realloc() allocates size bytes, similar to malloc(). If ptr is not a null pointer, then the value in ptr must be a pointer returned by a previous call to calloc(), malloc(), or realloc(), which has not yet been freed. (The operation of freeing will be discussed next in conjunction with the free() function.) If these conditions are not met, the behavior of the function is not defined.

The realloc() function returns a pointer to the beginning of the newly allocated space. If space cannot be allocated, a null pointer is returned and the object to which ptr points is unmodified. If size is zero, the realloc() function returns a null pointer. Furthermore, a zero size frees the space occupied by the object to which ptr points.

Let us consider another example. In C, array sizes are static. That is, the defining definition for each array must specify the size in a form that can be determined at compile time. It is possible to use the dynamic memory allocation functions to simulate dynamic arrays. To create a dynamic array of n characters (where n is a variable whose value is not known until run time), the calloc(), malloc(), or realloc() function can be used to allocate enough space for n times the size of one character. These functions return a pointer to void, which must be cast to a pointer to a char. This block of memory is then treated and accessed as an array. Dynamic arrays of other types are created in an analogous fashion.

```
#include <stdio.h>
#include <stdlib.h>

const int no_to_allocate = 25;

main()
{
    float *grades;
    float *temp_ptr;
    float score;
    long int no_grades, j;

    grades = (float *) NULL  /* make grades a null pointer */

    printf("Please enter the grades, one per line. \n");
    printf("Enter a negative grade to terminate. \n");

    no_grades = 0;
    do
    {
    /* This if statement will determine when more space is needed.
       When no_grade % no_to_allocate == 0, all the memory previously
```

Program 11.2. Use of realloc() to average test scores (continues)

```
      allocated has been used. It is time to allocate no_to_allocate
      more.*/
   if ( ( no_grades % no_to_allocate ) == 0 )
   {
     temp_ptr = grades;
     grades = realloc( grades,
       no_to_allocate*( no_grades/no_to_allocate+1) * sizeof(float)
     if ( grades == NULL)
     {
             printf( "No more space available." );
             printf( " More scores cannot be entered.\n");
             printf( "Processing of grades entered so far");
             printf( " will continue.\n");

             /* Restore grades to last area of memory. */
             grades = temp_ptr;
             break; /* exit input loop */
     }
   }
   scanf( "%f", &score );
   if (score >= 0)
   {
     grades[no_grades] = score;
   }
   no_grades++;
 } while (score >= 0.0);
 no_grades--; /* Do not count the negative number entered to termina

 /*Remainder of program to sort, average and print out the test score

 for( j=0; j < no_grades; j++)
 {
     printf( "%f\n", grades[j]);
 }

  exit(0);
} /* end main() */
```

Program 11.2. (continued)

Programs 11.2 and 11.3 demonstrate this method of creating a dynamic array. The key to this is C's flexibility in the equivalence between an array name and a pointer to the first byte of that array. This permits a variable to act as a pointer to a block of memory and also to be used as an array name in accessing that same memory.

   In Program 11.2, the realloc() function is used to guarantee that there is always sufficient space for the grades in the input loop. Additional space is allocated in units of 25 floats. Since the pointer grades is initially a null pointer, the first execution of realloc() will point grades to a block of memory that is sufficient for 25 floats. [The first evaluation of the boolean expression "(no-grades % no_to_ allocate) = = 0" gives true as no-grades is initially zero.] The realloc() function is called again when the space that was previously allocated has been exhausted. A new block of memory is allocated that is large enough for the previous grades array plus space for 25 more floats. Since the size of the block allocated continues to increase, previously input values will be preserved. If the call to realloc() ever returns a null pointer, then the reallocation failed. In this situation, control leaves the input loop because of the break statement. (The break statement causes the innermost loop in which the break statement resides to be terminated and process-ing to continue after the loop. This break statement will be more fully explained in Chapter 12.)

The reader should also notice that grades is declared as a pointer type. This variable is assigned a value by realloc(), which points to the newly allocated memory. After this allocation, grades is treated as an array. An index is used to increment through the data structure.

The *free(void *ptr)* function returns (i.e. deallocates) the space previously allocated by the allocation functions. This space is then available to be allocated to another object. This function requires one parameter, which is a pointer to the space to be freed. If it is a null pointer, this function does nothing. The pointer must have been generated by a previous call to one of the allocation functions. If it was not generated in this manner, or if its space was previously freed, the behavior of this function is undefined. Space that has been freed should not be referenced again since the system may reuse this space at any time. The function free() returns no value.

Program 11.3 illustrates the use of free(). This program expands Program 11.2

```
#include <stdio.h>
#include <stdlib.h>

const int no_to_allocate = 25;

main()
{
    float *grades;
    float *temp_ptr;
    float score;
    long int no_grades;
    int j, ch;
```

Program 11.3. Use of realloc() and free() (continues)

```
char answer;

do
{
grades = (float *) NULL; /* make grades a null pointer */

printf("Please enter the grades, one per line. \n");
printf("Enter a negative grade to terminate. \n");

no_grades  = 0;
do
{
    if ( ( no_grades   % no_to_allocate ) == 0 )
    {
      temp_ptr = grades;
      grades = realloc( grades, no_to_allocate*
            (no_grades/no_to_allocate +1) * sizeof(float));
      if ( grades == NULL)
      {
          printf( "No more space available." );
          printf( " More scores cannot be entered.\n");
          printf( "Processing of grades entered so far");
          printf( " will continue.\n");

          grades = temp_ptr; /* Restore grades to previous value. *
          break; /* exit input loop */
      } /* end if */
    } /* end if */
    scanf( "%f", &score );
    if (score >= 0)
    {
      grades[no_grades ] = score;
    }

    no_grades ++;
} while (score >= 0.0);

no_grades--; /* Adjust for negative sentinel grade. *?/

  /*Remainder of program to sort, average and print out the test
scores. */

for( j=0; j<no_grades; j++)
{
    printf( "%f\n", grades[j] );
}
```

Program 11.3. (continued)

```
      free( grades ); /* deallocates the memory to which grades points i
                         preparation for the grades of the   next class.

      printf( "Is there another class to average? (Enter y or n ):");
      scanf( "\n%c", &answer); /* get new-line and answer */

   } while (answer == 'y');

   exit(0);
} /* end main */
```

Program 11.3. (continued)

by permitting the program to handle multiple sets of test scores. After one group
of scores is entered, sorted, averaged, and printed, the space for the array grades
is freed. This returns the space to the run-time system for later reuse. Then space
for another set of data is incrementally allocated if necessary.

Further Examples of the Use of Dynamic Memory Allocation

Another very common dynamic data structure is a linked list. This is a data
structure that is an ordered collection of data similar to an array. The distinction is
that an array is allocated as contiguous memory locations, whereas a dynamic
linked list consists of a group of (possibly) noncontiguous memory locations. A
linked list is always accessed sequentially. (An array can be accessed both in
sequential order and in a random order.) Each component of the linked list stores,
in addition to the data, a pointer to the next component of the ordered list as
shown in Figure 11.4. A special pointer, the head, gives access to this data
structure by pointing to the beginning of the list.

A linked list has several advantages over an array. First, as a dynamic data
structure, a linked list has all the advantages of flexibility. The programmer does
not need to know the length of the list during design. Arrays are static and hence
are less flexible. Second, the linked list can be modified more easily. If a new
component is to be added in the middle of a list, the process involves modifying
two pointers. (In an array, it involves shifting a large number of elements to make
room.)

Deletions are a similarly simple process. The process of inserting and deleting
from a linked list will now be illustrated by means of an example. In this example,
we will present a group of functions that can be used to build a linked list. These
functions can be used in many situations. They are designed to maintain a linked
list of structures in alphabetic order by one particular field of this structure. To use
these functions in another program, the structure will have to be modified to fit
the needs of that program. However, the algorithms will remain the same.

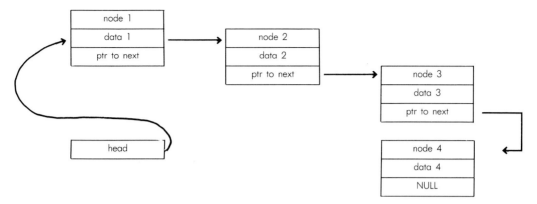

Figure 11.4. A linked list

    The primary tasks involved in maintaining a linked list are insertions and
deletions. We will first consider insertions. The general algorithm for insertion is
this:

1. Find the place in this list at which the new node is to be inserted. (If the list
    is ordered by some data field, the appropriate spot in the list is located by an
    examination of this field.) Maintain a pointer to the node just before the
    point of insertion.
2. Change the next node pointer of the new node to point to the list node
    following the insertion point.
3. Change the next node pointer of the node just before the point of insertion to
    point to the new node.

    Figure 11.5 illustrates the insertion of a node in a linked list.
    The perceptive reader will notice that there are two cases that require special
handling: (1) insertion into an empty list, and (2) insertion at the beginning of the
list. The algorithm needs to recognize these cases and to handle them gracefully.
Although these minor adjustments to the algorithm can be made, a more elegant
solution can be obtained by avoiding these special cases. By adding a special node
called the head or root that contains no valid data, but does point to the first node
in the list, these special cases are avoided. (This node's data field is not used in
any comparisons.) Rather than being a pointer to the first element of the list, head
is now a pointer to a complete node whose next field points to the actual first node
of the list. This node is often called a "dummy" node since it is not used to record
any data. The advantage of using this dummy node is that there is never a
completely empty list as this head node is always present. Insertion at the
beginning of the list is not a problem, as this is actually an insertion after the head
node.

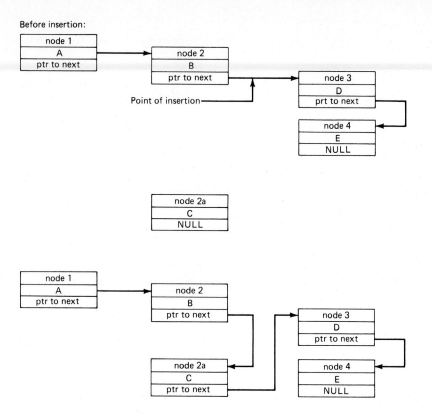

Figure 11.5. Insertion into a linked list

In designing any list algorithm, the programmer should always ascertain that the algorithm works correctly on these two special cases. They are a common source of error. Two other cases that often require special handling are any manipulation of the last node in the list and the situation in which the node to be manipulated is not in the list. Neither of these is a problem for the insertion algorithm. An insertion at the end of the list is identical to an insertion elsewhere. The latter situation is not a problem in an insert algorithm as we are not searching for an already existing node in the list, but just for a location at which to insert the new node. This will be a potential problem for deletion, modification, and find algorithms.

Now consider the C implementation of this insertion algorithm. The special head node has to be created just once when the program begins. The init_list() function in Figure 11.6 accomplishes this simple task. Its prototype declaration is

```
node *init_list( void  );
```

This function will allocate and return (by reference) the head node. This function is called as

```
node *head_ptr;
head_ptr = init_list();
```

The insertion algorithm itself is coded in the function list_insert() whose prototype declaration is

```
int list_insert( node * head, node student );
```

The parameter head points to the beginning of the list. The parameter student is a structure that is to be inserted in alphabetic order in this list. The type node and the actual parameter corresponding to the formal parameter head must be declared in the calling program. Figure 11.6 gives the code for this insertion function.

```
#include <stdio.h>
#include <stdlib.h>
#include <string.h>
#include "node.h"

/* This function allocates space for the root node   */
/* It returns a pointer to this new root node, or    */
/* NULL if out of memory                             */
node *init_list( void )
{
    node *head_ptr;

    head_ptr = (node *) malloc( sizeof(node) );
    if (head_ptr != (node *) NULL )
    {
        head_ptr->next = (node *) NULL;
    }

    return( head_ptr );

}

/* Adds a node to its proper place in the linked list. */

int list_insert( node *head, node student)
{
    int i;
    node *temp_ptr, *prev_ptr;
```

Figure 11.6. The list_insert() function (continues)

```
      node *new_student;

/* Find the location in which to insert the new node. */
      temp_ptr = head->next;
      prev_ptr = head;
      while( ( temp_ptr != NULL )
            && ( strcmp( temp_ptr->name, student.name) < 0 ) )
      {
      /* We have not yet reached the location at which to insert. */
      /* prev_ptr will point to the node previous to the one to   */
      /* which temp_ptr points.                                   */
      prev_ptr = temp_ptr;
      temp_ptr = temp_ptr->next;
      }

      if ( strcmp( temp_ptr->name, student.name) == 0 )
      {
      printf( "ERROR! A record with this name already exists.\n");
      printf( "Insertion aborted!");
      return( DUPLICATE_NAME );
      }


      /* We have found the location at which to insert. */

      /* Allocate memory for the new list element. */
      new_student = (node *) malloc( sizeof( node ) );

      if (new_student == (node *) NULL )
      {
      printf( "ERROR! Space cannot be allocated for another node.\n");
      return( OUT_OF_MEMORY );

      }

      *new_student = student;   /* copy the structure into the  */
                                /* newly allocated space.       */

      prev_ptr->next = new_student;
      new_student->next = temp_ptr;

      return( SUCCESS );

} /* end list_insert */
```

Figure 11.6. (continued)

This function uses a technique that is quite common in list processing. It maintains two list pointers: one (temp_ptr) points to the node under consideration; the other (prev_ptr) points to the previous node. In this function, the insertion occurs between these two nodes. Figure 11.7 illustrates these variables in this insertion in relation to the insertion point.

Insertion at the end is recognized if the while loop is terminated with temp_ptr equal to NULL. This means that the entire list was examined without finding a name greater than the new name in the node to be inserted. The same code that is used to insert in the middle of a list will insert at the end of a list.

The data structure, node, defined in node.h and used to represent each node of this list requires some special examination since it is a *self-referencing structure*. Its definition is shown again:

```
typedef struct list_node
{
  char name[20];
  int test_scores[4];
  int final_exam;
  char final_grade;
  struct list_node *next;
} node;
```

The member *next* is a pointer to the same structure type using the structure's tag. (While a self-referencing structure is quite useful, a structure cannot have a member that references that same structure. A reference to the structure tag is legitimate; the structure itself is not.) That is, the *next* member is a pointer to the next node in the list. Note the method of declaration for this node. It has type "struct list_node*." This works because the identifier list_node has already been mentioned on the first line of this declaration. The compiler knows what kind of identifier this is. The example of declaration of this structure given in Figure 11.8 will cause a syntax error since the identifier node is not defined when it is used in the declaration of *next*.

There is a method by which the typedef identifier can be used inside the structure. Figure 11.9 demonstrates this technique. The first structure definition is an *incomplete declaration* that gives the compiler sufficient information about the meaning of node to allow it to be used in the complete declaration of the struc-

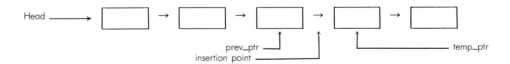

Figure 11.7. Operation of function list_insert()

```
typedef struct
{
char *name;
int test_scores[4];
int final_exam;
char final_grade;
node *next;     /* Syntax error here. Node is not defined yet */
} node;
```

Figure 11.8. Incorrect declaration of a self-referencing structure

```
typedef struct list_node node; /* An incomplete, but syntactically*/
                               /* correct declaration which tells  */
                               /* the compiler some information    */
                               /* about node.                      */
typedef struct list_node
{
char *name;
int test_scores[4];
int final_exam;
char final_grade;
node *next;                    /* This is correct now since    */
                               /* the compiler knows about node */

} node;
```

Figure 11.9. A correct declaration of a self-referencing structure using a typedef

ture. This technique is most useful when declaring two structures that refer to each other, as demonstrated in Figure 11.10.

In Figure 11.10, the incomplete declaration of node2 is necessary so that the member node_ptr1 of node1 can be declared.

The list_delete() function for the linked list is presented in Figure 11.11. The general deletion algorithm for a list is the following.

1. Locate the node to be deleted by comparing names. Maintain a pointer to the previous node as well as one to the node to be deleted.
2. Modify the *next* member of the previous node to point to the node that follows the node to be deleted.
3. Free all the memory associated with the node to be deleted.

This function also uses the previous pointer technique. The function free() is used in list_delete() to deallocate memory when the appropriate node has been found. If it is not found, an error message is printed and processing is terminated.

```
                  typedef struct node2_type node2;
                  typedef struct node1_type
                  {
                        float data1;
                        node2 *node_ptr1;
                  } node1;

                  typedef struct node2_type node2
                  {
                        float data2;
                        node1 *node_ptr2;
                  } node2;
```

Figure 11.10. Declaration of structures that reference each other

Contents of node.h :

```
#define SUCCESS 0
#define OUT_OF_MEMORY 1
#define DUPLICATE_NAME 2
#define NOT_FOUND 3

typedef struct list_node
{
    char name[20];
    int test_scores[4];
    int final_exam;
    char final_grade;
    struct list_node *next;
} node;
```

Contents of delete.c:

```
#include <stdio.h>
#include <stdlib.h>
#include <string.h>
#include "node.h"


int list_delete( node * head, char * name)
{
    node *delete_student;
    int i;
    node *temp_ptr, *prev_ptr;

    /* Find the node to delete. */
```

Figure 11.11. The list_delete() function (continues)

```
    temp_ptr = head->next;
    prev_ptr = head;
    while( (temp_ptr != (node *) NULL) &&
           ( strcmp( temp_ptr->name, name ) < 0 ) )

    {

    /* We have not yet reached the location of the node to be deleted.
    /* prev_ptr will point to the node previous to the one to which
    /* temp_ptr points .
        prev_ptr = temp_ptr;
        temp_ptr = temp_ptr->next;

    } /* end while */

    if ( strcmp( temp_ptr->name, name) == 0 )
    {
    /* Node found. Now delete it. */
    /* temp_ptr points to the node to be deleted.
    /* prev_ptr points to the node just prior to this. */

        prev_ptr->next = temp_ptr->next;
        free( temp_ptr );
        return( SUCCESS );
    } /* end if */


    /* If we exit the while loop with temp_ptr == NULL or with
    /* temp_ptr->name > name, then the node to be deleted is not prese

    if ( ( strcmp( temp_ptr->name, name) > 0 ) || ( temp_ptr == NULL )
    {
    /* The name for which we are searching is not present. */
        printf( "ERROR! Name not found in list. Deletion aborted!\n")
        return( NOT_FOUND );
    }

} /* end list_delete() */
```

Figure 11.11. (continued)

This function has two parameters: head is a pointer to the dummy node that points
to the beginning of the list; name is a string containing the name of the person to
be deleted.

In this function, deletion at the beginning of the list is not a special situation
because of the dummy head node. Deletion at the end of the list occurs through the
normal deletion mechanism. If the while loop is terminated with temp_ptr equal to
NULL, the end of the list was reached without finding the node to be deleted.

A more complex example of the use of dynamic memory allocation is the "phone directory" problem. (This problem is typical of many situations in which the dynamic data structure is ordered.) The purpose of this program is to store and retrieve names and corresponding telephone numbers. The requirements of this phone directory system are the following. The system should permit the insertion of new names and phone numbers, the deletion of a name and phone number pair, and the modification of a phone number for a given name. In addition to these directory maintenance features, the system should be able to produce the phone number for any given name. The program should have an easy-to-use, menu-driven interface.

In designing a solution to this problem, it is important to note that no maximum number of names was given. This is then an appropriate problem for the application of dynamic memory management. The solution will be built incrementally.

First, the main program, Program 11.4, is constructed. The requirements specify a menu-driven interface.

Contents of phone.h :

```
#define SUCCESS 0
#define OUT_OF_MEMORY 1
#define DUPLICATE_NAME 2
#define NOT_FOUND 3
#define EMPTY_TREE 4

typedef struct node_type
{
    char *name;
    char *phone_no;
    struct node_type *right_child;
    struct node_type *left_child;
} node;
```

Contents of phone.c :

```
#include <stdio.h>
#include <stdlib.h>
#include <string.h>
#include "phone.h"



main()
{
```

Program 11.4. Main program for phone directory (continues)

```c
    void print_menu(void );
    int insert( node ** );
    int delete( node ** );
    int modify( node ** );
    int find( node * );
    int print_tree(node *);
    int get_response( void );

    node * phone_directory;
    int response;

    do
    {
        print_menu();
        response = get_response();
        switch ( response )
        {
            case 'I' :
            case 'i' : insert(&phone_directory); break;
            case 'M' :
            case 'm' : modify(&phone_directory); break;
            case 'D' :
            case 'd' : delete(&phone_directory); break;
            case 'F' :
            case 'f' : find(phone_directory); break;
            case 't' : print_tree( phone_directory );
                    break;  /* This is a special command inserted
                                    for debugging purposes only.*/
            case 'Q' :
            case 'q' : break;
            default: printf("ERROR. Not a valid choice!\n");
                    printf("Enter I, M, D, F, or Q\n");
        }

    } while ( ( response != 'Q') && (response != 'q')  );

    exit(0);
} /* end main */

void print_menu(void)
{
    printf( "Insert -------------> I\n");
    printf( "Delete -------------> D\n");
    printf( "Modify -------------> M\n");
    printf( "Find Phone Number --> F\n");
    printf( "Quit ---------------> Q\n");
    printf( "Enter your choice --> ");
```

Program 11.4. (continued)

```
}

int get_response(void)
{
    int response;

    response = getchar();
    if (response != '\n')      /* read remaining characters on */
    {                           /* this line */
        while ( getchar() != '\n' );
    }
    return( response );
} /* end of get_response() */

int modify( node ** phone_directory)
{
    printf( "In modify.\n");
} /* end modify */

int delete( node ** phone_directory )
{
    printf("In delete.\n");
} /* end delete */
```

Program 11.4. (continued)

Notice that Program 11.4, in addition to providing the menu and getting the
user's choice, also includes a typedef for a node that will contain one name and
phone number. This node also contains two pointer members, one to point to the
left child and the other to point to the right child. We have made a design decision
to maintain the directory as a *binary search tree*. This tree allows a binary rather
than sequential search of a dynamic data structure. A binary search tree is a data
structure with the properties that each element of that data structure includes a
pointer to two other elements, that there are no loops possible in following these
pointers, and that each element (node) of the data structure has precisely one
pointer to it from another node. Furthermore, the nodes are arranged so that the
name at the left child is always alphabetically less than that of the parent, and the
name at the right child is always greater than that of the parent. The diagram in
Figure 11.12 pictures one such tree.

The next function to be written is insert(). This function has the responsibility
of creating a new node and inserting it in the correct spot in the tree. Thus, insert()
must maintain the order prescribed for a search tree. This function is presented as
Figure 11.13.

The call to malloc() in this function could be replaced by the following call to
calloc():

```
new_node = (node *) calloc( 1, sizeof( node ) );
```

The use of calloc() versus malloc() is moot as this algorithm allocates space for only one node at a time and as the insert function assigns values to all the new node's components. If all components were not assigned a value, the initialization to zero feature of calloc() might have proved useful. Conversely, malloc() is slightly more efficient than calloc().

The modify() function is comparable in difficulty to the insert() function and is left as an exercise. The most difficult function is delete(). The problem is that, when a node is removed from the tree, the remaining right and left subtrees of the deleted node have to be rearranged to maintain the search tree characteristics. This is discussed in a problem at the end of this chapter. An alternative to true deletion is simply to mark deleted nodes as inactive. This requires that we add another member to each node structure. This member would contain true or false (0 or 1) depending on whether this node is active or not. The process of deletion is to change this active field from true to false. The tree, in this situation, would continually grow. If the number of deletions are relatively few, then this is an acceptable solution.

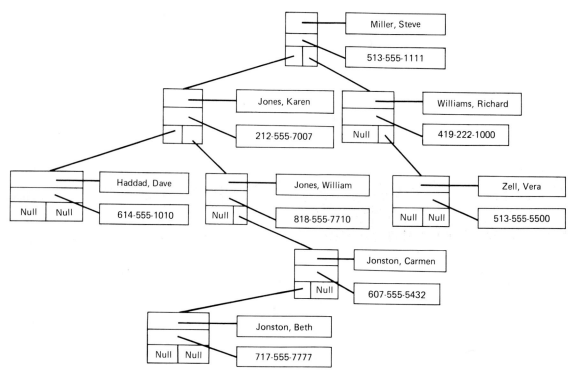

Figure 11.12. Sample phone directory binary search tree

```c
#include <ctype.h>
#include <stdarg.h>
#include <stdio.h>
#include <string.h>
#include "phone.h"


/* This function obtains a name from the user. */

char *get_name( void )
{
    #define MAX_NAME_SIZE  80
    static char name[MAX_NAME_SIZE+1];
    int ch, len;

    printf( "Enter the name.\n");
    printf( "(Maximum of %d characters.)\n", MAX_NAME_SIZE);

    len = 0;

    while( ( ch = getchar()) != '\n')
    {
        if (len < MAX_NAME_SIZE)
        {
            name[len++] = ch;
        } /* end if */
    } /* end while */
    for( ; len <= MAX_NAME_SIZE; len++)
    {
        name[len] = '\0';
    }

    return( name );

} /* end get_name() */


/* This function obtains a telephone number from the user. */

char *get_number()
{
    #define MAX_NUMBER_SIZE 13
    typedef int boolean;

    static char ph_no[MAX_NUMBER_SIZE+1];
    int ch, len, i;
    boolean valid;
```

Figure 11.13. The insert function for the phone directory problem (continues)

```
do
{
      printf( "Enter the phone number in the form 111-555-1212.\n")
      printf( "(Maximum of %d characters.)\n", MAX_NUMBER_SIZE);

      len = 0;

      while( ( ch = getchar()) != '\n')
      {
            if (len < MAX_NUMBER_SIZE)
            {
                  ph_no[len++] = ch;
            }   /* end if */
      } /* end while */

      /* error checking */
      valid = TRUE;
      for( i=0; i<3; i++)
      {
            if ( !isdigit( ph_no[i] ))
            {
                  valid = FALSE;
            }
      }
      if ( ph_no[3] != '-' )
      {
            valid = FALSE;
      }
      for( i=4; i<7; i++)
      {
            if ( !isdigit( ph_no[i]) )
            {
                  valid = FALSE;
            }
      }
      if ( ph_no[7] != '-' )
      {
            valid = FALSE;
      }
      for( i=8; i<12; i++)
      {
            if ( !isdigit( ph_no[i]) )
            {
                  valid = FALSE;
            }
      }
```

Figure 11.13. (continued)

```
        if ( !valid)
        {
              printf("Error in format. Please re-enter.\n");
        }

} while (! valid );

for( ; len <= MAX_NUMBER_SIZE; len++)
{
      ph_no[len] = '\0';
}
return( ph_no );

} /* end get_number() */


/* This function inserts a new name and telephone number
at the correct position in the search tree. */

int insert(node ** phone_directory )
{
    char *name;
    char *ph_no;
    node *new_node;

    node *back_ptr, *temp_ptr;
    /* temp_ptr will eventually point to the node to be deleted    */
    /* back_ptr will then point to the parent of that node.        */

    name = get_name();

    temp_ptr = *phone_directory;

    /* Find the location in tree in which the  is to be inserted.*/
    while (temp_ptr != NULL )
    {
        back_ptr = temp_ptr;   /* back_ptr always points to the parent.

        if (strcmp( temp_ptr -> name, name ) == 0 )
        {
              printf( "Error. This name is already present!" );
              printf( "Insertion aborted!");
              return ( DUPLICATE_NAME );
        }
        if (strcmp( temp_ptr -> name, name ) > 0 )
        {
```

Figure 11.13. (continued)

```
                temp_ptr = temp_ptr->left_child;
        } else
        {
                temp_ptr = temp_ptr->right_child;
        }

    } /* end while */

    /* Correct position found. Now allocate memory and connect the
    /* new node to the appropriate location. */

    ph_no = get_number();

    /* Allocate space  and fill in name, phone_no fields and
    child fields. */
    if((( new_node = (node *) malloc( sizeof(node) ) ) != (node *) NUL
    (( new_node->name = (char *) malloc( strlen( name) * sizeof(char))
            !=(char *) NULL) &&
    (( new_node->phone_no = (char *) malloc( strlen(ph_no) * sizeof(ch
            !=  (char *)  NULL) )
    {
            strcpy( new_node->name, name);
            strcpy( new_node->phone_no, ph_no);

            new_node -> right_child = NULL;
            new_node -> left_child = NULL;

            /* An empty tree is a special case. */
            if (*phone_directory == (node *) NULL )
            {
                    *phone_directory = new_node;
                    return ( SUCCESS );
            }

            if (strcmp( back_ptr->name, name ) > 0 )
            {
                    back_ptr->left_child = new_node;
            } else
            {
                    back_ptr->right_child = new_node;
            } /*end if*/
    } /* end if */
    else
    {
            printf( "Error. Not enough memory available. Insertion aborte
    }

} /*end insert*/
```

Figure 11.13. (continued)

The find() function has the task of recovering a telephone number given a name. The code for this function is given in Figure 11.14.

The programmer may find it useful to construct a print_tree() function to print the contents of the tree during debugging and testing. A recursive implementation of this function is included in Figure 11.15. The recursive nature of this algorithm produces a short, elegant algorithm. This particular function uses the spaces parameter to determine how many spaces to print before a name or telephone number. As a result of this parameter, the names of the left and right children of a node are printed beginning in the same column, and are indented two columns from the beginning of their parent's name.

The function print_tree() tests for an empty tree and then calls print_tree_body(), which is the recursive function that prints the names and telephone numbers in the tree.

These dynamic allocation and deallocation functions can allow the programmer to create data structures and algorithms which are difficult to solve in any other manner. However, debugging of programs which use dynamic allocation and deallocation can be quite difficult and complex.

This concludes our discussion of C's dynamic memory management functions. The next topic is the C facilities for support of variable numbers of function parameters.

11.3 VARIABLE NUMBER OF ARGUMENTS TO A C FUNCTION

C provides the ability to write functions for which the number and type of parameters vary at run time. The classical C example is the printf() function. This function, which is provided in the standard I/O library, can print out the value of several variables. As discussed in Chapter 8, the first parameter of this function is the specification that tells how to print the values of the expressions that follow. The number of arguments that follow the specification argument are not limited (except that each expression must have a conversion specification). This gives a generic output function that can be used in many circumstances. For example, some uses of printf() are: printf("Hello \n"), printf("x = %d\n", x), and printf("%c = %u\n", c, c). The alternatives to variable argument lists for printf() are repeatedly to use an output function that prints only one expression of one fixed type, or to have a set of functions each of which prints a fixed number of expressions of a fixed list of types.

To write a function that allowed a variable number of parameters prior to the introduction of the ANSI standard, programmers had to know many of the details of how parameters were handled by the execution environment. For example, some systems place all actual parameters on the run-time stack. These are

```
#include <stdio.h>
#include <string.h>
#include "phone.h"

int find( node *phone_directory)
{
    char * get_name(void);
    node *temp_ptr;
    /* temp_ptr will eventually point to the node to be deleted      */

    char *name;
    char *ph_no;

    name = get_name();

    /* An empty tree is a special case. */
    if (phone_directory == (node *) NULL )
    {
        printf("ERROR. No names in directory!\n");
        return( NOT_FOUND) ;
    }

    temp_ptr = phone_directory;

/* Find the location in tree of the node with desired name. */
    while ( temp_ptr != (node *) NULL )
    {
        if (strcmp( temp_ptr -> name, name ) == 0 )
        {
            printf( "Name = %s\n", temp_ptr->name );
            printf( "Telephone number = %s\n", temp_ptr->phone_no);
            return( SUCCESS );
        }
        if (strcmp( temp_ptr -> name, name ) > 0 )
        {
            temp_ptr = temp_ptr->left_child;
        } else
        {
            temp_ptr = temp_ptr->right_child;
        }

    } /* end while */

    printf("ERROR. Name not found in directory!\n");
    return( NOT_FOUND );

} /*end find() */
```

Figure 11.14. Tree find() function

```c
#include <stdio.h>
#include "phone.h"

int print_tree( node *phone_directory )
{
    int i;
    void print_tree_body( node *,  int);

    if ( phone_directory == (node *) NULL )
    {
        printf( "Tree Empty\n" );
        return( EMPTY_TREE );
    }

    print_tree_body( phone_directory , 0 );

    return( SUCCESS );

} /* end print_tree */

void print_tree_body( node *tree_ptr, int spaces)
{
    int i;

    for ( i=0; i < spaces; i++ )
    {
     printf( " " );
    }

    printf( "name= %s number = %s\n", tree_ptr->name,
                      tree_ptr->phone_no );

    if ( tree_ptr->left_child !=( node *) NULL)
    {
    print_tree_body( tree_ptr->left_child, spaces+2);
    }

    if (tree_ptr->right_child != NULL)
    {
    print_tree_body( tree_ptr->right_child, spaces+2);
    }

} /* end print_tree() */
```

Figure 11.15. The recursive print_tree() function

followed on the stack by all the automatic variables needed by this function. To access the parameters, the programmer had to find the address of the last item to be pushed on to the stack, then index down the stack to find the actual parameters. By knowing the address of the first parameter to be pushed onto the stack, a variable number of parameters can be recovered. This is complicated by the fact that some systems build the stack from lower addresses to higher addresses, whereas other compilers build the stack in the reverse order. Some compilers push the parameters onto the stack in the order in which they occur in the parameter list; others push them on in reverse order. These compiler-dependent details are not the subject of this book. However, knowledge of this type of implementation detail was necessary before the introduction of the ANSI standard functions. The result of this type of coding is a great loss of portability in the use of a variable number of arguments. The introduction of the standard variable argument type, function, and macros, which are the subject of this section, provide the ability to use variable parameter lists in a portable manner. Furthermore, these features are much easier to use. It is no longer necessary for the programmer to understand the details of each implementation.

Purpose of a Variable Number of Arguments

A function that can handle multiple numbers of arguments encapsulates the abilities of several functions. This can often make a program more understandable. It is better for the reader of a program to study one generic function than to have to understand and keep track of several closely related functions. (Using variable arguments to collect several unrelated functions into one larger function is a confusing misuse of this facility.) The result of a careful and disciplined use of variable argument list is a generic function that can be used in many places.

C Support for Variable Argument Lists

The standard library *stdarg.h* provides the necessary definitions of a type, two macros, and a function to support the use of a variable number of parameters. The type is *va_list,* which is an array type and is used to contain information about the variable argument list to be used by the other function and macros.

   The macro *va_start()* is used to set up the process of retrieving the arguments. The macro *va_arg()* is used repeatedly to retrieve subsequent arguments. The function *va_end()* is used to clean up the environment at the completion of the argument retrieval. The number of arguments to these macros and their use will be discussed in the next subsection.

Method of Using the Variable Argument Type and Functions

A function that will have a variable number of arguments must also have a subset of required parameters. These required formal parameters are specified first in the function header definition and are called the normal parameters. There must be at least one of these normal parameters. The last (right-most) of these normal parameter is used by the macro va_start() to set up the recovery of the unnamed parameters. This last normal parameter should not be declared as a register storage class. If it is, the behavior is undefined. (Many compilers will use the address of this last normal parameter to find the unnamed parameters.)

This last normal parameter is followed by three dots to denote the presence of a variable number of parameters to follow. Figure 11.16 illustrates the definition of a function with a variable number of parameters.

In the function, there must be a variable declared with type va_list. As

```c
#include <stdio.h>
#include <stdarg.h>

void sample( int n, ...)
{
  va_list arg_ptr;
  int i;
  int A[20];

  va_start( arg_ptr, n);
  for( i=0; i<n; i++)
  {
    A[i] = va_arg(arg_ptr, int);
  }

  va_end( arg_ptr);
  for( i=0; i< n; i++)
  {
    printf( "i = %d   A[i] = %d \n", i, A[i]);
  }
  return;
}

main()
{
    sample( 3, 7, 8, 9);
}
```

Figure 11.16. A sample function with a variable number of arguments

discussed above, this type describes an array that is used by the variable argument function and macros. In this discussion, we will call this array arg_ptr.

The macro va_start() must be called before any attempt is made to access the unnamed arguments. The first of the two arguments to this macro is arg_ptr; the second is the last-named parameter, n, in this case. This parameter is used by va_start() to find the location of the unnamed parameters that follow in the actual parameter list. The data structure arg_ptr is initialized by this macro. This macro returns no value.

The purpose of the macro va_arg() is to access arg_ptr in order to return the next of the unnamed function arguments. The first call retrieves the first unnamed argument; the second call retrieves the second unnamed argument, and so on. The macro va_arg() also requires two parameters. The first is arg_ptr. The second is the type of the unnamed argument to be recovered. The value returned is that of the next unnamed argument to be retrieved. The type that forms the second argument to va_arg must agree, after default promotions, with that of the corresponding unnamed argument in the call to the function. In the absence of type agreement, the behavior is undefined by the ANSI standard.

The function that uses variable arguments must understand the number of unnamed parameters. The macro va_arg() should be called the correct number of times. Frequently, one of the normal parameters is used as a count of the number of unnamed parameters. The parameter n serves this purpose in the example of Figure 11.16. The program also has to know the type of each of the unnamed arguments. In Figure 11.16, all of the unnamed parameters have type int. However, the types of the unnamed parameters are not restricted to having identical types. In the most general case, the number and type of these unnamed parameters are given in one or more of the normal parameters. The conversion specification parameter of printf() serves this purpose.

The va_end() function permits a normal return from a function that has used a variable number of arguments. It modifies va_list so that it cannot be used again until after another call to va_start(). The one parameter to va_end() is arg_ptr; va_end() returns no value. Its cleanup functionality is vital. If it is not called before a return statement, the behavior of the program is undefined.

Figure 11.17 gives a more complete demonstration of the definition of a function with a variable number of floating-point parameters.

```
#include <stdio.h>
#include <stdarg.h>
#include < math.h>

double pow( double exp, double x )
{
```

Figure 11.17. A polynomial evaluation function with a variable number of arguments (continues)

```
    int i;
    int n ;
    double result = 1.0;

    n= (int) exp;
    for ( i=0; i<n; i++ )
    {
      result = result * x;
    }

    return( result );
} /* end pow */

double evaluate( float x, int num_terms, ...)
{
  va_list arg_ptr;
  int i, n;
  double coefficient[10];
  double value = 0.0;

  va_start( arg_ptr, num_terms );
  for( i=0; i<num_terms; i++)
  {
    coefficient[i] = va_arg( arg_ptr, double );
  }

  for (i=0; i< num_terms; i++)
  {
    n = num_terms - (i+1);
    value = value + coefficient[i]*pow( (double) n, (double) x);
    printf( "coef = %f\n", coefficient[i] );
  }

  va_end( arg_ptr );
  return( value );
} /* end evaluate */

main()
{
  double result;

  result = evaluate( 2.0, 3, 1.0, 1.0, 1.0);

  printf( "result = %f\n", result );

  exit(0);
} /*end main */
```

Figure 11.17. (continued)

In the example in Figure 11.17, the variable parameters are assumed to be double. In general, there is no requirement about the type of unnamed parameters, except that the user of the function must be cognizant of the type of each parameter to the function. The evaluate() function first recovers all these unnamed parameters, then manipulates them. Notice that this function has two fixed, named parameters. The second gives the number of unnamed parameters to follow. The first parameter is a normal parameter that can be used as in any other function. To use this function, it would be declared in the caller as

```
extern float evaluate( double, int, . . . );
```

Then to call it, use, for example,

```
evaluate( 5.7, 4, 7.75, 4.578, 0.0, 3.40e-2);.
```

This function call would have the effect of evaluating the polynomial

$$7.75x^3 + 4.578x^2 + 0.034$$

when x has the value 5.7. (Notice that the next to the last coefficient is zero to denote the absence of the term with degree one.)

The function in Figure 11.18 extends the standard string function strcat() to concatenate more than two strings.

```
#include <string.h>
#include <stdarg.h>
#include <stdio.h>
#include <stdlib.h>

/* This function concatenates the string parameters, returning the
concatenated string as the value of the function. It requires at least
string as a parameter. The last parameter must be NULL. */

char *concat( char * str1, ... )
{
    va_list arg_ptr;
    int len;
    char *str;
    char *result;
    char *temp;

    if ( str1 == (char *) NULL )
    {
     return( NULL );
    }
```

Figure 11.18. Concatenation of a varying number of strings (continues)

```
va_start( arg_ptr, str1 );

result = (char *) malloc( strlen( str1 ) * sizeof(char) );
if (result == (char *) NULL)
{
 printf("Error! Out of memory in concat().\n");
 return( str1 );
}

strcpy( result, str1);
while( (str= va_arg( arg_ptr, char *)) != NULL )
{
len = strlen( str ) + strlen( result );

temp = result;
result = (char *) realloc( result, len * sizeof(char) );
if ( result == NULL )
{
     printf("Error! Out of memory in concat().\n");
     printf("The value returned is a partial concatenation.\n");
     return( temp );
}
 result = strcat( result, str );
} /* end while */

return( result );

} /* end concat() */
```

Figure 11.18. (continued)

The concat() function in Figure 11.18 differs from strcat() in two ways. The first is that concat() can concatenate any number of strings. The second is that concat() allocates memory for the new string. In calling strcat(), the calling function is responsible for providing sufficient space to contain the concatenated string. With concat(), the calling program only has to provide a pointer to a char, which will point to the concatenated string. The concatenated string is returned in that parameter, with appropriate space allocated. A valid call to this function is

```
char * result;
result = concat( 4, "abc", "defg", "hijk", "lmnop");
```

After this call, result has the value "abcdefghijklmnop".

The examples of the variable argument facilities of ANSI standard C have illustrated that the number of parameters can be varied. The example in Figure 11.19 demonstrates that the type of a parameter can vary from function call to

```c
#include <stdio.h>
#include <stdarg.h>
#include <stdlib.h>

const int true = 1;
const int false = 0;

void print_menu( char return_type, int num_choices, ... )
{
    typedef int boolean;

    va_list arg_ptr;
    char * str;
    int i;
    boolean valid;

    va_start( arg_ptr, num_choices);
    for ( i=0; i< num_choices; i++)    /* Print Menu */
    {
        printf( "\t%s\n", va_arg( arg_ptr, char *  ) );
    }

    if (return_type == 'c')
    {
        char * valid_ch;
        char ch_response;
        char *result;

        /* Place address of result parameter in variable result. */
        result = va_arg( arg_ptr, char*);


        valid_ch = (char *) malloc( num_choices * sizeof( char ) );

        /* Recover valid responses */
        for ( i=0; i< num_choices; i++)
        {
            valid_ch[i] = va_arg( arg_ptr, int );
        }

        do
        {
            valid = true;
            printf( "Please enter one of these: %c", valid_ch[0]);
            for ( i=1; i< num_choices ; i++)
            {
```

Figure 11.19. Function print_menu with varying parameter types (continues)

```
                              putchar( ',');
                              putchar( valid_ch[i] );
                        }
                        printf( "  ");
                        ch_response = getchar();

                        /* read past end of line */
                        while ( getchar() != '\n');

                        valid = false;
                        for ( i=0; i< num_choices ; i++)
                        {
                              if (ch_response == valid_ch[i])
                              {
                                    valid = true;
                              }
                        }
                        if ( !valid )
                        {
                              printf( "Error in input. Please re-enter.\n");
                        }
                  } while ( ! valid);
                  free( valid_ch );
                  *result = ch_response;

            } /* end if */
            else if (return_type == 'i')
            {
                  int * valid_int;
                  int int_response;
                  int *result;

/* Place address of result parameter in variable result. */
                  result = va_arg( arg_ptr, int *);
                  valid_int = (int *) malloc( num_choices * sizeof( int ) );

                  /* Recover valid responses */
                  for ( i=0; i< num_choices ; i++)
                  {
                        valid_int[i] = va_arg( arg_ptr, int );
                  }
                  do
                  {
                        valid = true;
                        printf( "Please enter one of these: %d", valid_int[0]);
```

Figure 11.19. (continued)

```
            for ( i=1; i< num_choices ; i++)
            {
                    putchar( ',');
                    printf( "%d", valid_int[i] );
            }
            printf( "   ");
            scanf( "%d", &int_response);
            valid = false;
            for ( i=0; i< num_choices ; i++)
            {
                    if ( int_response == valid_int[i])
                    {
                            valid = true;
                    }
            }
            if ( !valid )
            {
                    printf( "Error in input. Please re-enter.\n");
            }
      } while (! valid);

      free( valid_int );

      *result = int_response;

   } /* end if */

   return;
} /* end print_menu() */
```

Figure 11.19. (continued)

function call. This function accepts a description of a menu, the expected type for the choice to be entered, and the valid responses from the menu. It displays the menu, accepts a response, and error checks this response.

Consider the following function call to print_menu().

```
char result;
print_menu('c', 3, &result, "Insert.", "Delete.", "Quit.", 'I', 'D', 'Q');
```

This function call produces the following menu.

```
      Insert.
      Delete.
      Quit.
      Please enter one of these: I, D, Q.
```

This function will then accept a character from the user, and will assure that it is one of the characters "I," "D," or "Q."

This same function could be called with the following call.

```
int result
print_menu( 'i', 3, &result, "1. Insert.", "2. Delete.",
"3. Quit.", 1, 2, 3 );
```

Notice that this call inputs an integer from the user. The first parameter is used to determine the types of some of the other parameters. A value of i indicates an integer, 'c' indicates a character. In particular, the type of the third parameter, and of the last three parameters in this call, is determined from the value of the first parameter.

This print_menu() function may remind you of the printf() function. To use the printf() function, the programmer gives the type of the variables to be printed in the conversion specification. In this output function, the number of unnamed parameters is not explicitly given. But the user should notice that the number of parameters and the types of these parameters are implicitly given in the conversion specification. Thus, the prototype for the printf() function has the following form.

```
int printf( const char *, . . . );
```

The variable argument facilities of ANSI standard C permit the construction of a portable printf() function. This function examines the conversion specification to determine the number and the type of each of the unnamed parameters that follow. Since the possibilities in this conversion specification are so many, the printf() function body is quite complex. However, the result is a generic output function that can be used to output a varying number of values of many different types.

11.4 PORTABILITY AND SOFTWARE ENGINEERING ISSUES

The use of the dynamic allocation and deallocation functions of C must be disciplined to avoid some potentially difficult-to-repair errors. The two primary classes of errors are *dangling references* and the creation of *garbage*. Suppose that two pointers are pointing to the same block of memory. If this memory is freed using one pointer, but is subsequently accessed through the other pointer, the result is a dangling reference. The behavior of such a reference is undefined. It depends on what the system does with this block of memory when it is freed.

Figure 11.20 illustrates this problem. The pointer p2 is a dangling reference

```
int *p1, *p2;

p1 = (int *) malloc( 100 * sizeof (int) );
p2 = p1;

free( p1 );
```

Figure 11.20. A dangling reference

after the call to free(). This is not a syntax error, but will generally cause an error at run time. This should be avoided by explicitly freeing memory only when the last access path to that memory is to be lost.

Garbage is memory to which all access paths have been lost before the memory was freed. This can happen if a pointer to a block of memory is explicitly assigned another memory location. If the original memory locations have not been freed, and if this was the only access path to this block, then the programmer can never access or free this memory. The only way that the system can recover this memory during program execution is through a garbage collection algorithm that follows every pointer to determine which memory is accessible, and, by inference, which is inaccessible. C does not provide a garbage collection function. The example in Figure 11.21 demonstrates that garbage can be created quite easily.


```
char *p1, *p2;

p1 = (char *) malloc(1);
p2 = (char *) malloc(1);

*p1 = 'A';
*p2 = 'B';

/Creation of garbage */

Memory Map Before Assignment Statement "p1 = p2;"

Name        Address         Contents

p1          1068            2448
p2          1079            2704

*p1         2448            'A'

*p2         2704            'B'
```

Figure 11.21. Creation of garbage (continues)

```
Memory Map After Assignment Statement "p1 = p2;"

Name        Address              Contents

p1          1068                 2704
p2          1079                 2704

            2448                 'A'

*p2         2704                 'B'
```

Figure 11.21. (continued)

Access to the address 2448 has been lost. Since the programmer does not know that 'A' was stored at location 2448, there is no way for the programmer to recover or access this memory. There are more obscure ways of creating garbage. The example in Figure 11.22 illustrates this.

The free() function calls in the example of Figure 11.22 deallocate the structure to which str_ptr points. This includes the space occupied by the pointer in the member str_ptr->name. However, it does not free the memory to which this name pointer points. Consequently, there is no access to these 25 characters.

Generally, the creation of garbage is not as serious a problem as are dangling references. Garbage only becomes a problem if a large percentage of memory becomes garbage, leaving too little memory for the program to operate.

The advantages of the use of a variable number of arguments to a function have been discussed earlier in this chapter. These advantages center on the fact that a

```c
typedef struct
{
    char *name;
    int id;
} str_type;

str_type *str_ptr;

str_ptr = (str_type *) malloc( sizeof( str_type) );
str_ptr->name = (char *) malloc( 25*sizeof(char) );

/* processing of the structure */

free( str_ptr );    /* Creation of garbage because the name */
                    /* space is not freed.                  */
```

Figure 11.22. Creation of garbage

generic function that can be used in many circumstances may help to reduce, or at least hide, the complexity of a program solution. The programmer should be guided by the goal of controlling complexity. If the use of a variable argument list creates more confusion and complexity than it controls, it should not be used. The programmer should avoid the combination of functions with different purposes into a single function by the use of a variable argument list merely for the purpose of reducing the number of functions. Each function should accomplish a single task. Mixing of several tasks in one function actually increases the complexity.

Old-style C (prior to the introduction of the ANSI standard for C) had no features comparable to va_list, va_arg(), va_start(), and va_end(). The processing of variable-length argument lists was a responsibility of the programmer with knowledge of the implementation's parameter passing method. This leads to obvious portability problems as different C compilers will generally use differing methods and protocols for parameter passing.

The functions and header files described in this chapter (except malloc.h) are those specified in the C standard. These functions are present in many compilers that are not ANSI-compliant. However, the names of the header files are often different. On many UNIX machines, the variable argument type declaration, macro definition, and function prototype are given in the header file varargs.h. The memory allocation function prototypes are listed in the file malloc.h. For other compilers, consult the documentation to see if these functions are available, and, if so, which header files to use with them.

11.5   SUMMARY

This chapter discussed some of the dynamic mechanisms provided by C. The purposes and advantages of dynamic behavior were presented first. Then the uses of dynamic memory allocation and deallocation functions were explained. The allocation functions are malloc(), calloc(), and realloc(). The prototypes are given in stdlib.h. These functions take integers parameters that are used to describe the amount of memory to allocate at run time. Each function returns a pointer to that block of memory. This pointer then should be coerced to the appropriate type. The free() function takes a pointer to previously allocated memory and returns it to the system for reuse. These functions were illustrated by an extensive example. This program uses a search tree to store and retrieve names and telephone numbers.

The next major topic of this chapter was the C mechanism to permit functions to have a variable number of parameters. The standard library contains a type (va_list); two macros [va_start(), va_arg()]; and a function [va_end()], which can be used to implement variable parameter lists. The type and function prototypes are given in the standard header file stdarg.h.

The final section of this chapter was a discussion of software engineering considerations of the dynamic allocation functions, and of the use of a variable number of parameters. This includes the creation of dangling references and garbage.

Keywords

allocation	realloc()
binary search tree	self-referencing structure
calloc()	static
dangling references	stdarg.h
deallocation	stdlib.h
dynamic	va_arg()
free()	va_end()
garbage	va_list
incomplete declaration	va_start()
malloc()	variable argument list

References

Draft American National Standard x3.159-198x, Programming Language C. This is the ultimate authority on questions of syntax and semantic of the C language. Copies may be obtained from Global Engineering Documents, Inc., 2805 McGaw, Irvine, CA 92714.

Horowitz, E., and S. Sahni, 1984. *Fundamental of Computer Algorithms,* Rockville, Md.: Computer Science Press. This book describes many dynamic data structure algorithms, including tree algorithms.

Kernighan, B., and D. Ritchie, 1988. *The C Programming Language,* (2nd ed.). Englewood Cliffs, N.J.: Prentice-Hall. This updated version of a classic C reference contains a brief explanation of the use of a variable number of parameters.

Sedgewick, R. 1988. *Algorithms* (2nd ed.); Reading, Mass.: Addison Wesley. This book describes many dynamic data structure algorithms, including tree algorithms.

Singh, B., and T. L. Naps. 1985. *Introduction to Data Structures,* St. Paul, Minn.: West Publishing. This book describes many dynamic data structures and algorithms for their manipulation.

Discussion Questions

1. Why might one of the allocation functions fail?

2. Characterize each of the following as dynamic or static:
   a. Using scanf() to give a value to a variable.
   b. Giving a variable an initial value in the declaration of that variable.
   c. Memory allocation for an array as in "int scores[100];."
   d. Calculating a value in an arithmetic expression.
   e. The length of a file.
   f. The length of an array.
   g. Memory allocation using malloc().

3. Differentiate between the following pairs of functions:
   a. calloc() and malloc()?
   b. realloc() and malloc()?

4. Under what conditions are the function free() necessary and/or unnecessary?

5. Why are the variable argument macros necessary to make functions that use a variable number of parameters portable.

6. Discuss the advantages of a doubly linked list over a singly linked list. A doubly linked list is a list in which each member node has a pointer to the previous node in addition to the pointer to the next node. Are insertion and deletion substantially more difficult in such a list? Or are they easier?

7. What, if any, are the differences among the following declarations and statements?

```
char *carray1, *carray2, *carray3;
carray1 = malloc( 20 );
carray2 = malloc( 20 * sizeof( char ) );
carray3 = (char*) malloc( 20 * sizeof( char) );
```

   Is any of these preferable over the others? Why?

8. How does printf() determine the number and type of its parameters?

Exercises

1. a. Write a small section of code that creates garbage. (This is generally something to avoid. But it is useful to try this exercise in order to understand the problem better.)
   b. Write a small section of code to produce a dangling reference.

2. The function realloc() can be used to accomplish the same task as free() if the parameters are chosen appropriately. Write a call to the function realloc() that effectively frees the memory to which the pointer mem_ptr points. [Assume that mem_ptr is declared as a pointer to a character, and that space has been previously allocated by malloc() or calloc().]

3. Arrays can be created dynamically using malloc(). For example, the following code allocates an array of max characters.

```
char *array;
array = (char*) malloc( max*sizeof(char) );
```

Give two different ways to refer to the *i*th element of this array, one using [] and the other using*.

4. Allocate a dynamic array that will hold 500 long ints.

5. Write a structure declaration for a doubly linked list. (Doubly linked lists are discussed in Discussion Question 6.) The members are

```
char data[ max ];
previous pointer;
next pointer;
```

6. Write an insertion function that will insert a node into a double linked list. The parameters to this function are a pointer to the dummy head node and the new data to insert.

7. Write a function that will accept a pointer to the first node of a doubly linked list and will deallocate (free) the memory of all of the nodes in the list.

8. Write a function average() that accepts a variable number of ints and returns their average. The normal argument should be a count of the number of ints to be averaged.

9. Write a simple version of printf(). This function, simple_printf(), should accept a control string that consists of %s, %d, or other ordinary characters. The ordinary characters are output as given. The %s and %d are replaced by the value of corresponding string and int parameters.

Programming Problems

1. Complete the phone directory example of the section Further Examples of the Use of Dynamic Memory Allocation by writing the modify() function.

2. Rewrite insert() in the phone directory problem to traverse the tree recursively.

3. Rewrite the print_tree() function in a nonrecursive fashion.

4. a. In C, dynamic arrays are not permitted. That is, the array declaration that allocates memory (the defining declaration) has to have a size that is known during compilation. The equivalence between pointers and array names can give dynamic arrays. Write a C program that inputs a value for the int variable num_names. Then allocate enough space for num_names names of 25 characters each. This allocation process will return a pointer to a character. Reference this memory in array notation. Input num_names names into this array, sort the array, and print the names in alphabetic order.

   b. Now modify this program to add more names to the array after the original list has been input, sorted, and output. Use realloc() to increase the size of the array. Then input additional names, sort all the names, and print out the newly sorted list.

5. The tasks of memory allocation can be understood better by simulating these functions for yourself. Write a program that declares a large array of memory. Then write your own versions of malloc(), calloc(), realloc(), and free() to allocate and deallocate memory from this array. For example, the call

```
carray = (char*) malloc(25);
```

would return a pointer to a free portion of the large array from which you are allocating memory. You will have to keep track of which portions of the large array have been allocated and which are free. You will have to decide what to do with the memory that is freed later.

6. Reverse Polish notation (RPN) is a method for specifying arithmetic expressions in which the operator follows the operand. Generally, we use an in-fix notation in which the operator comes between the operands. RPN is very useful as parentheses are never required. Expressions in in-fix notation can be converted to RPN by the use of a stack. (A stack is a data structure that can store a collection of objects, like an array. It differs from an array in that there is no "random access" to elements. Elements are accessed in a last-out, first-in, or LIFO, manner. Generally, the operation push() is used to add an element to the top of the stack; the operation pop() is used to remove the element that is on top of the stack.)

   The algorithm for this task is given in pseudocode:

```
while not end of line do
begin
    read a character (ch)
    if ch is a variable then print it out
    elsif ch = '(' then push ch
    elsif if ch is an operator then
    begin
        Compare the precedence of the operator ch with
        that of the operator on top of the stack.
        If operator ch has a precedence that is less than or
        equal to that of the op on top of the stack, then
        begin
            Output the operator on top of stack;
            Push operator ch
        end
        else
        begin
            Push operator ch
        end
        elsif ch = ')' then pop the stack and print the operators until
                    a '(' is found
    end
end

Pop all the operators off the stack and print them out.
```

Write a program to convert an expression from in-fix to RPN. Use an operator stack that is implemented by means of pointers and dynamically allocated nodes. Thus, each element of the stack will contain the operator and a pointer to the next element of the stack. There will be a special pointer to the top of the stack. The functions pop() and push() will operate on this stack. You may also want a function IsEmpty() to determine if the stack is empty.

7. Write a program that solves the phone directory program in the text by using a linked list of records containing a name and telephone number. Maintain this list in alphabetic order. The program should allow insertions, deletions, modifications, and finding a telephone number.

8. Complete the phone directory problem that was begun in this chapter. (See Figures 11.13 through 11.15 and Program 11.4.) In particular, write the list_delete() and modify() functions. Write a deletion function that actually deletes and frees the memory associated with the deleted node.

   This deletion algorithm is somewhat complicated. There are four cases to consider. These are illustrated in Figures 11.23 through 11.26. The simplest is the case in which the deleted node is a "leaf" node. (A leaf node is one that has no children.) The solution in this case is merely to delete the node and replace the pointer to it in the parent by NULL.

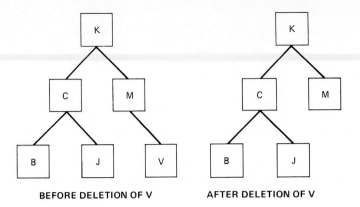

BEFORE DELETION OF V   AFTER DELETION OF V

Figure 11.23. Case 1: the deletion of a node with no children

The second case is when the node to be deleted has a left child but no right child. The solution here is fairly simple also. The left child is connected to the parent of the deleted node in place of that deleted node. This maintains the order in the tree since the left node of the deleted node has the same relationship to the parent of the deleted node as the deleted node had to its

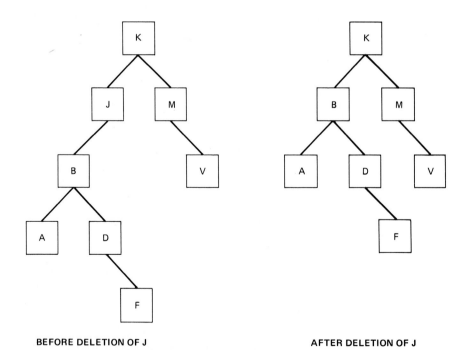

BEFORE DELETION OF J   AFTER DELETION OF J

Figure 11.24. Case 2: deletion of a node with a left child but no right child

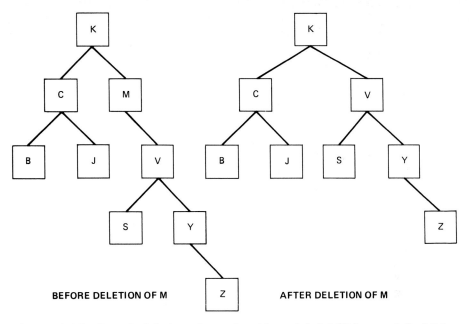

BEFORE DELETION OF M   AFTER DELETION OF M

Figure 11.25. Case 3: deletion of a node with a right child but no left child

parent. (That is, if the deleted node was less than its parent, then the left child of the deleted node is less than the deleted node's parent. If the deleted node was greater than its parent, then the left child of the deleted node is greater than the parent of the deleted node.) Draw a few sample trees to convince yourself.

Case 3 is the symmetric situation in which the left child is missing and the right child is present. This time, the right child is connected to the parent of the deleted node.

The most complex situation is the fourth, in which a node to be deleted has both a right and a left child. A solution to this is to find the smallest node in the right subtree of the deleted node. This can be obtained by following the right_child pointer from the node to be deleted. Then begin following left_child pointers of the children nodes until you reach a node with NULL for a left_child. This node is guaranteed to be the smallest node in the right subtree of the node to be deleted. (This is true because we initially followed the right_child pointer from the node to be deleted, then followed left_child pointers. Again, a few drawings will convince you of this.) This node can then be used to replace the deleted node since everything in the right subtree is greater than this node. By the method of choice, we know that this replacement node has no left_child. But it may have a right_child. This right_child can be attached to the tree in the location vacated by the replacement node. The tree's order will be maintained.

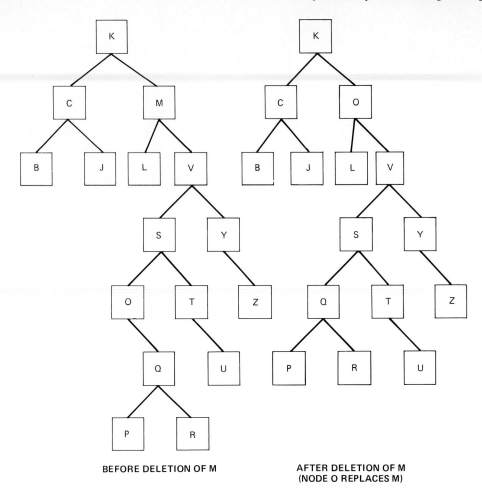

BEFORE DELETION OF M

AFTER DELETION OF M
(NODE O REPLACES M)

Figure 11.26. Case 4: deletion of a node with both left and right children

9. Finish the phone directory as described in Problem 8 except that the list_
delete() function should be implemented by marking a node as deleted rather
than actually deleting it. This method of deletion is not as efficient in its use of
storage, but is an easier algorithm to implement since it does not involve the
special cases discussed in Problem 8.

12 Advanced Control Flow

The control logic of most algorithms is adequately expressed using the C language statements if, for, while, switch, and do. The facility to decompose a program is provided by the function and the function call operator.

There are unusual cases, such as the need to react to an event such as a software or hardware interrupt, when the normal flow of control of a program must be interrupted. This chapter will examine the standard C statements and functions that are used to interrupt the normal flow of control in C programs. The discussion will cover local gotos, nonlocal gotos, and the signal (interrupt) processing functions. We will also reexamine pointers to functions and the ways that these can be used as function parameters and to construct dispatch (jump) tables.

12.1   POINTERS TO FUNCTIONS

The topic of a pointer to a function emerged in Chapters 6 and 10 when we discussed the standard library functions qsort() and bsearch(). In this section, we will further examine the use of these pointers. We will begin by reviewing the order of binding of the various attributes in a declaration.

Declaring Pointers to Functions

The attributes of pointer *, function (), and array [] bind in a declaration in the order that the precedence rule prescribes the order of execution of these operators in an expression. The precedence of the unary operators is shown in Table 12.1, with highest precedence at the top of the table.

Notice that the array and function reference operators have higher precedence then the pointer operators (& and *). Thus, the declaration

```
int *funct(void);
```

is interpreted as a *function* that returns a *pointer* to an integer, since the function attribute binds first, followed by the pointer attribute.

Table 12.1. Unary Operator Precedence

[], (), ., ->	Array reference, function call, structure reference
++ --	Postfix increment and decrement
++ -- sizeof (cast)	Prefix increment/decrement, sizeof, type
~, !, -, &, *	Bitwise not, logical not, negation, address of, indirection

```
int (*dispatch[]) () ;
```

Figure 12.1. An array of pointers to functions

The default binding can be changed by using parentheses, as in

```
int (*funct) (void)
```

which means a pointer to a function, since the * punctuator is now applied first, followed by the function punctuator.

Consider the declaration shown in Figure 12.1. This declaration is interpreted as an array of pointers to functions that return int values. The attributes within parentheses are applied first. Within the parentheses, the array attribute is applied before the pointer attribute. This is so because the [] operator has higher precedence than the * operator. The function attribute is then applied.

The following section considers some uses of pointers to functions.

Using Pointers to Functions

We have seen in Chapter 10 that qsort() and bsearch() accept an argument that is a pointer to a function. Program 12.1 is repeated from Program 10.9 as an example.

Program 12.1 sorts the array named list and then searches that array for a particular value.

A pointer to the function test_int() is passed to qsort() and bsearch(), as the last parameter to both functions. Test_it() is then called from within qsort() and bsearch() to perform comparisons of two of the elements of the list being sorted and searched.

To see how this pointer is used, consider the prototype declaration for qsort() shown in Figure 12.2.

Examine the last parameter in the declaration

```
int (*compar) (void *pl, void *p2)
```

```
#include <stdio.h>
#include <stdlib.h>

int list[] = {5, -102, 75, -44, 455, -203, -244, 211,
              105, -2, 52 };

main()
{
    extern int test_int(int *x, int *y);   /* comparison function */

    int key_value, i, item_number;
    int list_size = sizeof(list)/sizeof(list[0]);
    int *keyptr;

    qsort(list, list_size, sizeof(list[0]), test_int);

    printf("array has been sorted, new order is:\n");
    for (i = 0; i < list_size; i++)
    {
        printf("element %d = %d\n",i,list[i]);
    }

    printf("searching for item %d\n",key_value = 211);

    keyptr = (int *)bsearch(&key_value, list, list_size,
                sizeof(list[0]), test_int);
    item_number = (int)(keyptr - list);

    printf("Element located at element %d\n",item_number);
    exit(0);
}

int test_int(int *x, int *y)
{
    return(*x - *y);
}
```

Program 12.1. Using a pointer to a function

This declaration says that compar is a pointer to a function that accepts two parameters. To call this function within qsort(), we will use the expression

```
(*compar) ( p1, p2 )
```

The subexpression *compar is first evaluated. This is a reference to the function whose address is stored in compar. Next, the function call operator () is applied, passing two parameters to the function indicated by *compar.

```
void qsort(void *base, size_t nmemb, size_t size,
           int (*compar) (void *pl, void *p2) );
```

> This function sorts the array to which *base* points. The list contains *nmemb* elements. Each element consists of *size* bytes. *Compar* is a pointer to a function that accepts pointers to two array elements as parameters. Compar returns negative, zero, or positive according to whether the value of the object addressed by p1 is less than, equal to, or greater than the value addressed by p2.

Figure 12.2. The qsort() function

Let us consider a modified implementation of qsort() in order to illustrate the use of the function pointer parameter. We will implement a function called quick_sort() that will accept an array of values and sort that array into ascending order. We will use the declaration illustrated in Figure 12.3.

Notice that this function requires two function pointers: one to exchange values in the array and the other to compare two array values.

For the sort algorithm, we will use quick sort. The algorithm was developed by C. A. R. Hoare in 1960. It is popular because of its elegance. The algorithm works by selecting a particular element of the array called the pivot element and placing that element into its proper (sorted) location in the array. In the process of finding the proper place for the pivot element, the algorithm exchanges other array elements so that all elements to the left of the pivot element are less than it and all values to the right of the pivot element are greater. The pivot position is finally located and the element is put in the correct final position. Next the array is partitioned into two pieces, the unsorted elements to the left of the pivot and those to its right. To sort these two smaller arrays, the algorithm calls itself recursively. The pseudocode for the algorithm is shown in Figure 12.4.

```
quick_sort(void *first, void *last, int size,
           (*swap) (void *x, void *y),
           (*test) (void *x, void *y) ) ;
```

> *first* is a pointer to the first element in the array.
> *last* is a pointer to the last element of the array.
> *size* is the size in bytes of each element of the array.
> *swap* is a pointer to a function that exchanges the values addressed by its two parameters.
> *test* is a pointer to a function that compares the values addressed by its two parameters. It returns negative, zero, or positive if the *x < *y, *x == *y, or *x > *y respectively. [* is used here loosely.]

Figure 12.3. The quick_sort function

IF there is more than one element to be sorted THEN
    select a pivot element within the array
    rearrange the array, placing the pivot element into the proper (sorted) location
    sort the array elements to the left of the pivot using quik_sort
    sort the elements to the right of the pivot using quik_sort

Figure 12.4. Quik sort algorithm

    The key to the quick sort algorithm is the rearrangement algorithm. To accomplish the rearrangement, we will use two pointers: a left pointer, which begins at the left-most element of the array and moves right as long as elements are less than the pivot, and a right pointer, which begins with the right-most element of the array and moves to the left as long as elements in the list are greater than the pivot. Both left and right stop when they find an element out of order. When this happens, the two elements are exchanged and the algorithm continues until the right pointer moves to the left of the left pointer. This determines the proper location of the pivot element.

    Consider the unsorted list shown below.

    10 4 2 14 67 2 11 33 1 15

We will select as the pivot the left-most element and then set the left pointer to the next element in the list. (Any element could have been chosen as the pivot.) The right pointer is initialized to point to the last element in the list. Thus, the sort begins with

    Next, the algorithm determines the proper place for the pivot element (10) in the sorted list, and in the process exchanges any out-of-sequence elements. The left pointer moves until an item greater than the pivot is encountered, and the right pointer is moved until it finds a value less than the pivot. These elements must be exchanged because they are not in their proper position with respect to the final location of the pivot element. The diagram below shows the positions at which left and right will stop during the first iteration.

    Now the left and right elements are exchanged and the movement of left and right continues:

```
10  4  2  1  67  2  11  33  14  15
|              |__ left       |__ right
|__ pivot
```

The next stopping place is

```
10  4  2  1  67  2  11  33  14  15
|        left __|  |__ right
|__ pivot
```

After the exchange, the list appears as

```
10  4  2  1  2  67  11  33  14  15
|        left __|  |__ right
|__ pivot
```

The left and right pointers again move, but this time they cross—this indicates that the sorted position of the pivot has been located.

```
10  4  2  1  2  67  11  33  14  15
|        right __|  |__ left
|__ pivot
```

Finally, the element to which right points and the pivot are exchanged.

```
2  4  2  1  10  67  11  33  14  15
|        right __|  |__ left
|__ pivot
```

Now the pivot element is in the proper position, and all elements to the left of it are less in value and the elements to the right greater in value. The algorithm is then recursively called to sort the elements to the left of the pivot and to the right of the pivot.

Program 12.2 presents the quik_sort() function, along with a main() program and the swap() and test() functions.

Refer to Program 12.2. The call to quik_sort() in main() is

```
quik_sort(&list[0], &list[9], sizeof(int), change, compar)

&list[0] — address of first array element
&list[9] — address of last array element
sizeof(int) — size of an array element
change — address of element exchange function
compar — address of element comparison function
```

```
#include <stdio.h>
#include <stdlib.h>

int list[] = {10, 4, 2, 14, 67, 2, 11, 33, 1, 15 };

main()
{
    extern void change(int *x, int *y);
    extern int compare(int *x, int *y);
    extern void quik_sort(void *f, void *l, int size,
     void (*swap)(int *x, int *y),
     int (*compare)(int *x, int *y));
    int i;

    quik_sort(&list[0], &list[9], sizeof(int), change, compare);

    for(i=0; i<10; i++)
     printf("list[%d] = %d\n",i,list[i]);

    exit(0);
}

void
change(int *x, int *y)
{
    int temp;

    temp = *x;
    *x = *y;
    *y = temp;
}

int
compare(int *x, int *y)
{
    return(*x - *y);
}

void
quik_sort(void *first, void *last, int size,
        void (*swap)(int *x, int *y),
        int (*test)(int *x, int *y))
{
    char *pivot;
    char *left;
    char *right;
```

Program 12.2. Using pointers to functions in quik sort (continues)

```
if (first < last)
{
 pivot = (char *)first;
 left = (char *)first + size;
 right = (char *)last;

 do
 {
     while ((left <= right) &&
         ((*test)((int *)left, (int *)pivot) <= 0))
       left += size;
     while ((right >= left) &&
         ((*test)((int *)right, (int *)pivot) >= 0))
       right -= size;
     if (left < right) (*swap)((int *)left, (int *)right);
 } while (right >= left);

 (*swap)((int *)pivot, (int *)right);

 quik_sort(first, right-size, size, swap, test);
 quik_sort(right+size, last, size, swap, test);
}
```

Program 12.2. (continued)

Change and compar must have been previously defined or declared as functions in order for C to realize that these are the addresses of functions.

Inside quik_sort(), the element exchange function is called using the expression

```
(*swap) ( (int *)pivot, (int *)right)
```

and the comparison function is called using the expression

```
(*test) ( (int *)right, (int *)pivot)
```

The cast operations in both of these examples are used so that the type of the actual parameters would match that of the formal parameters for these functions.

The output from Program 12.2 is shown in Figure 12.5.

When using quick sort, one must be aware of possible performance problems. One potential problem is due to the algorithm's use of recursion. If the algorithm recurses too deeply, the C runtime stack (or its equivalent) may become exhausted. A second problem is that the performance of quick sort, although generally good (uses about 2NlnN comparisons), degrades to $N^2 2$ comparisons and deep recursion when used on an already sorted file.

```
list[0] = 1
list[1] = 2
list[2] = 2
list[3] = 4
list[4] = 10
list[5] = 11
list[6] = 14
list[7] = 15
list[8] = 33
list[9] = 67
```

Figure 12.5. Output from Program 12.2

Another application of pointers to functions is to build a dispatch or jump table of functions, and then call the function based upon some key value. This is illustrated in the next section.

Arrays of Pointers to Functions

A dispatch table is a table of addresses to which control is sent based upon some input transaction. For example, consider the simple menu-driven interface for the mailing list database system shown in Figure 12.6.

Suppose that the database system has been implemented so that a function has been coded to process each of the menu selections. A menu selection could then be processed using the switch statement illustrated in Figure 12.7.

An alternative to the code in Figure 12.7 is to create a dispatch table that contains the address of each of the functions. Then the proper function can be called using the menu selection as an index into the dispatch table. This is illustrated in Figure 12.8.

```
1 — Add a list entry
2 — Delete a list entry
3 — Display the list
4 — Print the list
5 — Sort the list
6 — Exit
```

Figure 12.6. Simple menu interface

```
choice = getchar() - '0';
switch (choice)
{
     case 1:
           result = add_entry();
           break;
     case 2:
           result = delete_entry();
           break;
     case 3:
           result = display_list();
           break;
     case 4:
           result = print_list();
           break;
     case 5:
           result = sort_list();
           break;
     case 6:
           result = close_db();
           break;
     default:
           result = errormst();
}
```

Figure 12.7. Processing a menu choice with switch.

Notice the declaration of the array dispatch

```
int (*dispatch[]) ()
```

Within the parentheses, the array symbol binds before the pointer indirection symbol (since [] has higher precedence than * in an expression). The function symbol binds last because it is outside of the parentheses. Thus, this dispatch table is an array of pointers to functions that each return an int. The parentheses around *dispatch[] are required. Without them, the declaration would attempt to declare an array of functions that return pointers to ints.

The array dispatch in Figure 12.8 is initialized with six pointers. The value of a function name without the call operator is the address of the entry point to the function. For the C compiler to realize that the names in the initialization list for dispatch are functions, they must have been previously defined or declared (as was done in Figure 12.8 with the extern declaration).

To call one of the functions in the array, the expression

```
(*dispatch[choice]) ()
```

```
extern int add_entry(void), delete_entry(void),
        display_list(void), print_list(void),
        sort_list(void), close_db(void), errormsg(void);

int (*dispatch[])() = {
    add_entry,
    delete_entry,
    display_list,
    print_list,
    sort_list,
    close_db
};

/* executable code follows */

choice = getchar() - '1';   /* map character '1' - '6' to int 0 - 5 */

if (choice < 0 || choice > (sizeof(dispatch)/sizeof(dispatch[0])))
{
    result = errormsg();
}
else
{
    result = (*dispatch[choice])();
}
```

Figure 12.8. Using an array of function pointers

is used. As in the declaration, the parentheses around *dispatch[] are required because the function call operator has higher precedence than the indirection operator. Within the parentheses, the array indirection operator has highest precedence. Thus, the order of application of the operators is array reference, indirection, and function call.

The example in Figure 12.8 utilized functions with no parameters. This is not a restriction, and, in fact, we have seen in the section Using Pointers to Functions that we can use a pointer to call functions with parameters. When a dispatch table is used, the functions should be written so that they all require the same number of arguments, since a single call is coded for all of the functions.

In this example a dispatch table and a switch statement can be used interchangeably. A dispatch table produces highly compact executable code, and may also produce more efficient code in the absence of compiler optimization. The reader of a switch statement, however, may find the operation of the executable code a bit more obvious than a function call using a dispatch table, since the purpose of a statement like (*dispatch[choice]) () may not be obvious. In general, switch statements are much more common.

12.2 LOCAL JUMPS: GOTO, BREAK, AND CONTINUE

The Goto Statement

The goto statement can be used to transfer control to any statement within the enclosing function. The statement to which control is transferred must have an associated label. The syntax for using gotos and labels is illustrated in Figure 12.9.

   Gotos are useful for handling errors within a function. Program 12.3 illustrates the use of the goto statement so that all of the exit() calls for the function are gathered at the end of the code. The program copies one file to another where the file names are specified on the command line.

```
    goto  label_name;
           .
           .
           .
label_name:  statement
```

Figure 12.9. The goto statement and label usage

```
#include <stdio.h>

/* File copy utility program */
main(int argc, char *argv[])
{
  FILE *in, *out;
  int ch;

  if (argc != 3)
  {
     printf("Usage: copy file1 file2\n");
     goto error_return;
  }
if ((in = fopen(argv[1],"r")) == NULL)
{
   printf("Cannot open file %s\n",argv[1]);
   goto error_return;
}

if ((out = fopen(argv[2],"w")) == NULL)
{
```

Program 12.3. Using goto and labels (continues)

```
                    printf("Canot open file %s\n",argv[2]);
                    goto error_return;
            }

        while (!feof(in))
        {
            ch = fgetc(in);
            if (!ferror(in))
            {
                    fputc(ch, out);
                    if ferror(out)
                    {
                            printf("Error writing to file\n");
                            goto error_return;
                    }
            }
            else
            {
                    printf("Error reading from file\n");
                    goto error_return;
            }
        }
        fclose(in);
        fclose(out);
        exit(0);

        /* Here after an error is detected */
        error_return:

        printf("Program terminated abnormally\n");
        exit(1);
    }
```

Program 12.3. (continued)

The use of the goto statement should be avoided when possible. The presence
of gotos generally complicates program control flow, and thus readability and
maintainability. Gotos can also restrict compiler optimizations. The best usage of
gotos is to branch down in a program in order to recover from errors or to handle
exceptions, as was illustrated in Program 12.3. Harbison and Steele in *A C
Reference Manual* present the following guidelines for using the goto statement.

1. Do not branch into the then or else portion of an if statement from outside of
   the if statement.

2. Do not branch from the then portion of an if to the else portion or back.
3. Do not branch into the body of a switch or iteration statement from outside the statement.
4. Do not branch into a compound statement (block) from outside the statement.

To exit an iteration or switch statement, or to skip the remainder of an iteration statement, a restricted form of the goto can be used. This is discussed next.

The Break and Continue Statements

The break statement was introduced in the discussion of the switch statement. In general, break can be used to jump out of the innermost do, for, switch, or while statement in which it is used. The continue statement can be used in do, for, or while statements to jump to the end of the loop body, and to continue the next iteration, skipping any intervening statements in the loop. Figure 12.10 illustrates

Using break

```
for ( ... )
{
    /* statements */
    if ( ... )
    {
        break;
    }
    /* statements */
}

/* statements */
```

Goto equivalent

```
    for ( ... )
    {
        /* statements */
        if ( ... )
        {
            goto break_label;
        }
        /* statements */
    }
break_label:
    /* statements */
```

Using continue

```
for ( ... )
{
    /* statements */
    if ( ... )
    {
        continue;
    }
    /* statements */
}
```

Goto equivalent

```
    for ( ... )
    {
        /* statements */
        if ( ... )
        {
            goto cont_label;
        }
        /* statements */
    cont_label:
    }
```

Figure 12.10. Action of break and continue statements

the operation of break and continues by comparing them with equivalent code using gotos.

Break and continue can be used in a similar way within while and do-while statements. Break can be used in switch statements to terminate processing in a case statement, as was illustrated previously.

Like goto, break and continue are useful to handle exceptions when they occur in a loop. Break and continue are better than goto from a maintenance standpoint because their actions are more restricted than that of the goto.

12.3 NONLOCAL JUMPS

Programs are often designed with many levels of functions. Consider the hierarchy chart in Figure 12.11, which represents the structure of a database management system that supports the functions of adding, deleting, and displaying records.

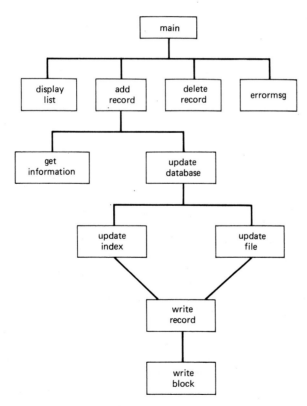

Figure 12.11. Deep function call hierarchy

Suppose that each of the boxes in the hierarchy chart of Figure 12.11 represent functions. In Figure 12.11, we have shown the complete hierarchy for the add function only. Display and delete would also have subordinate functions.

The function write block in Figure 12.11 is the function that will initiate the transfer of data to the secondary storage device (such as a disk drive). Suppose that an unrecoverable I/O error were detected in that function. Write block could return an error code to write record. Write record could return that code to update file, which, in turn, would return it to update database. Update database could return the error code to add record and add record could then return the code to main. Main might then call errormsg to output an error message to the user, and then terminate processing.

Two functions are provided in the standard C library that can be used in instances such as this to return directly from one function to another while bypassing intermediate functions. The first function, setjmp(), establishes the return point for the second function, longjmp(). These two functions are declared in the file setjmp.h and are described in Table 12.2.

Referring to Figure 12.11, we could call setjmp() in main. Then, when an unrecoverable I/O error is detected in write block, longjmp() can be called and control will transfer directly to main(), bypassing all of the intermediate functions. This is illustrated in Figure 12.12.

Table 12.2 Setjmp() and longjmp()

```
# include <setjmp.h>
int setjmp(jmp_buf env)
```

Establishes a return point for longjmp(). Here, *env* is a buffer in which the current execution environment (program counter, register values, and return address) is stored for later reference by longjmp(). The type of *env*, jmp_buf, is a type declared in setjmp.h.

An unusual aspect of setjmp() is that control in the program resumes after its call for two reasons: (1) setjmp() has been called to set the return location, or (2) longjmp() has been called. If the return is from the call to setjmp(), then zero is returned. If the return is from longjmp(), then a value given in the longjmp() call is returned.

```
void longjmp(jmp_buf env, int val)
```

longjmp() causes control to transfer from the point of a call to setjmp(). The point to which control is transferred is determined by the contents of *env*, which must have been set by a prior setjmp() call. The value of *val* is used as the value returned to setjmp().

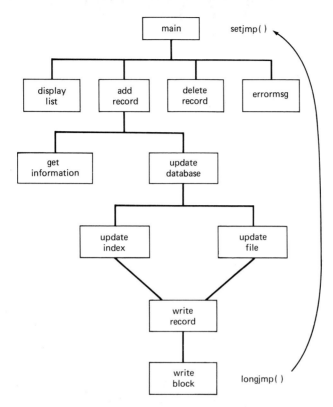

Figure 12.12. Operation of setjmp() and longjmp()

Program 12.4 implements the structure shown in Figure 12.12, including the use of setjmp() and longjmp().

Notice the call to setjmp() in main(). This call saves the execution environment into the buffer environ, including the address of the setjmp() call for later use by longjmp(); setjmp() will return from the first call with a return value of zero. If longjmp() is called with the argument environ, setjmp() will again return to this point in main(). However, the return value will not be zero, but the value of the second parameter in the call to longjmp().

Notice the code in Program 12.4. When it executes, it will display the entry message from each of the stub functions. If control returns normally, we should then see the corresponding exit messages displayed. However, if the longjmp() call is executed from write_block(), none of the exit messages will display. Instead, control will transfer directly to main(), where the return value from setjmp() will again be tested. A nonzero return value from setjmp indicates that a longjmp() has transferred control to that point—in this case, because of

```c
#include <stdio.h>
#include <setjmp.h>

jmp_buf environ;   /* defined externally for reference
                      by setjmp() and longjmp() */
#define IOERROR -10

main()
{
    int setj_code, result;
    int add_record(void);
    int opendb(void), closedb(void); /* hypothetical functions
                                        that open and close the
                                        database system */


    if ((setj_code = setjmp(environ)) != 0)
    {
        /* Here if the return is from longjmp() */
        printf("Hard error number %d\n", setj_code);
        printf("Attempting to recover...\n");
        closedb();
        printf("Data may have been lost, check the database\n");
        printf("Would you like to continue (y or n) ");
        result = getchar();  getchar();
        if (result == 'n')
        {
            exit(1);
        }
    }
    else
    {
        /* Here if return is from setjmp() */
    }
    /* Open database system */
    if (opendb() != 1)
    {
        printf("Cannot initialize database. Fatal Error\n");
        exit(2);
    }
    /* Here to process database commands.
     * Add record is used as an example.
     */
    add_record();
    printf("Program terminated normally\n");
    exit(0);
```

Program 12.4 Using setjmp() and longjmp() (continues)

```
}

/* open the database */
int opendb(void)
{
    /* code to initialize the database */
    printf("Database Initialized\n");
    return(1);
}

/* close the database */
int closedb(void)
{
    /* code to close the database */
    return(1);
}

/* Driver function for add operation */
int add_record(void)
{
    int update_database(void);

    printf("Entered add_record\n");
    update_database();
    printf("Exiting add_record\n");
}

/* Function to update the database */
int update_database(void)
{
    int update_file(void);

    printf("Entered update_database\n");
    update_file();
    printf("Exiting update_database\n");
}

/* Function to update a file in the database */
int update_file(void)
{
    int write_record(void);

    printf("Entered update_file\n");
    write_record();
    printf("Exiting update_file\n");
}
```

Program 12.4 (continued)

```
/* Function to write a record to a file */
int write_record(void)
{
    int write_block(void);

    printf("Entered write_record\n");
    write_block();
    printf("Exiting write_record\n");
}

/* Function to write a block of records into the database */
int write_block(void)
{
    printf("Entered write_block\n");

    /* Simulate a hard I/O error and
     * call longjmp() to attempt recovery.
     */
    longjmp(environ,IOERROR);

    printf("Exiting write_block\n"); /* should never execute */
}
```

Program 12.4 (continued)

a simulated hard error condition. The code detects this and attempts to recover.

The output from Program 12.4 is shown in Figure 12.13. Notice that none of the exit messages are displayed in Figure 12.13 because the longjmp() call bypasses the normal function return mechanisms. However, it does free any space utilized by function parameters and automatic variables in intervening function activations. It restores the execution environment to the state at the point of the corresponding setjmp() call.

The function in which the setjmp() is enclosed need not be the main() function, as was illustrated above. However, the enclosing function must still be active when longjmp() is called. It should not have returned. Also, when using setjmp(), the call should not be embedded in complex expressions. This is so because intermediate results of an expression may not be retained when control resumes in the expression due to a longjmp() call. Simple expressions, such as in a simple assignment statement or conditional expression, are the best uses for setjmp().

The primary use of setjmp() and longjmp() is to leave a deep sequence of function calls when a processing error or an interrupt is detected. Interrupts are discussed in the next section.

```
Database initialized
Entered add_record
Entered update_database
Entered update_file
Entered write_record
Entered write_block
Hard error number -10
Attempting to recover . . .
Data may have been lost, check the database
Would you like to continue (y or n) y
Database Initialized
Entered add_record
Entered update_database
Entered update_file
Entered write_record
Entered write_block
Hard error number -10
Attempting to recover . . .
Data may have been lost, check the database
Would you like to continue (y or n) n
```

Figure 12.13. Output from Program 12.4

12.4 SIGNAL PROCESSING

Interrupts and Signals

Most computers have a mechanism whereby a peripheral, such as an I/O device, or an abnormal event, such as an illegal memory reference or an attempt to divide by zero, can get the immediate attention of the computer's processor. This allows the processor to respond to a condition immediately, and later return to the normal flow of processing. These are called hardware interrupts.

Interrupts can also be generated by software, that is, by the operating system or by a program. Like hardware interrupts, a software interrupt will disrupt the normal flow of control in a program, so that the program can immediately respond to some extraordinary event. For example, an interactive program could be coded to respond to an attention signal from the operating system (or command processor), such as control-C or control-break, entered from the user's keyboard. In a multiuser system, a parent process might spawn a child, wait for the child to terminate, and then be notified of the child process's death via a software interrupt.

In C, interrupts are called *signals*. The standard C library contains functions that allow a program to detect and respond to certain hardware- and software-generated signals.

Signal Types

The act of detecting a signal is called *trapping*. To send a signal, that particular signal is *raised*. The standard header file *signal.h* defines constants that represent the types of signals that can be handled in C, along with functions that are used to trap and raise signals. The standard specifies the signal types listed in Table 12.3. A particular implementation might support additional types.

We recommend that readers consult their documentation (or <signal.h>) to ascertain the signal types supported in their own environment.

Signal Processing Functions

A program can be coded to respond in three possible ways to the receipt of a signal:

1. Follow default action, specified by the implementation.
2. Ignore the signal.
3. Trap and respond to the signal locally within the program.

The default processing of a signal is described by the local implementation and host operating system. For example, a particular signal might cause immediate termination of a program in one implementation but be ignored in another. The user should consult local documentation for specifics concerning default processing.

Table 12.3. Signal Types

SIGABRT	Generated by abnormal program termination, such as by a call to abort().
SIGFPE	Generated by an erroneous arithmetic operation, such as division by zero.
SIGILL	An illegal function image (executable format).
SIGINT	An interactive attention signal.
SIGSEGV	Invalid memory reference.
SIGTERM	A termination request sent to the program. This could be generated by the raise() function from within the program or from a parent process (shell) in a multiuser environment.

We will examine trapping and ignoring of signals using the signal handling functions. Table 12.4 describes these functions.

Trapping and Handling Signals

Program 12.5 illustrates the use of signal() to specify a function to be invoked in the case of an attempted floating-point zero divison. Under default signal processing, the program might be terminated by the host operating system if a division by zero was detected. The use of signal() allows the program to trap and attempt to recover from the signal without causing termination.

The call to signal() in Program 12.5 specifies that the function trapper() is to be called when a zero divide is detected. The output from Program 12.5 is shown in Figure 12.14.

After responding to the signal, it may or may not be possible to continue executing the program at the point at which it was interrupted. This depends on the particular type of signal. For most signals, the signal processing function will be able to return control to the point of the interrupt by executing the return statement. For computational exceptions like SIGFPE, the signal handler may be restricted to execution of abort(), exit(), or longjmp(), as was illustrated in Program 12.5. This is implementation-defined behavior. In either case, the use of

Table 12.4. Signal Processing Functions

```
#include <signal.h>
void (*signal(int signal_type,
     void (*func) (int x)))(int y)
```

The signal() function specifies how a *signal_type* is to be processed: either default, ignored, or trapped. *signal_type* is one of the values from Table 12.3. *func* is either one of the values:

  SIG_DFL—for default processing

  SIG_IGN—to ignore the signal

or it is a pointer to a function to be invoked when the specified *signal_type* is received. This *traps* the signal.

Signal() returns the value of func that was previously in effect before the call, or SIG_ERR if the signal handling request cannot be honored. The return type of signal() is a pointer to a function that accepts a single integer parameter.

```
int raise(int signal_type)
```

Generates a signal of type *signal_type* to the executing program. Returns zero if successful, and nonzero if not successful.

```
#include <stdio.h>
#include <signal.h>
#include <setjmp.h>

jmp_buf environ;

main()
{
    int trapper(int sig_val);    /* Function to be invoked when
                                  * the signal is detected */
    float x = 1.0, y = 0.0;

    /* Save environment for longjmp() */
    if (setjmp(environ) != 0)
    {
        /* Here when longjmp() is called */
        printf("Returned to main() after interrupt\n");
        printf("Restarting processing in main\n");
    }

    /* Initiate trapping of floating point exception */
    if (signal(SIGFPE, trapper) == SIG_ERR)
    {
        printf("Cannot process signal\n");
        abort();
    }

    /* Generate a floating point exception */
    x = x/y;

    /* This code should never be executed */
    printf("In main, after divide\n");
    exit(0);
}

/* Here when a floating point zero divide signal is generated */
int trapper(int sig_val)
{
    printf("Signal received, value = %d\n",sig_val);
    longjmp(environ,1);
}
```

Program 12.5. Processing SIGFPE

```
Signal received, value = 2
Returned to main( ) after interrupt
Restarting processing in main
                    .
                    .
                    .
```

Figure 12.14. Output from Program 12.5

the signal handler allows the programmer to provide a more user-friendly response than would be provided by the typical default signal response.

Program 12.6 shows a program that traps a software interrupt, SIG_INT. This
is generated when the user enters an attention signal such as control-C from the
keyboard.

The output from Program 12.6 is shown in Figure 12.15. Notice several
techniques in Program 12.6. The first executable statement in the signal trapping
function, attention(), is a call to signal() to ignore control-C interrupts: signal(SI-
GINT, SIG_IGN). This is needed because once a signal occurs, its handling is set
to the default behavior (automatically). On our system, the default processing for
control-C is to terminate the program. Notice also that the trapping function
allows the user to choose either to terminate execution or to continue execution of
the program. Execution of the return statement will return control to the point
where the program was interrupted (the while(1) statement) and processing could
continue. If the user elects to continue processing, signal() is once more called to
reinstitute control-C trapping, and return is executed.

Raising Signals

The raise() function can be used to send a signal within a program. Signals can be
raised from within a program in order to invoke an exception-handling function
when an error is detected. Program 12.7 illustrates a program that detects an
attempt to divide by zero and invokes an exception handler instead of allowing the
hardware to do this.

12.5 PORTABILITY AND SOFTWARE ENGINEERING ISSUES

The use of pointers to functions, nonlocal gotos, and signal processing will make
a program more difficult to read and understand, and thus more difficult to
maintain. When calling a function using a pointer stored in a pointer variable, it is

```c
#include <stdio.h>
#include <signal.h>

main()
{
    int attention(int sig_val);   /* Function to trap control-C */

    printf("In main, starting execution\n");
    signal(SIGINT, attention);
    while (1)
    {
        printf("Executing, type control-C to interrupt\n");
    }
}

/* Trapping function for Control-C */
int attention(int sig_val)
{
    int result;

    /* Ignore control-C in the interrupt trapper */
    signal(SIGINT, SIG_IGN);

    printf("Signal received, value = %d\n",sig_val);
    printf("Would you like to continue (y or n)?");
    result = getchar(); getchar();
    if (result == 'y')
    {
        /*
         * Signal must be called again to re-establish
         * trapping of control-C.
         */
        signal(SIGINT, attention);
        return;
    }
    else
    {
        abort();
    }
}
```

Program 12.6. Processing control-C

```
        In main, starting execution
        Executing, type control-C to interrupt
        Executing, type control-C to interrupt
                .
                .
                .
        ^C
        Signal received, value = 10
        Would you like to continue (y or n)?
```

Figure 12.15. Output from Program 12.6

```c
#include <stdio.h>
#include <signal.h>

main()
{
  void trapper(void);
  double x = 4.0, y = 0.0;

  /* Initiate trapping of floating point exceptions */
  if (signal(SIGFPE, trapper) == SIG_ERR)
  {
      printf("Cannot trap memory reference signal\n");
      abort();
  }

  /* Code to check for zero divide */

  if (y == 0.0)
  {
      /* Invoke exception handler using signal() */
      raise(SIGFPE);
  }
  else
  {
      printf("%f/%f = %f\n",x,y,x/y);
      exit(0);
  }
}

/* Signal trapping function for zero division */
void trapper(void)
{
    printf("Detected attempt to divide by zero\n");
    printf("Process terminated\n");
    exit(1);
}
```

Program 12.7. Using raise()

not obvious as to which actual function will be invoked by looking at the source code. Using nonlocal gotos and signal processing bypasses the normal function call and return mechanisms, thus obscuring the flow of control within the program. Because of these difficulties, all three capabilities should be used only when necessary, and the source code should be commented on appropriately. For example, a comment at a longjmp() indicating the destination of the jump would aid a reader of the source. A banner comment at the top of a module that utilizes signal processing, notifying the reader of signals that are processed and the type of processing applied to each, will provide assistance to a maintenance programmer.

The types of signals generated by a host environment and the default processing applied to each signal are implementation-defined characteristics. Thus, an application that utilizes signals may be expected to require modification when ported between host environments. If signals are utilized, their use should be carefully documented within the source code.

Some operating systems support signal processing between processes that are executing concurrently on a multiprocessing system. For example, processes within the same family on a UNIX-based system (parent/child processes) can send and receive signals to one another. Signals can thus be used as an interprocess communication mechanism for synchronizing the execution of cooperating processes. The use of signals in this context is not addressed in this text. Interested readers are referred to their local system documentation.

12.6 SUMMARY

In this chapter, we reexamined the use of variables that contain pointers to functions, including arrays of such pointers. We noted that the declaration of these variables required an extra set of parentheses, as in

```
int (*funct) ()  ;
int (*dispatch[5])();
```

because of the relative order of binding of the *, [], and () attributes.

We examined how an array of pointers to functions can be used as a dispatch table for calling a function based upon some transaction value such as a menu selection. In applicable situations, this technique makes it possible to replace a long switch statement with a few lines of code.

Local goto statements were presented. The best use of the goto statement is to send control to the end of a function in order to handle common exception processing. Break and continue statements are a restricted form of the local goto statement. Gotos should be avoided when possible as they add to the complexity of a program.

Table 12.5. Nonlocal Goto and Signal Processing Functions

```
#include <setjmp.h>

int setjmp (jmp_buf enf)
```

Establish a return environment for longjmp().

```
void longjmp(jmp_buf env, int val)
```

Transfer control from this point to the location determined by setjmp(). Bypass the usual function return mechanisms. Use *val* as the value returned by setjmp().

```
#include <signal.h>

int raise(int signal_type)
```

Generate a signal of type *signal_type*.

```
void (*signal(int signal_type,
void (*func) (int x)))(int y)
```

Specifies how the signal *signal_type* is to be handled.

The functions in Table 12.5 were presented.

The use of the functions summarized in Table 12.5 cause the standard function call and return mechanisms to be bypassed. For this reason, these functions are used infrequently and their usage should be well documented.

The use of signal processing can cause particular difficulty when porting software as a result of implementation-defined behavior. Signal processing should also be carefully documented in the source code.

Keywords

binding, order of
break statement
continue statement
dispatch table
execution environment
goto
interrupt

labels
nonlocal goto
pointer, to a function
quick sort
raise a signal
signal
trapping signals

References

Harbison, S. P., and G. L. Steele. 1984. *A C Reference Manual,* Englewood Cliffs, N.J.: Prentice-Hall, p. 225.

Hoare, C. A. R. 1961. "Partition (Algorithm 63), Quicksort (Algorithm 64), and Find (Algorithm 65)", *CACM,* 4(7): July 1961, 321–322.

Reynolds, F. 1987. "Signals in UNIX," *The C J.,* 3(2): 45–48. Info-Pro Systems, Denville, N.J.

Discussion Questions

1. C declarations can become quite cryptic. Discuss the interpretation of declarations that utilize the combinations of the *, [], and () attributes. Compare attribute binding with operator precedence.

2. Discuss a disciplined usage of the goto statement. When is a goto appropriate and when is it not appropriate?

3. To terminate the execution of a loop prematurely, it was suggested that break is superior to goto. Discuss the reasoning behind this statement.

4. Application programs communicate with the operating system through an interrupt mechanism. Typically, there is a machine instruction that generates an interrupt and passes an integer value to the operating system. Each interrupt value is interpreted by the operating system as a particular kind of request for services (I/O, memory, program termination, etc.). Discuss the way that an array of pointers to functions could be used in the operating system's interrupt handler.

5. The setjmp() function saves the current execution environment for possible restoration at a later time by a call to longjmp(). What information would need to be saved by setjmp()? Consider the use of local variables, registers, and the address to which longjmp() returns.

6. It was suggested in the text that a use for setjmp() and longjmp() is for branching to a function to do error recovery. Considering a program structure such as illustrated in Figure 12.11 where a deep level of function call is used, how might the use of longjmp() simplify the code in each of the functions in the hierarchy?

7. In many UNIX-based systems, the parent process to all of the application processes that run on a multiuser system is the init process. Init starts a process that waits for input on each of the system's terminal ports. This is the getty process. When getty detects terminal activity, a login process is started, and finally a command processor is initiated. Thus, each user's command processor is a child process of init. When the user decides to log out, the command processor terminates its execution, and init must then restart the whole chain of processes, beginning with the getty program. What mechanism could be used by init so that it can detect the termination of the command processor (or any of its children)?

8. Suppose that you are reading the source code for a program and you come across the statement

```
longjmp(oldenv);
```

How would you go about locating the place to which control will transfer upon execution of the statement?

Exercises

1. Consult your local C language library documentation and determine which signal types are supported and the default processing. List and summarize this information.

2. Obtain a listing of setjmp.h. What information is stored in the jmp_buf data structure?

3. The following function was written to handle signals of type SIGFPE.

```
void matherr(int sig)
{
    printf("Erroneous arithmetic operation detected\n");
    printf("Continuing with processing\n");
    return;
}
```

If it is intended that this function be able to respond more than once to a signal of the given type, what additional code should be added to that shown?

4. Write a statement that explains the meaning of each of the following C declarations:
   a. `float *func();`
   b. `int (*func) ();`

    c. `char (*array[]) ();`
    d. `double *(*func) ();`

5. Given the declaration

   ```
   int (*func)() = smooth;
   ```

   state a reasonable declaration for the object smooth.

6. List the three possible ways in which signals can be processed by a C program.

7. Obtain a listing of signal.h. List the signal types that are defined in that file.

8. If you are using a UNIX system, find a description of the functions fork(), exec(), and wait(). How is this combination of functions more powerful than the system() function described in Chapter 10?

9. Consider the following statements.

   ```
   for (i = 1; i < MAX; i++)
   {
        statement-1;
        while (!done)
        {
             statement-2;
             if (condition)
             {
                  break;
             }
             statement-3
        }
        statement-4;
   }
   statement-5;
   ```

   Answer these questions about this code fragment.
   a. If the break statement is executed, to what statement will control be transferred?
   b. If the break statement is replaced with a continue statement and it is executed, to what statement will control be transferred?

Programming Problems

1. Write a program that can be used to exercise the following math library functions.

double cosh(double x)	hyperbolic cosine
double sinh(double x)	hyperbolic sine

double tanh(double x)	hyperbolic tangent
double ceil(double x)	smallest integer
double fabs(double x)	absolute value
double floor(double x)	largest integer
double sqrt(double x)	square root
double acos(double x)	arc cosine
double asin(double x)	arc sine
double atan(double x)	arc tangent
double cos(double x)	cosine
double sin(double x)	sine
double tan(double x)	tangent

You should display a menu to allow the user to select the desired function. Accept a menu selection, and then a value to operate upon. Use the menu selection to call the function through the use of a dispatch table. The dispatch table should be an array of pointers, one pointer to each of the above functions. Use another array of pointers to characters that reference an appropriate output message for each of the math functions. For example, selecting sqrt and entering 64 might result in the response:

> The square root of 64.00 is 8.00.

Following the output of an answer, redisplay the menu and allow the user to make another selection. Include in your menu an option to terminate the program.

2. Many C libraries have functions in addition to system() that can be used to execute a program from within a C program. These functions might be called fork(), exec(), and wait(), on UNIX, or spawn(), on some PC systems. If these functions are available, write an implementation of system() using the alternative functions available on your system.

3. Develop a simplified command processor similar to Figure 12.8. Make a command processor that could be used by beginning programmers. For example, the menu selections might be

Edit a file.
Print a listing.
Compile a program.
Execute a program.
List files on disk.
Log out.

Use a dispatch table to call a function that carries out each function, or use a function such as system(). On a UNIX system, you might want to utilize the fork(), exec(), and wait() library functions.

4. Modify Program 12.4 so that when the simulated hard error is detected, the program raises the signal SIGTERM. Write a trapping function to trap this signal, and modify the main() function to initiate trapping of the signal. Have the trapper function output an appropriate diagnostic, and then longjmp() back to main().

Appendix A
Standard Library
Functions

A.1 STANDARD HEADER FILES

`assert.h`	Macros used for debugging.
`ctype.h`	Character processing and testing macros.
`errno.h`	Macros (EDOM and ERANGE) and the lvalue errno used in error reporting.
`float.h`	Ranges for floating-point data types.
`limits.h`	Ranges for integer data types.
`locale.h`	Used to specify locale-specific behavior of functions of certain library functions.
`math.h`	Declaration of double precision math functions.
`setjmp.h`	Declaration of nonlocal goto functions.
`signal.h`	Declaration of signal processing functions.
`stdarg.h`	Macros and functions for functions that process a variable number of parameters.
`stddef.h`	Catchall file that includes various commonly used macros and types that are also defined in other header files. stddef.h contains ptrdiff_t, size_t, NULL, offsetof(), and errno.
`stdio.h`	Declaration of standard I/O macros and functions.
`stdlib.h`	Declaration of utility functions and macros.
`string.h`	Declaration of string processing functions and macros.
`time.h`	Declaration of time and date functions and macros.

A.2 DEBUGGING

```
#include <assert.h>
```

Macros and Declarations

NDEBUG   If this macro is defined before the inclusion of assert.h, then the assert() is given a benign definition.

`void assert(int expression)`   Causes programs to output diagnostics. If the value of expression is zero (false), then the assert() macro outputs a diagnostic line to the standard error stream as follows:

```
Assertion failed: expression, file filename, line xx
```

The program is then terminated by calling the abort() function.

A.3 CHARACTER PROCESSING AND TRANSLATION

```
#include <ctype.h>
```

Macros and Declarations

For the ASCII character set, the printing characters are those with hexadecimal codes 0x20 (space) through 0x7E (tilde). Control characters have hexadecimal codes 0 through 0x1F.

`int isalnum(int c)`	Nonzero (true) if c is the code for an alphanumeric character.
`int isalpha(int c)`	Nonzero (true) if c is the code for an alphabetic character.
`int iscntrl(int c)`	Nonzero (true) if c is the code for a control character (any nonprinting character).
`int isdigit(int c)`	Nonzero (true) if c is the code for a decimal digit.
`int isgraph(int c)`	Nonzero (true) if c is the code for a graphic character (any printing character other than space).
`int islower(int c)`	Nonzero (true) if c is the code for a lowercase alphabetic character.
`int isprint(int c)`	Nonzero (true) if c is the code for a printing character (any character that is not a control character).
`int ispunct(int c)`	Nonzero (true) if c is the code for any nonalphanumeric printing character.
`int isspace(int c)`	Nonzero (true) if c is the code for a white space character.
`int isupper(int c)`	Nonzero (true) if c is the code for an uppercase alphabetic character.
`int isxdigit(int c)`	Nonzero (true) if c is the code for a hexadecimal digit (0–9, A–F, or a–f).
`int tolower(int c)`	Maps only uppercase characters to lowercase; otherwise returns the parameter unchanged.
`int toupper(int c)`	Maps only lowercase characters to uppercase, otherwise returns the parameter unchanged.

A.4 LOCALE-SPECIFIC BEHAVIOR

```
#include <locale.h>
```

Macros and Declarations

LC_ALL	The programs entire locale
LC_COLLATE	Affects strcoll() functions
LC_CTYPE	Affects character handling functions
LC_NUMERIC	Affects formatted I/O functions (decimal point)
LC_MONETARY	Affects monetary formatting information returned by localeconv()
LC_TIME	Affects strftime() function

Other implementation-specific macros

struct lconv   Atype. See localconv() below.

Functions

```
char *setlocale(int category, const char *value)
```

Set locale-specific behavior for various functions. The first parameter, category, is one of the above macros. The second parameter is an implementation-defined value that affects the operation of the function(s) specified by the first parameter. For example, the LC_NUMERIC parameter can be used to change the character that is used to represent the decimal point in the formatted I/O functions. The programmer is advised to see the translator's documentation to determine the operations supported by setlocale().

```
struct lconv *localeconv(void)
```

Returns a pointer to a structure of type struct lconv. This structure gives the current values used for formatting of numeric values by the formatted output functions. The structure contains the following members. The types char* are pointers to strings. Types of char are integer values.

```
char *decimal_point;      /*decimal point character*/
char *thousands_sep;      /*character to separate groups of digits*/
char *grouping;           /*size of each group of digits*/
char *int_curr_symbol;    /*international currency symbol*/
char *currency_symbol;    /*local currency symbol*/
char *mon_decimal_point;  /*decimal point for monetary quantities*/
char *mon_thousands_sep;  /*separator of groups of digits to left of
                            decimal*/
```

```
char *mon_grouping;      /*size of each group of digits for monetary
                           quantities*/
char *positive_sign;     /*string to indicate nonnegative monetary
                           quantity*/
char *negative_sign;     /*string to indicate negative monetary
                           quantity*/
char int_frac_digits;    /*number of digits to right of decimal, in-
                           ternational*/
char frac_digits;        /*number of digits to right of decimal, local*/
char p_cs_precedes;      /*1 or 0 if currency symbol precedes or suc-
                           ceeds value*/
char p_sep_by_space;     /*1 or 0 if currency symbol is or is not sepa-
                           rated by a space*/
char n_cs_precedes;      /*1 or 0 if currency symbol precedes or suc-
                           ceeds value for negative*/
char n_sep_by_space;     /*1 or 0 if currency symbol is or is not sepa-
                           rated by a space for negative*/
char p_sign_posn;        /*position of positive sign for monetary value*/
char n_sign_posn;        /*position of negative sign for monetary
                           value*/
```

A.5 DOUBLE PRECISION MATHEMATICAL FUNCTIONS

`#include <math.h>`

Macros and Declarations

`errno`	a modifiable integer used to hold an error code value.
`EDOM`	errno is set to this value if an input parameter is outside of the domain of the function. The function also returns an implementation-defined value.
`ERANGE`	errno is set to this value of the result of a function cannot be represented as a double value. The function also returns HUGE_VAL.
`HUGE_VAL`	Value returned by functions when the result cannot be represented as a double value.

Functions

Exponential and Logarithmic Functions

`double exp(double x)`	Computes the exponential of x with the base e.
`double frexp(double x, int *exp)`	Converts x into a fraction in the range [0.5,1) and a power of two. The fraction is returned as the value of the expression, and the power of two is returned into the location to which exp points. If x is zero, both returned values are zero.
`double ldexp(double x, int exp)`	Determines the value of x times 2 to the exp power.
`double log(double x)`	Determines the natural logarithm of x.
`double log10(double x)`	Determines the base-10 logarithm of x.
`double modf(double x, double *iptr)`	Breaks x into integral and fractional parts. Returns the fractional part as the value of the function and returns the integral part into the location to which iptr points. Both returned values have the sign of x.

Hyperbolic Functions   The input to these functions is in radians.

    double cosh(double x)   Returns the hyperbolic cosine of x.
    double sinh(double x)   Returns the hyperbolic sine of x.
    double tanh(double x)   Returns the hyperbolic tangent of x.

Nearest Integer, Absolute Value, and Remainder

    double ceil(double x)   Returns the smallest integer not
                                         less than x as type double.
    double fabs(double x)   Returns the absolute value of x.
    double floor(double x)   Returns the largest integer not
                                         greater than x as type double.
    double fmod(double x, double y)   Returns the remainder of x / y,
                                         where the remainder is computed
                                         as $x - i * y$ for some integer i where
                                         i is the largest integer such that
                                         |remainder| < |y|. The result is
                                         implementation defined if y is 0.

Power and Square Root Functions

    double pow(double x, double y)   Returns x raised to the y power. A
                                         domain error (EDOM) occurs if x is
                                         zero and y is less than or equal to
                                         zero, or if x is negative and y is not
                                         an integer.
    double sqrt(double x)   Returns the nonnegative square root
                                         of x. A domain error (EDOM)
                                         occurs if x is negative.

Trigonometric Functions   The value returned from the trigonometric functions is
measured in radians.

    double acos(double x)   Returns the arc cosine of x for x
                                         in the range of [−1, 1]. The result
                                         is in the range [0, π].
    double asin(double x)   Returns the principal value of the
                                         arc sine of x, where x is in the
                                         range [−1, 1]. The result is in the
                                         range [− π/2, π/2].
    double atan(double x)   Returns the principal value of the
                                         arc tangent of x. The result is the
                                         range [-π/2, π/2].

`double atan2(double y, double x)`	Returns the principal value of the arc tangent of y/x using the signs of both y and x to determine the quadrant of the return value. A domain error is generated if x and y are zero. The result is in the range $[-\pi, \pi]$.
`double cos(double x)`	Returns the cosine of x, where x is measured in radians.
`double sin(double x)`	Returns the sine of x, where x is measured in radians.
`double tan(double x)`	Returns the tangent of x, where x is measured in radians.

A.6 NONLOCAL GOTOS

```
#include <setjmp.h>
```

Macros and Declarations

jmp_buf   A type. Used to hold information returned by setjmp().

Functions

```
int setjmp(jmp_buf env)
```

Establishes a return point for longjmp(). *env* is a buffer in which the current execution environment (program counter, register values, and return address) is stored for later reference by longjmp(). The type of *env*, jmp_buf, is a type declared in setjmp.h.

   An unusual aspect of setjmp() is that control in the program resumes after its call for two reasons: (1) setjmp() has been called to set the return location, or (2) longjmp() has been called. If the return is from the call to setjmp(), then zero is returned. If the return is from longjmp(), then a value given in the longjmp() call is returned.

```
void longjmp(jmp_buf env, int val)
```

longjmp() causes control to transfer from the point of the call to a call to setjmp(). The point to which control is transferred is determined by the contents of *env*, which must have been set by a prior setjmp() call. The value of *val* is used as the value returned to setjmp(). A value of zero should not be used for *val*. If it is, 1 is used in its place.

A.7 SIGNAL PROCESSING

```
#include <signal.h>
```

Macros and Declarations

sig_atomic_t A type for an atomic entity. Such objects are modified as atomic entities.

The following two values can be used as the value of the second argument to signal().

SIG_DFL Specifies default signal processing.

SIG_IGN Specifies that a signal is to be ignored.

SIG_ERR Return value from signal() if request cannot be honored. The object errno is also set to indicate an error.

The following values are signal-types used as the first argument of signal() and raise().

SIGABRT Abnormal termination signal.

SIGFPE Erroneous arithmetic operation signal.

SIGILL Invalid execution, such as an illegal instruction.

SIGINT Interactive attention signal.

SIGSEGV Invalid storage access signal.

SIGTERM Termination request signal.

Other implementation-defined signal types.

Functions

```
void (*signal(int signal_type, void (*func)(int x)))(int y)
```

The signal() function specifies how a *signal_type* is to be processed: either default, ignored, or trapped. *signal_type* is one of the signal type values listed above. func is either one of the values

SIG_DFL—for default processing

SIG_IGN—to ignore the signal

or it is a pointer to a function to be invoked when the specified *signal_type* is received. This *traps* the signal.

signal() returns the value of func that was previously in effect before the call, or SIG_ERR if the signal-handling request cannot be honored. The return type of signal() is a pointer to a function that accepts a single integer parameter.

```
int raise(int signal_type)
```

Generates a signal of type *signal_type* to the executing program. Returns zero if successful, and nonzero if not successful. Signal types are SIGABRT, SIGFPE, SIGILL, SIGINT, SIGSEGV, SIGTERM, and other implementation-defined signal types.

A.8   VARIABLE PARAMETER LIST PROCESSING

```
#include <stdarg.h>
```

Macros and Declarations

va_list   A type of an array that hold information used by the va_args, va_end, and va_start macros.

```
void va_start(va_list ap, lastparm)
```

Prepares for access to optional parameters by initializing ap for use by va_arg() and va_end(). The parameter ap must point to an object of type va_list. lastparm is the name of the last-named parameter in the formal parameter list (before the . . .).

```
type-name va_arg(va_list ap, type-name)
```

Fetches the value of each optional parameter. The type name is a type that must agree with the type of each actual parameter. Following the invocation of va_start(), the first invocation of va_arg returns the first optional parameter, and successive invocations return subsequent parameter values.

```
va_end(va_list ap)
```

Should be invoked before returning from a function that has utilized variable parameter list processing.

A.9   INPUT/OUTPUT PROCESSING

```
#include <stdio.h>
```

Macros and Constants

FILE	A type used to recording information needed for I/O operations to a stream.
fpos_t	A type used to record the position within a file for I/O operations.
_IOFBF	Indicates full buffering (see setvbuf()).
_IOLBF	Indicates line buffering (see setvbuf()).
_IONBF	Indicates no buffering (see setvbuf()).
BUFSIZ	Default buffer size (see setbuf()).
EOF	Negative integer used to indicate end-of-file.
errno	A modifiable int set to an error code value.
FOPEN_MAX	Maximum number of files that can be opened simultaneously.
FILENAME_MAX	Maximum length for a file name.
L_tmpnam	Size of a temporary file name.
NULL	Null pointer.
OPEN_MAX	Guaranteed minimum number of files that can be simultaneously open.
SEEK_CUR	Seek from current position (see fseek()).
SEEK_END	Seek from end-of-file (see fseek()).
SEEK_SET	Seek from the beginning of the file (see fseek()).
TMP_MAX	Guaranteed minimum number of unique file names that can be produced by tmpnam().
size_t	Type of value returned by the sizeof operator.
stderr	Standard error stream.
stdin	Standard input stream.
stdout	Standard output stream.

Functions

File Access

```
FILE *fopen (const char *file_specification, const char *mode);
```

Returns a pointer to an object of type FILE, or null pointer in case of failure. The macro NULL in stdio.h can be used to represent a null pointer. *mode* is a pointer to a string (or string constant). Valid modes are:

`"r"`	open a text file for input only.
`"w"`	create and open a text file for output. Destroy existing contents.
`"a"`	open a text file for output at the end of the file.
`"rb"`	open a binary file for input only.
`"wb"`	create and open a binary file for output. Destroy existing contents.
`"r+"`	open a text file for input and output (update).
`"w+"`	create and open a text file for input and output (update). Destroy existing contents.
`"a+"`	open a text file for input/output (update), writing at end of file.
`"rb+"`	open a binary file for input/output (update).
`"wb+"`	create and open a binary file for input/output (update).
`"ab+"`	open a binary file for input/output (update), writing at end of file.

("r+b", "w+b", and "a+b" can be used in place of the above three strings.)

```
int fclose( FILE *stream);
```

Returns zero if successful, and nonzero otherwise. Also flushes data in any buffers.

```
int feof(FILE *stream)
```

Returns nonzero (true) if the end-of-file indicator is set for the stream; otherwise feof() returns zero (false).

```
freopen(const char *file_specification, const char *mode,
        FILE *stream)
```

Attempts to close any file associated with stream, and then to open the specified file and associate it with the given stream. Returns stream if successful, and a null pointer for failure.

Character I/O Functions

`int fgetc(FILE *stream)`	Get the next character (if present) from the input stream.
`int getc(FILE *stream)`	A (possibly) macro implementation of fgetc().
`int getchar()`	getc(stdin)
`int fputc(int c, FILE *stream)`	Write the character specified by c to the output stream.
`int putc(int c, FILE *stream)`	A (possibly) macro implementation of fputc().
`int putchar(int c)`	putc(stdout, c)
`int ungetc(int c, FILE *stream)`	Push the character c back into the input stream. The character will be input by the next input function call. The character is not actually written into the file, but kept in a

buffer. Pushing back more than one character without intervening input operations is not guaranteed to work. Once end of file is reached, characters cannot be pushed back.

Line I/O Functions

```
char *fgets(char *s, int n, FILE *stream)
```

Reads at most n-1 characters from the stream into the array pointed to by s, or read up to the next new-line or end-of-file (whichever comes first). If read, a new-line is retained. A null byte is appended to the data. On EOF, a null pointer is returned.

```
char *gets(char *s)
```

Reads characters from stdin into the array pointed to by s until a new-line or end-of-file is encountered. If read, a new-line is discarded. A null byte is appended to the data. On EOF, a null pointer is returned.

```
int fputs(const char *s, FILE *stream)
```

Writes to the indicated stream the string to which s points. The terminating null byte is not written. If successful, it returns nonzero (true), and zero (false) if not successful.

```
int puts(const char *s)
```

Writes to stdout the string to which s points. The null byte is not written, but a new-line (or host-dependent line terminator character(s)) is written in its place. It returns nonzero (true) for success and zero (false) for failure.

Formatted I/O Functions

```
int fprintf(FILE *stream, const char *format, . . .)
```

Writes output to the indicated stream and converts values under control of the format control string. Returns the number of characters transmitted or a negative integer for an output error.

```
int fscanf(FILE *stream, const char *format, . . .)
```

Reads input from the indicated stream and converts values under control of the format control string. Returns the number of input items assigned or EOF if an I/O error occurs.

```
int sprintf(char *array, const char *format, . . .)
```

Converts values from the . . . list of parameters to characters and stores these characters into the array. Returns the number of characters stored into the array, excluding the terminating null byte.

```
int sscanf(const char *array, const char *format, . . .)
```

Converts characters from the array to internal format and assigns these values to the locations specified in the . . . list. Returns EOF if a conversion failure occurs. Otherwise, it returns the number of input items assigned.

```
vfprintf(FILE *stream, const char *format, va_list parm)
vprintf(const char *format, va_list parm)
vsprintf(char *s, const char *format, va_list parm)
```

vfprintf(), vprintf(), and vsprintf() are equivalent to fprintf(), printf(), and sprintf(), respectively, with the variable parameter list being replaced by parm. Parm must be initialized by the va_start macro. None of these three functions invokes the va_end macro.

Direct I/O Functions

```
size_t fread(void *ptr, size_t size, size_t nblks,
             FILE *stream);
```

Inputs *nblks* (blocks), each containing *size* bytes, each into the array ptr. Returns the number of blocks successfully read.

```
size_t fwrite(const void *ptr, size_t size,
              size_t nblks, FILE *stream);
```

Outputs *nblks* (blocks), each containing *size* bytes, from the array *ptr* to the indicated stream. Returns the number of blocks successfully written.

File Positioning Functions

```
int fgetpos(FILE *stream, fpos_t *pos)
```

Stores the current value of the file pointer for the indicated stream into the object to which pos points. Returns zero if successful, and nonzero for failure. On a failure, also stores an error code in errno.

```
int fseek(FILE *stream, long int offset, int whence)
```

Sets the file position indicator for the file designated by stream. For *binary mode* files, the offset can be either relative to the current position or an offset from the start or end of the file. The meaning of the offset is determined by the value of the whence parameter. The possible values for this parameter are the following macros:

```
whence == SEEK_SET   from the beginning of the file
whence == SEEK_CUR   from the current position in the file
whence == SEEK_END   from the end of the file
```

For *text mode* files, the offset is either zero or a value returned by the ftell() function.

Notice that binary mode files afford more flexibility in setting the internal file pointer as compared with text mode files. This is attributable to the possible discrepancy between internal and external representations of text mode files. This discrepancy does not exist for binary mode files. fseek() returns nonzero in case of failure.

```
fsetpos(FILE *stream, const fpos_t *pos)
```

Sets the file pointer for the indicated stream to the value of the object to which pos points. This value must have been previously returned by a call to fgetpos(). Returns zero for success, and nonzero otherwise. For errors, also sets errno.

```
long int ftell(FILE *stream)
```

Returns the value of the internal file pointer. Values returned from ftell() can be used in calls to fseek(). ftell() returns –1L in case of failure.

```
void rewind(FILE *stream)
```

Equivalent to the call (void)fseek(stream, OL, SEEK_SET) followed by clearerr (stream). That is, it sets the file pointer to the beginning of the file and the error indicator is cleared.

Operations on Files

```
int remove(const char *filename)
```

Delete the specified file name. Returns zero if successful, and nonzero otherwise. The result of an attempt to remove an open file is implementation dependent.

```
int rename(const char *old, const char *new)
```

Rename the file specified by the string old to the name specified in the string new. Returns zero for success, and nonzero for failure.

```
FILE *tmpfile(void)
```

Creates and opens for update a temporary file that will be automatically deleted when it is closed or the program terminates. Returns a pointer to the stream for the file if successful, or a null pointer in case of failure.

```
char *tmpnam(char *array)
```

Generates a file name that is different from any existing files. Generates a different name each time it is called. Two possible returns are possible: If the array pointer is null, then tmpnam() returns a pointer to an object in memory containing the new name. If array is not null, the name is returned into that array.

The array should be declared as char array[L_tmpnam]. L_tmpnam is defined in stdio.h.

Error-Handling Functions

```
void clearerr(FILE *stream)
```

Clears the value of the error indicator for the stream.

```
int ferror(FILE *stream)
```

Returns nonzero (true) if the error indicator for stream is set; otherwise it returns zero (false).

```
void perror(const char *s)
```

Using the current value in errno, maps this error code to an error message string. It writes the string to the standard error stream. If the parameter s is not null, then the error message is prepended with the string to which s points, followed by a colon.

Functions to Control Buffering

```
void setbuf(FILE *stream, char *buf)
```

See setvbuf(). The following calls are equivalent.

```
setbuf(stream, NULL)      setvbuf(stream, NULL, _IONBF, 0);
setbuf(stream, buf)       setvbuf(stream, buf, _IOFBF, BUFSIZ);
                          setbuf() returns no value. See setvbuf() for
                          details.
```

```
int setvbuf(FILE *stream, char *buf, int mode, size_t size);
```

setvbuf() must be called after a file has been opened but before performance of any I/O operations on the file. It is used to specify the desired type of buffering, using the following macros for the *mode* parameter (macros are defined in stdio.h):

- `_IOFBF` Full buffering. Fill the entire buffer when possible.
- `_IOLBF` Uses line buffering. Buffers are flushed when new-lines are read or written.
- `_IONBF` No buffering.

If the parameter *buf* is not null, then the array to which it points may be used as the buffer instead of the system supplied buffer. The parameter *size* gives the size of this buffer. See local documentation for additional details. setvbuf() returns zero if successful, and nonzero for failure.

```
int fflush(FILE *stream)
```

Causes any buffered data to be written to the stream. For input streams, the effect is undefined (see local documentation). Returns nonzero if a write error occurs.

A.10   UTILITY FUNCTIONS

```
#include <stdlib.h>
```

Macros and Declarations

`div_t`	Type of a structure used by div().
`errno`	Modifiable integer used to hold an error code.
`ldiv_t`	Type of a structure used by ldiv().
`size_t`	Type generated by the sizeof operator.
`ERANGE`	Value stored in errno by some string conversion functions to indicate overflow or underflow conditions.
`EXIT_FAILURE`	Argument to exit().
`EXIT_SUCCESS`	Argument to exit().
`HUGE_VAL`	Value returned by some string conversion functions to indicate overflow.
`RAND_MAX`	Maximum value returned by rand().

Functions

Base 10 String Conversion Functions

```
double atof(const char *sptr);   /* ASCII-to-float*/
```

Converts the string to which sptr points to double representation. Returns zero (false) if no conversion could be performed.

```
int atoi(const char *sptr)       /* ASCII-to-integer */
```

Converts the string to which sptr points to int representation. Returns zero (false) if no conversion could be performed.

```
long int atol(const char *sptr)  /* ASCII-to-long */
```

Converts the string to which sptr points to long int representation. Returns zero (false) if no conversion could be performed.

```
double strtod(const char *nptr, char **endptr)
```

Converts the initial part of the string to which *nptr* points to double. Returns a pointer to the part of the string after the converted value in *endptr*. Returns zero (false) if no conversion was performed or if the value would cause underflow. Returns 1 plus or minus HUGE_VAL (according to the sign of the value to be converted) if the value is too large to convert (overflow). Sets errno to ERANGE for overflow or underflow errors.

String Conversion, Other Bases

```
long int strtol(const char *sptr, char **endptr, int base)
unsigned long int strtoul(const char *sptr, char **endptr,
int base)
```

Both strtol() and strtoul() convert the digits in the string addressed by *sptr* to long and unsigned long representation respectively. The parameter *base* is a value between 2 and 36 that represents the radix of the digit string. The letters from a (or A) through z (or Z) are used for digits between 10 and 35. The parameter *endptr* is used to hold a pointer that points to any text after from the *sptr* string that follows the values converted.

Random Number Generation Functions

```
void srand(unsigned int seed);
```

Causes the next random number produced by rand() to be computed using the value in seed.

```
int rand(void)
```

Generates a pseudorandom number between 0 and RAND_MAX (inclusive) based upon the last random number so generated. The first random number generated is based upon the value of the seed set by srand(). If srand() has not been called, a seed of 1 is used. RAND_MAX is defined in stdlib.h

Memory Management Functions

```
void *calloc(size_t nmemb, size_t size)
```

Allocates memory for an array of nmemb objects each of which is size bytes long. The allocated memory is initialized to zero bits. Returns a pointer to the lowest byte address of the allocated space if successful, and returns a null pointer for failure.

```
void free(void *ptr)
```

Deallocates the memory to which ptr points. The memory must have been previously allocated by a call to calloc(), malloc(), or realloc().

```
void *malloc(size_t size)
```

Allocates size bytes and returns a pointer to the lowest address byte of the allocated space. Returns a null pointer for failure.

```
void *realloc(void *ptr, size_t size)
```

Changes the amount of allocated memory to which *ptr* points to the indicated *size*. *ptr* must be either NULL or contain a pointer previously returned by calloc(), malloc(), or realloc(). Returns a NULL pointer for failure and leaves ptr unchanged. If *size* is zero, then the space to which *ptr* points is freed.

Communication with the Host Environment
```
void abort(void)
```

Causes abnormal termination of the current program. It is implementation-defined value indicating unsuccessful termination is returned to the host operating system.
```
int atexit(void (*func)(void))
```

Registers functions to be executed at normal program termination. Returns zero if registration succeeds, nonzero otherwise.
```
void exit(int status)
```

Causes normal program termination. If the value of status is zero, or EXIT_SUCCESS successful termination is returned to the host operating system. If status in EXIT_FAILURE, unsuccessful termination is returned to the host operating system. Causes any registered functions to be executed in reverse order of their registration. Flushes and closes any open output streams. Removes any temporary files created by tmpfile().
```
char *getenv(const char *name)
```

Searches the host operating system's environment for the string to which *name* points. Returns a point to the string associated with the specified environment name (if found) or a NULL pointer if the name is not found.
```
int system(const char *string)
```

Executes the host operating system command to which string points. If string is NULL, system() returns nonzero to indicate that there is a command processor or zero (false) if there is not. If string is not NULL, it returns an implementation-defined value.

Sorting and Searching
```
void *bsearch(const void *key, const void *base,
              size_t nmemb, size_t size,
              int (*compar)(void *p1, void *p2))
```

Returns a pointer to the matching member of the array or NULL if no match is found.
key is a pointer to the value to be located.
base is a pointer to the start of the array to be searched. The array must be in ascending order.
nmemb is the number of elements in the array.
size is the size in bytes of each array element.
compar() is a pointer to a function that will compare two of the array elements. compar() returns negative if *p1 < *p2; it returns zero if *p1 == *p2, and positive if *p1 > *p2. (The expressions *p1 and *p2 are used loosely here to indicate the objects to which p1 and p2 point.)

```
/* quick-sort */
void qsort(void *base, size_t nmemb, size_t size,
           int (*compar)(const void *p1, const void *p2))
```

qsort() does not return a value.

base is a pointer to the start of the array to be sorted.

nmemb is the number of elements in the array.

size is the size in bytes of each array element.

compar() is a pointer to a function that will compare two array elements. compar() returns negative if *p1 < *p2, zero if *p1 == *p2, and positive if *p1 > *p2. (The expressions *p1 and *p2 are used loosely here to indicate the objects to which p1 and p2 point.)

Integer Mathematics Functions

```
int abs(int x)
```

Returns the absolute value of x.

```
div_t div(int numer, int denom)
```

Returns the quotient and remainder of the division (numer/denom) into the structure of type div_t. div_t has the following members:

```
struct {
    int quot;
    int rem;
};
```

```
long int labs(long int j)
```

Returns the absolute value of j.

```
ldiv_t ldiv(long int numer, long int denom)
```

Similar to div() shown above. Returns the quotient and remainder of (numer/denom) into the structure of type ldiv_t with members quot and rem.

A.11   STRING FUNCTIONS

```
#include <string.h>
```

Macros

size_t   Type of the value generated by sizeof.
NULL   A null pointer.

Functions

In the following descriptions, the functions whose names begin with *mem* operate upon "generic" strings that do not require null termination. The functions whose names begin with *str* deal with null terminated strings.

String Copy

```
void *memcpy(void *target, const void *source, size_t n)
```

Copies n bytes from *source* to *target*. If the source and target objects overlap, the result is implementation dependent. Returns the value of *target*.

```
void *memmove(void *target, const void *source, size_t n)
```

Copies n bytes from *source* to *target*. The source and target strings may overlap in memory. Returns the value of *target*.

```
char *strcpy(char *target, const char *source)
```

Copy the null terminated string to which *source* points to *target*. If the source and target strings overlap, the result is implementation dependent. Returns the value of *target*.

```
char *strncpy(char *target, const char *source, size_t n)
```

Copies not more than *n* bytes from the null terminated *source* string to the *target*. If the two strings overlap, the result is implementation dependent. Returns the value of *target*.

String Concatenation

```
char *strcat(char *target, const char *source)
```

Appends a copy of the null terminated string to which *source* points to the end of the *target* string. Returns the value of *target*.

```
char *strncat(char *target, const char *source, size_t n)
```

Appends not more than *n* characters from the null terminated *source* string to the end of the *target* string. The resulting string is always null terminated. Returns the value of target.

String Comparison

When comparing characters, the collating sequence of the particular character set determines the result of comparisons.

```
int memcmp(const void *sl, const void *s2, size_t n)
```

Compares the first *n* characters of the object to which *s1* points with that pointed by *s2*. Returns a negative integer if s1 < s2, zero if s1 == s2, or positive integer if s1 > s2. s1 and s2 here indicate the strings, not the pointers themselves!

```
int strcmp(const char *sl, const char *s2)
```

Compares the null terminated strings to which *s1* and *s2* point. Returns a negative integer if s1 < s2, zero if s1 == s2, and positive if s1 > s2. Here, s1 and s2 refer to the strings to which these parameters point.

```
int strncmp(const char *sl, const char *s2, size_t n)
```

Compares not more than *n* characters of the null terminated strings to which *s1* and *s2* point. Returns a negative integer if s1 < s2, zero if s1 == s2, or a positive integer if s1 > s2 (the strings, not the pointers).

```
int strcoll(const char *SI, const char *S2)
```

Compares the string pointed to by *S1* and *S2*, both interpreted as indicated by the LC_COLLATE category of the current locale. Returns negative, zero, or positive according to whether *S1* is greater than, equal to, or less than *S2*.

```
size_t strxfrm(char *target, size_t size, const char *source)
```

Takes the string to which *source* points and transforms it so that it can be correctly compared by memcmp() or strcmp(). The transformed string is stored into *target*. The parameter *size* specifies the maximum length of the transformed string. Returns the length of the transformed string if it did not exceed the size, or zero otherwise. strxfrm() can be controlled by the setlocale() function. This function is provided so that string comparisons can be properly performed for implementations that use character sets whose numeric codes do not correspond to the desired collating sequence. (Such as certain European character sets.)

String Searching

```
void *memchr(const void *s, int c, size_t n)
```

Returns a pointer to the first occurrence of the character *c* in the string to which *s* points. Searchs at most n bytes. Returns a null pointer if c is not found.

```
char *strchr(const char *s, int c)
```

Returns a pointer to the first occurrence of the character c in the string to which s points. Returns a null pointer if the character was not found.

```
size_t strcspn(const char *s, const char *not)
```

Returns the length of the initial part of the *s* string that consists entirely of characters not contained in the string *not*.

```
char *strpbrk(const char *s, const char *tofind)
```

Returns a pointer to the first occurrence of any character in *s* that is also in the string *tofind*. Returns a null pointer if none of the characters in *tofind* are in *s*.

```
char *strrchr(const char *s, int c)
```

Locates the last occurrence of the character *c* in the string *s*. Returns a null pointer if *c* is not found in *s*.

```
size_t strspn(const char *s, const char *tofind)
```

Returns the length of the initial part of the string to which *s* points that consists entirely of characters contained in the string pointed to by *tofind*.

```
char *strstr(const char *s, const char *tofind)
```

Returns a pointer to the start of the substring within *s* that matches the string to which *tofind* points.

```
char *strtok(char *s, const char *delimit)
```

Successive calls return pointers to the start of tokens within the string *s* that are delimited by any character contained within the string to which *delimit* points. Delimiters are overwritten with nulls so that the tokens are null terminated. Returns a null pointer if no token is found.

Miscellaneous String Functions

```
void *memset(void *s, int c, size_t n)
```

Copies the value of the character *c* into each of the first *n* bytes of the string to which *s* points. Returns the original value of the pointer *s*.

```
char *strerror(int error)
```

Returns a pointer to an error message string. The string is created based upon the value of *error*.

```
size_t strlen(const char *s)
```

Returns the length of the string to which s points. The null byte is not counted.

A.12   DATE AND TIME FUNCTIONS

```
#include <time.h>
```

Macros and Constants

CLK_TCK	The granularity of the processor clock. The type clock_t is in the unit (1/CLK_TCK) seconds.
clock_t	The type of the processor time [see clock()].
time_t	The type of the encoded calendar time [see time()].
struct tm	A structure containing elements of the broken-down time. The structure is

```
struct tm {
  int tm_sec;           /* seconds after the minute - [0,60] */
  int tm_min;           /* minutes after the hour - [0,59] */
  int tm_hour;          /* hours since midnight - [0,23] */
  int tm_mday;          /* day of the month - [1,31] */
  int tm_mon;           /* months since January - [0,11] */
  int tm_year;          /* years since 1900 */
  int tm_wday;          /* days since Sunday - [0,6] */
  int tm_yday;          /* days since January 1 - [0,365] */
  int tm_isdst;         /* daylight savings time flag */
                        /* positive => daylight savings time */
                        /* zero => not daylight savings time */
                        /* negative => no information */
};
```

Functions

```
clock_t clock(void)
```

Returns the amount of processor time used by the program since its invocation. The value (clock_t)(–1) is returned if the time is not available.

```
time_t time(time_t *timer)
```

Returns the current encoded calendar time. The parameter can be either a NULL or a pointer to a variable of type time_t. If this parameter is not NULL, the encoded time is also stored at the given location. The value (time_t)(–1) is returned if the time cannot be determined.

```
double difftime(time_t time1, time_t time0)
```

Returns the value (time1–time0) in seconds. *time*0 and *time*1 are encoded calendar times returned by time() or mktime().

```
struct tm *localtime(const time_t *timeptr);
```

Accepts a pointer to an encoded time and returns a pointer to a structure containing the broken-down time that corresponds to the given encoded time value. The pointer points to a single static structure so that if localtime() is called again, the same pointer is returned that points to the updated structure.

```
char *asctime(const struct tm *timeptr)
```

Accepts a pointer to the tm structure containing a date and time and then returns a pointer to a string with the form:
    Mon Jan 01 08:30:23 1988\n\0
The values in the string are determined by the values in the structure pointed to by timeptr.

```
char *(time (const time_t *timer)
```

Accepts a pointer to an encoded calendar and returns a pointer to a string of the same form as asctime().

```
struct tm *gmtime(const time_t *timeptr)
```

Like localtime(), but converts the encoded time to the broken-down format expressed in Coordinated Universal Time (UTC).

```
time_t mktime(struct tm *timeptr)
```

Accepts a pointer to a broken-down time structure and returns the corresponding encoded calendar time.

```
size_t strftime(char *s, size_t size,
            const char *format, const struct tm *timeptr)
```

Takes time values out of the structure to which *timeptr* points and stores them into the string to which *s* points. The conversion is done under control of the format string, similar to the sprintf() function. The format control string can consist of ordinary characters or conversion specifications. The parameter *size* specifies the maximum number of characters to be stored into the string *s*. Conversion strings are replaced with date or time information, as follows:

%a	Abbreviated weekday name
%A	Full weekday name
%b	Abbreviated month name
%B	Full month name
%c	Local date and time
%d	Decimal (01–31) day of month
%H	Decimal (00–23) hour
%I	Decimal (01–12) hour
%j	Decimal (001–366) day of year

%m   Decimal (01–12) month
%M   Decimal (00–59) minute
%p   AM or PM
%S   Decimal (00–59) second
%U   Decimal (00–52) week of the year, using Sunday as the first day of the week
%w   Decimal (0–6) weekday
%W   Decimal (00–53) week of the year, using Monday as the first day of the week
%x   Date
%X   Time
%y   Decimal (00–99) year without century
%Y   Decimal year with century
%Z   Time zone name
%%   Replaced with %

strftime () returns the number of characters written into the array *s* if the number is not more than *size*. Otherwise zero is returned.

A.13   IMPLEMENTATION LIMITS

The files limits.h and float.h specify maximum and minimum magnitudes and precisions for the various types. The names of the constants are listed here, but the reader is referred to the local implementation for specific values in their environment.

```
#include <limits.h>

CHAR_BIT            /* bits in a character */
CHAR_MAX            /* max value (integer) for char type */
CHAR_MIN            /* min value (integer) for a char type */
INT_MAX             /* int max value */
INT_MIN             /* int min value */
LONG_MAX            /* long int max value */
LONG_MIN            /* long int min value */
SCHAR_MAX           /* signed char max value */
SCHAR_MIN           /* signed char min value */
SHRT_MAX            /* short int max value */
SHRT_MIN          /* short int min value */
UCHAR_MAX           /* unsigned char max value */
UINT_MAX            /* unsigned int max value */
ULONG_MAX           /* unsigned long max value */
USHRT_MAX           /* unsigned short max value */

#include <float.h>

DBL_DIG             /* max precision for a double value */
DBL_EPSILON         /* min double value such that */
                    /* 1.0 + DBL_EPSILON != 1.0 */
DBL_MANT_DIG        /* max digits in base FLT_RADIX double mantissa */
DBL_MAX             /* max magnitude double value */
DBL_MAX_10_EXP      /* max power of 10 for double values */
DBL_MAX_EXP         /* max power of FLT_RADIX for double values */
DBL_MIN             /* min positive double value */
DBL_MIN_10_EXP      /* min negative power of 10 for doubles */
DBL_MIN_EXP         /* min negative power of FLT_RADIX for doubles */
FLT_DIG             /* max precision for a float value */
FLT_EPSILON         /* min float value such that */
                    /* 1.0 + FLT_EPSILON != 1.0 */
FLT_MANT_DIG        /* max digits in base FLT_RADIX float mantissa */
FLT_MAX             /* max magnitude float value */
FLT_MAX_10_EXP      /* max power of 10 for float values */
FLT_MAX_EXP         /* max power of FLT_RADIX for float values */
FLT_MIN             /* min positive float value */
FLT_MIN_10_EXP      /* min negative power of 10 for floats */
FLT_MIN_EXP         /* min negative power of FLT_RADIX for floats */
FLT_RADIX           /* radix of exponent representation (2 or 16) */
FLT_ROUNDS          /* rounding mode in use. A value > 0 implies */
                    /* implementation defined rounding; 0 implies */
                    /* chops, and -1 implies mode unknown */
```

```
LDBL_DIG           /* max precision for a long double value */
LDBL_EPSILON       /* min double value such that */
                   /* 1.0 + LDBL_EPSILON != 1.0 */
LDBL_MANT_DIG      /* max digits in base FLT_RADIX long */
                   /* double mantissa */
LDBL_MAX           /* max magnitude long double value */
LDBL_MAX_10_EXP    /* max power of 10 for long double values */
LDBL_MAX_EXP       /* max power of FLT_RADIX for long */
                   /* double values */
LDBL_MIN           /* min positive long double value */
LDBL_MIN_10_EXP    /* min negative power of 10 for long doubles */
LDBL_MIN_EXP       /* min negative power of FLT_RADIX for */
                   /* long doubles */
```

Appendix B
ASCII and EBCDIC
Character Codes

B.1 ASCII CONTROL CHARACTERS

Decimal	Binary	Hex	Character	Meaning	
00	?0000000	00		Null	
01	?0000001	01	Control-A	Start of heading	(SOH)
02	?0000010	02	Control-B	Start of text	(STX)
03	?0000011	03	Control-C	End of test	(ETX)
04	?0000100	04	Control-D	End of transmission	(EOT)
05	?0000101	05	Control-E	Enquiry	(ENQ)
06	?0000110	06	Control-F	Acknowledge	(ACK)
07	?0000111	07	Control-G	Bell	(BEL)
08	?0001000	08	Control-H	Backspace	(BS)
09	?0001001	09	Control-I	Horizontal tab	(HT)
10	?0001010	0A	Control-J	New line	(LF)
11	?0001011	0B	Control-K	Vertical tab	(VT)
12	?0001100	0C	Control-L	Form feed	(FF)
13	?0001101	0D	Control-M	Carriage return	(CR)
14	?0001110	0E	Control-N	Shift out	(SO)
15	?0001111	0F	Control-O	Shift in	(SI)
16	?0010000	10	Control-P	Data link escape	(DLE)
17	?0010001	11	Control-Q	Device control 1	(DC1)
18	?0010010	12	Control-R	Device control 2	(DC2)
19	?0010011	13	Control-S	Device control 3	(DC3)
20	?0010100	14	Control-T	Device control 4	(DC4)
21	?0010101	15	Control-U	Negative acknowledge	(NAK)
22	?0010110	16	Control-V	Synchronous idle	(SYN)
23	?0010111	17	Control-W	End of trans. block	(ETB)
24	?0011000	18	Control-X	Cancel	(CAN)
25	?0011001	19	Control-Y	End of medium	(EM)
26	?0011010	1A	Control-Z	Substitute	(SUB)
27	?0011011	1B	Escape	Escape	(ESC)
28	?0011100	1C		File separator	(FS)

ASCII Control Characters (continued)

Decimal	Binary	Hex	Character	Meaning	
29	?0011101	1D		Group separator	(GS)
30	?0011110	1E		Record separator	(RS)
31	?0011111	1F		Unit separator	(US)

Printable Characters

Decimal	Binary	Hex	Character
32	?0100000	20	Space
33	?0100001	21	!
34	?0100010	22	"
35	?0100011	23	#
36	?0100100	24	$
37	?0100101	25	%
38	?0100110	26	&
39	?0100111	27	'
40	?0101000	28	(
41	?0101001	29	)
42	?0101010	2A	*
43	?0101011	2B	+
44	?0101100	2C	,
45	?0101101	2D	-
46	?0101110	2E	.
47	?0101111	2F	/
48	?0110000	30	0
49	?0110001	31	1
50	?0110010	32	2
51	?0110011	33	3
52	?0110100	34	4
53	?0110101	35	5
54	?0110110	36	6
55	?0110111	37	7
56	?0111000	38	8
57	?0111001	39	9
58	?0111010	3A	:
59	?0111011	3B	;
60	?0111100	3C	<

(continued)

Printable Characters (continued)

Decimal	Binary	Hex	Character
61	?0111101	3D	=
62	?0111110	3E	>
63	?0111111	3F	?
64	?1000000	40	@
65	?1000001	41	A
66	?1000010	42	B
67	?1000011	43	C
68	?1000100	44	D
69	?1000101	45	E
70	?1000110	46	F
71	?1000111	47	G
72	?1001000	48	H
73	?1001001	49	I
74	?1001010	4A	J
75	?1001011	4B	K
76	?1001100	4C	L
77	?1001101	4D	M
78	?1001110	4E	N
79	?1001111	4F	O
80	?1010000	50	P
81	?1010001	51	Q
82	?1010010	52	R
83	?1010011	53	S
84	?1010100	54	T
85	?1010101	55	U
86	?1010110	56	V
87	?1010111	57	W
88	?1011000	58	X
89	?1011001	59	Y
90	?1011010	5A	Z
91	?1011011	5B	[
92	?1011100	5C	\
93	?1011101	5D	]
94	?1011110	5E	^
95	?1011111	5F	_
96	?1100000	60	'
97	?1100001	61	a
98	?1100010	62	b
99	?1100011	63	c
100	?1100100	64	d

(continued)

Printable Characters (continued)

Decimal	Binary	Hex	Character
101	?1100101	65	e
102	?1100110	66	f
103	?1100111	67	g
104	?1101000	68	h
105	?1101001	69	i
106	?1101010	6A	j
107	?1101011	6B	k
108	?1101100	6C	l
109	?1101101	6D	m
110	?1101110	6E	n
111	?1101111	6F	o
112	?1110000	70	p
113	?1110001	71	q
114	?1110010	72	r
115	?1110011	73	s
116	?1110100	74	t
117	?1110101	75	u
118	?1110110	76	v
119	?1110111	77	w
120	?1111000	78	x
121	?1111001	79	y
122	?1111010	7A	z
123	?1111011	7B	{
124	?1111100	7C	|
125	?1111101	7D	}
126	?1111110	7E	~
127	?1111111	FF	Delete (DEL)

B.2 EBCDIC CHARACTER CODES

Decimal	Binary	Hex	Character	Meaning
000	0000 0000	00	NUL	Null
001	0000 0001	01	SOH	Start of Heading
002	0000 0010	02	STX	Start of Text
003	0000 0011	03	ETX	End of Text
004	0000 0100	04	SEL	Select

(continued)

Decimal	Binary	Hex	Character	Meaning
005	0000 0101	05	HT	Horizontal Tab
006	0000 0110	06	RNL	Required New Line
007	0000 0111	07	DEL	Delete
008	0000 1000	08	GE	Graphic Escape
009	0000 1001	09	SPS	Superscript
010	0000 1010	0A	RPT	Repeat
011	0000 1011	0B	VT	Vertical Tab
012	0000 1100	0C	FF	Form Feed
013	0000 1101	0D	CR	Carriage Return
014	0000 1110	0E	SO	Shift Out
015	0000 1111	0F	SI	Shift In
016	0001 0000	10	DLE	Data Line Escape
017	0001 0001	11	DC1	Device Control 1
018	0001 0010	12	DC2	Device Control 2
019	0001 0011	13	DC3	Device Control 3
020	0001 0100	14	RES/ENP	Restore/Enable Presentation
021	0001 0101	15	NL	New Line
022	0001 0110	16	BS	Backspace
023	0001 0111	17	POC	Program-Operator Communication
024	0001 1000	18	CAN	Cancel
025	0001 1001	19	EM	End of Medium
026	0001 1010	1A	UBS	Unit Backspace
027	0001 1011	1B	CU1	Customer Use 1
028	0001 1100	1C	IFS	Interchange File Separator
029	0001 1101	1D	IGS	Interchange Group Separator
030	0001 1110	1E	IRS	Interchange Record Separator
031	0001 1111	1F	IUS/ITB	Interchange Unit Separator/Transmission Block
032	0010 0000	20	DS	Digit Select
033	0010 0001	21	SOS	Start of Significance
034	0010 0010	22	FS	Field Separator
035	0010 0011	23	WUS	Word Underscore
036	0010 0100	24	BYP/INP	Bypass/Inhibit Presentation
037	0010 0101	25	LF	Line Feed
038	0010 0110	26	ETB	End of Transmission Block
039	0010 0111	27	ESC	Escape
040	0010 1000	28	SA	Set Attribute
041	0010 1001	29	SFE	Start Field Extended
042	0010 1010	2A	SM/SW	Set Mode/Switch
043	0010 1011	2B	CSP	Control Significance Prefix
044	0010 1100	2C	MFA	Modify Field Attribute

(continued)

Decimal	Binary	Hex	Character	Meaning
045	0010 1101	2D	ENQ	Enquiry
046	0010 1110	2E	ACK	Acknowledge
047	0010 1111	2F	BEL	Bell
048	0011 0000	30		
049	0011 0001	31		
050	0011 0010	32	SYN	Synchronous Idle
051	0011 0011	33	IR	Index Return
052	0011 0100	34	PP	Presentation Position
053	0011 0101	35	TRN	Transparent
054	0011 0110	36	NBS	Numeric Backspace
055	0011 0111	37	EOT	End of Transmission
056	0011 1000	38	SBS	Subscript
057	0011 1001	39	IT	Indent Tab
058	0011 1010	3A	RFF	Required Form Feed
059	0011 1011	3B	CU3	Customer Use 3
060	0011 1100	3C	DC4	Device Control 4
061	0011 1101	3D	NAK	Negative Acknowledge
062	0011 1110	3E		
063	0011 1111	3F	SUB	Substitute
064	0100 0000	40	SP	Space
065	0100 0001	41	RSP	Required Space
066	0100 0010	42		
067	0100 0011	43		
068	0100 0100	44		
069	0100 0101	45		
070	0100 0110	46		
071	0100 0111	47		
072	0100 1000	48		
073	0100 1001	49		
074	0100 1010	4A	¢	
075	0100 1011	4B	.	
076	0100 1100	4C	<	
077	0100 1101	4D	(	
078	0100 1110	4E	+	
079	0100 1111	4F	|	
080	0101 0000	50	&	
081	0101 0001	51		
082	0101 0010	52		
083	0101 0011	53		
084	0101 0100	54		
085	0101 0101	55		
086	0101 0110	56		

(*continued*)

Decimal	Binary	Hex	Character	Meaning
087	0101 0111	57		
088	0101 1000	58		
089	0101 1001	59		
090	0101 1010	5A	!	
091	0101 1011	5B	$	
092	0101 1100	5C	.	
093	0101 1101	5D	)	
094	0101 1110	5E	;	
095	0101 1111	5F	¬	
096	0110 0000	60	-	
097	0110 0001	61	/	
098	0110 0010	62		
099	0110 0011	63		
100	0110 0100	64		
101	0110 0101	65		
102	0110 0110	66		
103	0110 0111	67		
104	0110 1000	68		
105	0110 1001	69		
106	0110 1010	6A	|	
107	0110 1011	6B	,	
108	0110 1100	6C	%	
109	0110 1101	6D	_	
110	0110 1110	6E	>	
111	0110 1111	6F	?	
112	0111 0000	70		
113	0111 0001	71		
114	0111 0010	72		
115	0111 0011	73		
116	0111 0100	74		
117	0111 0101	75		
118	0111 0110	76		
119	0111 0111	77		
120	0111 1000	78		
121	0111 1001	79	`	
122	0111 1010	7A	:	
123	0111 1011	7B	#	
124	0111 1100	7C	@	
125	0111 1101	7D	'	
126	0111 1110	7E	=	
127	0111 1111	7F	"	
128	1000 0000	80		

(continued)

Decimal	Binary	Hex	Character	Meaning
129	1000 0001	81	a	
130	1000 0010	82	b	
131	1000 0011	83	c	
132	1000 0100	84	d	
133	1000 0101	85	e	
134	1000 0110	86	f	
135	1000 0111	87	g	
136	1000 1000	88	h	
137	1000 1001	89	i	
138	1000 1010	8A		
139	1000 1011	8B		
140	1000 1100	8C		
141	1000 1101	8D		
142	1000 1110	8E		
143	1000 1111	8F		
144	1001 0000	90		
145	1001 0001	91	j	
146	1001 0010	92	k	
147	1001 0011	93	l	
148	1001 0100	94	m	
149	1001 0101	95	n	
150	1001 0110	96	o	
151	1001 0111	97	p	
152	1001 1000	98	q	
153	1001 1001	99	r	
154	1001 1010	9A		
155	1001 1011	9B		
156	1001 1100	9C		
157	1001 1101	9D		
158	1001 1110	9E		
159	1001 1111	9F		
160	1010 0000	A0		
161	1010 0001	A1	~	
162	1010 0010	A2	s	
163	1010 0011	A3	t	
164	1010 0100	A4	u	
165	1010 0101	A5	v	
166	1010 0110	A6	w	
167	1010 0111	A7	x	
168	1010 1000	A8	y	
169	1010 1001	A9	z	
170	1010 1010	AA		

(continued)

Decimal	Binary	Hex	Character	Meaning
171	1010 1011	AB		
172	1010 1100	AC		
173	1010 1101	AD		
174	1010 1110	AE		
175	1010 1111	AF		
176	1011 0000	B0		
177	1011 0001	B1		
178	1011 0010	B2		
179	1011 0011	B3		
180	1011 0100	B4		
181	1011 0101	B5		
182	1011 0110	B6		
183	1011 0111	B7		
184	1011 1000	B8		
185	1011 1001	B9		
186	1011 1010	BA		
187	1011 1011	BB		
188	1011 1100	BC		
189	1011 1101	BD		
190	1011 1110	BE		
191	1011 1111	BF		
192	1100 0000	C0	{	
193	1100 0001	C1	A	
194	1100 0010	C2	B	
195	1100 0011	C3	C	
196	1100 0100	C4	D	
197	1100 0101	C5	E	
198	1100 0110	C6	F	
199	1100 0111	C7	G	
200	1100 1000	C8	H	
201	1100 1001	C9	I	
202	1100 1010	CA	SHY	Syllable Hyphen
203	1100 1011	CB		
204	1100 1100	CC	⌐	
205	1100 1101	CD		
206	1100 1110	CE	Ч	
207	1100 1111	CF		
208	1101 0000	D0	}	
209	1101 0001	D1	J	
210	1101 0010	D2	K	
211	1101 0011	D3	L	
212	1101 0100	D4	M	

(continued)

Decimal	Binary	Hex	Character	Meaning
213	1101 0101	D5	N	
214	1101 0110	D6	O	
215	1101 0111	D7	P	
216	1101 1000	D8	Q	
217	1101 1001	D9	R	
218	1101 1010	DA		
219	1101 1011	DB		
220	1101 1100	DC		
221	1101 1101	DD		
222	1101 1110	DE		
223	1101 1111	DF		
224	1110 0000	E0	\	
225	1110 0001	E1	NSP	Numeric Space
226	1110 0010	E2	S	
227	1110 0011	E3	T	
228	1110 0100	E4	U	
229	1110 0101	E5	V	
230	1110 0110	E6	W	
231	1110 0111	E7	X	
232	1110 1000	E8	Y	
233	1110 1001	E9	Z	
234	1110 1010	EA		
235	1110 1011	EB		
236	1110 1100	EC	⊣	
237	1110 1101	ED		
238	1110 1110	EE		
239	1110 1111	EF		
240	1111 0000	F0	0	
241	1111 0001	F1	1	
242	1111 0010	F2	2	
243	1111 0011	F3	3	
244	1111 0100	F4	4	
245	1111 0101	F5	5	
246	1111 0110	F6	6	
247	1111 0111	F7	7	
248	1111 1000	F8	8	
249	1111 1001	F9	9	
250	1111 1010	FA	|	
251	1111 1011	FB		
252	1111 1100	FC		
253	1111 1101	FD		
254	1111 1110	FE		
255	1111 1111	FF	EO	Eight Ones

Appendix C
Keywords and Operator Precedence and Associativity

C.1 KEYWORDS

auto	default	float	register	switch
break	do	for	return	typedef
case	double	goto	short	union
char	else	if	signed	unsigned
const	enum	int	sizeof	void
continue	extern	long	static	volatile
		noalias	struct	while

C.2 OPERATOR PRECEDENCE AND ASSOCIATIVITY

Operator		Associativity
Reference	() [] . ->	left to right
Postfix	++ --	right to left
Unary	!~+- ++ -- (type) * & sizeof	right to left
Multiplicative	* / %	left to right
Additive	+-	left to right
Bitwise shift	<< >>	left to right
Relational	<<= >>=	left to right
Equality	== !=	left to right
Bitwise AND	&	left to right
Bitwise XOR	^	left to right
Bitwise OR	|	left to right
Logical AND	&&	left to right
Logical OR	||	left to right
Ternary	? :	right to left
Assignment	= += -= *= /= %= >>= <<= &= ^= |=	right to left
Comma	,	left to right

Operator precedence
(Listed from highest to lowest precedence)

Appendix D
Syntax Diagrams
(C Language and
Preprocessor)

Some Preprocessor diagrams are based upon those developed by David Smith and used by permission of David Smith and AGS Computers, Inc.

FILE INCLUSION

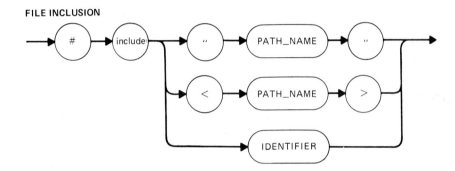

TOKEN REPLACEMENT

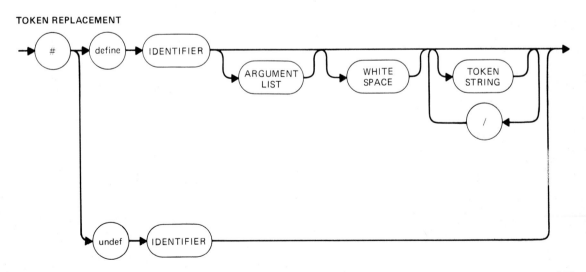

CONDITIONAL COMPILATION

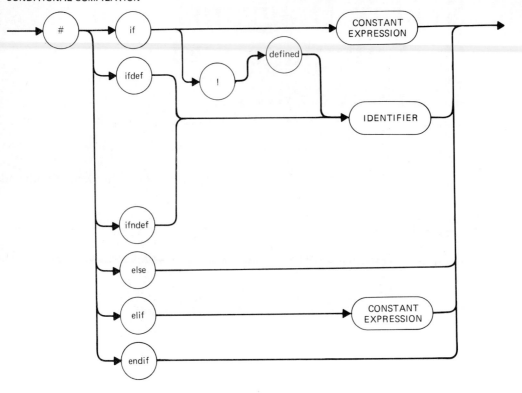

 # LINE DIRECTIVE

 # ERROR DIRECTIVE

 # PRAGMA DIRECTIVE

PREDEFINED MACROS

——DATE——	date of translation
——FILE ——	current source file
——LINE ——	current source line number
——STDC——	ANSI conformance flag. 1 = conformance
——TIME——	time of translation

PREPROCESSOR OPERATORS

#	enclose in double quotes
##	token concatenation

PROGRAM

MODULE

TYPE DEFINITION

DEC LIST

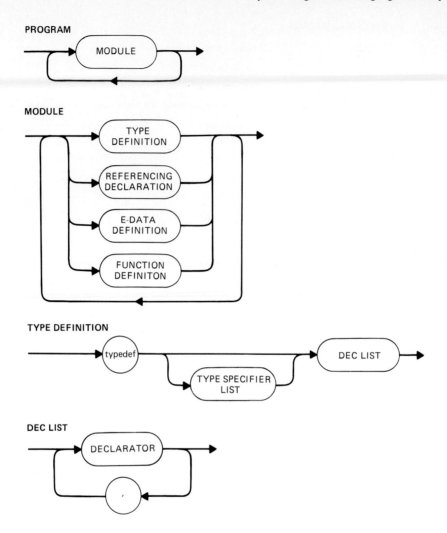

REFERENCING DECLARATION

E-DATA DEFINITION

FUNCTION DEFINITION

DECLARATOR

INIT DEC LIST

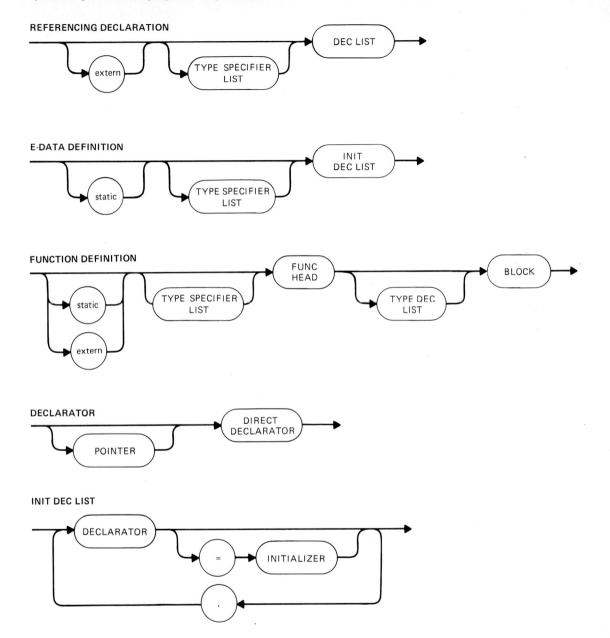

TYPE SPECIFIER

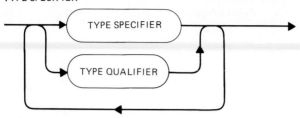

TYPE QUALIFIER

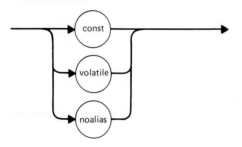

TYPE DEC LIST

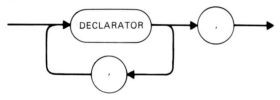

TYPE SPECIFIER

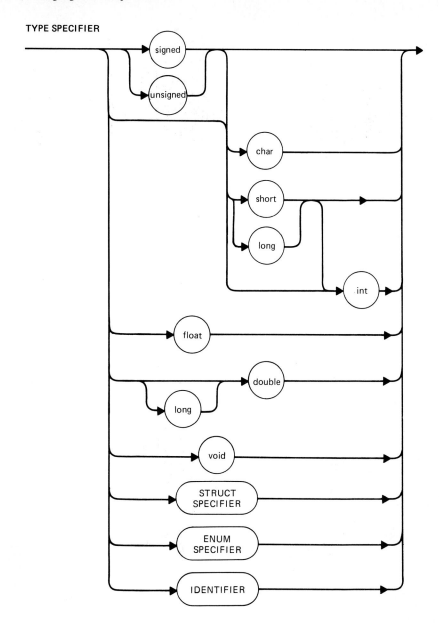

DIRECT DECLARATOR

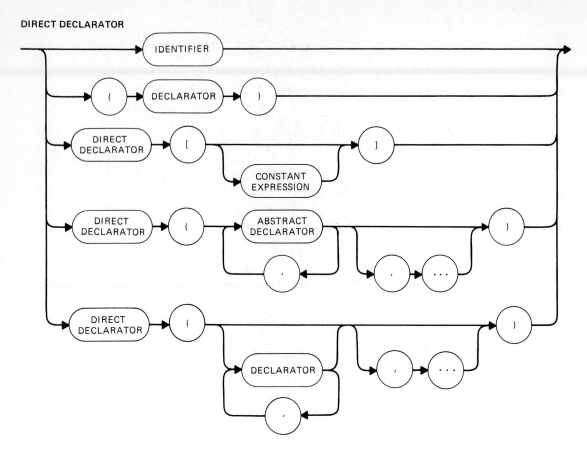

FUNC HEAD

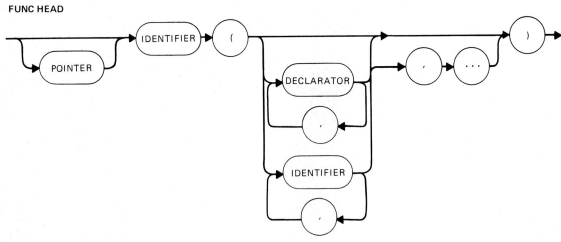

POINTER

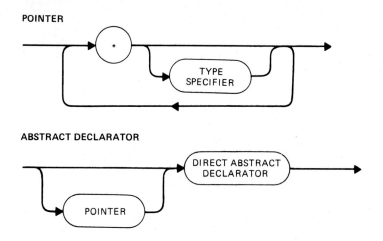

ABSTRACT DECLARATOR

DIRECT ABSTRACT DECLARATOR

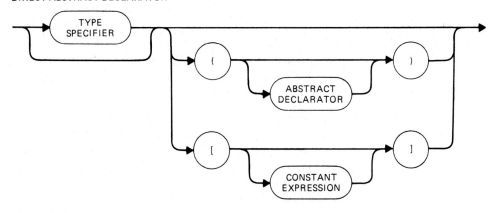

BLOCK

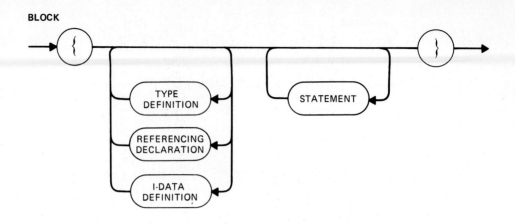

I-DATA DEFINITION

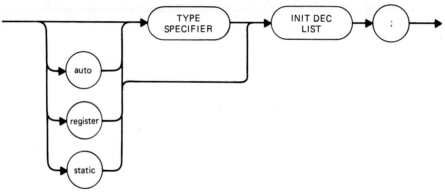

INITIALIZER

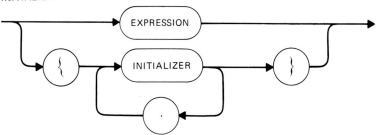

STRUCT SPECIFIER

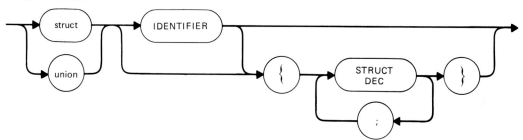

STRUCT DEC

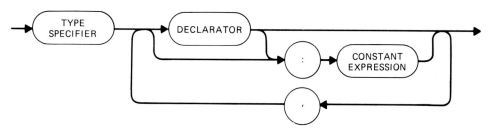

ENUM SPECIFIER

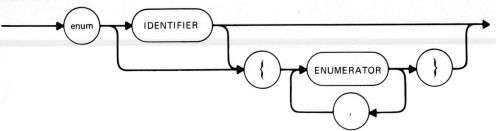

ENUMERATOR

STATEMENT

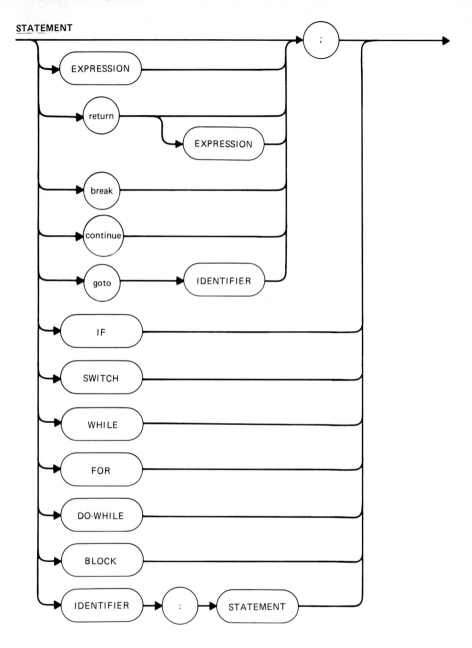

IF

SWITCH

CASE STATEMENT

WHILE

FOR

DO-WHILE

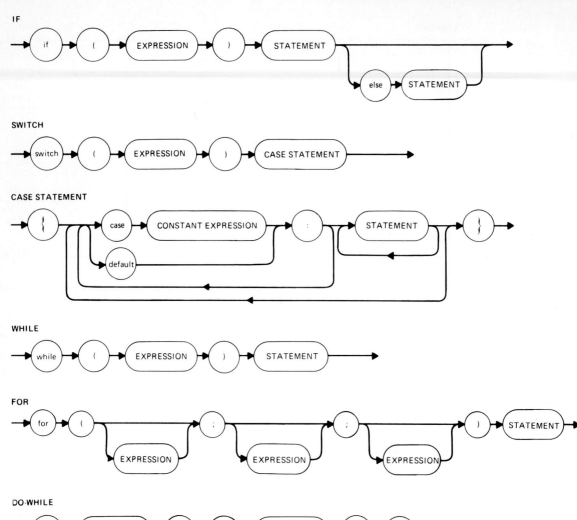

EXPRESSION

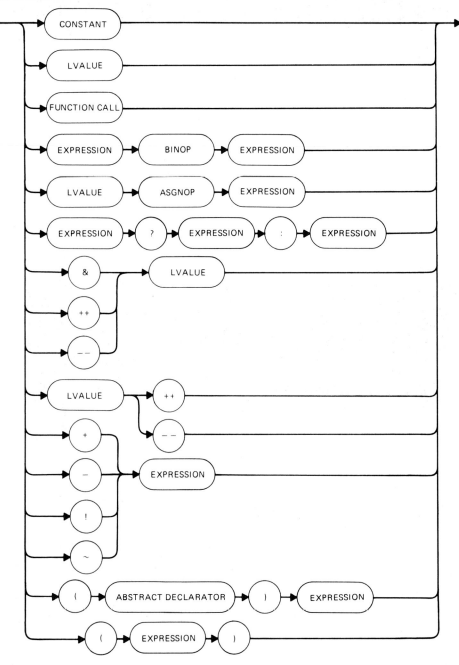

LVALUE

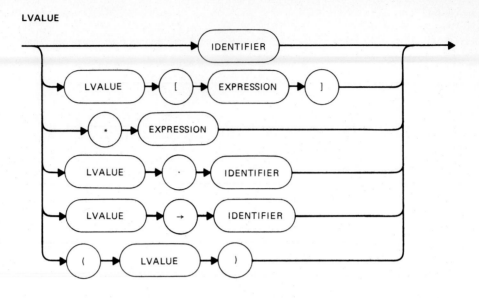

FUNCTION CALL

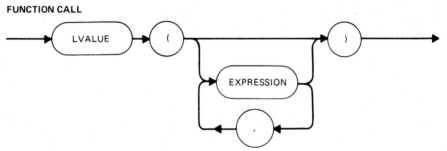

BINOP

ASGNOP

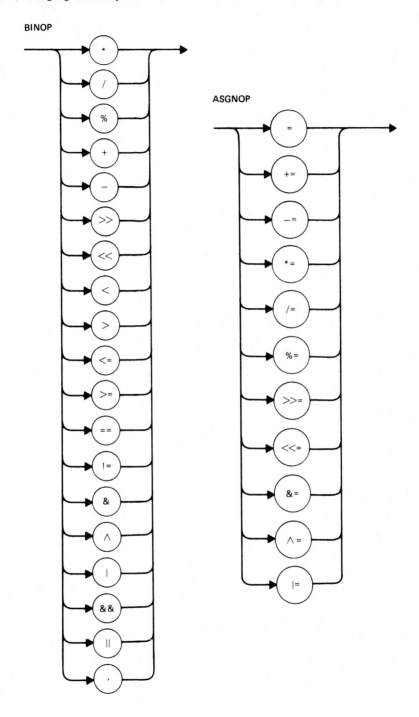

CONSTANT EXPRESSION

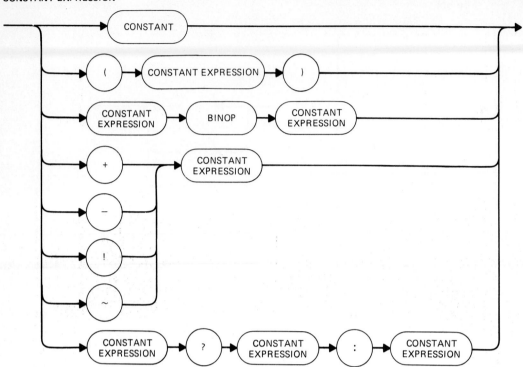

SIZE OF EXPRESSION

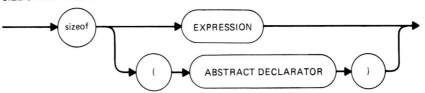

CONSTANT

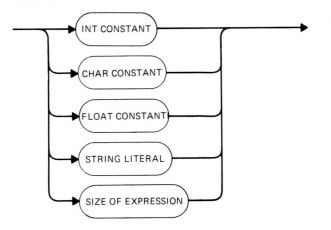

INT CONSTANT

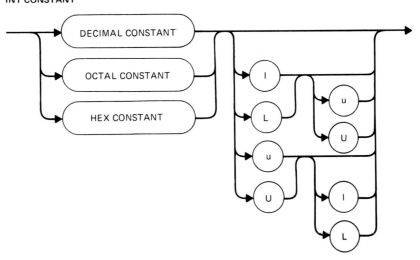

CHAR CONSTANT

STRING LITERAL

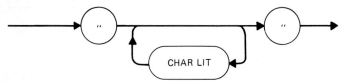

FLOAT CONSTANT

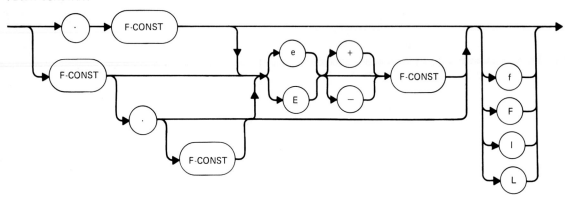

F-CONST

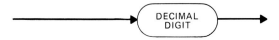

DECIMAL CONSTANT

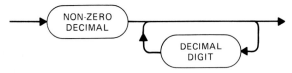

DECIMAL DIGIT

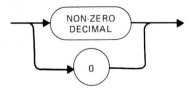

NON-ZERO DECIMAL

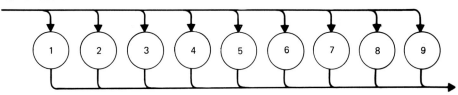

OCTAL CONSTANT

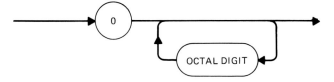

OCTAL DIGIT

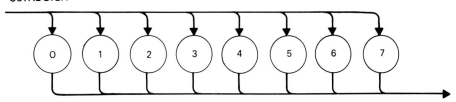

HEX CONSTANT

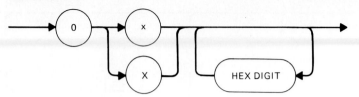

HEX DIGIT

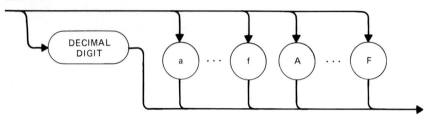

ENUMERATION CONSTANT

IDENTIFIER

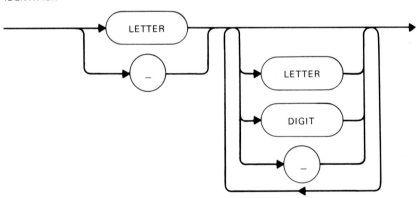

LETTER

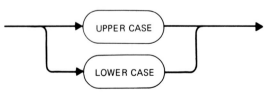

UPPER CASE

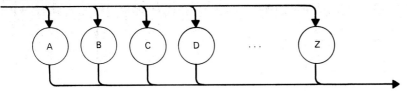

LOWER CASE

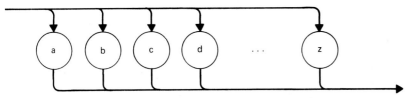

CHAR LIT

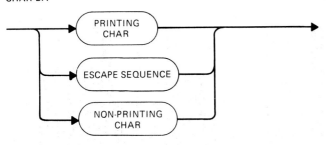

PRINTING CHAR

any printible character from the execution environment character set

ESCAPE SEQUENCE

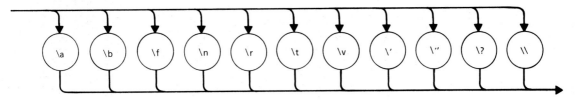

COMMENT

NON COMMENT CHARACTER

any character from the translation environment except the sequence */

NON PRINTING CHAR

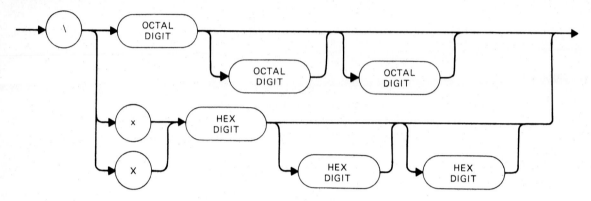

Index

541